Quinton

in the mid-1800s

"A most dark and wicked place..."

To Pat
Best wishes
Michael Hall

Michael Hall

Cobham
25-6-2019

ISBN 978-0-9551921-2-8

[A shorter version of this study entitled *Dark and Wicked Place – Quinton in the mid-1800* (ISBN 0 9509662 8 2), by the same author, exploring only Ridgacre tithe map and apportionments, was published in 2000.]

Printed by:

www.biddles.co.uk

Published by:

Quinton Local History Society

Dedication

For Sue
and all who live, have lived, or will live
within the borders of the Quinton tithe maps.

*"Look to the rock from which you were cut
And to the quarry from which you were hewn."*

Isaiah 51.1

*"Some there are who have left behind them a name to be commemorated in story.
Others are unremembered;
they have perished as though they had never existed, as though they had never been born."*

Ecclesiasticus 44. 8-9

Contents

Acknowledgments

Catherine L. Hughes and Simon A. Hughes – *for creating the new version of the tithe maps of Ridgacre and Quinton's enclaves in Warley Wigorn included in this book.*
Malcolm K. Read – *for his 2007 re-drawing of the Ridgacre tithe map.*

Professor Carl Chinn, MBE, PhD – *for his very gracious foreword.*

Jeff Bedford – *for photograph of Red Lion Inn*
Catherine & John Cooper – *for the statutory declarations made by Benjamin Yates in 1857.*
Joyce Eccles – *for her gift of the Presentation Address to John Chambers and "The Basket of Flowers."*
Patricia Evans – *for information relating to the family of her ancestor, Thomas Smith (plot 46).*
Public Record Office – *for permission to reproduce Quinton's Ecclesiastical Census returns.*
Bernard Taylor & Quinton Local History Society – *for conveyances relating to Quinton farms.*
Ann Tullis – *for transcribing the reports of the trial of Thomas Taylor and the inquest on Amy Read; information regarding the Hall, Jones and Read families – see footnote 353*
University of Birmingham – *for permission to quote from the novels of Francis Brett Young.*
Birmingham Museum and Art Gallery (Photo © Birmingham Museums Trust) – for *permission to use W.J. Pringle's painting "The Birmingham Post Passing Quinton Gate, 1842."*
Vina Campbell – *for photographs of cottage, plot 46 after restoration; plot 47, Inglenook Cottage.*
Viscount Cobham – *for permission to use the portrait of George William, 4th Baron Lyttelton*
Kate Creed – *for permission to use W. Nicholls' painting of Hawthorn Farm*
Enid Dawson – *for her gift of the painting of Quinton Rectory by Beatrice May Phillips.*
Diabolus in Musica & members of the cast – *for the recording of "Meet the Quinton Ancestors".*
David Eades – *for photograph of Richard Brindley Hone.*
Englesea Brook Chapel & Museum – *for permission to use the image of carved head of Hugh Bourne.*
John Hadley – *for pen and ink drawing of a nail-maker at work.*
Jonathan Hall – *for photographs of William & Eleanor Spurrier's tombstone, Old Church, Smethwick; Samuel Chatwin's tombstone Christ Church The Quinton; help with plot co-ordinates.*
Rev John S. Hope – *for photographs of Quinton Toll House; Ambrose Foley's Preaching House; Pax Hall; Monckton Farmhouse; cottage, plot 46 before 21st century restoration; cottage, plot 38.*
Julian Hunt – *Information relating to Land Tax and Dudley Register of Electors 1836.*
Bernard Taylor & Quinton Local History Society – *for photographs of Bogs Farmhouse; Quinton National School; Rev Christopher Oldfield; Four Dwellings Farmhouse; Redhall Farmhouse; Worlds End Farmhouse; Beech Tree Inn; Ivy House Farmhouse; cottage, plot 223. Plans of Four Dwellings Farm; Windmill Farm; Mockbeggar Farm; Lower Ridgacre Farm; Tinkers Farm; New Burial Ground.*
Nick Utting & Blamire Trust – *for permission to use the silhouette of William Blamire.*
H.R. Wilson – *paintings/drawings of: Hales Owen Free School; Greenhill Farm; Samuel Chatwin's farmhouse & barn; Hagg Farm; Quinton Tollgate base stone; various nails; copies of David Parkes' sketches of Belle Vue and Ambrose Foley.*

Dudley Archives and Local History Centre; Library of Birmingham; National Archives; Public Record Office; Shropshire Archives; Walsall Local History Centre; Worcester Archive and Archaeology Service.

Dr Lindsey Hall – *for her painstaking proof-reading of the text.*

1   Foreword   *Professor Carl Chinn MBE PhD*

The Reverend James Jones, the vicar of Christ Church, Quinton and chairman of the parish council, was a formidable figure. Distinguished by his top hat, a carefully-groomed moustache and white mutton-chop whiskers flowing down the sides of his face, it was he who pushed through the annexation of the district by Birmingham in 1909. Although Halesowen was nearer, Reverend Jones argued forcefully that Quinton received its gas and food from the city, where 111 Quintonians worked as opposed to 128 locally. Moreover, the population of the village and its farms was more likely to visit Birmingham for their shopping and entertainment facilities.

Perhaps the clinching argument arose from the local dissatisfaction with the water supply and drainage system as well as concerns over the high cost of a proposed sewerage scheme by Halesowen. By contrast, Birmingham could supply Quinton's needs more cheaply through its renowned water supplies and drainage board. The cause of annexation was further helped by Councilor J. S. Nettlefold. A wealthy industrialist, he was chairman of Birmingham's Housing Department and knew that Birmingham needed plenty of farmland if well-laid out housing estates for its people were to be developed.

There was strong opposition from Halesowen and the Stourbridge Guardians, who levied a poor rate on Quinton's 1,100 people, but in a vote, 180 out of 224 electors voted for annexation. Thus, on 9 November 1909, Quinton became part of Birmingham. In a speech of welcome, the Lord Mayor, Sir George Kendrick, declared that Quinton had "green fields and tree-clad hills" everywhere. That rural scene would soon be transformed.

Within a year of its annexation, Quinton was included in Birmingham's first town planning scheme along with east Birmingham, where there was to be a mixed development of houses and industrial premises. Contrarily, Quinton would be a residential district because it was upwind of the select middle-class suburb of Edgbaston, in which lived many councilors - and they did not want the smells and smokes of manufacturing drifting downwind towards their homes. The scheme was approved by Parliament in 1913. The first of its kind in the country, it became a model for other local authorities.

During both the inter-war years and after 1945, there was widespread building of private and council houses in Quinton. This urbanisation swept away most of its green spaces, although part of Quinton Meadows remains as a site of importance for nature conservation. Little else remains of rural Quinton, other than Christ Church, built in 1841, and intriguing names like Four Dwellings School and Spies Lane. Yet though it is an outwardly twentieth-century creation, Quinton boasts one of the most active local history societies in the West Midlands and also an exceptional local historian – Dr Michael Hall. His doctoral thesis examining the Birmingham of the novelist Francis Brett Young was outstanding and this work on Quinton in the mid-1800s emphasises his qualities as an indefatigable researcher and talented historian. Most importantly, through delving deeply into the past, he has brought into view those previously hidden in the shadows. In so doing, he has emphasised the importance of understanding Quinton's history before its annexation. This book is a remarkable achievement and Dr Hall should be congratulated on it.

2   Introduction

The mid-1800s is the first moment in history when anything approaching a complete roll of those who lived in Quinton, an area of 943 acres on the high Midland Plateau, divided between the townships of Ridgacre and Warley Wigorn, was set down. That history, however, began some 4.5 billion years earlier with a fragment from a dying star spinning through space, warming and cooling through numberless millennia, eventually giving birth to the Midland Plateau. Formed largely of Upper Coal Measures, Bunter Pebble Beds, Bunter and Keuper Sandstone, this main watershed of England is bordered by the valleys of Trent, Severn, Avon and their tributaries. At one of the Plateau's highest points, Quinton lies some 735' above sea level. Just south of the Plateau, the Clent Ridge rises to 1036' at Walton Hill. These geographical features are cited by novelist Francis Brett Young to identify Tilton, his fictional portrait of Quinton. "An escarpment, eight hundred feet above sea-level, which is, in fact, the brim of the high Midland plateau: the watershed between the cold, sodden lands drained by Trent's tributaries and the warm brooklands of Severn. The plateau reaches its highest point and its end in the village of Tilton, where the contrast between these two worlds is magnificently revealed."[1]

The first humans (homo erectus) probably crossed the land bridge into Britain some 500,000 years ago, before the First Ice Age, followed by Neanderthals 225,000 years ago and homo sapiens 190,000 years later. Archaeology, however, places the beginning of civilisation at the end of the Last Ice Age around 10,000BCE. The tundra bequeathed by the Ice Age eventually gave way to forest, mostly lime trees on the fringe of the Midland Plateau, an area grazed by red and roe deer, elk, horse, wild cattle and pigs. Around 6,500BCE the neck of marshy land linking South East England to Europe was submerged and Britain became an island, still largely covered by forest and valleys of dense undergrowth and swamp. The Midland Plateau was perhaps first colonised around this time by settlers arriving via the valleys of Trent and Tame. From its earliest occupation, the Midlands Plateau formed a dividing line: first between Iron Age tribes – Cornovii, Silures and Dobunni; in the later Roman administration between Britannia Superior and Britannia Inferior.

Did any of these early settlers occupy those 943 acres which by the mid-1800s were known as Quinton? Whilst there is scant evidence to confirm that they did, it is idle to conclude that the Iron Age builders of the 7½ acre fort on Wychbury Hill, just 5 miles away never strayed as far as Quinton, or that, following Julius Caesar's invasion of Britain in 55BCE, Romans garrisoned at Metchley on Rycknield Street, a mere 3 miles distant never ventured this far. Indeed, the name Quinton has been used to suggest Roman connections either from *quintana*, the market of a camp or *quintana via*, a road used by soldiers. A third alternative is that offered by T. R. Nash[2] who favoured derivation from the Roman sport, descended through medieval chivalric training, part of which involved tilting at the quintain, a cross beam on an upright pole, at which a rider with a lance would test both his own and his horse's agility. The object was to strike the broad end of the cross beam with the lance and avoid being hit by the heavy weight which would consequently spin round on the central swivel. Francis Brett Young's choice of Tilton as his name for Quinton suggests a preference for this option, as does a late 19th century comment by Quintonian Henry Dingley: "We think it very possible that the military tournaments of the Romans took place in [Bourne] College Park for two reasons - this is the finest

---

[1] Young, F.B. (1940) *Mr Lucton's Freedom*, pp 64-65
[2] Nash, T.R. (1781) *Collections for the History of Worcestershire*, Vol 1, p509

space for picturesque surroundings in the vicinity, and would therefore be chosen as the site most excellently suited for the purpose. And again, the old Roman road, or as we should now term it, the turnpike road, then ran alongside the College Park."[3] Less romantic, but probably more reliable than the Roman exposition is the Saxon interpretation, suggesting that Quinton derives from the Old English Cwēningtūn – the farm or manor of cwēna (the woman) or cwēn (the queen). The record of such a female role at this early period is a significant landmark in Quinton's history.

The name Quinton, however, was rarely used in early records,[4] when the township was identified as Ridgacre, with its variants of Rudge acre, Rugacre, Rugaker, Rugeacre, Rugeacur, Ruggacre, Rughacre and Rughaker. This Saxon name meaning ploughed land on the ridge offers an apt description of geographical features which supersede the vagaries of history. Thus, the name survived as the descriptor of the 1844 tithe map and the census enumeration districts of 1841-61 with which this study is concerned. Upper and Lower Quinton appear only as addresses within Ridgacre and The Quinton (the format usually adopted in legal documents) as the title of the ecclesiastical parish. Also Saxon in origin is Warley (Wearley, Weireleye, Werioleye, Wernlegh, Werwelie), from the suffix *leah* = wood or clearing, the prefix suggesting the imposition of a covenant, presumably the result of an earlier land dispute.[5] The addition of the Latin Wigorn (Wigorniensis = of Worcester) distinguishing the township from the neighbouring Warley Salop which as its name indicates lay in Shropshire.

The departure of the Romans in the 5th century gave way to the Dark Ages, so called through the lack of surviving archaeology. However, by the mid-7th century much of central England was under Anglo-Saxon rule, as the kingdom of Mercia, a territory with fluid borders, which took its name from the Anglo-Saxon *mierce* = boundary. Thus, the natural role of the Midland Plateau was continued. This period saw the appearance of place names which, like Quinton, have survived, as with Birmingham which recalls the *ham* (settlement) of Beorma's *inga* (people). The Anglo-Saxon Chronicle[6] records the establishment of shires in southern England prior to 892BCE, though Mercian shires were evidently a later creation, the first mention of Worcestershire being in 1038. For administrative purposes, the shires were divided into Hundreds, each with its own court, dealing with criminal cases and land transactions. A Hundred consisted of 100 hides, each measuring 120 acres.[7] Like other counties, Worcestershire was divided into 12 Hundreds. The requirement to fit a shire exactly to this size frequently resulted in boundaries ignoring natural geographical barriers and ecclesiastical dioceses. Ridgacre, within Worcestershire's Clent Hundred, at the time of Edward the Confessor (1042-1066), as part of Hales Owen, was held by Olwin (also called Wulfwin), Thane of Edwin, Earl of Mercia. Similarly, Warley Wigorn was held by Aethelward, though there is confusion as to whether it was located in Clent

---

[3] Dingley, H. (1892) "Recollections of Quinton and its Surroundings" *Bourne College Chronicle Vol IV*, pp 132-133. Bourne College, a Primitive Methodist School was located in Quinton from 1882 to 1928, when it became Quinton Hall, an old men's home, closing c1980.

[4] A.N. Rosser has identified Quenton in the 1221 *Assize Rolls;* Quinton in the 1275 *Lay Subsidy Rolls*; Queynton in the 1665 *Index Pedum Finium pro com Wigorn – The Quinton and Round About Vol I* (1998) p 1

[5] See Mills, A.D. (1991) *Dictionary of Place-Names*, OUP

[6] Created in the late 9th century, probably in Wessex, during the reign of Alfred the Great.

[7] A hide was measured as the amount of land that could be cultivated by a team of eight oxen.

or Came Hundred.[8] This township did not consist of one unified piece; rather it was scattered in small patches, some no more than single fields, dispersed through neighbouring townships. The confusion continued into the mid-1800s and explains the patchwork intrusion of Warley Wigorn into Ridgacre, together creating the area identified as Quinton.

The arrival of the Normans was followed, in 1085-6, by a thorough investigation into the lands William had conquered. "At Gloucester at midwinter the King had deep speech with his counsellors and sent men all over England to each shire to find out what or how much each landowner held and what it was worth."[9] The information was collected at Winchester and copied by one writer into a single volume.[10] Though included only as part of a larger whole, the 943 acres of Quinton with which we are concerned, direct us to two entries in the Worcestershire folio of Domesday Book: 14.1 and 23.6.

> "14.1 In CLENT Hundred Earl Roger holds one manor, Halas, from the King. 10 hides... In lordship 4 ploughs; 36 villagers, 18 smallholders, 4 riders and a church with 2 priests; between them they have 41½ ploughs. 8 male and 2 female slaves. Roger Hunter holds 1½ hides of this land from the Earl; he has 1 plough. 6 villagers and 5 smallholders, with 5 ploughs. Value 25s. Value of this manor before 1066 £24; now £15. Wulfwin held it and had a salt-house at Droitwich and 1 house at 12d in Worcester."

> "23.6 In CAME Hundred William, son of Ansculf holds Werwelie from the King. Alfhelm holds from him. Aethelward held it. ½ hide... In lordship 1 plough; 2 villagers and 8 smallholders with 4½ ploughs. 2 slaves. Value before 1066, 17s; now 10s."[11]

Ansculf, perhaps something of an opportunist, from Picardy, fought with William at Hastings, for which, in addition to Werwelie, he was rewarded with numerous detached fragments of land spread through south and central England.[12] William, Ansculf's son, who held Werwelie in 1086, also held Dudelei, the Domesday entry commenting briefly "his castle is there." According to some sources, Earl Roger also fought at Hastings, commanding the Norman right flank;[13] others suggest that though remaining in Normandy, assisting Duchess Mathilde to govern the duchy in William's absence, he contributed 60 ships towards the invasion.[14] Whatever the reality, he was rewarded with the earldom of Shrewsbury, most of Shropshire, Halas and manors across eight counties.[15] In the early 12th century, Roger annexed

---

[8] In their transcription of the Worcestershire volume of Domesday Book, Frank and Caroline Thorn recognise the difficulty of missing headings, noting specifically with regard to William Son of Ansculf's holding, "In Clent Hundred: The heading inserted in the margin at 23,8 should certainly have included 23,7 Churchill which is on the far side of Clent from its boundary with Came, and probably 23,6 Warley which is adjacent to the Clent-Came boundary." Thorn, F. & C. (1982) *Domesday Book 16 Worcestershire*, notes

[9] *Anglo-Saxon Chronicle* cited by Morris, J (1982) Introduction to *Domesday Book 16: Worcestershire*

[10] Cumberland and Westmorland were not included in the survey; Durham and Northumberland were not transcribed; Norfolk, Suffolk and Essex appeared in a second volume.

[11] Thorn, F & C (eds) (1982), 14.1, 23.6

[12] Apart from in Worcestershire, Ansculf held land in Warwickshire, Staffordshire, Northamptonshire, Rutland, Berkshire, Buckinghamshire, Hertfordshire, Oxfordshire, Middlesex and Surrey.

[13] E.g. Robert Wace, *Roman de Rou,* a 12th century verse chronicle commissioned by King Henry II.

[14] E.g. *Brevis Relatio de Origine Willelmi Conquestoris*, composed in reign of Henry I

[15] Surrey, Hampshire, Wiltshire, Middlesex, Gloucestershire, Cambridgeshire, Warwickshire and Staffordshire.

his small Worcestershire Manor to his larger holding in Shropshire and so Halas became a part of that county, administered via the Brimstree Hundred. In 1844, shortly after the tithe map was drawn, Hales Owen was returned from Salop to Worcestershire and the Clent Hundred. The areas of Warley Wigorn shown on the 19th century Quinton tithe map are those lands which were not included in the grant to Earl Roger, having been possessions of Aethelward rather than Wulfwin before the Conquest.

Late in 1086, shortly after the Domesday survey, King William returned to Normandy, where he died the following year, to be succeed by his son, William Rufus. In 1100, when William Rufus died, his brothers, Henry and Robert fought for the crown. The Earl of Shrewsbury, successor to Earl Roger, supported Robert. Upon Henry's victory, Shrewsbury's lands were confiscated. At the end of the twelfth century, Henry II granted Halas to his brother-in-law, David ap Owen, who died after adding his own name to that of Halas. Thus, the manor reverted to the crown, until King John granted it to Bishop Peter of Winchester in 1214.

> "John, by the grace of God… to Archbishops, Bishops, Abbots etc… Know ye, that for the good of our souls, and our ancestors we have given, granted etc. to Peter, Lord Bishop of Winton, our Manor of Hales, with all its appurtenances for the building of a religious house, of whatsoever order he shall think fit. Wherefore we will and firmly decree, that the religious men whom the aforementioned Lord Bishop shall have placed there, do have and hold the said Manor with its appurtenances… its Tenements and Hereditaments, in wood and plain; in meadows and pastures; in fishponds and pools; in water and in mills etc. free from all servitude and secular exactions… In testimony whereof we bear witness: -
>
> William, Lord Bishop of Worcester,   Edward, Lord Bishop of Hereford,
> William, Earl of Warenne,   Samuel, Earl of Winton.
>
> Given by the hand of Master Richard de Marisco, at London, being the 28th day of October, in the 16th year of our reign."[16]

A Premonstratensian[17] Abbey was completed in 1218 and survived, with never more than twenty monks until the Dissolution of the Monasteries. The respective rights and responsibilities of the abbey and its tenants included that tenants "ought to grind their corn at the abbot's mill in Hales, unless there was a defect in the mill," and "they should do for the abbot six days ploughing and six days harrowing every Lent for every virgate; and those who hold less land shall do less service." The abbot agreed that "neither he nor his successors are able to exact other or more services than those aforesaid," and "that no-one need attend the abbot's market at Hales unless he wished."[18] Some 33 years later, rights of inheritance and marriage were clarified. "On the decease of every tenant, the best beast was due for a heriot, except a mare. And the king used to have half the goats, hogs and bees, and all the colts not broken in. On entering his father's land, the heir was to pay for a relief two year's rent of the same. If anyone married his daughter outside the manor, he paid 2s; if inside 12s."[19]

---

[16] Cited from Somers, F & KM (1932) *Halas Hales Hales Owen*, Appendix i

[17] The Premonstratensian order (known as white canons from their colour of their habit) had been founded at Prémontré in France in 1120. Their first English abbey was established at Newhouse in Lincoln c1143.

[18] *Placita de Banco*, 27 Henry III, roll xiii (1242) cited by Amphlett, J. (1910) *Court Rolls of the Manor of Hales* Vol 1, p xiii

[19] 4 Edward I, (1275) Amphlett, J. (1910) *Court Rolls of the Manor of Hales*, Part I, pp xiv, xv

Warley Wigorn, meanwhile, had passed from William, son of Ansculf, possibly by the marriage of his daughter Beatrice, to Fulke Paganel and, then to the de Somery family, who held the manor by direct line of succession throughout the 13th century. On the death of John de Somery in 1321, his estate was inherited by his sisters Margaret, wife of Sir John de Sutton and Joan, wife of Sir John Bottetourt of Weoley Castle. Seven years later, Lady Joan, by a licence in mortmain,[20] granted the manor of Weireleye to the abbot and convent of Hales Owen in return for prayers for her soul.

Following the dissolution of Hales Owen Abbey in 1538 Henry VIII granted its land to John Dudley[21], who lost it, along with his head, for his attempt to place his daughter-in-law, Lady Jane Grey, on the throne after the death of Edward VI. Dudley's widow successfully claimed the Hales Owen manor as her inheritance and in due course it passed to her son, Robert Dudley, who sold the estate to his land agent, George Tuckey, in partnership with another 'esquire,' Thomas Blount, for £3,000.

> *"THIS INDENTURE MADE the XXVIIth day of marche in the fourth and fyth years of the reignes of our Souverynes Lorde and Ladye Phyllip and Mary by the grace of God King and Quene of England… BETWEEN Sir Robt. Dudley Knyght and Dame Amye his ladye on the one parte and Thomas Blount and George Tukye, Esquires on the other parte WITNESSETH that the said Robt. Dudley and Dame Amye for the some of thre thousand pounds of lawful money of England to them payd by the said Thomas and George… do hereby bargayne sell gyve and grannte unto the sayd Thomas and George all that their Manor of Halsowyn with the appurtenances in the Counties of Salopp and Worcester… lying and beyng in the Townes, fields, parishes or hamlettes of Halsowyn, Halsboroughe, Ramsley, Honyngton, Ylley, Hasbury Hallen, Hyllgrange, Lapoole, Hyll, Rudge acre, Ludley, Walloxhall, Warley Oldebury and Kackmore in the sayd countie of Salopp and in Warley, Cradeley in the sayd Countie of Worcester except such parte, parcelles and members of the premysses as be and do lye in Oldebury and Walloxhall alias Langley Walloxhall in the sayd Countie of Salopp… IN WYTNESSE whereof as well the sayd Sir Robt. Dudley and Dame Amye hys wyf, as the sayd Thomas Blounte and George Tuckye to this Indenture their seales interchangeably have sett dated the day and yere first above written.*
>
> $\qquad\qquad\qquad\qquad\qquad\qquad\qquad\qquad\qquad\qquad\qquad$ *R. Duddley $\qquad$ Amye Duddley."*[22]

The involvement of Robert and Amy Dudley brought intrigue at the very highest level to the manor. Robert Dudley married Amy Robsart in 1550, eight years before Elizabeth became queen. In the early years of her reign Elizabeth and Dudley were romantically involved, generating suspicion that they would marry, were Dudley free. In 1560 Amy was found dead at the foot of the stairs at Cumnor, the Dudley home near Oxford. A coroner's jury returned a verdict of accidental death, but rumour rapidly implicated Dudley in her murder. Whether or not the residents of Quinton knew anything of this at the time, their descendants in in the mid-1800s who were literate could certainly have read all about it in Walter Scott's highly romanticised account which forms the main plot of *Kenilworth*, published in 1821. Subsequently, Blount and Tuckey leased many of the farms to their sitting tenants, before selling the

---

[20] As the abbey, not the abbot became the legal owner of the land, it was held in perpetuity as the abbey would not die and therefore its property would not revert to the crown, as in cases where there was no legal heir. For land to be granted as Joan Bottetourt wished, a *licence in mortmain* from the king was required.

[21] John Dudley was raised to the Dukedom of Northumberland by Edward VI in 1551.

[22] Cited from Somers, F & KM (1932) Appendix iii

residue of the manor in 1558 for £2,000 to John Lyttelton of Frankley, 6x great grandfather of George William, 4th Baron Lyttelton, Lord of the Manor in the mid-1800s. By that date further parcels of land had been sold, resulting in the 38 Quinton landowners: 20 in Ridgacre, 8 in Warley Wigorn and 10 owning land in both townships.

Insights into the lives of Quinton inhabitants during these changing years are offered by the court rolls. Disputes over boundaries regularly occurred, sometimes moving beyond field to township boundary. In 1305 William Osbern complained that John Freeman, a Warley Wigorn tenant, had annexed Salop land worth 12d into Worcestershire. Considering the way in which plots in Ridgacre and Warley Wigorn were interconnected, this cannot have been a unique occurrence. Courts had a responsibility for keeping the peace. Where local disagreements looked likely to end in bloodshed, or a felony had been committed, the "hue and cry" might be raised. Not to raise it when there was just cause and raising it when there was not, were both punishable offences. In 1276, Richard Cok of Ridgacre reported that Richard, brother of Matilda le Felawes raised hue on her behalf against William, son of Richard de Tewenhal, and John, son of Richard Cok, raised hue against Matilda on behalf of his father. Consequently, all were to be arrested and brought before the next court. Constables, as law officers are first mentioned in the Great Court[23] of Wednesday 14th October 1293, when Thomas Harald paid the Lord 6d to be excused from serving in this role. By the mid-1800s a constable was elected annually for Warley Wigorn and a deputy (Benjamin Hill in 1843) for Ridgacre.

Some offenders though regularly summoned to court, failed to appear. In March 1301, Thomas Green of Ridgacre was charged with trespass[24] by Roger Fokerham; of damaging corn belonging to Henry Simmond; and the non-payment of an outstanding debt. At the next court, four months later, Green was again charged by Fokerham for non-payment and failed to appear to answer this or the trespass charge. On July 22nd, he again failed to appear, even though a young bullock had been distrained from him to ensure his attendance. At this court, he was also charged with trespass by Geoffrey of Warley, though on August 9th, he was found not guilty of that charge; fined 6d for defaulting on previous fines; and faced a new trespass charge from Geoffrey Osborn. Following another failure to attend court on October 2nd, finally on October 25th, Thomas Green was fined 6d for bringing false charges against Roger Fokerham and 4d for trespass on Geoffrey Warley's land. Four years later, Green was again in court, accused of skinning a dead horse belonging to Thomas Sygrim. Evidence was presented that while Sygrim had gone to seek help, Green found the horse and skinned it himself. The value of the skin was 6d. Green was ordered to compensate Sygrim 6d plus 12p fine. He was further fined 3s 4d payable to the Lord of the Manor.[25]

That some of Ridgacre's copyhold tenants who, in earlier years would have been serfs, had become wealthy, is illustrated by the case of Thomas Bird, whose widowed mother surrendered to him in 1281, all the land she held within Ridgacre and other places. In return, he agreed to build her a timber house, measuring 30' by 14'. Furthermore, he would pay to her annually, at Michaelmas and again eight days

---

[23] Great Courts were held twice a year, usually in April and October. Two representatives of each township were required to attend to make the necessary representations

[24] Trespass usually meant allowing animals to wander and graze on another persons' land.

[25] Courts 142, 143, 144, 145, 147,148, 171,172

before Christmas, a quarter of wheat, a quarter of oats and a bushel of peas; on All Saints Day five cart-loads of sea-coal; on Good Friday and at Midsummer a quarter of wheat and a quarter of oats; at Pentecost five shillings of good money.[26]

In the years following the Black Death in the mid-14th century, re-marriage amongst England's peasant class who lost their wives was commonplace. Juliana, wife of Philip Boury of Ridgacre died in 1378; his second wife died in 1382 and in the same year he married his third wife, who was constantly brought before the courts for brewing ale without a licence.[27] Rapid re-marriage of widowed nail-makers remained a practice commonly observed in Quinton in the mid-1800s.

The court rolls also reveal something of Quinton's early infrastructure. In 1305 an Edgbaston man was given permission to build a house in *Rugacre ex oposito tenement Ricardi le Feys que est triangula inter duas vias que ducunt de Hales versus Birmyngham*.[28] Only rarely are there clues as to exactly where people lived, so the identification of this building plot, opposite Richard Fey's tenement, where two roads from Hales Owen to Birmingham meet at an angle, is particularly important. The only possibilities for these two sites are at and opposite what would become plot 58 on the tithe map – the toll house. In 1307, the verdict of a Great Court *dicit quod quedam via apud Rugacre Tounewelle deteriorate per Willelmum de Chyselhurst,* confirms that Ridgacre did have a town well, by which the road, damaged by William Chiselhurst, passed.[29]

The use of surnames in the 13th and 14th century court rolls is not common: most people were identified by their baptismal name coupled with a family relationship – daughter of, brother of etc – or place of origin, such as Nicholai de Ridgacre in 1278 and Felicia de Ridgacre in 1281. Exceptions, as we have already seen, included Thomas Bird, Thomas Sygrim and Thomas Green. For 16 years during the reigns of Henry VII and Henry VIII, Hales Owen churchwardens received annually from "John P'kys of Rugeacur two shillings for the hyr of a cowe." In 1503 John's wife, Elizabeth, bequeathed 4d to Hales Owen Parish Church and in 1519 John P'yks bequeathed 6d to the church "to ye hye light."[30]

By the mid-17th century, when Hales Owen church registers identify addresses within the parish,[31] the combination of baptismal and surname is commonplace, enabling the tracing of possible family links over a protracted period. The litigious 14th century Thomas Green may well be an ancestor of a 17th century Thomas, "the son of William Green by Margery his wife of Ridgaker" born September 15th and baptised September 25th 1659. A century later, Mary, daughter of Samuel and Susanna Green of Ridgacre was buried at Hales Owen on December 29th 1752. In the mid-1800s, Alice Green of Ridgacre worked at the Red Lion Inn and Benjamin Green of Warley Wigorn married Mary Harvey. By the mid-1800s, Quinton residents shared some 277 surnames, of which 28 had been present in the mid-1700s

---

[26] Court 79, October 28th 1281, Feast Day of the Apostles Simon and Jude; *9Edw*
[27] Various courts, 1382-1396
[28] Court 174 June 26th 1305, Sunday next after the Feast of the Birth of John the Baptist
[29] Great Court 193, April 26th 1307
[30] Somers, F. (ed) (1952) *Hales Owen Churchwarden's Accounts (1487-1582)* Part 1
[31] The earliest identifiable entry on April 15th 1637, is of "Isabella, daughter of Roger Quinton by Katherine his wife." Five days later the register records the burial of "Isabella Quinton, an infant." References to Warley predate this Quinton entry by some 68 years.

and just nine in the mid-1600s. On September 20th 1658, John Hadley of The Quintain was buried; on February 2nd 1753, Mary daughter of William and Mary Hadley of Ridgacre was baptised. In the mid-1800s Hadley families could be found at some eight Quinton plots. Though, at just three, Hodgetts households were less numerous, they too had been present for at least 200 years: "Joseph, the son of Homfrey Hodgetts jun by Elizabeth his wife of Ridgacre" was born on February 11th 1658 and baptised on March 5th. Even though the register noted that no certificate was brought," Sarah Hodgits, infant of Ridgacre was buried in Hales Owen on April 2nd 1759. Perhaps Katherine Partridge, daughter of Mary Partridge spinster of Warley Wigerne, who was married in Hales Owen Parish Church in 1654, was related to Esther, wife of William Partridge of Warley Wigorn, buried in December 1752,[32] and to the family of Thomas Partridge who lived at plot W1 in the mid-1800s.

Quinton in the mid-1800s visits a particular place at a particular time. The time begins in 1840 and ends in 1861. This encompasses the compiling of tithe maps and apportionments, and four national enumerations: the general censuses of June 6th 1841, March 30th 1851 and April 7th 1861, along with the unique ecclesiastical census of March 30th 1851. Enumerators of the 1841 census were directed to round down the ages of all persons over 15 to the nearest 5 (thus people aged 15-19 were to be recorded as 15, etc). Though the enumerator for Warley Wigorn adhered to the principle, Ridgacre's enumerator was inconsistent, rounding down in some cases and recording actual ages in others. The place is that 943 acres contained in the 1844 tithe map of Ridgacre, with the enclaves of Warley Wigorn, which that map left blank, inserted. These encompass areas listed in censuses as Quinton, Upper Quinton, Hawthorn, Worlds End, Four Dwellings, Lower Dwellings and Hagg. Included also, from Warley Wigorn's 1845 tithe map, in the north west corner, is the remainder of Hagg Farm, parts of which were in Ridgacre. The tithe map area of 21st century Quinton, traversed by the A458 Hagley Road West (following the route of the turnpike road in the mid-1800s) stretches from Balden Road at plot 214 in the east to Narrow Lane at plot 7 in the west. Where there is more than ribbon development to the north of the turnpike road, the modern-day limit at plot W184 is approximately Hurst Green Road. The southern boundary remains exactly as it was in the mid-1800s – Bourn Brook, at the edge of Woodgate Valley Country Park.

The hand-written apportionments accompanying the tithe maps list residents and landowners with details of the plots which they respectively occupied or owned. For Ridgacre, 88 entries catalogue three churches, 76 households, five absentee tenants and four void properties. The relevant sections of the Warley Wigorn apportionments contain 14 households, all of which were occupied and no public buildings. Censuses of 1841 and 1851 show a slightly different picture, the earlier giving a total of 105 households (87 in Ridgacre and 18 in Warley Wigorn) and the later 103 households (with one less in each township). The 1851 census lists 547 inhabitants (458 in Ridgacre and 89 in Warley Wigorn) just 20 less than in the previous census which returned 465 inhabitants in Ridgacre and 102 in Warley Wigorn's Quinton enclaves. The composite tithe map, newly drawn for this study from the 1844 tithe map of Ridgacre and 1845 tithe map of Warley Wigorn, is itself a valuable artefact. More important, by virtue of colour, it offers what the original maps could not, showing at a glance, land utilization in Quinton in the mid-1800s.

---

[32] Gregory, K. (ed) *Parish Registers of Hales Owen Commonwealth Period 1652-1611*; Thompson, A. Registers of the Church of St John the Baptist, Hales Owen,1736-1761

Though many residents had spent the whole of their lives within Ridgacre and Warley Wigorn townships, records also indicate significant mobility. At least 277 surnames shared by Quinton residents during the mid-1800s, compared with the few inherited from earlier centuries, confirm an influx of new-comers. Such migrants had arrived from close at hand - the surrounding townships of Harborne, Hill, Lapal Northfield and Warley Salop; from Hales Owen and Birmingham, and also from much greater distances: English counties as widespread as Yorkshire and Hampshire, Herefordshire and Norfolk. Some had journeyed from Wales and Scotland and even crossed the sea from Ireland.

Counties of Origin of Quinton Residents in the mid-1800s

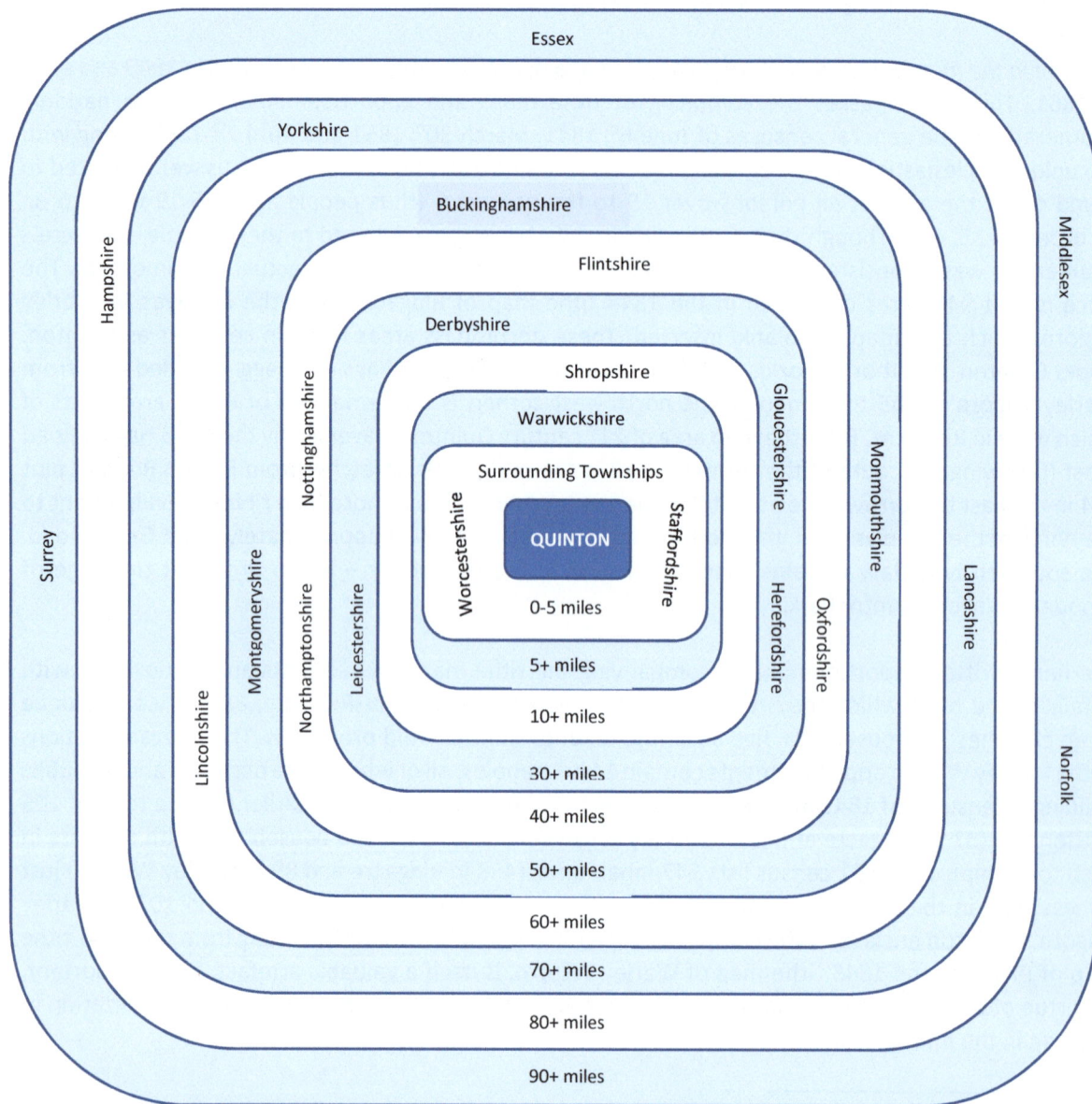

Essex

Yorkshire

Buckinghamshire

Flintshire

Derbyshire

Shropshire

Warwickshire

Surrounding Townships

Worcestershire **QUINTON** Staffordshire

0-5 miles

5+ miles

10+ miles

30+ miles

40+ miles

50+ miles

60+ miles

70+ miles

80+ miles

90+ miles

Hampshire

Middlesex

Surrey

Lincolnshire

Montgomeryshire

Northamptonshire

Nottinghamshire

Leicestershire

Gloucestershire

Herefordshire

Monmouthshire

Oxfordshire

Lancashire

Norfolk

Plot occupancy in Quinton in the mid-1800s varied in 1841/1851 between such single person households as those of Richard Holloway and Sarah Hill and the 14-member-households of the Davenport and Hadley/Haycock families. By 1861 the largest occupancy lagged only slightly behind with 13 in the Wood household. 101 Quinton families had between one and nine children living at home during the period, the average being 3.5. 27 families had five or more resident children, though from extant records it is not possible to say how many children may have left home or died in infancy.

Children per Family

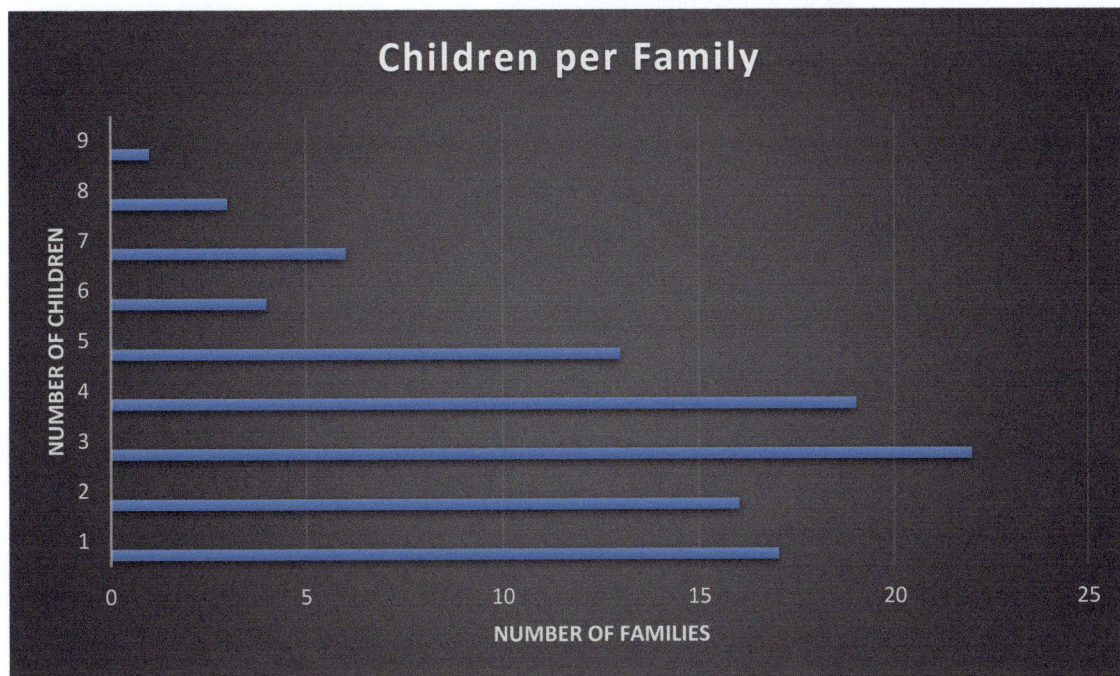

Though the colourful patchwork of pasture and arable revealed by the tithe map suggests a bucolic idyll, dark, satanic mills loomed and reality in the mid-1800s was less than pastoral. From its vantage point on the Midland Plateau, Quinton overlooked both Birmingham and the Black Country, in an age when the latter name was apt. Again, Francis Brett Young offers a vibrant topographical portrait. "A sunless, treeless waste, within a crescent of mournful hills from whose summits a canopy of eternal smoke was suspended above a slagged desert, its dead surface only variegated by conglomerations of brick surrounding the forges and pit-heads and brick-yards and furnaces in which the smoke was brewed; by drowned clay-pits and sullen canals whose surface appropriately reflected an apocalyptic sky."[33] To this portrait Quinton added, with its numerous nail-making households, the smoke from which, where, in some cases, entire families toiled away from dawn to dusk, would certainly have increased the general grime of the Black Country. At least 1,040 people lived in the area covered by the tithe map - 516 males and 524 females of whom 395 were under 10, but only 50 over 65. Of these, the censuses state occupations for 575.

---

[33] Young, F.B. (1936) *Far Forest*, pp 27-28

Quinton Occupations in mid-1800s

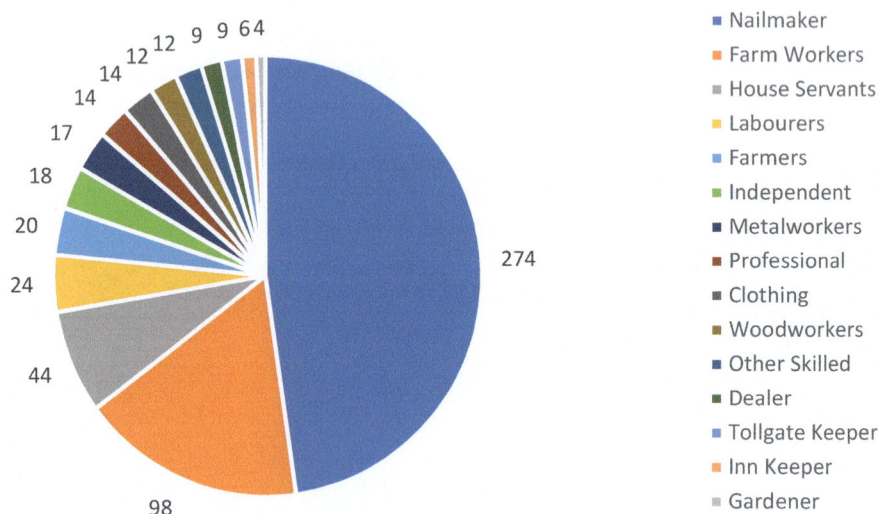

Legend:
- Nailmaker
- Farm Workers
- House Servants
- Labourers
- Farmers
- Independent
- Metalworkers
- Professional
- Clothing
- Woodworkers
- Other Skilled
- Dealer
- Tollgate Keeper
- Inn Keeper
- Gardener

Values shown on chart: 274, 98, 44, 24, 20, 18, 17, 14, 14, 12, 12, 9, 9, 6, 4

Farm Workers include waggoners and carters; House Servants include housekeeper, cook, nursemaids, washer-woman and char-woman; Independent includes those living on annuities; Metalworkers include blacksmiths, whitesmiths, file-cutters and grinder, puddler, steel-pin-maker, crank iron forger, brass founder, iron bedstead maker, screw wrench filers, tally maker; Professional includes clergymen, schoolteachers, accountant; Clothing includes dress-makers, tailors, cordwainers/shoemakers, glover; Woodworkers include cabinet makers, carpenters and joiner; Other Skilled includes wheelwrights, gun-finisher, lapidary, miners, stonemasons, varnish maker; Dealer includes provisions, cattle and horse dealers. The working-class status of Quinton in the mid-1800s is thus confirmed by its range of occupations which, with very few exceptions (clergy, schoolteachers, accountant, i.e. 14 out of 575 or 2.4%) are ranked in the lower to lowest divisions of the HISCO scale of occupations.[34]

If mid-1800s Birmingham and the Black Country generally were made dark by fumes from seemingly numberless smoking chimneys, of both huge furnaces and tiny hearths, then they were also frequently made wicked by the lawless and violent lives of many whose labours produced the smoke. That Quinton was no exception is confirmed by various sources. Describing the route of the turnpike road, passing through Quinton on its way from Birmingham to Hales Owen, William Hutton saw it as "like the life of man, chequered with good and evil; chiefly the latter."[35] That the road, on its journey through Quinton, was indeed a centre of mischief was confirmed when "one of the oldest men of the village remembered the time when the most barbarous sports were kept up on the main

---

[34] Historical International Standard Classification of Occupations (2013): a scale divided into 9 major groups: (1) Professional & technical; (2) Administrative & managerial; (3) Clerical; (4) Sales; (5) Services; (6) Agricultural; (7,8,9) Production, transport, labourers.
[35] Hutton, W. (1819) *The History of Birmingham*, p 409

road for Birmingham."[36] John Chambers, who lived just outside Quinton in Hill township, in 1842 was graphic in his condemnation – "the Quinton, a most dark and wicked place."[37] 20 years later, the Rector of Quinton, Rev C.H. Oldfield, expressed his dismay concerning current wickedness in a lengthy diatribe. "So much has happened in our Parish lately, that I must break silence. I beg everyone who has the good name of Quinton at heart, to reflect on what I say, (that) our Parish shall not become a bye-word of disgrace. I pass by the sins which I have often publicly and from house to house, entreated you to forsake. One evil that had previously worked in darkness and secrecy has lately come to light under circumstances so cruel and disgraceful that it must be exposed. It is witchcraft…"[38] That perhaps little had changed by the late-1800s is suggested by article in the *Bourne College Chronicle* stating that Quinton's "inhabitants number a little over 500 and are generally of somewhat primitive habits."[39]

The narrow parameters of geography and history confining the lives of Quinton's 1,040 residents on their 943 acres may too readily encourage a parochial view of this small community, overlooking the obvious fact that Quinton was part of a much wider world. Though the degree to which this outside world impinged upon the lives of those who lived in this small township remains a matter for conjecture, it is important not to neglect the wider context against which those lives were set.

The mid-1800s was the era of the young Queen Victoria, who had married her prince, Albert, in 1840. Six Prime Ministers served during this period: Lord Melbourne, replaced by Sir Robert Peel in 1841, in turn succeeded by Lord John Russell in 1846. The Earl of Derby held office twice (1852; 1858-59). Lord Aberdeen succeeded Derby's first government and was himself succeeded by Viscount Palmerston in 1855. Palmerston's government, briefly interrupted by Derby's second term, continued into the 1860s.

For 30 years since the ending of the Napoleonic Wars, England had enjoyed peace and stability, though this would change in the later mid-1800s with war in the Crimea and mutiny in India. At home, worsening trading conditions, poor harvests, high food prices, declining industrial activity and unemployment, paved the way for the General Enclosure Act of 1845,[40] designed to encourage large-scale farming, and the Repeal of the Corn Laws in 1846. Awareness that an increasing population needed to be fed, revealed a middle class in the wake of the Great Reform Act (1832), aspiring to political maturity. Also designed to provide food and other supplies at fair prices for the working classes, the Co-operative Movement began in Rochdale in 1844. Four years later John Stuart Mill published his *Political Economy* and Marx and Engels brought out their *Communist Manifesto*. Even had they heard of them, few of Quinton's residents would have been able to read them.

However, for those who could read, communications were improving in the mid-1800s. *Punch* magazine was launched in 1841 and *News of the World* in 1843. Three years later, *Daily News* was

---

[36] Middleton, G. (1888) *Bourne College Chronicle*, p 27

[37] Chambers, J. (1842) "An Epitome of the History of Primitive Methodism at The Quinton" in Bourne, H, & Flesher, J. *Primitive Methodist Magazine*

[38] Oldfield, C.H. (August 5th 1862) in Minutes of Vestry & Annual Parish Meeting: Christ Church The Quinton

[39] Middleton, G. (1888) *Bourne College Chronicle*, p 27

[40] Quinton was never subject to parliamentary enclosure - see Reynolds, S. (1964) "Agriculture" in Stephens, W.B., *A History of the Country of Warwick VII*, p 249

founded, with Charles Dickens as editor. Little dreaming that his innovation would grow into a multi-million-pound industry, in 1843 John Callcot Horsley designed the first Christmas card, though perhaps few people in Quinton received one, even though Rowland Hill had introduced the Penny Post in 1840. Six years later the Electric Telegraph Company made reality out of a previous dream of messages sent at speed. For those with leisure, of which there was surely little in Quinton, Thomas Cook organised his first outing – for a temperance group – from Leicester to Loughborough in July 1841.

English Literature enjoyed a particularly vigorous period of expression during the mid-1800s: the age of Anthony Trollope's *Barchester* novels, Elizabeth Gaskell's *Cranford*, Alfred, Lord Tennyson's *Charge of the Light Brigade* and William Wordsworth's *The Prelude*. Within one short year, high on the Yorkshire Moors, three young sisters proved that a lonely parsonage and a sheltered upbringing were no barrier to imagination's soaring flight. In 1847 Anne Brontë published *Agnes Grey*, Emily published *Wuthering Heights* and Charlotte published *Jane Eyre*. In the mid-1800s Charles Dickens produced both the story destined to become inextricably linked with the image of Victorian humbug reformed - *A Christmas Carol* (1843) and *Hard Times* (1854) castigated by Macaulay[41] for its sullen socialism.

If developments in literature had been happening far away from Quinton, a momentous event in the world of music was to occur right on its doorstep in the mid-1800s. Before an audience of 2,000 on August 26th 1846, Felix Mendelssohn conducted the first ever performance of his oratorio *Elijah* in Birmingham Town Hall. Could it be that amongst that large audience that day was any resident of Quinton? If so, they would have heard Birmingham-born composer Edward Bache[42] playing in the orchestra. Is it possible that the cottage dwellers of Ridgacre and Warley Wigorn were even remotely aware that Fryderyk Chopin, poet of the piano, died in 1849 or that Richard Wagner produced *Tannhäuser* in 1845 and *Lohengrin* in 1850?

In the art world, J.M.W. Turner, exhilarating exponent of light and colour, was still shocking the public in the mid-1800s with his use of yellow. As the age of Turner came to an end with his death in 1850, a new movement was born with the foundation in 1848 of the Pre-Raphaelite Brotherhood. Dante Gabriel Rossetti, William Holman Hunt and John Everett Millais, famed for their choice of religious and romantic subjects, rebelled against the pomp and grand manner of Raphael and the later Renaissance, and sought to return in style to the simplicity of the early fifteenth century. Did their concern for the purity of their art have any opportunity to strike chords with the residents of Quinton, the majority of whom had time and energy for little else than work?

Great advances in the mid-1800s were made in science and technology. Did they impinge on the nail forgers, agricultural workers and others who dwelt on Quinton's tithe map? Did they eat any of Huntley and Palmer's biscuits, which were first produced in 1841? Did any intrepid Quinton travellers make the journey down to London to marvel at Nelson's Column which was completed in 1843? Were any of them aware of the maiden transatlantic crossing in 1845 of Brunel's *SS Great Britain*, the first large

---

[41] Historian, poet, politician Thomas Babington Macaulay (1800-59) author of *Lays of Ancient Rome* (1842) and History of England (vols 1-2, 1849, vols 3-4, 1855)

[42] Francis Edward Bache (1833-1858) studied with James Stimpson, organist at Birmingham Town Hall, and composed more than 60 works for piano.

ship to be fitted with a screw propeller? Would they have known of the discovery of the planet Neptune by German astronomer Johann Galle in 1846? Were their own lives improved and made safer by James Simpson's pioneering use of chloroform in an operation in 1847 or by Florence Nightingale's innovative nursing at Scutari in the next decade? Did any of them ever cross Robert Stevenson's Menai Bridge which opened in 1849? 11 years earlier, the first train from London Euston arrived in Birmingham; Snow Hill and New Street stations opened in 1852. However, it would be another decade before the possibilities of rail travel approached any closer to Quinton, with passenger services from Stourbridge to Cradley in 1863 and to Old Hill in 1866, a line eventually reaching Hales Owen in 1878. Did many Quinton residents of the mid-1800s take advantage of the mail coach which passed through the village, connecting in Birmingham with the 10.30am London train? Were any of them fortunate enough to visit that showcase of British achievement, the Great Exhibition of 1851? Were they amazed to read of David Livingstone's discovery in 1855 of Mosi-oa-Tunya – *the smoke that thunders* – which he re-named Victoria Falls? Were they shocked when Charles Darwin published *On the Origin of Species* in 1859? Did Quinton residents share in the general suffering when cholera swept the country in 1849, reaching epidemic proportions in July-September? This question need not remain rhetorical, for it can, in part, be answered. In this, the most severe outbreak of the disease the country had experienced, some 53,000 people died in England and Wales. Dudley registered 412 cholera deaths between August 21st and December 22nd and Stourbridge 413 between July 22nd and December 29th. Birmingham recorded "nearly complete immunity from cholera in its successive epidemics while neighbouring districts suffered severely."[43] Of the ten burials at Christ Church The Quinton between June 28th and December 18th 1849, only 43-year-old Isaac Dearn, of Bristnall Fields, Warley Wigorn, died of Asiatic Cholera. Clearly, Quinton's comparative isolation on the high Midland Plateau offered some immunity from the invasions of the outside world.

This, then, is the wider map on which some 1,040 folk lived in the mid-1800s. Objective assessment suggests that Quinton had little to commend it. It was the scene of no decisive historical battle, political intrigue or significant archaeological discovery. It had no ancient buildings of particular note or worth. Within its boundaries were no recognised beauty-spots or remarkable geographical features. In its new churchyard perhaps was laid no

> "Heart once pregnant with celestial Fire,
> Hands that the Rod of Empire might have sway'd,
> Or wak'd to Extacy the living Lyre."[44]

Nevertheless, Quinton in the mid-1800s takes its place as a story of the tragi-comedy of human life, revealing more than official listing's records of births, marriages, deaths, addresses and occupations. Contained within these 20 years are tales of work, poverty and unemployment; complex family relationships; assault, attempted rape, illness, timely and untimely death; clues as to who were the

---

[43] Heslop, T.P. (1866) "The Medical Aspects of Birmingham" in Timmins, S. *The Resources, Products and Industrial History of Birmingham and the Midland District*, p 689
[44] Gray, Thomas (1751) *An Elegy Written in a Country Church-Yard*

people of local influence – the *Village-Hampden, Milton and Cromwell*. The story reveals that though the historic ties of Ridgacre and Warley Wigorn were with the parish of Hales Owen, in the mid-1800s it was to Birmingham churches that those who chose not to be married at Quinton's Christ Church[45] turned, perhaps laying the foundations for Quinton severing its ties with Hales Owen and becoming part of Birmingham two generations later.[46]

Simply knowing that there were 274 nail-makers or 98 farm-labourers in Quinton at this time, fascinating ancestral narrative though it may be, gives little clue as to the reality of their lives. However, the insights of poets, novelists and surveyor in the introduction to each section of this study help to lift the veil, collapsing the interval of time and space separating us from them by illuminating the daily lives, craftsmanship, husbandry, skills and trades of the people we meet. The CD *Meet the Quinton Ancestors*[47] follows Rev William Skilton on a pastoral tour of his parish. Though the conversations are imaginary, they are plausible, for the people, their concerns, histories and activities are real.

History, of course, presents many conflicting narratives which may obscure reality, but L.P. Hartley was only partly right in his judgement that *the past is a foreign country*.[48] The 1,040 people who lived and died on the 943 acres of Ridgacre and Warley Wigorn together creating Quinton in the mid-1800s were four-dimensional people, leading four-dimensional lives in a four-dimensional world. The opportunity is given to those who inherit their narrative to ensure that they have not *perished as though they had never existed*, but have *left behind them a name to be commemorated in story* – the story of which all who live, have lived, or will live within the borders of the Quinton tithe map play their part.

Bourn Brook –
Quinton's only
natural boundary

---

[45] Neither the Wesleyan nor the Primitive Methodist Chapel was licensed for marriages.
[46] Quinton became part of the City of Birmingham in November 1909.
[47] Written and recorded in 2000, the CD deals only with Ridgacre township, within which context Redhall was the largest farm. Later research also corrects earlier misconceptions: Thomas White farmed at Lower Quinton not Lower Ridgacre; James Wragg farmed at (Upper) Ridgacre not Highfield, which did not exist by that name in the mid-1800s; paupers Thomas and Sarah Haycock lived at plot W87 not at plot 233.
[48] Opening of *The Go-Between* (1953).

3   Tithe Commission

By the 19th century tithes had been part of English taxation for over a millennium. This levy of one tenth of the gross produce of the land had much older antecedents. In the sagas and legends of the Old Testament, the patriarch Jacob promised God, "Of all that thou shalt give me, I will surely give the tenth unto thee."[49] By the time of the New Testament, pharisaic law required tithes even of mint and anise and cummin.[50] What began in England as voluntary contributions to the upkeep of the church had, in the 8th century, become compulsory and was enacted into the laws of King Canute before the Norman Conquest. That the church enforced this right is made clear by Geoffrey Chaucer in the 14th century, albeit in praising his good, though poor, parson, who, unlike some of his colleagues was unwilling to threaten tithe defaulters with excommunication: "Ful looth were hym to cursen for his tithes."[51] Popular resentment of tithes, particularly when appropriated to monks and the higher clergy, was focused by Shakespeare in the late 16th century, but in a scene set in the 13th century, when King John informs the Papal Legate: "No Italian priest/Shall tithe or toll in our dominions."[52]

At the 16th century dissolution of the monasteries, their tithes were first vested in the crown and then sold on, by which route the Lyttelton family acquired their tithe holdings in Quinton. Over a century later popular literature still deplored the whole concept of tithes. In 1691, John Dryden (appointed Poet Laureate by King Charles II) in his opera *King Arthur*, has three peasants singing: "We've cheated the parson, we'll cheat him again,/For why should a blockhead have one in ten?"[53] By the 18th century, the increasing value of tithes enabled the squirearchy to encourage their younger sons into livings within their gift, at the same time enhancing parsonages into lesser manor houses by such means as the addition of bay windows. Such actions only served to compound the general unpopularity of tithes with those farmers who had to pay them, for this was a selective tax and a burden not then shared by tradesmen, manufacturers and other wage-earners.

Tithes fell into three categories. Predial tithes were levied on the fruits of the earth – corn, fruit, hay, wood etc; agistment tithes payable on animal products – calves, colts, lambs, eggs, honey, milk, wool etc; personal tithes – gains of labour and industry, especially fishing and milling. Originally paid in kind, from the middle of the 17th century many payments had been commuted into money, by which time personal tithes, notoriously difficult to enforce, had declined. In the apportionments which follow in sections 2 & 3, tithes are divided into two categories: Great Tithes – those levied on grain, hay and wood, and Small (or Vicarial) Tithes – everything else which was liable. Variation in exact definition from place to place, however, was not uncommon according to the "custom of the parish."

By the 19th century resentment at the payment of tithes had reached its apogee. When corn prices were high in 1816, a Select Committee set payments, often invariable throughout a 14-year lease. Agricultural riots in the early 1830s brought the issue into sharp focus and the Great Reform Bill of 1832 paved the way for redress. The Tithe Commutation Act introduced by Lord John Russell in

---

[49] Genesis 28.22 (King James Version 1611)
[50] Matthew 23.23
[51] Chaucer, G. (c1387→) *The Canterbury Tales*: Prologue, l 486
[52] Shakespeare, W. (1591-1598) *King John*, act III, sc 1, l 153-154
[53] Dryden, J. (1691) *King Arthur*, act 5

February 1836 and passed into law in August of that year, replaced tithes in kind with a land rent charge adjusted annually according to the average price of wheat, barley and oats calculated over a seven-year period. England and Wales were divided into 14,829 tithe districts. In a number of these it was quickly established that tithes were no longer payable in 1836 and eventually 11,800 tithe appointments and maps were produced, two of which defined the townships of Ridgacre and Warley Wigorn. Three commissioners, supported by a team of assistants, were appointed with responsibility to confirm rent charges and apportion the fixed amount over the various land types of each district. The tithe on arable land was calculated at ⅕ of its rent value, whereas pasture was less than ⅛. Meetings were held within the districts, it being the responsibility of assistant commissioners to conduct local inquiries where disputes arose and to recommend the final confirmation of awards.

The apportionments were produced in standardized format on rolls of parchment sheets each measuring 21⅓" x 18¾". A preamble stated the articles of agreement for commutation, named the officials responsible and the title owners. This was followed by a schedule of apportionments, listing owners and occupiers of each parcel of land. A summary and, if necessary, any alterations completed the document. In addition, and bound in with the apportionments, was a tithe map which the commissioners had originally specified should be drawn to a scale of 3 chains to 1 inch (27.6" to 1 mile), should give accurate measurements of each parcel of land and show its state of cultivation. The tithe map needed to be sufficiently accurate to serve as legal evidence of boundaries, confirmed by a certificate of accuracy signed by two tithe commissioners. In reality, some districts relied on pre-existent maps of varying scales, and accuracy did not always reach the commissioners' expectations. The Ridgacre map shows no building on plot 233 identified in the apportionments as the home of Thomas Haycock; the Warley Wigorn map labels the township as in Salop, over-written as Worcester. Nor were the apportionments always strictly accurate. Listed Ridgacre landowner Aaron White (plots 24 & 25) had died in 1832, 12 years before the tithe award; listed Warley Wigorn occupier William Pritchett actually lived in Lapal township and evidently had an under-tenant at plot W125.

Within ten years of its establishment the Tithe Commission had completed 75% of all tithe awards and the last survey was finished in 1866.

3.01 Ridgacre Apportionments: Preamble

Know all Men by these presents that I, George Wingrove Cooke, of the Middle Temple Barrister at Law, having been duly appointed and sworn an Assistant Tithe Commissioner according to the provisions of the Act for the Commutation of Tithes in England and Wales and having been also duly appointed to ascertain and award the total sum to be paid by way of rent charge instead of the Tithes of the Township of Ridgacre in the parish of Hales Owen in the County of Salop do hereby award as follows that is to say:-

Whereas I have held divers Meetings in the said parish as touching the matter aforesaid, of which Meetings due notice was given for the information of the Landowners and Tithe owners of the said parish.

And whereas I have duly considered all the allegations and proofs tendered to me by all parties interested and have myself made all enquiries touching the promised subject which appeared to me to be necessary.

And whereas I find that the estimated quantity in statute measure of all the lands of the said Township, the whole of which are subject to the payment of Tithes in kind, amounts to five hundred and forty-nine acres and thirty poles which are cultivated as follows, that is to say:
Two hundred and forty-seven acres three roods and twenty-three poles as Arable Land;
Two hundred and seventy-nine acres three roods and seventeen poles as pasture and Twenty-one acres one rood and thirty poles as gardens.

And whereas I have estimated the clear annual value of the said Tithes in the manner directed by the said Act of Parliament and have also taken into account the rates and assessments paid in respect of such Tithes during the seven years of average prescribed by the said Act.

And whereas I find that the Right Honourable George, Lord Lyttelton is Impropriator of all the Great Tithes of the said Township

And that the Vicar of the parish of Hales Owen for the time being is entitled to all the Small Tithes thereof.

Now know ye that I, the said George Wingrove Cooke, do hereby award that the annual sum of twenty-two pounds by way of rent charge subject to the provisions of the said Act shall from the first day of January next following the confirmation of the Apportionments of the said rent charge be paid to the said Impropriator, his heirs or assigns or to the persons entitled in remainder or reversion after him, instead of all the Great Tithes arising from all the Lands of the said Township.

And that the annual sum of forty pounds also by way of rent charge and subject to the provisions and to commence from the time aforesaid shall be paid to the Vicar of Hales Owen for the time being instead of all the Small Tithes arising from all the Lands of the said Township of Ridgacre.

In Testimony whereof I have hereunto set my hand this thirteenth day of February in the year of our Lord one thousand eight hundred and forty-four.

Signed Geo. Wingrove Cooke

Now I, Jeremiah Mathews, of Kidderminster in the County of Worcestershire,
having been duly appointed Valuer to apportion the total Sum awarded to be paid by way of Rent Charge in lieu of Tithes amongst the several Lands of the said Township of Ridgacre

Do hereby apportion the Rent Charges as follows: -
GROSS RENT CHARGES payable to the Tithe Owner in lieu of tithes for the Township of Ridgacre in the Parish of Hales Owen in the County of Salop:

Sixty-two pounds viz.

To the Vicar of Hales Owen:	40.0.0
To Lord Lyttelton, Impropriator:	22.0.0
	62.0.0

Value in Imperial Bushels and Decimal Parts of an Imperial Bushel of Wheat, Barley and Oats:

Crop:	Price per Bushel:	Bushels and Decimal Parts:
WHEAT	7/0¼d	58,87240
BARLEY	3/11¼d	104,42105
OATS	2/9d	150,30303

3.02 Ridgacre Apportionments in order of Plan Numbers

Plan	Landowner	Occupier	Address	Cultivation
1	White, John	Farmer, Jonathan	In Nobles Innage	Pasture
2	White, John	Farmer, Jonathan	New Innage	Pasture
3	White, John	White, Thomas	Cotterill's Innage	Arable
4	White, John	Farmer, Jonathan	In the First Innage	Arable
5	White, John	Farmer, Jonathan	Foredrove	
6	Lyttelton, Lord	White, Thomas	Part of Far Quinton Field	Pasture
7	Grosvenor, John	Grosvenor, John	House, Shop, Garden	
7	Grosvenor, John	Hunt, James	House, Shop, Garden	
8	Foley, John	Foley, John	In The Field	Pasture
9	Foley, John	Foley, John	In The Field	Pasture
10	White, John	Farmer, Jonathan	In First Quinton Field	Pasture
11	White, John	Farmer, Jonathan	In First Quinton Field	Pasture
12	Foley, John	Foley, John	Kings Leasow	Arable
13	Foley, John	Foley, John	Lower Meadow	Pasture
14	Yates, John	Yates, John	Garden	
15	Lyttelton, Lord	White, Thomas	Jack Clerk's Meadow	Arable
16	Lyttelton, Lord	White, Thomas	Further Mancroft	Arable
17	Lyttelton, Lord	White, Thomas	Four Acres	Arable
18	Lyttelton, Lord	White, Thomas	Mancroft Meadow	Pasture
19	White, John	Farmer, Jonathan	Lower Cutlers Leasow	Pasture
20	White, John	Farmer, Jonathan	Middle Cutlers Leasow	Pasture
21	white, John	Farmer, Jonathan	Little Cutlers Leasow	Pasture
22	Lyttelton, Lord	White, Thomas	Marl Pit	
23	Lyttelton, Lord	White, Thomas	Far Rough Meadow	Arable
24	White, Aaron	White, Thomas	Upper Golds Meadow	Pasture
25	White, Aaron	White, Thomas	Lower Golds Meadow	Pasture
26	Lyttelton, Lord	White, Thomas	Rough Meadow	Pasture
27	Lyttelton, Lord	White, Thomas	Part of Foldyard	
28	Lyttelton, Lord	White, Thomas	The Close	Pasture
29	Millward, Ann	Millward, Ann	House & Garden	
30	White, John	Yates, John	Pleck	Pasture
31	White, Ann	Yates, Benjamin	House & Garden	
32	White, John	Farmer, Jonathan	Garden	Arable
33	Powers, Sally	Goode, Joseph	House & Garden	
33	Powers, Sally	Yates, John	House & Garden	
34	White, John	Male, James	House & Garden	
35	Lyttelton, Lord	Void	House & Garden	
35	Lyttelton, Lord	Wheeler, Benjamin	House & Garden	
36	Glebe		Garden	
37	Darby, Joseph	Andrews, Thomas	House & Garden	

Plan	Landowner	Occupier	Address	Cultivation
37	Darby, Joseph	Mason, Mary	House & Garden	
37	Darby, Joseph	Read, John	House & Garden	
38	Darby, Joseph	Prady, James	House & Garden	
38	Darby, Joseph	Sadler, John	House & Garden	
39	White, John	Farmer, Jonathan	Barn & Yard	
40	White, John	Farmer, Jonathan	Cutlers Meadow	Pasture
41	White, John	Smith, Edward	House & Garden	
41	White, John	Yeomans, Thomas	House & Garden	
42	Lyttelton, Lord	White, Thomas	Hither Mancroft	Arable
43	Hill, Timothy	Guest, John	House, Shop & Garden	
44	Bissell, James	Price, James	House, Shop & Garden	
45	Bissell, James	Hall, John	House, Shop & Garden	
45	Bissell, James	Rose, William	House, Shop & Garden	
46	Smith, Thomas	Smith, David	House, Shop & Garden	
46	Smith, Thomas	Smith, Thomas	House, Shop & Garden	
47	Cutler, James	Cutler, James	House, Shop & Garden	
47	Taylor, Francis	Hallen, John	House, Shop & Garden	
48	Glebe		Big Leasow	Pasture
49	Glebe		Parsonage & Garden	
50	Glebe		Church, Yard, School	
51	Bissell, James	Cooper, James	Upper Stony Cross	Arable
52	Bissell, James	Cooper, James	Lower Stony Cross	Pasture
53	Bissell, James	Cooper, James	Little Stony Cross	Pasture
54	Foley, John	Foley, John	Top Meadow	Pasture
55	Foley, John	Foley, John	House, Yard, Barn	
55	Foley, John	Hall, James	House	
56	Foley, John/Ambrose	Foley, John/Ambrose	Chapel & Yard	
57	Lyttelton, Lord	Hall, James	House, Shop & Garden	
58	Turnpike Commissioners	Turnpike Commissioners	Tollhouse & Yard	
59	Foley, Ambrose	Foley, John	Garden	
59	Foley, Ambrose	Hall, George	Garden	
60	Macdonald, H. Foley	Westwood, Benjamin	House, Shop & Garden	
61	Lyttelton, Lord	Powers, Sarah	House & Garden	
62	Foley, John	Foley, John	Garden	
63	Foley, John/Ambrose	Mason, John	House, Shop, Garden	
64	Lyttelton, Lord	White, Thomas	Foredrove	
65	Foley, Ambrose	Foley, John	Little Meadow	Pasture
66	Foley, Ambrose	Foley, John	Church Leasow	Pasture
67	Foley, Ambrose	Foley, John	Little Middle Leasow	Pasture
68	Foley, Ambrose	Foley, John	Little Wood Leasow	Arable

Plan	Landowner	Occupier	Address	Cultivation
69	Foley, Ambrose	Foley, John	Big Wood Leasow	Arable
70	Foley, Ambrose	Foley, John	Big Middle Leasow	Arable
71	Foley, Ambrose	Foley, John	Barn Close	Pasture
72	Foley, Ambrose	Hadley, Benjamin	House & Shop	
73	Foley, Ambrose	Foley, John	House & Farm Buildings	
74	Macdonald, H. Foley	Clay, Benjamin	House, Shop & Garden	
74	Macdonald, H. Foley	Macdonald, H. Foley	House & Garden	
74	Macdonald, H. Foley	Robinson, James	House, Shop & Garden	
75	Grainger, David	Underhill, Richard	House, Buildings, Garden	
76	Grainger, David	Underhill, Richard	Near High Leasow	Pasture
77	Grainger, David	Underhill, Richard	Far High Leasow	Arable
78	Grainger, David	Underhill, Richard	Far Middle Leasow	Arable
79	Grainger, David	Underhill, Richard	Near Middle Leasow	Arable
80	Grainger, David	Underhill, Richard	Meadow	Pasture
81	Foley, John	Cooper, James	Meadow	Pasture
82	Foley, John	Cooper, James	Middle Leasow	Arable
83	Foley, John	Cooper, James	Lower Leasow	Arable
84	Foley, John	Cooper, James	Top Leasow	Arable
85	Foley, John	Void	House (in ruins) & Garden	
86	Foley, John	Cooper, James	Slough Leasow	Arable
87	Spurrier, William	Davenport, John	Meadow	Pasture
88	Hill, Ann	Nicholls, Henry	Great Hill	Pasture
89	Bissell, James	Cooper, James	Red Lion Inn Stable Yard & Garden	
90	White, John	Read, Daniel	House & Garden	
91	White, John	Hadley, Samuel	House & Garden	
91	White, John	Record, Joseph	House & Garden	
92	White, John	Farmer, Jonathan	The Hill	Pasture
93	Cooper, James	Harris, Joseph	House, Shop & Garden	
94	Lyttelton, Lord	Sadler, Joseph	House, Shop & Garden	
95	Hill, Ann	Nicholls, Henry	Shop Close	Pasture
96	White, John	Farmer, Jonathan	The Long Hills	Pasture
97	Grazebrook, William	Tomlinson, Richard	Mill Field	Arable
98	Grazebrook, William	Tomlinson, Richard	Middle Piece	Pasture
99	Grazebrook, William	Tomlinson, Richard	Bottom Piece	Arable
100	Grazebrook, William	Tomlinson, Richard	Barn Piece	Pasture
101	Grazebrook, William	Tomlinson, Richard	Farm House Building	
102	Grazebrook, William	Tomlinson, Richard	Rump Piece	Pasture
103	Lyttelton, Lord	White, Thomas	Taylor's Close	Arable
104	Grazebrook, William	Tomlinson, Richard	Rickyard Piece	Arable
105	Lyttelton, Lord	White, Thomas	Windmill Piece	Arable

Plan	Landowner	Occupier	Address	Cultivation
106	Lyttelton, Lord	White, Thomas	Bonfire Leasow	Arable
107	Grazebrook, William	Ragg, James	Far Meadow	Pasture
108	Lyttelton, Lord	White, Thomas	Taylor's Croft	Arable
109	Lyttelton, Lord	White, Thomas	The Park	Pasture
110	Lyttelton, Lord	White, Thomas	Little Leasow	Pasture
111	Grazebrook, William	Ragg, James	Old House Meadow	Pasture
112	Grazebrook, William	Coley, Thomas	House & Gardens	
112	Grazebrook, William	Gould, William	House & Gardens	
112	Grazebrook, William	Read, Elijah	House & Gardens	
113	Grazebrook, William	Ragg, James	House & Farm Building	
114	Grazebrook, William	Ragg, James	Lane	
115	Grazebrook, William	Ragg, James	Ridgacre Meadow	Pasture
116	Birch, John	Birch, John	Garden	
117	Birch, John	Birch, John	Tenements, Building, Yard	
118	Birch, John	Birch, John	Garden	
119	Lyttelton, Lord	White, Thomas	The Meadow	Pasture
120	Lyttelton, Lord	White, Thomas	Farm House Building	
121	Lyttelton, Lord	White, Thomas	Dafodil Leasow	Arable
122	Birch, John	Birch, John	Middle Meadow	Pasture
123	Birch, John	Birch, John	Pit Leasow	Arable
124	Birch, John	Birch, John	Upper Meadow	Pasture
125	Birch, John	Birch, John	Second Cow Leasow	Pasture
126	Birch, John	Birch, John	Cow Leasow	Pasture
127	Birch, John	Birch, John	Fog Leasow	Arable
128	Birch, John	Birch, John	Clover Leasow	Pasture
129	Grazebrook, William	Ragg, James	Yell Leasow	Arable
130	Grazebrook, William	Ragg, James	Upper Ridgacre Field	Arable
131	Grazebrook, William	Ragg, James	Lower Ridgacre Field	Arable
132	Grazebrook, William	Ragg, James	Old Meadow	Pasture
133	Grazebrook, William	Ragg, James	Smooth Moor	Arable
134	Grazebrook, William	Ragg, James	Big Rye Hill	Arable
135	Grazebrook, William	Ragg, James	The Sling	Pasture
136	Grazebrook, William	Ragg, James	Rushy Piece	Arable
137	Grazebrook, William	Ragg, James	Little Rye Hill	Arable
138	Grazebrook, William	Ragg, James	Brickkiln Leasow	Arable
139	Grazebrook, William	Ragg, James	Broad Leasow	Arable
140	Grazebrook, William	Ragg, James	Piece behind Powells	Arable
141	Grazebrook, William	Ragg, James	The Warms	Pasture
142	Greaves, Richard	Jakeman, John	Long Leasow	Arable
143	Greaves, Richard	Jakeman, John	Little Leasow	Arable
144	Greaves, Richard	Jakeman, John	Spring Leasow	Arable

Plan	Landowner	Occupier	Address	Cultivation
145	Greaves, Richard	Jakeman, John	Broad Leasow	Pasture
146	Greaves, Richard	Jakeman, John	Well Leasow	Arable
147	Greaves, Richard	Jakeman, John	Clover Leasow	Arable
148	Greaves, Richard	Jakeman, John	Head Piece	Pasture
149	Greaves, Richard	Jakeman, John	Five Acres	Arable
150	Greaves, Richard	Jakeman, John	Brickkiln Piece	Pasture
151	Greaves, Richard	Jakeman, John	Plant Leasow	Pasture
152	Greaves, Richard	Jakeman, John	Garden Leasow	Pasture
153	Greaves, Richard	Jakeman, John	Jones's Leasow	Pasture
154	Greaves, Richard	Jakeman, John	World's End Leasow	Pasture
155	Greaves, Richard	Jakeman, John	Big Meadow	Pasture
156	Greaves, Richard	Jakeman, John	House, Building & Garden	
157	Greaves, Richard	Jakeman, John	The Croft	Pasture
158	Whitehouse, John	Coley, Josiah	Croft	Pasture
159	Whitehouse, John	Coley, Josiah	House & Garden	
159	Whitehouse, John	Lane, David	House & Garden	
160	Penn, William	Johnson, William	Pleck	Pasture
161	Hales Owen Poor	Wakeman, Joseph	Parish Ground	Pasture
162	King, William	Wakeman, Joseph	Little Meadow	Pasture
163	King, William	Wakeman, Joseph	House & Garden	
164	King, William	Wakeman, Joseph	Well Leasow	Pasture
165	King, William	Wakeman, Joseph	Peters Piece	Arable
166	King, William	Wakeman, Joseph	Wood Leasow	Arable
167	King, William	Wakeman, Joseph	Wood Leasow	Pasture
168	King, William	Wakeman, Joseph	Holly Meadow	Pasture
169	Penn, William	Johnson, William	Old Road	
170	Hales Owen Poor	Wakeman, Joseph	Potatoe Leasow	Pasture
171	Hales Owen Poor	Void	House & Garden	
172	Hales Owen Poor	Wakeman, Joseph	Orchard	Pasture
173	Birch, George	Birch, George	World's End Meadow	Pasture
174	Lyttelton, Lord	Hill, Isaac	House, Shop, Garden	
175	Lyttelton, Lord	Deeley, George	House & Garden	
176	Birch, George	Birch, George	Lower Hannah Green	Arable
177	Birch, John	Birch, John	Lunt Coppy	Pasture
178	Birch, John	Birch, John	Wood Leasow	Pasture
179	Birch, John	Birch, John	Long Leasow	Pasture
180	Birch, John	Birch, John	Old Lane	
181	Birch, George	Birch, George	Big Leasow	Pasture
182	Birch, George	Birch, George	Lunt Leasow	Arable
183	Birch, George	Birch, George	Field	Arable
184	Birch, George	Birch, George	World's End Leasow	Arable

Plan	Landowner	Occupier	Address	Cultivation
185	Birch, George	Birch, George	Ewes Well Leasow	Arable
186	Birch, George	Birch, George	Pits Wood Leasow	Arable
187	Birch, George	Birch, George	The Sling	Arable
188	Hill, Timothy	Hill, Benjamin	House, Shop & Garden	
189	Hill, Timothy	Hill, Benjamin	Little Meadow	Pasture
190	Hill, Timothy	Hill, Benjamin	Big Meadow	Pasture
191	Lyttelton, Lord	White, Thomas	Gosty Leasow	Pasture
192	Lyttelton, Lord	White, Thomas	Lower Leasow	Arable
193	Lyttelton, Lord	White, Thomas	Upper Leasow	Pasture
194	Grazebrook, William	Tomlinson, Richard	Cow Leasow	Arable
195	Lyttelton, Lord	White, Thomas	Bridge Leasow	Arable
196	Grazebrook, William	Tomlinson, Richard	Daleday Math	Pasture
197	Grazebrook, William	Tomlinson, Richard	The Meadow	Pasture
198	Hill, Ann	Nicholls, Henry	Roundabout	Pasture
199	Birch, George	Birch, George	Aldridge Meadow	Pasture
200	Birch, George	Birch, George	The Muttons	Arable
201	Lyttelton, Lord	Hadley, Samuel	House & Garden	
202	Hill, Timothy	Dixon, Joseph	Close	Pasture
203	Birch, George	Birch, George	Great Ox Leasow	Arable
204	Hill, Timothy	Dixon, Joseph	Close	Pasture
205	Hill, Timothy	Partridge, James	House & Garden	
206	Birch, George	Birch, George	Two Hill Leasow	Pasture
207	Birch, George	Birch, George	Ox Leasow	Arable
208	Birch, George	Birch, George	Little Meadow	Pasture
209	Birch, George	Birch, George	Redhall Farmhouse &c	
210	Birch, George	Birch, George	House Meadow	Pasture
211	Birch, George	Birch, George	Barn Close	Pasture
212	Birch, George	Birch, George	Great Wood Leasow	Arable
213	Birch, George	Birch, George	Second Wood Leasow	Arable
214	Lyttelton, Lord	Birch, George	Redhill Piece	Arable
215	Lyttelton, Lord	Milner, James	Garden	
216	Lyttelton, Lord	Milner, James	House & Garden	
217	Lyttelton, Lord	Woodbridge, Joseph	House, Smith's Shop & Garden	
218	Lyttelton, Lord	Dixon, Joseph	Garden	
219	Hill, Timothy	Dixon, Joseph	Beech Tree Inn Garden	
220	Hill, Timothy	Branton, Richard	House & Garden	
221	Lyttelton, Lord	Branton, Richard	Garden	
222	Lyttelton, Lord	Cutler, Widow	Garden	
222	Lyttelton, Lord	Fox, John	Garden	
222	Lyttelton, Lord	Taylor, John	Garden	

Plan	Landowner	Occupier	Address	Cultivation
223	Hill, Timothy	Cutler, Esther	House & Garden	
223	Hill, Timothy	Fox, John	House & Garden	
223	Hill, Timothy	Taylor, John	House & Garden	
224	Birch, George	Birch, George	Upper Tolly Leasow	Arable
225	Birch, George	Birch, George	Square Leasow	Arable
226	Birch, George	Birch, George	Smart's Leasow	Pasture
227	Birch, George	Birch, George	Smart's Piece	Pasture
228	Birch, George	Smart, Edward	House & Garden	
229	Birch, George	Fox, William	House & Garden	
230	Birch, George	Hall, Thomas	Garden	
231	Birch, George	Birch, George	Road Leasow	Pasture
232	Birch, George	Page, Thomas	House & Garden	
232	Birch, George	Partridge, Thomas	House & Garden	
233	Birch, George	Haycock, Thomas	House & Garden	
234	Birch, George	Adams, James	Holly Bush Inn & Garden	
235	Cutler, Ann	Cutler, Ann	House, Shop & Garden	
236	Lyttelton, Lord	Birch, George	Redhill Piece	Arable
237	Hill, Ann	Nicholls, Henry	Upper Sawpit Leasow	Arable
238	Hill, Ann	Nicholls, Henry	Lower Sawpit Leasow	Arable
239	Hill, Ann	Nicholls, Henry	Coneygre Leasow	Pasture
240	Boulton, Samuel	Void	House & Garden	
241	Boulton, Samuel	Boulton, Samuel	House & Garden	
242	Hill, Ann	Nicholls, Henry	Pleck	Arable
243	Hill, Ann	Nicholls, Henry	House & Farm Buildings	
244	Hill, Ann	Nicholls, Henry	Barn Close	Pasture
245	Hill, Ann	Nicholls, Henry	Hither Leys	Arable
246	Hill, Ann	Nicholls, Henry	Home Meadow	Pasture
247	Hill, Ann	Nicholls, Henry	Little Leys	Arable
248	Hill, Ann	Nicholls, Henry	Top of the Meadow	Arable

3.03 Ridgacre Apportionments in order of Occupiers

Plan	Landowner	Occupier	Address	Cultivation
234	Birch, John	Adams, James	Holly Bush Inn & Garden	
37	Darby, Joseph	Andrews, Thomas	House & Garden	
173	Birch, George	Birch, George	World's End Meadow	Pasture
176	Birch, George	Birch, George	Lower Hannah Green	Arable
181	Birch, George	Birch, George	Big Leasow	Pasture
182	Birch, George	Birch, George	Lunt Leasow	Arable
183	Birch, George	Birch, George	Field	Arable
184	Birch, George	Birch, George	World's End Leasow	Arable
185	Birch, George	Birch, George	Ewes Well Leasow	Arable

Plan	Landowner	Occupier	Address	Cultivation
186	Birch, George	Birch, George	Pits Wood Leasow	Arable
187	Birch, George	Birch, George	The Sling	Arable
199	Birch, George	Birch, George	Aldridge Meadow	Pasture
200	Birch, George	Birch, George	The Muttons	Arable
203	Birch, George	Birch, George	Great Ox Leasow	Arable
206	Birch, George	Birch, George	Two Hill Leasow	Pasture
207	Birch, George	Birch, George	Ox Leasow	Arable
208	Birch, George	Birch, George	Little Meadow	Pasture
209	Birch, George	Birch, George	Redhall Farmhouse &c	
210	Birch, George	Birch, George	House Meadow	Pasture
211	Birch, George	Birch, George	Barn Close	Pasture
212	Birch, George	Birch, George	Great Wood Leasow	Arable
213	Birch, George	Birch, George	Second Wood Leasow	Arable
214	Lyttelton, Lord	Birch, George	Redhill Piece	Arable
224	Birch, George	Birch, George	Upper Tolly Leasow	Arable
225	Birch, George	Birch, George	Square Leasow	Arable
226	Birch, George	Birch, George	Smart's Leasow	Pasture
227	Birch, George	Birch, George	Smart's Piece	Pasture
231	Birch, George	Birch, George	Road Leasow	Pasture
236	Lyttelton, Lord	Birch, George	Redhill Piece	Arable
116	Birch, John	Birch, John	Garden	
117	Birch, John	Birch, John	Tenements, Building &c	
118	Birch, John	Birch, John	Garden	
122	Birch, John	Birch, John	Middle Meadow	Pasture
123	Birch, John	Birch, John	Pit Leasow	Arable
124	Birch, John	Birch, John	Upper Meadow	Pasture
125	Birch, John	Birch, John	Second Cow Leasow	Pasture
126	Birch, John	Birch, John	Cow Leasow	Pasture
127	Birch, John	Birch, John	Fog Leasow	Arable
128	Birch, John	Birch, John	Clover Leasow	Pasture
177	Birch, John	Birch, John	Lunt Coppy	Pasture
178	Birch, John	Birch, John	Wood Leasow	Pasture
179	Birch, John	Birch, John	Long Leasow	Pasture
180	Birch, John	Birch, John	Old Lane	
241	Boulton, Samuel	Boulton, Samuel	House & Garden	
220	Hill, Timothy	Branton, Richard	House & Garden	
221	Lyttelton, Lord	Branton, Richard	Garden	
74	Macdonald, H. Foley	Clay, Benjamin	House, Shop & Garden	
158	Whitehouse, John	Coley, Josiah	Croft	Pasture
159	Whitehouse, John	Coley, Josiah	House & Garden	
112	Grazebrook, William	Coley, Thomas	House & Gardens	

Plan	Landowner	Occupier	Address	Cultivation
51	Bissell, James	Cooper, James	Upper Stony Cross	Arable
52	Bissell, James	Cooper, James	Lower Stony Cross	Pasture
53	Bissell, James	Cooper, James	Little Stony Cross	Pasture
81	Foley, John	Cooper, James	Meadow	Pasture
82	Foley, John	Cooper, James	Middle Leasow	Arable
83	Foley, John	Cooper, James	Lower Leasow	Arable
84	Foley, John	Cooper, James	Top Leasow	Arable
86	Foley, John	Cooper, James	Slough Leasow	Arable
89	Bissell, James	Cooper, James	Red Lion Inn Stable Yard & Garden	
235	Cutler, Ann	Cutler, Ann	House, Shop & Garden	
223	Hill, Timothy	Cutler, Esther	House & Garden	
47	Cutler, James	Cutler, James	House, Shop & Garden	
222	Lyttelton, Lord	Cutler, Widow	Garden	
87	Spurrier, William	Davenport, John	Meadow	Pasture
175	Lyttelton, Lord	Deeley, George	House & Garden	
202	Hill, Timothy	Dixon, Joseph	Close	Pasture
204	Hill, Timothy	Dixon, Joseph	Close	Pasture
218	Lyttelton, Lord	Dixon, Joseph	Garden	
219	Hill, Timothy	Dixon, Joseph	Beech Tree Inn Garden	
1	White, John	Farmer, Jonathan	In Nobles Innage	Pasture
2	White, John	Farmer, Jonathan	New Innage	Pasture
4	White, John	Farmer, Jonathan	In the First Innage	Arable
5	White, John	Farmer, Jonathan	Foredrove	
10	White, John	Farmer, Jonathan	In First Quinton Field	Pasture
11	White, John	Farmer, Jonathan	In First Quinton Field	Pasture
19	White, John	Farmer, Jonathan	Lower Cutlers Leasow	Pasture
20	White, John	Farmer, Jonathan	Middle Cutlers Leasow	Pasture
21	White, John	Farmer, Jonathan	Little Cutlers Leasow	Pasture
32	White, John	Farmer, Jonathan	Garden	Arable
39	White, John	Farmer, Jonathan	Barn & Yard	
40	White, John	Farmer, Jonathan	Cutlers Meadow	Pasture
92	White, John	Farmer, Jonathan	The Hill	Pasture
96	White, John	Farmer, Jonathan	The Long Hills	Pasture
8	Foley, John	Foley, John	In The Field	Pasture
9	Foley, John	Foley, John	In The Field	Pasture
12	Foley, John	Foley, John	Kings Leasow	Arable
13	Foley, John	Foley, John	Lower Meadow	Pasture
54	Foley, John	Foley, John	Top Meadow	Pasture
55	Foley, John	Foley, John	House, Yard, Barn	
59	Foley, Ambrose	Foley, John	Garden	

Plan	Landowner	Occupier	Address	Cultivation
62	Foley, John	Foley, John	Garden	
65	Foley, Ambrose	Foley, John	Little Meadow	Pasture
66	Foley, Ambrose	Foley, John	Church Leasow	Pasture
67	Foley, Ambrose	Foley, John	Little Middle Leasow	Pasture
68	Foley, Ambrose	Foley, John	Little Wood Leasow	Arable
69	Foley, Ambrose	Foley, John	Big Wood Leasow	Arable
70	Foley, Ambrose	Foley, John	Big Middle Leasow	Arable
71	Foley, Ambrose	Foley, John	Barn Close	Pasture
73	Foley, Ambrose	Foley, John	House & Farm Buildings	
56	Foley, John/Ambrose	Foley, John/Ambrose	Chapel & Yard	
222	Lyttelton, Lord	Fox, John	Garden	
223	Hill, Timothy	Fox, John	House & Garden	
229	Birch, George	Fox, William	House & Garden	
33	Powers, Sally	Goode, Joseph	House & Garden	
112	Grazebrook, William	Gould, William	House & Gardens	
7	Grosvenor, John	Grosvenor, John	House, Shop, Garden	
43	Hill, Timothy	Guest, John	House, Shop & Garden	
72	Foley, Ambrose	Hadley, Benjamin	House & Shop	
91	White, John	Hadley, Samuel	House & Garden	
201	Lyttelton, Lord	Hadley, Samuel	House & Garden	
59	Foley, Ambrose	Hall, George	Garden	
55	Foley, John	Hall, James	House	
57	Lyttelton, Lord	Hall, James	House, Shop & Garden	
45	Bissell, James	Hall, John	House, Shop & Garden	
230	Birch, George	Hall, Thomas	Garden	
47	Taylor, Francis	Hallen, John	House, Shop & Garden	
93	Cooper, James	Harris, Joseph	House, Shop & Garden	
233	Birch, John	Haycock, Thomas	House & Garden	
188	Hill, Timothy	Hill, Benjamin	House, Shop & Garden	
189	Hill, Timothy	Hill, Benjamin	Little Meadow	Pasture
190	Hill, Timothy	Hill, Benjamin	Big Meadow	Pasture
174	Lyttelton, Lord	Hill, Isaac	House, Shop, Garden	
7	Grosvenor, John	Hunt, James	House, Shop, Garden	
142	Greaves, Richard	Jakeman, John	Long Leasow	Arable
143	Greaves, Richard	Jakeman, John	Little Leasow	Arable
144	Greaves, Richard	Jakeman, John	Spring Leasow	Arable
145	Greaves, Richard	Jakeman, John	Broad Leasow	Pasture
146	Greaves, Richard	Jakeman, John	Well Leasow	Arable
147	Greaves, Richard	Jakeman, John	Clover Leasow	Arable
148	Greaves, Richard	Jakeman, John	Head Piece	Pasture
149	Greaves, Richard	Jakeman, John	Five Acres	Arable

Plan	Landowner	Occupier	Address	Cultivation
150	Greaves, Richard	Jakeman, John	Brickkiln Piece	Pasture
151	Greaves, Richard	Jakeman, John	Plant Leasow	Pasture
152	Greaves, Richard	Jakeman, John	Garden Leasow	Pasture
153	Greaves, Richard	Jakeman, John	Jones's Leasow	Pasture
154	Greaves, Richard	Jakeman, John	World's End Leasow	Pasture
155	Greaves, Richard	Jakeman, John	Big Meadow	Pasture
156	Greaves, Richard	Jakeman, John	House, Building & Garden	
157	Greaves, Richard	Jakeman, John	The Croft	Pasture
160	Penn, William	Johnson, William	Pleck	Pasture
169	Penn, William	Johnson, William	Old Road	
159	Whitehouse, John	Lane, David	House & Garden	
74	Macdonald, H. Foley	Macdonald, H. Foley	House & Garden	
34	White, John	Male, James	House & Garden	
63	Foley, John/Ambrose	Mason, John	House, Shop, Garden	
37	Darby, Joseph	Mason, Mary	House & Garden	
29	Millward, Ann	Millward, Ann	House & Garden	
215	Lyttelton, Lord	Milner, James	Garden	
216	Lyttelton, Lord	Milner, James	House & Garden	
88	Hill, Ann	Nicholls, Henry	Great Hill	Pasture
95	Hill, Ann	Nicholls, Henry	Shop Close	Pasture
198	Hill, Ann	Nicholls, Henry	Roundabout	Pasture
237	Hill, Ann	Nicholls, Henry	Upper Sawpit Leasow	Arable
238	Hill, Ann	Nicholls, Henry	Lower Sawpit Leasow	Arable
239	Hill, Ann	Nicholls, Henry	Coneygre Leasow	Pasture
242	Hill, Ann	Nicholls, Henry	Pleck	Arable
243	Hill, Ann	Nicholls, Henry	House & Farm Buildings	
244	Hill, Ann	Nicholls, Henry	Barn Close	Pasture
245	Hill, Ann	Nicholls, Henry	Hither Leys	Arable
246	Hill, Ann	Nicholls, Henry	Home Meadow	Pasture
247	Hill, Ann	Nicholls, Henry	Little Leys	Arable
248	Hill, Ann	Nicholls, Henry	Top of the Meadow	Arable
232	Birch, John	Page, Thomas	House & Garden	
205	Hill, Timothy	Partridge, James	House & Garden	
232	Birch, John	Partridge, Thomas	House & Garden	
61	Lyttelton, Lord	Powers, Sarah	House & Garden	
38	Darby, Joseph	Prady, James	House & Garden	
44	Bissell, James	Price, James	House, Shop & Garden	
107	Grazebrook, William	Ragg, James	Far Meadow	Pasture
111	Grazebrook, William	Ragg, James	Old House Meadow	Pasture
113	Grazebrook, William	Ragg, James	House & Farm Building	
114	Grazebrook, William	Ragg, James	Lane	

Plan	Landowner	Occupier	Address	Cultivation
115	Grazebrook, William	Ragg, James	Ridgacre Meadow	Pasture
129	Grazebrook, William	Ragg, James	Yell Leasow	Arable
130	Grazebrook, William	Ragg, James	Upper Ridgacre Field	Arable
131	Grazebrook, William	Ragg, James	Lower Ridgacre Field	Arable
132	Grazebrook, William	Ragg, James	Old Meadow	Pasture
133	Grazebrook, William	Ragg, James	Smooth Moor	Arable
134	Grazebrook, William	Ragg, James	Big Rye Hill	Arable
135	Grazebrook, William	Ragg, James	The Sling	Pasture
136	Grazebrook, William	Ragg, James	Rushy Piece	Arable
137	Grazebrook, William	Ragg, James	Little Rye Hill	Arable
138	Grazebrook, William	Ragg, James	Brickkiln Leasow	Arable
139	Grazebrook, William	Ragg, James	Broad Leasow	Arable
140	Grazebrook, William	Ragg, James	Piece behind Powells	Arable
141	Grazebrook, William	Ragg, James	The Warms	Pasture
90	White, John	Read, Daniel	House & Garden	
112	Grazebrook, William	Read, Elijah	House & Garden	
37	Darby, Joseph	Read, John	House & Garden	
91	White, John	Record, Joseph	House & Garden	
74	Macdonald, H. Foley	Robinson, James	House, Shop & Garden	
45	Bissell, James	Rose, William	House, Shop & Garden	
38	Darby, Joseph	Sadler, John	House & Garden	
94	Lyttelton, Lord	Sadler, Joseph	House, Shop & Garden	
228	Birch, George	Smart, Edward	House & Garden	
46	Smith, Thomas	Smith, David	House, Shop & Garden	
41	White, John	Smith, Edward	House & Garden	
46	Smith, Thomas	Smith, Thomas	House, Shop & Garden	
222	Lyttelton, Lord	Taylor, John	Garden	
223	Hill, Timothy	Taylor, John	House & Garden	
97	Grazebrook, William	Tomlinson, Richard	Mill Field	Arable
98	Grazebrook, William	Tomlinson, Richard	Middle Piece	Pasture
99	Grazebrook, William	Tomlinson, Richard	Bottom Piece	Arable
100	Grazebrook, William	Tomlinson, Richard	Barn Piece	Pasture
101	Grazebrook, William	Tomlinson, Richard	Farm House Building	
102	Grazebrook, William	Tomlinson, Richard	Rump Piece	Pasture
104	Grazebrook, William	Tomlinson, Richard	Rickyard Piece	Arable
194,	Grazebrook, William	Tomlinson, Richard	Cow Leasow	Arable
196	Grazebrook, William	Tomlinson, Richard	Daleday Math	Pasture
197	Grazebrook, William	Tomlinson, Richard	The Meadow	Pasture
58	Turnpike Commissioners	Turnpike Commissioners	Tollhouse & Yard	
75	Grainger, David	Underhill, Richard	House, Buildings, Garden	

Plan	Landowner	Occupier	Address	Cultivation
76	Grainger, David	Underhill, Richard	Near High Leasow	Pasture
77	Grainger, David	Underhill, Richard	Far High Leasow	Arable
78	Grainger, David	Underhill, Richard	Far Middle Leasow	Arable
79	Grainger, David	Underhill, Richard	Near Middle Leasow	Arable
80	Grainger, David	Underhill, Richard	Meadow	Pasture
35	Lyttelton, Lord	Void	House & Garden	
85	Foley, John	Void	House (in ruins) & Garden	
171	Hales Owen Poor	Void	House & Garden	
240	Boulton, Samuel	Void	House & Garden	
161	Hales Owen Poor	Wakeman, Joseph	Parish Ground	Pasture
162	King, William	Wakeman, Joseph	Little Meadow	Pasture
163	King, William	Wakeman, Joseph	House & Garden	
164	King, William	Wakeman, Joseph	Well Leasow	Pasture
165	King, William	Wakeman, Joseph	Peters Piece	Arable
166	King, William	Wakeman, Joseph	Wood Leasow	Arable
167	King, William	Wakeman, Joseph	Wood Leasow	Pasture
168	King, William	Wakeman, Joseph	Holly Meadow	Pasture
170	Hales Owen Poor	Wakeman, Joseph	Potatoe Leasow	Pasture
172	Hales Owen Poor	Wakeman, Joseph	Orchard	Pasture
60	Macdonald, H. Foley	Westwood, Benjamin	House, Shop & Garden	
35	Lyttelton, Lord	Wheeler, Benjamin	House & Garden	
3	White, John	White, Thomas	Cotterill's Innage	Arable
6	Lyttelton, Lord	White, Thomas	Part of Far Quinton Field	Pasture
15	Lyttelton, Lord	White, Thomas	Jack Clerk's Meadow	Arable
16	Lyttelton, Lord	White, Thomas	Further Mancroft	Arable
17	Lyttelton, Lord	White, Thomas	Four Acres	Arable
18	Lyttelton, Lord	White, Thomas	Mancroft Meadow	Pasture
22	Lyttelton, Lord	White, Thomas	Marl Pit	
23	Lyttelton, Lord	White, Thomas	Far Rough Meadow	Arable
24	White, Aaron	White, Thomas	Upper Golds Meadow	Pasture
25	White, Aaron	White, Thomas	Lower Golds Meadow	Pasture
26	Lyttelton, Lord	White, Thomas	Rough Meadow	Pasture
27	Lyttelton, Lord	White, Thomas	Part of Foldyard	
28	Lyttelton, Lord	White, Thomas	The Close	Pasture
42	Lyttelton, Lord	White, Thomas	Hither Mancroft	Arable
64	Lyttelton, Lord	White, Thomas	Foredrove	
103	Lyttelton, Lord	White, Thomas	Taylor's Close	Arable
105	Lyttelton, Lord	White, Thomas	Windmill Piece	Arable
106	Lyttelton, Lord	White, Thomas	Bonfire Leasow	Arable
108	Lyttelton, Lord	White, Thomas	Taylor's Croft	Arable
109	Lyttelton, Lord	White, Thomas	The Park	Pasture

Plan	Landowner	Occupier	Address	Cultivation
110	Lyttelton, Lord	White, Thomas	Little Leasow	Pasture
119	Lyttelton, Lord	White, Thomas	The Meadow	Pasture
120	Lyttelton, Lord	White, Thomas	Farm House Building	
121	Lyttelton, Lord	White, Thomas	Dafodil Leasow	Arable
191	Lyttelton, Lord	White, Thomas	Gosty Leasow	Pasture
192	Lyttelton, Lord	White, Thomas	Lower Leasow	Arable
193	Lyttelton, Lord	White, Thomas	Upper Leasow	Pasture
195	Lyttelton, Lord	White, Thomas	Bridge Leasow	Arable
217	Lyttelton, Lord	Woodbridge, Joseph	House, Smith's Shop & Garden	
31	White, Ann	Yates, Benjamin	House & Garden	
14	Yates, John	Yates, John	Garden	
30	White, John	Yates, John	Pleck	Pasture
33	Powers, Sally	Yates, John	House & Garden	
41	White, John	Yeomans, Thomas	House & Garden	
36	Glebe		Garden	
48	Glebe		Big Leasow	Pasture
49	Glebe		Parsonage & Garden	
50	Glebe		Church, Yard, School	

3.04   Ridgacre Apportionments in order of Landowners

Plan	Landowner	Occupier	Address	Cultivation
173	Birch, George	Birch, George	World's End Meadow	Pasture
176	Birch, George	Birch, George	Lower Hannah Green	Arable
181	Birch, George	Birch, George	Big Leasow	Pasture
182	Birch, George	Birch, George	Lunt Leasow	Arable
183	Birch, George	Birch, George	Field	Arable
184	Birch, George	Birch, George	World's End Leasow	Arable
185	Birch, George	Birch, George	Ewes Well Leasow	Arable
186	Birch, George	Birch, George	Pits Wood Leasow	Arable
187	Birch, George	Birch, George	The Sling	Arable
199	Birch, George	Birch, George	Aldridge Meadow	Pasture
200	Birch, George	Birch, George	The Muttons	Arable
203	Birch, George	Birch, George	Great Ox Leasow	Arable
206	Birch, George	Birch, George	Two Hill Leasow	Pasture
207	Birch, George	Birch, George	Ox Leasow	Arable
208	Birch, George	Birch, George	Little Meadow	Pasture
209	Birch, George	Birch, George	Redhall Farmhouse &c	
210	Birch, George	Birch, George	House Meadow	Pasture
211	Birch, George	Birch, George	Barn Close	Pasture
212	Birch, George	Birch, George	Great Wood Leasow	Arable

Plan	Landowner	Occupier	Address	Cultivation
213	Birch, George	Birch, George	Second Wood Leasow	Arable
224	Birch, George	Birch, George	Upper Tolly Leasow	Arable
225	Birch, George	Birch, George	Square Leasow	Arable
226	Birch, George	Birch, George	Smart's Leasow	Pasture
227	Birch, George	Birch, George	Smart's Piece	Pasture
228	Birch, George	Smart, Edward	House & Garden	
229	Birch, George	Fox, William	House & Garden	
230	Birch, George	Hall, Thomas	Garden	
231	Birch, George	Birch, George	Road Leasow	Pasture
116	Birch, John	Birch, John	Garden	
117	Birch, John	Birch, John	Tenements, Building, Yard	
118	Birch, John	Birch, John	Garden	
122	Birch, John	Birch, John	Middle Meadow	Pasture
123	Birch, John	Birch, John	Pit Leasow	Arable
124	Birch, John	Birch, John	Upper Meadow	Pasture
125	Birch, John	Birch, John	Second Cow Leasow	Pasture
126	Birch, John	Birch, John	Cow Leasow	Pasture
127	Birch, John	Birch, John	Fog Leasow	Arable
128	Birch, John	Birch, John	Clover Leasow	Pasture
177	Birch, John	Birch, John	Lunt Coppy	Pasture
178	Birch, John	Birch, John	Wood Leasow	Pasture
179	Birch, John	Birch, John	Long Leasow	Pasture
180	Birch, John	Birch, John	Old Lane	
232	Birch, John	Page, Thomas	House & Garden	
232	Birch, John	Partridge, Thomas	House & Garden	
233	Birch, John	Haycock, Thomas	House & Garden	
234	Birch, John	Adams, James	Holly Bush Inn & Garden	
44	Bissell, James	Price, James	House, Shop & Garden	
45	Bissell, James	Hall, John	House, Shop & Garden	
45	Bissell, James	Rose, William	House, Shop & Garden	
51	Bissell, James	Cooper, James	Upper Stony Cross	Arable
52	Bissell, James	Cooper, James	Lower Stony Cross	Pasture
53	Bissell, James	Cooper, James	Little Stony Cross	Pasture
89	Bissell, James	Cooper, James	Red Lion Inn Stable Yard & Garden	
240	Boulton, Samuel	Void	House & Garden	
241	Boulton, Samuel	Boulton, Samuel	House & Garden	
93	Cooper, James	Harris, Joseph	House, Shop & Garden	
235	Cutler, Ann	Cutler, Ann	House, Shop & Garden	
47	Cutler, James	Cutler, James	House, Shop & Garden	
37	Darby, Joseph	Andrews, Thomas	House & Garden	

Plan	Landowner	Occupier	Address	Cultivation
37	Darby, Joseph	Mason, Mary	House & Garden	
37	Darby, Joseph	Read, John	House & Garden	
38	Darby, Joseph	Prady, James	House & Garden	
38	Darby, Joseph	Sadler, John	House & Garden	
59	Foley, Ambrose	Foley, John	Garden	
59	Foley, Ambrose	Hall, George	Garden	
65	Foley, Ambrose	Foley, John	Little Meadow	Pasture
66	Foley, Ambrose	Foley, John	Church Leasow	Pasture
67	Foley, Ambrose	Foley, John	Little Middle Leasow	Pasture
68	Foley, Ambrose	Foley, John	Little Wood Leasow	Arable
69	Foley, Ambrose	Foley, John	Big Wood Leasow	Arable
70	Foley, Ambrose	Foley, John	Big Middle Leasow	Arable
71	Foley, Ambrose	Foley, John	Barn Close	Pasture
72	Foley, Ambrose	Hadley, Benjamin	House & Shop	
73	Foley, Ambrose	Foley, John	House & Farm Buildings	
8	Foley, John	Foley, John	In The Field	Pasture
9	Foley, John	Foley, John	In The Field	Pasture
12	Foley, John	Foley, John	Kings Leasow	Arable
13	Foley, John	Foley, John	Lower Meadow	Pasture
54	Foley, John	Foley, John	Top Meadow	Pasture
55	Foley, John	Foley, John	House, Yard, Barn	
55	Foley, John	Hall, James	House	
62	Foley, John	Foley, John	Garden	
81	Foley, John	Cooper, James	Meadow	Pasture
82	Foley, John	Cooper, James	Middle Leasow	Arable
83	Foley, John	Cooper, James	Lower Leasow	Arable
84	Foley, John	Cooper, James	Top Leasow	Arable
85	Foley, John	Void	House (in ruins) & Garden	
86	Foley, John	Cooper, James	Slough Leasow	Arable
56	Foley, John/Ambrose	Foley, John/ Ambrose	Chapel & Yard	
63	Foley, John/Ambrose	Mason, John	House, Shop, Garden	
36	Glebe		Garden	
48	Glebe		Big Leasow	Pasture
49	Glebe		Parsonage & Garden	
50	Glebe		Church, Yard, School	
75	Grainger, David	Underhill, Richard	House, Farm Building, Tenement, Garden	
76	Grainger, David	Underhill, Richard	Near High Leasow	Pasture
77	Grainger, David	Underhill, Richard	Far High Leasow	Arable
78	Grainger, David	Underhill, Richard	Far Middle Leasow	Arable
79	Grainger, David	Underhill, Richard	Near Middle Leasow	Arable

Plan	Landowner	Occupier	Address	Cultivation
80	Grainger, David	Underhill, Richard	Meadow	Pasture
97	Grazebrook, William	Tomlinson, Richard	Mill Field	Arable
98	Grazebrook, William	Tomlinson, Richard	Middle Piece	Pasture
99	Grazebrook, William	Tomlinson, Richard	Bottom Piece	Arable
100	Grazebrook, William	Tomlinson, Richard	Barn Piece	Pasture
101	Grazebrook, William	Tomlinson, Richard	Farm House Building	
102	Grazebrook, William	Tomlinson, Richard	Rump Piece	Pasture
104	Grazebrook, William	Tomlinson, Richard	Rickyard Piece	Arable
107	Grazebrook, William	Ragg, James	Far Meadow	Pasture
111	Grazebrook, William	Ragg, James	Old House Meadow	Pasture
112	Grazebrook, William	Coley, Thomas	House & Gardens	
112	Grazebrook, William	Gould, William	House & Gardens	
112	Grazebrook, William	Read, Elijah	House & Gardens	
113	Grazebrook, William	Ragg, James	House & Farm Building	
114	Grazebrook, William	Ragg, James	Lane	
115	Grazebrook, William	Ragg, James	Ridgacre Meadow	Pasture
129	Grazebrook, William	Ragg, James	Yell Leasow	Arable
130	Grazebrook, William	Ragg, James	Upper Ridgacre Field	Arable
131	Grazebrook, William	Ragg, James	Lower Ridgacre Field	Arable
132	Grazebrook, William	Ragg, James	Old Meadow	Pasture
133	Grazebrook, William	Ragg, James	Smooth Moor	Arable
134	Grazebrook, William	Ragg, James	Big Rye Hill	Arable
135	Grazebrook, William	Ragg, James	The Sling	Pasture
136	Grazebrook, William	Ragg, James	Rushy Piece	Arable
137	Grazebrook, William	Ragg, James	Little Rye Hill	Arable
138	Grazebrook, William	Ragg, James	Brickkiln Leasow	Arable
139	Grazebrook, William	Ragg, James	Broad Leasow	Arable
140	Grazebrook, William	Ragg, James	Piece behind Powells	Arable
141	Grazebrook, William	Ragg, James	The Warms	Pasture
194	Grazebrook, William	Tomlinson, Richard	Cow Leasow	Arable
196	Grazebrook, William	Tomlinson, Richard	Daleday Math	Pasture
197	Grazebrook, William	Tomlinson, Richard	The Meadow	Pasture
142	Greaves, Richard	Jakeman, John	Long Leasow	Arable
143	Greaves, Richard	Jakeman, John	Little Leasow	Arable
144	Greaves, Richard	Jakeman, John	Spring Leasow	Arable
145	Greaves, Richard	Jakeman, John	Broad Leasow	Pasture
146	Greaves, Richard	Jakeman, John	Well Leasow	Arable
147	Greaves, Richard	Jakeman, John	Clover Leasow	Arable
148	Greaves, Richard	Jakeman, John	Head Piece	Pasture
149	Greaves, Richard	Jakeman, John	Five Acres	Arable
150	Greaves, Richard	Jakeman, John	Brickkiln Piece	Pasture

Plan	Landowner	Occupier	Address	Cultivation
151	Greaves, Richard	Jakeman, John	Plant Leasow	Pasture
152	Greaves, Richard	Jakeman, John	Garden Leasow	Pasture
153	Greaves, Richard	Jakeman, John	Jones's Leasow	Pasture
154	Greaves, Richard	Jakeman, John	World's End Leasow	Pasture
155	Greaves, Richard	Jakeman, John	Big Meadow	Pasture
156	Greaves, Richard	Jakeman, John	House, Building & Garden	
157	Greaves, Richard	Jakeman, John	The Croft	Pasture
7	Grosvenor, John	Grosvenor, John	House, Shop, Garden	
7	Grosvenor, John	Hunt, James	House, Shop, Garden	
161	Hales Owen Poor	Wakeman, Joseph	Parish Ground	Pasture
170	Hales Owen Poor	Wakeman, Joseph	Potatoe Leasow	Pasture
171	Hales Owen Poor	Void	House & Garden	
172	Hales Owen Poor	Wakeman, Joseph	Orchard	Pasture
88	Hill, Ann	Nicholls, Henry	Great Hill	Pasture
95	Hill, Ann	Nicholls, Henry	Shop Close	Pasture
198	Hill, Ann	Nicholls, Henry	Roundabout	Pasture
237	Hill, Ann	Nicholls, Henry	Upper Sawpit Leasow	Arable
238	Hill, Ann	Nicholls, Henry	Lower Sawpit Leasow	Arable
239	Hill, Ann	Nicholls, Henry	Coneygre Leasow	Pasture
242	Hill, Ann	Nicholls, Henry	Pleck	Arable
243	Hill, Ann	Nicholls, Henry	House & Farm Buildings	
244	Hill, Ann	Nicholls, Henry	Barn Close	Pasture
245	Hill, Ann	Nicholls, Henry	Hither Leys	Arable
246	Hill, Ann	Nicholls, Henry	Home Meadow	Pasture
247	Hill, Ann	Nicholls, Henry	Little Leys	Arable
248	Hill, Ann	Nicholls, Henry	Top of the Meadow	Arable
43	Hill, Timothy	Guest, John	House, Shop & Garden	
188	Hill, Timothy	Hill, Benjamin	House, Shop & Garden	
189	Hill, Timothy	Hill, Benjamin	Little Meadow	Pasture
190	Hill, Timothy	Hill, Benjamin	Big Meadow	Pasture
202	Hill, Timothy	Dixon, Joseph	Close	Pasture
204	Hill, Timothy	Dixon, Joseph	Close	Pasture
205	Hill, Timothy	Partridge, James	House & Garden	
219	Hill, Timothy	Dixon, Joseph	Beech Tree Inn Garden	
220	Hill, Timothy	Branton, Richard	House & Garden	
223	Hill, Timothy	Cutler, Esther	House & Garden	
223	Hill, Timothy	Fox, John	House & Garden	
223	Hill, Timothy	Taylor, John	House & Garden	
162	King, William	Wakeman, Joseph	Little Meadow	Pasture
163	King, William	Wakeman, Joseph	House & Garden	
164	King, William	Wakeman, Joseph	Well Leasow	Pasture

Plan	Landowner	Occupier	Address	Cultivation
165	King, William	Wakeman, Joseph	Peters Piece	Arable
166	King, William	Wakeman, Joseph	Wood Leasow	Arable
167	King, William	Wakeman, Joseph	Wood Leasow	Pasture
168	King, William	Wakeman, Joseph	Holly Meadow	Pasture
6	Lyttelton, Lord	White, Thomas	Part of Far Quinton Field	Pasture
15	Lyttelton, Lord	White, Thomas	Jack Clerk's Meadow	Arable
16	Lyttelton, Lord	White, Thomas	Further Mancroft	Arable
17	Lyttelton, Lord	White, Thomas	Four Acres	Arable
18	Lyttelton, Lord	White, Thomas	Mancroft Meadow	Pasture
22	Lyttelton, Lord	White, Thomas	Marl Pit	
23	Lyttelton, Lord	White, Thomas	Far Rough Meadow	Arable
26	Lyttelton, Lord	White, Thomas	Rough Meadow	Pasture
27	Lyttelton, Lord	White, Thomas	Part of Foldyard	
28	Lyttelton, Lord	White, Thomas	The Close	Pasture
35	Lyttelton, Lord	Void	House & Garden	
35	Lyttelton, Lord	Wheeler, Benjamin	House & Garden	
42	Lyttelton, Lord	White, Thomas	Hither Mancroft	Arable
57	Lyttelton, Lord	Hall, James	House, Shop & Garden	
61	Lyttelton, Lord	Powers, Sarah	House & Garden	
64	Lyttelton, Lord	White, Thomas	Foredrove	
94	Lyttelton, Lord	Sadler, Joseph	House, Shop & Garden	
103	Lyttelton, Lord	White, Thomas	Taylor's Close	Arable
105	Lyttelton, Lord	White, Thomas	Windmill Piece	Arable
106	Lyttelton, Lord	White, Thomas	Bonfire Leasow	Arable
108	Lyttelton, Lord	White, Thomas	Taylor's Croft	Arable
109	Lyttelton, Lord	White, Thomas	The Park	Pasture
110	Lyttelton, Lord	White, Thomas	Little Leasow	Pasture
119	Lyttelton, Lord	White, Thomas	The Meadow	Pasture
120	Lyttelton, Lord	White, Thomas	Farm House Building	
121	Lyttelton, Lord	White, Thomas	Dafodil Leasow	Arable
174	Lyttelton, lord	Hill, Isaac	House, Shop, Garden	
175	Lyttelton, Lord	Deeley, George	House & Garden	
191	Lyttelton, Lord	White, Thomas	Gosty Leasow	Pasture
192	Lyttelton, Lord	White, Thomas	Lower Leasow	Arable
193	Lyttelton, Lord	White, Thomas	Upper Leasow	Pasture
195	Lyttelton, Lord	White, Thomas	Bridge Leasow	Arable
201	Lyttelton, Lord	Hadley, Samuel	House & Garden	
214	Lyttelton, Lord	Birch, George	Redhill Piece	Arable
215	Lyttelton, Lord	Milner, James	Garden	
216	Lyttelton, Lord	Milner, James	House & Garden	

Plan	Landowner	Occupier	Address	Cultivation
217	Lyttelton, Lord	Woodbridge, Joseph	House, Smith's Shop & Garden	
218	Lyttelton, Lord	Dixon, Joseph	Garden	
221	Lyttelton, Lord	Branton, Richard	Garden	
222	Lyttelton, Lord	Cutler, Widow	Garden	
222	Lyttelton, Lord	Fox, John	Garden	
222	Lyttelton, Lord	Taylor, John	Garden	
236	Lyttelton, Lord	Birch, George	Redhill Piece	Arable
60	Macdonald, H. Foley	Westwood, Benjamin	House, Shop & Garden	
74	Macdonald, H. Foley	Clay, Benjamin	House, Shop & Garden	
74	Macdonald, H. Foley	Macdonald, H. Foley	House & Garden	
74	Macdonald, H. Foley	Robinson, James	House, Shop & Garden	
29	Millward, Ann	Millward, Ann	House & Garden	
160	Penn, William	Johnson, William	Pleck	Pasture
169	Penn, William	Johnson, William	Old Road	
33	Powers, Sally	Goode, Joseph	House & Garden	
33	Powers, Sally	Yates, John	House & Garden	
46	Smith, Thomas	Smith, David	House, Shop & Garden	
46	Smith, Thomas	Smith, Thomas	House, Shop & Garden	
87	Spurrier, William	Davenport, John	Meadow	Pasture
47	Taylor, Francis	Hallen, John	House, Shop & Garden	
58	Turnpike Commissioners	Turnpike Commissioners	Tollhouse & Yard	
24	White, Aaron	White, Thomas	Upper Golds Meadow	Pasture
25	White, Aaron	White, Thomas	Lower Golds Meadow	Pasture
31	White, Ann	Yates, Benjamin	House & Garden	
1	White, John	Farmer, Jonathan	In Nobles Innage	Pasture
2	White, John	Farmer, Jonathan	New Innage	Pasture
3	White, John	White, Thomas	Cotterill's Innage	Arable
4	White, John	Farmer, Jonathan	In the First Innage	Arable
5	White, John	Farmer, Jonathan	Foredrove	Pasture
10	White, John	Farmer, Jonathan	In First Quinton Field	Pasture
11	White, John	Farmer, Jonathan	In First Quinton Field	Pasture
19	White, John	Farmer, Jonathan	Lower Cutlers Leasow	Pasture
20	White, John	Farmer, Jonathan	Middle Cutlers Leasow	Pasture
21	White, John	Farmer, Jonathan	Little Cutlers Leasow	Pasture
30	White, John	Yates, John	Pleck	Pasture
32	White, John	Farmer, Jonathan	Garden	Arable
34	White, John	Male, James	House & Garden	
39	White, John	Farmer, Jonathan	Barn & Yard	
40	White, John	Farmer, Jonathan	Cutlers Meadow	Pasture

Plan	Landowner	Occupier	Address	Cultivation
41	White, John	Smith, Edward	House & Garden	
41	White, John	Yeomans, Thomas	House & Garden	
90	White, John	Read, Daniel	House & Garden	
91	White, John	Hadley, Samuel	House & Garden	
91	White, John	Record, Joseph	House & Garden	
92	White, John	Farmer, Jonathan	The Hill	Pasture
96	White, John	Farmer, Jonathan	The Long Hills	Pasture
158	Whitehouse, John	Coley, Josiah	Croft	Pasture
159	Whitehouse, John	Coley, Josiah	House & Garden	
159	Whitehouse, John	Lane, David	House & Garden	
14	Yates, John	Yates, John	Garden	

3.05   Warley Wigorn Apportionments: Preamble

Apportionment of the rent charges in lieu of tithes in the township of Warley Wigorn in the parish of Hales Owen in the county of Worcester.

Provisional Articles of Agreement for the commutation of the tithes of the township of Warley Wigorn in that part of the parish of Hales Owen which lies in the county of Worcester in pursuance of the Act for the Commutation of Tithes in England and Wales made and executed at a meeting duly called and holden in the said parish and adjourned and holden by adjournment on the thirteenth day of November in the year of our Lord one thousand eight hundred and thirty-nine.

By and between the several persons owners of land within the said township of Warley Wigorn by whom or by whose agents duly authorised in that behalf these presents are executed and the interests of which landowners in the lands of the said township is not less than two thirds to the land therein subject to tithes of the first part.

Elizabeth Curtis of the borough of Walsall in the county of Stafford, widow, impropriator of great tithes of such part of the said township of Warley Wigorn as mentioned in the schedule hereunder written or hereunto annexed marked A of the second part.

Hubert John Barclay Galton of Portman Square in the county of Middlesex, esquire, impropriator of great tithes of such part of the said township of Warley Wigorn as mentioned in the schedule hereunder written or hereunto annexed marked B of the third part.

Ann Hill of 49 Park Road, Grosvenor Square in the county of Middlesex, widow, impropriator of great tithes of such part of the said township of Warley Wigorn as mentioned in the schedule hereunder written or hereunto annexed marked C of the fourth part.

John Monckton [E][54] of Fireshade near Wansford in the county of Northampton, esquire, impropriator of lands of such part of the said township of Warley Wigorn as mentioned in the schedule hereunder written or hereunto annexed marked D of the fifth part.

---

[54] As owner of freehold land in both Ridgacre & Warley Wigorn townships. See 13.01

The Right Honourable George William Lord Lyttelton as impropriator of great tithes of the lands of such part of the said township of Warley Wigorn as mentioned in the schedule hereunder written or hereunto annexed marked E of the sixth part.

The said George William Lord Lyttelton as impropriator of the great tithes of all other lands of such part of the said township of Warley Wigorn which are not comprised in the said schedules A, B, C, D and E of the seventh part.

And Richard Brindley Hone who as Vicar of the said parish of Hales Owen is entitled absolutely to all the small tithes.

Whereas the said Elizabeth Curtis is the owner of lands mentioned in the schedule marked A;

And the said Hubert John Barclay Galton is the owner of lands mentioned in the schedule marked B;

And the said Ann Hill is the owner of lands mentioned in the schedule marked C;

And the said John Monckton is the owner of lands mentioned in the schedule marked D;

And the said Lord Lyttelton is the owner of lands mentioned in the schedule marked E;

And whereas the said Elizabeth Curtis, Hubert John Barclay Galton, Ann Hill, John Monckton and Lord Lyttelton are also respectively owners of estates in possession in fee simple or fee tail of the great tithes arising from the said lands within the township of Warley Wigorn comprised in the said schedules A, B, C, D and E so belonging to them as aforesaid

Now the said parties except Elizabeth Curtis do and each of them respectively doth declare their or his intention testified by their several and respective signatures and seals hereunto annexed that the said great tithes arising from their said respective lands shall henceforth be absolutely merged and extinguished in the freehold and inheritance of the said lands.

It is hereby agreed that the annual sum of two pounds by way of rent charge subject to the provisions of the said Act shall be paid to the said Elizabeth Curtis or the person or persons entitled in remainder or reversion after her instead of the great tithes of the said lands comprised in schedule A so belonging to the said Elizabeth Curtis in the township of Warley Wigorn subject to great tithes.

And that the annual sum of eighty pounds by way of rent charge subject to the provisions of the said Act shall be paid to George William Lord Lyttelton, his heirs and assigns or the person or persons entitled in remainder or reversion after her instead of the great tithes of all other lands within the said township subject to great tithes except those lands the great tithes arising from which are hereinbefore declared to be merged and instead of all Moduses and Compositions real or prescriptive or customary payments payable in respect of the great tithes of the land of the said township or the produce thereof other than the lands comprised in the said schedules marked A, B, C, D and E.

And the annual sum of one hundred and twenty pounds by way of rent charge subject to the provisions of the said Act shall be paid to the said Richard Brindley Hone and to his successors in the said vicarage instead of all the vicarial tithes of all the lands of the said township subject to tithes and instead of all Moduses and Compositions real or prescriptive or customary payments payable in respect of all the lands of the said township or produce thereof and also instead of all Easter offerings payable to the said vicar by the resident inhabitants of the said township.

A summary description of all the lands of the said township is contained in schedule F hereunder written or hereunto annexed.

And it is further agreed that the lands included in this agreement and not comprised in the schedules A, B, C, D and E[55] shall be discharged from the payment of great tithes. And the lands comprised in this agreement including the lands specified in the said schedules A, B, C, D and E shall be discharged from the payment of all vicarial tithes from the first day of October next preceding the confirmation of the Apportionment of the Rent charges herein before agreed on and that the first payment of such rent charges shall be made or be recoverable on the expiration of six calendar months from the time from which the said lands are discharged from the payment of tithes.

And it is further agreed by all parties hereto and particularly by the said George William Lord Lyttelton for himself his heirs and assigns that the expense of repairing and at all times for ever hereafter keeping in good and substantial repair the chancel of the parish church of Hales Owen aforesaid shall be wholly paid, sustained and borne by the said Lord Lyttelton his heirs and assigns and be charged upon the said annual rent charge of eighty pounds herein before made payable to him and them.

In testimony whereof we the said parties to these presents or their respective agents thereunto duly authorised in their names and on their behalves have to these presents subscribed and set their respective hands and seals this thirteenth day of November in the year of our Lord one thousand eight hundred and thirty-nine.

And whereas an award by way of supplement to the foregoing agreement was on the thirty-first day of December in the year of our Lord one thousand eight hundred and forty-four confirmed by the Tithe Commissioners for England and Wales of which supplemental award the following is a copy.

Whereas an agreement for the commutation of tithes of the township of Warley Wigorn in that part of the parish of Hales Owen which lies in the county of Worcester has been confirmed by us the Tithe Commissioners for England and Wales but the apportionment of the said rent charges has not yet been confirmed

And whereas it has been represented to us that an error has been committed in the said agreement by the insertion of the words first day of October next preceding instead of the words first day of January preceding the confirmation of the apportionment as the date of the commencement of the said rent charges

And whereas we have ascertained that the said error does really exist in the said agreement and that it should be amended accordingly.

Now we the undersigned Tithe Commissioners for England and Wales do hereby make this our separate award by way of supplement to the said hereinbefore mentioned agreement, that is to say

---

[55] Only schedule C – property of Ann Hill (including plots W7 & W8) and schedule E – property of Lord Lyttelton (including plots W83, W84, W88, W89, W90, W91, W135 & W136) relate to land within the Quinton area of Warley Wigorn.

We do hereby award that the said rent charges shall commence and be payable from the first day of January preceding the confirmation of the Apportionments of the said rent charges instead of on the first day of October preceding such confirmation as is in the said agreement erroneously specified.

In testimony whereof we have hereto subscribed our respective names this third day of December in the year of our Lord one thousand eight hundred and forty-four.

Wm Blamire

TW Buller.

Now I, Jeremiah Mathews, of Kidderminster in the County of Worcestershire,
having been duly appointed Valuer to apportion the total Sum awarded to be paid by way of Rent Charge in lieu of Tithes amongst the several Lands of the said Township of Warley Wigorn
Do hereby apportion the Rent Charges as follows: -
GROSS RENT CHARGES *payable to the Tithe Owner in lieu of tithes for the Township of Ridgacre in the Parish of Hales Owen in the County of Salop:*

Two hundred and four pounds viz.

To the Vicar:	122.0.0
To Lord Lyttelton:	80.0.0
To Elizabeth Curtis	2.00

January 1st 1845

Value in Imperial Bushels and Decimal Parts of an Imperial Bushel of Wheat, Barley and Oats:

Crop:	Price per Bushel:	Bushels and Decimal Parts:
WHEAT	7/0¼d	193.70920
BARLEY	3/11½d	343.57895
OATS	2/9d	494.54545

3.06 Warley Wigorn (Hagg, Upper Quinton, Quinton, Dwellings, Lower Dwellings, Worlds End, Hawthorn) Apportionments in order of Plan Numbers

Plan	Landowner	Occupier	Address	Cultivation
W1	Grazebrook, William	Partridge, Thomas	House, Shop & Garden	
W2	Grazebrook, William	Partridge, William	House, Shop & Garden	
W3	Grazebrook, William	Partridge, Thomas	Garden	
W4	Grazebrook, William	Pritchett, William	Finches Leasow	Pasture
W5	Grazebrook, William	Pritchett, William	Finches Leasow	Pasture
W6	Grazebrook, William	Pritchett, William	Finches Leasow	Arable
W7	Hill, Ann	Nicholls, Thomas	Lower Redhill	Pasture
W8	Hill, Ann	Nicholls, Thomas	Upper Redhill	Arable
W9	Penn, William	Penn, William	Plantation	Woodland
W10	Penn, William	Pearman, Joseph	Big Piece (In)	Pasture
W11	Penn, William	Penn, William	Pits Wood	Woodland

Plan	Landowner	Occupier	Address	Cultivation
W12	Penn, William	Pearman, Joseph	Upper Moor	Pasture
W13	Penn, William	Pearman, Joseph	Lower Moor	Pasture
W14	Penn, William	Pearman, Joseph	Middle Moor	Pasture
W15	Penn, William	Pearman, Joseph	Big Piece (In)	Pasture
W16	Penn, William	Penn, William	Pool Tail Planation	Woodland
W17	Penn, William	Pearman, Joseph	Wheat Field (In)	Pasture
W18	Penn, William	Pearman, Joseph	Lower Feston	Arable
W19	Penn, William	Penn, William	Feston Wood	Woodland
W20	Penn, William	Pearman, Joseph	Upper Feston	Arable
W21	Penn, William	Pearman, Joseph	Off Leasow (In)	Arable
W22	Penn, William	Penn, William	Bearlands Wood	Woodland
W23	Penn, William	Johnson, William	Upper Bears Land (part)	Arable
W24	Penn, William	Johnson, William	Bears Land	Pasture
W25	Penn, William	Johnson, William	Lower Bears Land (part)	Arable
W26	Penn, William	Penn, William	Bog Wood	Woodland
W27	Penn, William	Johnson, William	Little Hill	Pasture
W28	Penn, William	Johnson, William	Big Meadow	Pasture
W29	Penn, William	Johnson, William	Swale Well Leasow	Arable
W30	Penn, William	Johnson, William	Flat Piece	Pasture
W31	Penn, William	Johnson, William	The Hill	Arable
W32	Penn, William	Johnson, William	Shop Leasow	Pasture
W33	Penn, William	Johnson, William	House, Buildings, Garden	
W33a	Penn, William	Penn, William	Road	
W33b	Penn, William	Johnson, William	Road	
W34	Penn, William	Johnson, William	Peters Piece	Pasture
W35	Penn, William	Johnson, William	First Gorsty Leasow	Arable
W36	Penn, William	Johnson, William	Second Gorsty Leasow	Arable
W37	Penn, William	Johnson, William	Common Go	Arable
W38	Penn, William	Johnson, William	Garden Pleck	Arable
W39	Penn, William	Johnson, William	The Brake	Pasture
W40	Penn, William	Johnson, William	Little Meadow	Pasture
W41	Penn, William	Johnson, William	Big Well Leasow	Arable
W42	Penn, William	Johnson, William	Days Hill	Arable
W43	Penn, William	Johnson, William	Long Meadow	Pasture
W44	Penn, William	Johnson, William	Square Leasow	Arable
W45	Penn, William	Johnson, William	Three Cornered Piece	Pasture
W46	Spurrier, William	Davenport, Joseph	The Warms	Arable
W47	Spurrier, William	Davenport, Joseph	Holly Croft	Arable

Plan	Landowner	Occupier	Address	Cultivation
W48	Spurrier, William	Davenport, Joseph	Holly Croft	Pasture
W49	Spurrier, William	Davenport, Joseph	Little Meadow	Pasture
W50	Spurrier, William	Davenport, Joseph	Third Leasow	Arable
W51	Spurrier, William	Davenport, Joseph	Broad Meadow	Pasture
W52	Spurrier, William	Davenport, Joseph	Half Close	Pasture
W53	Spurrier, William	Davenport, Joseph	Half Close	Pasture
W54	Spurrier, William	Davenport, Joseph	Upper Leasow	Pasture
W55	Spurrier, William	Davenport, Joseph	Dun Leasow	Pasture
W56	Spurrier, William	Davenport, Joseph	Wall yard, farm buildings	
W57	Spurrier, William	Davenport, Joseph	Barn Leasow	Pasture
W58	Spurrier, William	Davenport, Joseph	Lower Leasow	Pasture
W58a	Spurrier, William	Davenport, Joseph	Holly Leasow	Arable
W59	Spurrier, William	Davenport, Joseph	Lower Long Meadow	Pasture
W60	Spurrier, William	Davenport, Joseph	Upper Long Meadow	Pasture
W61	Spurrier, William	Davenport, Joseph	Little White Close	Arable
W62	Spurrier, William	Davenport, Joseph	Gorsy Piece	Arable
W63	Spurrier, William	Davenport, Joseph	Ten Acres	Arable
W64	Spurrier, William	Davenport, Joseph	Well Close	Arable
W66	Spurrier, William	Davenport, Joseph	Marys Leasow	Pasture
W67	Spurrier, William	Davenport, Joseph	Four Dwellings Farmhouse	
W68	Spurrier, William	Davenport, Joseph	Harp Leasow	Pasture
W69	Spurrier, William	Davenport, Joseph	Massy Leasow	Arable
W70	Spurrier, William	Davenport, Joseph	Dunn	Arable
W73	Spurrier, William	Davenport, Joseph	Dwellings Meadow	Pasture
W74	White, Aaron	White, Thomas	Dwellings Big Meadow	Pasture
W75	White, Aaron	White, Thomas	Rough in Dwellings Big Meadow	
W76	White, Aaron	White, Thomas	House, Buildings & c	
W77	White, Aaron	White, Thomas	Pigsty Meadow	Pasture
W78	White, Aaron	White, Thomas	Pound Close	Arable
W79	White, Aaron	White, Thomas	Little Meadow	Pasture
W80	White, Aaron	White, Thomas	Long Meadow	Arable
W81	White, Aaron	White, Thomas	Coneybury	Arable
W82	White, Aaron	White, Thomas	Swans Field	Arable
W83	Lyttelton, Lord	White, Thomas	Further Green Croft	Arable
W84	Lyttelton, Lord	White, Thomas	Hither Green Croft	Arable
W85	White, George	White, Thomas	Top Croft	Pasture
W86	White, George	Clay, Charles	Garden	

Plan	Landowner	Occupier	Address	Cultivation
W87	White, George	Clay, Charles	House, shop, garden	
W87	White, George	Haycock, Thomas	House, shop, garden	
W88	Lyttelton, Lord	White, Thomas	Upper Meadow	Arable
W89	Lyttelton, Lord	White, Thomas	Big Meadow	Pasture
W91	Lyttelton, Lord	White, Thomas	House, Farm Buildings & c	
W92	Spurrier, William	Davenport, Joseph	House Meadow	Pasture
W93	Hall, Thomas	Hall, Thomas	Garden	
W94	Spurrier, William	Davenport, Joseph	Ivy House, Farm Buildings	
W95	Spurrier, William	Davenport, Joseph	Broad Leasow	Arable
W96	Spurrier, William	Davenport, Joseph	Ox Leasow	Arable
W96a	Spurrier, William	Davenport, Joseph	Windmill Leasow	Arable
W97	Spurrier, William	Davenport, Joseph	Great Birmingham Piece	Arable
W98	Spurrier, William	Davenport, Joseph	Little Birmingham Piece	Arable
W99	Haden, Edward	Yeomans, James	House, Shop & Garden	
W100	Haden, Edward	Yeomans, James	Big Meadow	Pasture
W102	Haden, Edward	Yeomans, James	Spring Meadow	Pasture
W103	Haden, Edward	Yeomans, James	Shop Leasow	Pasture
W111	Grainger, Daniel	Wakeman, Joseph	Great Hall Piece	Pasture
W112	Grainger, Daniel	Wakeman, Joseph	Pool Meadow	Arable
W113	Grainger, Stephen	Cooper, James	Big Piece	
W114	Grainger, Stephen	Cooper, James	Little Piece	
W115	Grainger, Stephen	Cooper, James	Long Meadow	
W116	Grainger, Stephen	Cooper, James	Near Piece	
W117	Hudson, Sarah	Salt, Joseph	House & Garden	
W118	Grainger, Stephen	Cooper, James	The Pleck	
W119	Grainger, Stephen	Cooper, James	House, Buildings, Garden	
W120	Grainger, Stephen	Cooper, James	Roundabout	
W121	Pritchett, William	Armes, Stephen	House, Shop, Garden	
W121	Pritchett, William	Coles, Samuel	House, shop, garden	
W122	Hales Owen School	Pritchett, William	Lower Quinton	
W123	Hales Owen School	Pritchett, William	Lower Field	
W124	Hales Owen School	Pritchett, William	House Field	
W125	Hales Owen School	Pritchett, William	House, Garden & c	
W126	Macdonald, H. Foley	Macdonald, H. Foley	Grotto & Pleck	
W127	White, John	White, Thomas	In Milestone Piece	Pasture
W128	White, John	White, Thomas	In Milestone Piece	Pasture
W129	White, George	White, Thomas	In Lower Horseletts	Arable
W130	White, George	White, Thomas	In Upper Quinton Field	Pasture

Plan	Landowner	Occupier	Address	Cultivation
W131	White, John	White, Thomas	In First Quinton Field	Pasture
W132	White, John	White, Thomas	In First Quinton Field	Pasture
W133	White, John	White, Thomas	In First Quinton Field	Pasture
W134	White, John	White, Thomas	In First Innage	Pasture
W135	Lyttelton, Lord	White, Thomas	Road	
W136	Lyttelton, Lord	White, Thomas	Duncemoor Wood	Arable
W137	White, John	Farmer, Jonathan	Wood Leasow	Arable
W138	White, John	Farmer, Jonathan	Middle Close	Arable
W139	White, John	Farmer, Jonathan	The Hill	Arable
W140	White, John	Farmer, Jonathan	Little Meadow	Pasture
W141	White, John	Farmer, Jonathan	Old Meadow	Arable
W142	White, John	Farmer, Jonathan	House, Buildings, Garden	
W143	White, John	Farmer, Jonathan	Cart Leasow	Pasture
W144	White, John	Farmer, Jonathan	Orchard	Pasture
W145	White, John	Farmer, Jonathan	House Piece	Pasture
W146	White, John	White, Thomas	The Lunt	Pasture
W147	White, John	White, Thomas	Noble's Innage	Pasture
W148	White, John	White, Thomas	Little Innage	Arable
W158	White, John	Farmer, Jonathan	The Lunt	Arable
W184	White, John	Farmer, Jonathan	Higgins Close	Pasture

3.07 Warley Wigorn (Hagg, Upper Quinton, Quinton, Dwellings, Lower Dwellings, Worlds End, Hawthorn) Apportionments in order of Occupiers

Plan	Landowner	Occupier	Address	Cultivation
W121	Pritchett, William	Armes, Stephen	House, shop, garden	
W86	White, George	Clay, Charles	Garden	
W87	White, George	Clay, Charles	House, shop, garden	
W121	Pritchett, William	Coles, Samuel	House, Shop, Garden	
W113	Grainger, Stephen	Cooper, James	Big Piece	
W114	Grainger, Stephen	Cooper, James	Little Piece	
W115	Grainger, Stephen	Cooper, James	Long Meadow	
W116	Grainger, Stephen	Cooper, James	Near Piece	
W118	Grainger, Stephen	Cooper, James	The Pleck	
W119	Grainger, Stephen	Cooper, James	House, Buildings, Garden	
W120	Grainger, Stephen	Cooper, James	Roundabout	
W46	Spurrier, William	Davenport, Joseph	The Warms	Arable
W47	Spurrier, William	Davenport, Joseph	Holly Croft	Arable

Plan	Landowner	Occupier	Address	Cultivation
W48	Spurrier, William	Davenport, Joseph	Holly Croft	Pasture
W49	Spurrier, William	Davenport, Joseph	Little Meadow	Pasture
W50	Spurrier, William	Davenport, Joseph	Third Leasow	Arable
W51	Spurrier, William	Davenport, Joseph	Broad Meadow	Pasture
W52	Spurrier, William	Davenport, Joseph	Half Close	Pasture
W53	Spurrier, William	Davenport, Joseph	Half Close	Pasture
W54	Spurrier, William	Davenport, Joseph	Upper Leasow	Pasture
W55	Spurrier, William	Davenport, Joseph	Dun Leasow	Pasture
W56	Spurrier, William	Davenport, Joseph	Wall yard, farm buildings	
W57	Spurrier, William	Davenport, Joseph	Barn Leasow	Pasture
W58	Spurrier, William	Davenport, Joseph	Lower Leasow	Pasture
W58a	Spurrier, William	Davenport, Joseph	Holly Leasow	Arable
W59	Spurrier, William	Davenport, Joseph	Lower Long Meadow	Pasture
W60	Spurrier, William	Davenport, Joseph	Upper Long Meadow	Pasture
W61	Spurrier, William	Davenport, Joseph	Little White Close	Arable
W62	Spurrier, William	Davenport, Joseph	Gorsy Piece	Arable
W63	Spurrier, William	Davenport, Joseph	Ten Acres	Arable
W64	Spurrier, William	Davenport, Joseph	Well Close	Arable
W66	Spurrier, William	Davenport, Joseph	Marys Leasow	Pasture
W67	Spurrier, William	Davenport, Joseph	Four Dwellings Farmhouse	
W68	Spurrier, William	Davenport, Joseph	Harp Leasow	Pasture
W69	Spurrier, William	Davenport, Joseph	Massy Leasow	Arable
W70	Spurrier, William	Davenport, Joseph	Dunn	Arable
W73	Spurrier, William	Davenport, Joseph	Dwellings Meadow	Pasture
W92	Spurrier, William	Davenport, Joseph	House Meadow	Pasture
W94	Spurrier, William	Davenport, Joseph	Ivy House, Farm Buildings	
W95	Spurrier, William	Davenport, Joseph	Broad Leasow	Arable
W96	Spurrier, William	Davenport, Joseph	Ox Leasow	Arable
W96a	Spurrier, William	Davenport, Joseph	Windmill Leasow	Arable
W97	Spurrier, William	Davenport, Joseph	Great Birmingham Piece	Arable
W98	Spurrier, William	Davenport, Joseph	Little Birmingham Piece	Arable
W137	White, John	Farmer, Jonathan	Wood Leasow	Arable
W138	White, John	Farmer, Jonathan	Middle Close	Arable
W139	White, John	Farmer, Jonathan	The Hill	Arable
W140	White, John	Farmer, Jonathan	Little Meadow	Pasture
W141	White, John	Farmer, Jonathan	Old Meadow	Arable
W142	White, John	Farmer, Jonathan	House, Buildings, Garden	
W143	White, John	Farmer, Jonathan	Cart Leasow	Pasture

Plan	Landowner	Occupier	Address	Cultivation
W144	White, John	Farmer, Jonathan	Orchard	Pasture
W145	White, John	Farmer, Jonathan	House Piece	Pasture
W158	White, John	Farmer, Jonathan	The Lunt	Arable
W184	White, John	Farmer, Jonathan	Higgins Close	Pasture
W93	Hall, Thomas	Hall, Thomas	Garden	
W87	White, George	Haycock, Thomas	House, shop, garden	
W23	Penn, William	Johnson, William	Upper Bears Land (part)	Arable
W24	Penn, William	Johnson, William	Bears Land	Pasture
W25	Penn, William	Johnson, William	Lower Bears Land (part)	Arable
W27	Penn, William	Johnson, William	Little Hill	Pasture
W28	Penn, William	Johnson, William	Big Meadow	Pasture
W29	Penn, William	Johnson, William	Swale Well Leasow	Arable
W30	Penn, William	Johnson, William	Flat Piece	Pasture
W31	Penn, William	Johnson, William	The Hill	Arable
W32	Penn, William	Johnson, William	Shop Leasow	Pasture
W33	Penn, William	Johnson, William	House, Buildings, Garden	
W33b	Penn, William	Johnson, William	Road	
W34	Penn, William	Johnson, William	Peters Piece	Pasture
W35	Penn, William	Johnson, William	First Gorsty Leasow	Arable
W36	Penn, William	Johnson, William	Second Gorsty Leasow	Arable
W37	Penn, William	Johnson, William	Common Go	Arable
W38	Penn, William	Johnson, William	Garden Pleck	Arable
W39	Penn, William	Johnson, William	The Brake	Pasture
W40	Penn, William	Johnson, William	Little Meadow	Pasture
W41	Penn, William	Johnson, William	Big Well Leasow	Arable
W42	Penn, William	Johnson, William	Days Hill	Arable
W43	Penn, William	Johnson, William	Long Meadow	Pasture
W44	Penn, William	Johnson, William	Square Leasow	Arable
W45	Penn, William	Johnson, William	Three Cornered Piece	Pasture
W126	Macdonald, H. Foley	Macdonald, H. Foley	Grotto & Pleck	
W7	Hill, Ann	Nicholls, Thomas	Lower Redhill	Pasture
W8	Hill, Ann	Nicholls, Thomas	Upper Redhill	Arable
W1	Grazebrook, William	Partridge, Thomas	House, Shop & Garden	
W3	Grazebrook, William	Partridge, Thomas	Garden	
W2	Grazebrook, William	Partridge, William	House, Shop & Garden	
W10	Penn, William	Pearman, Joseph	Big Piece (In)	Pasture
W12	Penn, William	Pearman, Joseph	Upper Moor	Pasture
W13	Penn, William	Pearman, Joseph	Lower Moor	Pasture

Plan	Landowner	Occupier	Address	Cultivation
W14	Penn, William	Pearman, Joseph	Middle Moor	Pasture
W15	Penn, William	Pearman, Joseph	Big Piece (In)	Pasture
W17	Penn, William	Pearman, Joseph	Wheat Field (In)	Pasture
W18	Penn, William	Pearman, Joseph	Lower Feston	Arable
W20	Penn, William	Pearman, Joseph	Upper Feston	Arable
W21	Penn, William	Pearman, Joseph	Off Leasow (In)	Arable
W9	Penn, William	Penn, William	Plantation	Woodland
W11	Penn, William	Penn, William	Pits Wood	Woodland
W16	Penn, William	Penn, William	Pool Tail Planation	Woodland
W19	Penn, William	Penn, William	Feston Wood	Woodland
W22	Penn, William	Penn, William	Bearlands Wood	Woodland
W26	Penn, William	Penn, William	Bog Wood	Woodland
W33a	Penn, William	Penn, William	Road	
W4	Grazebrook, William	Pritchett, William	Finches Leasow	Pasture
W5	Grazebrook, William	Pritchett, William	Finches Leasow	Pasture
W6	Grazebrook, William	Pritchett, William	Finches Leasow	Arable
W122	Hales Owen School	Pritchett, William	Lower Quinton	
W123	Hales Owen School	Pritchett, William	Lower Field	
W124	Hales Owen School	Pritchett, William	House Field	
W125	Hales Owen School	Pritchett, William	House, Garden & c	
W117	Hudson, Sarah	Salt, Joseph	House & Garden	
W111	Grainger, Daniel	Wakeman, Joseph	Great Hall Piece	Pasture
W112	Grainger, Daniel	Wakeman, Joseph	Pool Meadow	Arable
W83	Lyttelton, Lord	White, Thomas	Further Green Croft	Arable
W84	Lyttelton, Lord	White, Thomas	Hither Green Croft	Arable
W88	Lyttelton, Lord	White, Thomas	Upper Meadow	Arable
W89	Lyttelton, Lord	White, Thomas	Big Meadow	Pasture
W91	Lyttelton, Lord	White, Thomas	House, Farm Buildings & c	
W135	Lyttelton, Lord	White, Thomas	Road	
W136	Lyttelton, Lord	White, Thomas	Duncemoor Wood	Arable
W74	White, Aaron	White, Thomas	Dwellings Big Meadow	Pasture
W75	White, Aaron	White, Thomas	Rough in Dwellings Big Meadow	
W76	White, Aaron	White, Thomas	House, Buildings & c	
W77	White, Aaron	White, Thomas	Pigsty Meadow	Pasture
W78	White, Aaron	White, Thomas	Pound Close	Arable
W79	White, Aaron	White, Thomas	Little Meadow	Pasture
W80	White, Aaron	White, Thomas	Long Meadow	Arable
W81	White, Aaron	White, Thomas	Coneybury	Arable

Plan	Landowner	Occupier	Address	Cultivation
W82	White, Aaron	White, Thomas	Swans Field	Arable
W85	White, George	White, Thomas	Top Croft	Pasture
W129	White, George	White, Thomas	In Lower Horseletts	Arable
W130	White, George	White, Thomas	In Upper Quinton Field	Pasture
W132	White, John	White, Thomas	In First Quinton Field	Pasture
W127	White, John	White, Thomas	In Milestone Piece	Pasture
W128	White, John	White, Thomas	In Milestone Piece	Pasture
W131	White, John	White, Thomas	In First Quinton Field	Pasture
W133	White, John	White, Thomas	In First Quinton Field	Pasture
W134	White, John	White, Thomas	In First Innage	Pasture
W146	White, John	White, Thomas	The Lunt	Pasture
W147	White, John	White, Thomas	Noble's Innage	Pasture
W148	White, John	White, Thomas	Little Innage	Arable
W99	Haden, Edward	Yeomans, James	House, Shop & Garden	
W100	Haden, Edward	Yeomans, James	Big Meadow	Pasture
W102	Haden, Edward	Yeomans, James	Spring Meadow	Pasture
W103	Haden, Edward	Yeomans, James	Shop Leasow	Pasture

3.08 Warley Wigorn (Hagg, Upper Quinton, Quinton, Dwellings, Lower Dwellings, Worlds End, Hawthorn) Apportionments in order of Landowners

Plan	Landowner	Occupier	Address	Cultivation
W111	Grainger, Daniel	Wakeman, Joseph	Great Hall Piece	Pasture
W112	Grainger, Daniel	Wakeman, Joseph	Pool Meadow	Arable
W113	Grainger, Stephen	Cooper, James	Big Piece	
W114	Grainger, Stephen	Cooper, James	Little Piece	
W115	Grainger, Stephen	Cooper, James	Long Meadow	
W116	Grainger, Stephen	Cooper, James	Near Piece	
W118	Grainger, Stephen	Cooper, James	The Pleck	
W119	Grainger, Stephen	Cooper, James	House, Buildings, Garden	
W120	Grainger, Stephen	Cooper, James	Roundabout	
W1	Grazebrook, William	Partridge, Thomas	House, Shop & Garden	
W2	Grazebrook, William	Partridge, William	House, Shop & Garden	
W3	Grazebrook, William	Partridge, Thomas	Garden	
W4	Grazebrook, William	Pritchett, William	Finches Leasow	Pasture
W5	Grazebrook, William	Pritchett, William	Finches Leasow	Pasture
W6	Grazebrook, William	Pritchett, William	Finches Leasow	Arable
W99	Haden, Edward	Yeomans, James	House, Shop & Garden	

Plan	Landowner	Occupier	Address	Cultivation
W100	Haden, Edward	Yeomans, James	Big Meadow	Pasture
W102	Haden, Edward	Yeomans, James	Spring Meadow	Pasture
W103	Haden, Edward	Yeomans, James	Shop Leasow	Pasture
W122	Hales Owen School	Pritchett, William	Lower Quinton	
W123	Hales Owen School	Pritchett, William	Lower Field	
W124	Hales Owen School	Pritchett, William	House Field	
W125	Hales Owen School	Pritchett, William	House, Garden & c	
W93	Hall, Thomas	Hall, Thomas	Garden	
W7	Hill, Ann	Nicholls, Thomas	Lower Redhill	Pasture
W8	Hill, Ann	Nicholls, Thomas	Upper Redhill	Arable
W117	Hudson, Sarah	Salt, Joseph	House & Garden	
W83	Lyttelton, Lord	White, Thomas	Further Green Croft	Arable
W84	Lyttelton, Lord	White, Thomas	Hither Green Croft	Arable
W88	Lyttelton, Lord	White, Thomas	Upper Meadow	Arable
W89	Lyttelton, Lord	White, Thomas	Big Meadow	Pasture
W91	Lyttelton, Lord	White, Thomas	House, Farm Buildings & c	
W135	Lyttelton, Lord	White, Thomas	Road	
W136	Lyttelton, Lord	White, Thomas	Duncemoor Wood	Arable
W126	Macdonald, H. Foley	Macdonald, H. Foley	Grotto & Pleck	
W9	Penn, William	Penn, William	Plantation	Woodland
W10	Penn, William	Pearman, Joseph	Big Piece (In)	Pasture
W11	Penn, William	Penn, William	Pits Wood	Woodland
W12	Penn, William	Pearman, Joseph	Upper Moor	Pasture
W13	Penn, William	Pearman, Joseph	Lower Moor	Pasture
W14	Penn, William	Pearman, Joseph	Middle Moor	Pasture
W15	Penn, William	Pearman, Joseph	Big Piece (In)	Pasture
W16	Penn, William	Penn, William	Pool Tail Planation	Woodland
W17	Penn, William	Pearman, Joseph	Wheat Field (In)	Pasture
W18	Penn, William	Pearman, Joseph	Lower Feston	Arable
W19	Penn, William	Penn, William	Feston Wood	Woodland
W20	Penn, William	Pearman, Joseph	Upper Feston	Arable
W21	Penn, William	Pearman, Joseph	Off Leasow (In)	Arable
W22	Penn, William	Penn, William	Bearlands Wood	Woodland
W23	Penn, William	Johnson, William	Upper Bears Land (part)	Arable
W24	Penn, William	Johnson, William	Bears Land	Pasture
W25	Penn, William	Johnson, William	Lower Bears Land (part)	Arable
W26	Penn, William	Penn, William	Bog Wood	Woodland
W27	Penn, William	Johnson, William	Little Hill	Pasture

Plan	Landowner	Occupier	Address	Cultivation
W28	Penn, William	Johnson, William	Big Meadow	Pasture
W29	Penn, William	Johnson, William	Swale Well Leasow	Arable
W30	Penn, William	Johnson, William	Flat Piece	Pasture
W31	Penn, William	Johnson, William	The Hill	Arable
W32	Penn, William	Johnson, William	Shop Leasow	Pasture
W33	Penn, William	Johnson, William	House, Buildings, Garden	
W33a	Penn, William	Penn, William	Road	
W33b	Penn, William	Johnson, William	Road	
W34	Penn, William	Johnson, William	Peters Piece	Pasture
W35	Penn, William	Johnson, William	First Gorsty Leasow	Arable
W36	Penn, William	Johnson, William	Second Gorsty Leasow	Arable
W37	Penn, William	Johnson, William	Common Go	Arable
W38	Penn, William	Johnson, William	Garden Pleck	Arable
W39	Penn, William	Johnson, William	The Brake	Pasture
W40	Penn, William	Johnson, William	Little Meadow	Pasture
W41	Penn, William	Johnson, William	Big Well Leasow	Arable
W42	Penn, William	Johnson, William	Days Hill	Arable
W43	Penn, William	Johnson, William	Long Meadow	Pasture
W44	Penn, William	Johnson, William	Square Leasow	Arable
W45	Penn, William	Johnson, William	Three Cornered Piece	Pasture
W121	Pritchett, William	Coles, Samuel	House, Shop, Garden	
W121	Pritchett, William	Armes, Stephen	House, shop, garden	
W46	Spurrier, William	Davenport, Joseph	The Warms	Arable
W47	Spurrier, William	Davenport, Joseph	Holly Croft	Arable
W48	Spurrier, William	Davenport, Joseph	Holly Croft	Pasture
W49	Spurrier, William	Davenport, Joseph	Little Meadow	Pasture
W50	Spurrier, William	Davenport, Joseph	Third Leasow	Arable
W51	Spurrier, William	Davenport, Joseph	Broad Meadow	Pasture
W52	Spurrier, William	Davenport, Joseph	Half Close	Pasture
W53	Spurrier, William	Davenport, Joseph	Half Close	Pasture
W54	Spurrier, William	Davenport, Joseph	Upper Leasow	Pasture
W55	Spurrier, William	Davenport, Joseph	Dun Leasow	Pasture
W56	Spurrier, William	Davenport, Joseph	Wall yard, farm buildings	
W57	Spurrier, William	Davenport, Joseph	Barn Leasow	Pasture
W58	Spurrier, William	Davenport, Joseph	Lower Leasow	Pasture
W58a	Spurrier, William	Davenport, Joseph	Holly Leasow	Arable
W59	Spurrier, William	Davenport, Joseph	Lower Long Meadow	Pasture
W60	Spurrier, William	Davenport, Joseph	Upper Long Meadow	Pasture

Plan	Landowner	Occupier	Address	Cultivation
W61	Spurrier, William	Davenport, Joseph	Little White Close	Arable
W62	Spurrier, William	Davenport, Joseph	Gorsy Piece	Arable
W63	Spurrier, William	Davenport, Joseph	Ten Acres	Arable
W64	Spurrier, William	Davenport, Joseph	Well Close	Arable
W66	Spurrier, William	Davenport, Joseph	Marys Leasow	Pasture
W67	Spurrier, William	Davenport, Joseph	Four Dwellings Farmhouse	
W68	Spurrier, William	Davenport, Joseph	Harp Leasow	Pasture
W69	Spurrier, William	Davenport, Joseph	Massy Leasow	Arable
W70	Spurrier, William	Davenport, Joseph	Dunn	Arable
W73	Spurrier, William	Davenport, Joseph	Dwellings Meadow	Pasture
W92	Spurrier, William	Davenport, Joseph	House Meadow	Pasture
W94	Spurrier, William	Davenport, Joseph	Ivy House, Farm Buildings	
W95	Spurrier, William	Davenport, Joseph	Broad Leasow	Arable
W96	Spurrier, William	Davenport, Joseph	Ox Leasow	Arable
W96a	Spurrier, William	Davenport, Joseph	Windmill Leasow	Arable
W97	Spurrier, William	Davenport, Joseph	Great Birmingham Piece	Arable
W98	Spurrier, William	Davenport, Joseph	Little Birmingham Piece	Arable
W74	White, Aaron	White, Thomas	Dwellings Big Meadow	Pasture
W75	White, Aaron	White, Thomas	Rough in Dwellings Big Meadow	
W76	White, Aaron	White, Thomas	House, Buildings & c	
W77	White, Aaron	White, Thomas	Pigsty Meadow	Pasture
W78	White, Aaron	White, Thomas	Pound Close	Arable
W79	White, Aaron	White, Thomas	Little Meadow	Pasture
W80	White, Aaron	White, Thomas	Long Meadow	Arable
W81	White, Aaron	White, Thomas	Coneybury	Arable
W82	White, Aaron	White, Thomas	Swans Field	Arable
W85	White, George	White, Thomas	Top Croft	Pasture
W86	White, George	Clay, Charles	Garden	
W87	White, George	Clay, Charles	House, shop, garden	
W87	White, George	Haycock, Thomas	House, shop, garden	
W129	White, George	White, Thomas	In Lower Horseletts	Arable
W130	White, George	White, Thomas	In Upper Quinton Field	Pasture
W127	White, John	White, Thomas	In Milestone Piece	Pasture
W128	White, John	White, Thomas	In Milestone Piece	Pasture
W131	White, John	White, Thomas	In First Quinton Field	Pasture
W132	White, John	White, Thomas	In First Quinton Field	Pasture
W133	White, John	White, Thomas	In First Quinton Field	Pasture

Plan	Landowner	Occupier	Address	Cultivation
W134	White, John	White, Thomas	In First Innage	Pasture
W137	White, John	Farmer, Jonathan	Wood Leasow	Arable
W138	White, John	Farmer, Jonathan	Middle Close	Arable
W139	White, John	Farmer, Jonathan	The Hill	Arable
W140	White, John	Farmer, Jonathan	Little Meadow	Pasture
W141	White, John	Farmer, Jonathan	Old Meadow	Arable
W142	White, John	Farmer, Jonathan	House, Buildings, Garden	
W143	White, John	Farmer, Jonathan	Cart Leasow	Pasture
W144	White, John	Farmer, Jonathan	Orchard	Pasture
W145	White, John	Farmer, Jonathan	House Piece	Pasture
W146	White, John	White, Thomas	The Lunt	Pasture
W147	White, John	White, Thomas	Noble's Innage	Pasture
W148	White, John	White, Thomas	Little Innage	Arable
W158	White, John	Farmer, Jonathan	The Lunt	Arable
W184	White, John	Farmer, Jonathan	Higgins Close	Pasture

3.09   Tithe Commission Officials

3.09.01   William Blamire

Described by Poet Laureate Robert Southey as "half gentleman, half cattle-dealer,"[56] William Blamire (1790-1862) of Thackwood Nook and The Oaks near Dalston, Cumberland, was descended from a wealthy farming family. After education at Christ Church, Oxford, he developed his interests in the agriculture of his home county, where he was a considerable landowner and of which he was appointed High Sheriff in 1828. Though his sympathies lay with the Whig party and reform, he was actively involved with local associations to protect property during the *Captain Swing* riots[57] of 1830-31. Elected as Member of Parliament for Cumberland in 1831, he concerned himself mainly with property and the question of tithes, though his speeches in the House were rare. Immediately following *An Act for the Commutation of Tithes in England and Wales (6 & 7 William IV c71)* which received the royal assent on August 13th 1836, William Blamire was appointed commission chairman, which required him to resign his parliamentary seat. Much of the

---

[56] Curry, K. (1965) New Letters of Robert Southey, vol 2, p265

[57] So called after the name appended to several threatening letters written during the agricultural upheaval when labourers rioted over the introduction of new machinery and the consequent loss of their livelihoods.

tithe commission's work was London-based and in the 1841 census, Blamire is found living with his wife Dora and three servants in Upper Harley Street, Cavendish Square, Marylebone. In 1841 Blamire was appointed Commissioner for Copyholds in addition to his appointment with the Tithe Commission, and in 1845 he took charge of the commission dealing with enclosures of commons and waste. Though much of his work was involved with the production of official reports and statutes, far more than this, William Blamire is regarded as having undertaken work which forever changed the face of rural England.[58]

In the Quinton tithe apportionments, Wm Blamire was joint signatory to the award for Warley Wigorn and to the certification for both the Ridgacre and Warley Wigorn tithe maps.

3.09.02   Thomas Wentworth Buller

Appointed second tithe commissioner on August 22nd 1836 (the same day as William Blamire) Thomas Wentworth Buller (1792-1852) was born in Maidwell, Northamptonshire into a family with strong naval and military connections. He enlisted in the Royal Navy in 1806 and served in various engagements during the Napoleonic wars. After becoming Flag Lieutenant to the Port Admiral at Plymouth, Buller retired from the navy with the rank of commander in 1817. His own landed interests were in his native Northamptonshire and in Devon, where he became involved in promoting Whig politics, by which activity he attracted the attention of Lord John Russell.[59] However, like Blamire, Buller's responsibilities as a tithe commissioner required his presence in London. On census night 1841, Buller's wife and five children were enumerated at the family home in Whimple, Devon, where their needs were attended to by six female and three male servants. On the same night, Buller, whose occupation is given as Royal Navy rather than tithe commissioner, was resident in the capital at 79, Hanover Square, the home of Edward Divett, MP for Exeter, who also happened to be Buller's father-in-law. The degree of social distance between the tithe commissioners and Quinton's mid-19th century residents is reiterated by the 1851 census, by which time Thomas Wentworth Buller, RN, Tithe Commissioner, had his own home at 15 Sussex Gardens Marylebone. Here, in addition to himself, his household consisted of his wife, five children (whose ages ranged from 14-22), a butler, housekeeper, footman, lady's maid, cook and two housemaids.

In the Quinton tithe apportionments, T. W. Buller was joint signatory to the award for Warley Wigorn and to the certification for both the Ridgacre and Warley Wigorn tithe maps.

3.09.03   George Wingrove Cooke

Appointed one of a number of assistant tithe commissioners, George Wingrove Cooke (1814-1865), described in *Dictionary of National Biography* as a 'man of letters,' was born in Bristol. Educated at Jesus College Oxford and at London University, he was called to the bar of Middle Temple in 1835. Whilst still an undergraduate, he published *Memoirs of Lord Bolingbroke* (1835) written from the standpoint of a Whig sympathiser. Two further books, also representing his political interests, followed in rapid succession: *The Life of the First Earl of Shaftesbury* (1836) and *The History of Party from the*

---

[58] See, for example, Spring, D. (1963) *The English Landed Estate* in the 19th Century, p167
[59] Lord John Russell (1st Earl Russell) was the principal architect of the Great Reform Act of 1832. He served as Prime Minister 1846-1852 and 1865-1866.

George Wingrove Cooke

rise of the Whig and Tory factions in the reign of Charles II to the passing of the Reform Bill (1836-7). Employed under the commissions dealing with tithe commutation and enclosures, Cooke's work involved defining the principles and managing the application of tithe awards. These were subjects about which he also wrote: *Act for the Enclosure of Commons with a Treatise on the Law of Rights of Commons* (1846); *Treatise on the Law and Practice of Agricultural Tenancies* (1850); *Treatise on the Law and Practice of Copyhold Enfranchisement* (1853) all of which went through several editions. Other publications reflected his wide-ranging interests. *Inside Sebastopol* (1856) described his visit made during the Crimean War. The following year *The Times* sent him to China as its special correspondent to report on the Second Opium War. Twice unsuccessful in parliamentary elections (Colchester in 1850 and Marylebone in 1861), in 1862 Cooke was appointed a commissioner within the Copyhold Commission.

In the Quinton tithe apportionments, George Wingrove Cooke was appointed to ascertain and award the rents in Ridgacre township.

3.09.04   John Mee Mathew

Between August 1836 and January 1839, seven assistant commissioners for special purposes came into office. One such was John Mee Mathew whose appointment was announced in the London Gazette in March 1838.

The Tithe Commissioners for England and Wales have appointed John Mee Mathew, Esq. of Churchyard-court, Temple, Barrister at Law, an Assistant-Commissioner for an especial purpose; and he has taken the oath required by an Act, passed in the reign of His late Majesty, intituled "An Act for the commutation of tithes in England and Wales," before George Keene, Esq. a Master Extraordinary in Chancery, at Stafford, in the county of Stafford.

Born in Ashby-de-la-Zouche, Leicestershire in 1806/7, John Mathew, prior to his appointment as assistant commissioner had been employed as auditor and land agent to Earl Ferrers on his Staffordshire estates,[60] hence his accessibility to Stafford court. (Ferrers himself was manager of Lord Dudley's estates in Bilston, Dudley and Tipton.) By 1841, Mathew was clearly travelling as part of his job for the Tithe Commission, as the census finds him in Carrs Lane Birmingham, in company with 17 other residents whose stated occupations range from independent, iron-master, commercial, inn-keeper, maltster, coachman, groom, farrier to male and female servants. His overnight venue, the *Post Office Directory* reveals, was the Turk's Head Commercial Inn at 14 Carrs Lane, proprietor, Mrs Elizabeth Harrold.

---

[60] These included: Amerton-in-Stowe, Chartley, Colwich, Drointon, Field, Fradswell, Gayton, Grindley in Stowe, Lea Fields in Stowe, Hixon, Milwich, Newcastle-under-Lyme, Shirleywich.

Mathew's professional experience led him into print. Apart from editing *Justice of the Peace*, in 1845 he was the author of *A Practical Treatise on the Law of Landlord and Tenant*, reviewed by *Law Journal* as "the best and cheapest work (10s 6d) which treats upon the subject."[61]

By 1861, now living in Keston, Kent with his wife, Eleanor, and two children John and Francis, J.M. Mathew was described as "barrister-at-law, not in actual practice." In the intervening years he had ceased to work for the Tithe Commission (which had been wound up in 1851) but had obviously continued to travel. His elder son, John, had been born in Gravesend, Kent in 1848, whilst in 1850 Francis was born in Belgium, which presumably explains the family's absence from the census of 1851.

In the Quinton tithe apportionments, J. Mee Mathew was signatory to the certification for the Warley Wigorn tithe map.

3.09.05   Jeremiah Mathews

Jeremiah Mathews (1799-1883) was born in Hagley. At the time of his appointments as valuer for the Quinton tithe apportionments, he was living at Park Hall, Kidderminster, the residence of William Grazebrook, trustee to the Lea-Smith estate, third largest landowner in Quinton. Mathews was the estate's land agent. By 1851 he had moved to Edgbaston, Birmingham where, at various addresses in Hagley Road and Harborne Road he would remain for the rest of his life. Jeremiah Mathews obviously prospered in his career and was sufficiently wealthy to send his youngest son to Cambridge and to employ three resident domestic servants. Three of his sons also became land agents, and a fourth an attorney's clerk. Mathews' final home, at 68 Harborne Road, was a large house on the corner of Vicarage Road, where he gave his occupation as 'retired land surveyor' and where his unmarried daughter Marianne ('of private means') still lived in 1911.

In the Quinton tithe apportionments, Jeremiah Mathews was appointed to apportion the rent charges in both Ridgacre and Warley Wigorn townships.

3.10   Impropriators

3.10.01   Right Honourable George William, Lord Lyttelton

George William Lyttelton (1817-1876), 6 x great grandson of John Lyttelton who purchased the manor from Thomas Blount and George Tuckey in 1558, was a gifted classical scholar, somewhat eccentric and tactless, with flaming red hair, a Cambridge cricket blue and a keen interest in billiards. On succeeding to the barony in 1837, he assumed a life of public service, often with the assistance of his brother-in-law, W.E. Gladstone (who was Prime Minister four times between 1868 and 1894). Appointed Lord Lieutenant of Worcestershire in 1840, Lyttelton also served on the committee of the Society for the Propagation of the Gospel and as Governor of Queen's College, Birmingham. He was Vice President of the London Library and President of the Birmingham and Midland Institute and of Saltley Teachers' Training College. In 1862, he became a member of the Taunton Commission on Secondary Education and seven years later was appointed Chairman of the Commission for Endowed

---

[61] Cited from *Landlord and Tenant* (1845)

Schools, the same year in which he was made a Privy Councillor. Though an ardent Anglican, in his report on endowed schools he insisted on the insertion of a conscience clause for the benefit of Nonconformists. For a brief period in 1846, Lord Lyttelton held the office of Under Secretary for the Colonies, when Gladstone was Secretary. In addition, he had a long-term involvement with the Canterbury Association – an organisation aimed at creating a community of Anglican settlers in New Zealand – and was for thirty years a Sunday School teacher in Hagley. A generous benefactor to Quinton, Lyttelton not only donated the land on which church, school and parsonage were built, with glebe land to support the vicarage, he also headed the list of benefactors with a donation of £40 towards the cost of building the school.

George William, 4th Baron Lyttelton

Lyttelton's finances at this period were often precarious, with relatives visiting Hagley expected to contribute as paying guests. Most of George Lyttelton's income was derived from his land, which yielded approximately £1 per acre per annum, to a total of £7,000, when £10,000 was considered the absolute minimum necessary for a minor peer. Quinton's annual contribution of around £90, at a time when Hagley Hall's annual grocery bill was £70, was, therefore, a very insignificant portion of the Lord of the Manor's revenues.

Though not Quinton's largest landowner at the time of the tithe maps, Lord Lyttelton's holdings amounted to approximately 124 acres. This consisted of 99 acres of Lower Quinton Farm, let to George and Thomas White (plots 6, 15, 16, 17, 18, 22, 23, 26, 27, 28, 42, 64, 103, 105, 106, 108, 109, 110, 119, 120, 121, 191, 192, 193, 195, W83, W84, W88, W89, W91, W135, W136) and 22 acres of Redhall Farm let to George Birch (plots 214, 236). This leaves three acres distributed among 13 domestic plots: viz – two houses and gardens on the south edge of Redhall Farm (plots 174, 175, tenants: Isaac Hill, George Deeley); two houses and gardens on the north edge of Redhall Farm (plots 216, 217, tenants: James Milner, Joseph Woodbridge); a narrow strip of land on the south edge of the wedge-shaped enclave of Warley Wigorn township (plot 201, tenant: Samuel Hadley); the site of the Primitive Methodist Chapel (plot 57) two houses and gardens, one void, facing the south edge of the Glebe (plot 35, tenant: Benjamin Wheeler); two houses and gardens widely distributed along the turnpike road (plots 61, 94, tenants: Sarah Powers, Joseph Sadler) one garden at the very north-east extremity of the map (plot 215, tenant: James Milner) and three more gardens behind houses owned by absentee landlord Timothy Hill, also bordering the turnpike road at the north east of the map (plots 218, 221, 222, tenants: Joseph Dixon, Richard Branton, Esther Cutler, John Fox, John Taylor).

A dynastic family man, George William Lyttelton married twice; first Mary Glynne, who died in 1857, and second, Sybella Mildmay, who survived him. He had 15 children and 44 grandchildren. Following the death of his first wife, Lyttelton was increasingly prone to bouts of melancholia, which led to the taking of his own life in 1876.

Quinton tithe apportionments detail George William, 4th Baron Lyttelton as commutator of lands listed in Schedule E of the preamble to Warley Wigorn tithe awards and impropriator of the Great Tithes of both Ridgacre and Warley Wigorn townships.

3.10.02   Richard Brindley Hone

The first vicar (later rector) to whom the small tithes were assigned was Rev Richard Brindley Hone who was born on March 12th 1805 in Farringdon, Berkshire, the younger son of Joseph Terry Hone and named after his grandfather, Brindley Hone. Richard followed his elder brother, Joseph, to Oxford[62] and was awarded his BA in 1827 and MA in 1831. Curacies at Upton St Leonards, Gloucestershire and Portsmouth, Hampshire followed ordination in 1828. Richard Hone married Frances Rickman in September 1836, the year in which he was appointed Vicar of Hales Owen, where he would remain for the rest of his life. Such immobility, however, did not hinder his preferment within the church hierarchy: he was appointed a canon of Worcester Cathedral in 1846 and Archdeacon of Worcester in 1849.

Richard Brindley Hone (1805-1881)

Hone's immediate predecessor at Hales Owen's Church of St John the Baptist, Rev George Briggs who, though vicar for over 30 years, reputedly never visited the town, delegated his parochial responsibilities to a succession of curates. Hone inherited a scattered parish of around 1,700 souls, the needs of which he rapidly decided would best be met through a vigorous building programme which, in addition to refurbishment and restoration, would eventually embrace new churches, schools and vicarages. Indeed, within two years of his appointment, the press reported "the many excellent objects by which the pious and indefatigable vicar, Rev Richard Brindley Hone, is endeavouring to promote the welfare of his extensive parish."[63] Within this programme, Hone was not only initiator, but also a generous benefactor: £50 for the restoration of Hales Owen Church; £15 for new Sunday School rooms in Hales Owen; £50 for the building of a new church in Oldbury; £25 for the building of a new church in Blackheath; £10 for the building of a school at Quinton. Nor were his subscriptions restricted to the work of the established church - £8 in 1847 donated to Irish Famine Relief; £10 in 1869 to the Nailers' Relief Fund are just some of the benefactions listed in his note books. The new rectory at Hales Owen, presumably necessary to accommodate his large household, was also built at his own expense.

---

[62] Richard was at Brasenose, Joseph (who subsequently became Vicar of Tireley, Gloucestershire) at University College.
[63] *Wolverhampton Chronicle* (18.07.1838)

Richard and Frances Hone had eight children: one son, Evelyn Joseph (b 1837), educated at Harrow and Wadham College, Oxford, prior to ordination and a curacy at St George's, Doncaster;[64] and seven daughters: Catherine (b 1839); Augusta (b 1840); Anne (b 1841); Bertha (b 1843); Dora (b 1844); Edith (b 1849) and Alice (b 1850). Augusta, Bertha, Dora and Edith never married and were still living in the rectory with their father at the time of his death in 1881. Censuses of 1851 and 1861 show that the household also included a governess, cook housemaids and, in 1851 a nurse and under-nurse, and in 1861, a lady's maid, when Hone's mother and sister were also present. Thus, Hales Owen Rectory exemplified the stereotypical image of female satellites surrounding the paterfamilias, whose well-being was their raison d'être, such as was seen in the parsonage at Haworth, or indeed in its less famous counterpart in Quinton. (7.06)

Within Hales Owen parish, Archdeacon Hone was a leading figure in the Nailmakers' Protection Society, clearly aware of the penury and privation under which many of his parishioners toiled. Akin to this, in Worcester diocese, in March 1857, he convened a meeting of the archdeaconry which, amongst its recommendations, stressed that "the improvement of the dwellings of the poor is essential to the success of any efforts for their spiritual good."[65] He also found time to write, publishing in his early years in Hales Owen *The Lives of James Usher, Henry Hammond, John Evelyn, Thomas Wilson*, later providing an introduction to *Seventeen Years in the Yoruba Country*, a life of the missionary Anna Hinderer compiled by his daughters, in addition to many other instructive papers and pamphlets. Hone's notebooks reveal a lively interest in the history and progress of his parish: passages copied from Nash's *Collections for the History of Worcestershire*; lists of contributions made to various projects by notable parishioners; lists of books which his Sunday School teachers should read; an assessment of local poet William Shenstone: "amongst his poems there is a very dull ode for

THE

LIVES

OF

JAMES USHER, D.D.
ARCHBISHOP OF ARMAGH;

HENRY HAMMOND, D.D.
RECTOR OF PENSHURST, KENT;

JOHN EVELYN, ESQ.
AUTHOR OF "SYLVA," &c.;

AND

THOMAS WILSON, D.D.
BISHOP OF SODOR AND MAN.

BY THE REV. RICHARD B. HONE, M.A.
VICAR OF HALES OWEN, SHROPSHIRE,
AND CANON OF WORCESTER.

PUBLISHED UNDER THE DIRECTION OF
THE COMMITTEE OF GENERAL LITERATURE AND EDUCATION,
APPOINTED BY THE SOCIETY FOR PROMOTING
CHRISTIAN KNOWLEDGE.

THE SIXTH EDITION.

LONDON:
JOHN W. PARKER, WEST STRAND.
M.DCCC.XLVI.

Dr Brettle and the Hales Owen citizens… In Elegy XXIII, a portion of St Kenelm's story is related in moderate verse."[66] Details concerning the populations of Hales Owen's various townships include the note that in 1839 the population of Quinton (which he gives as 2,138) are spread some one-and-a-half to four miles from Hales Owen's school and parsonage,[67] obviously a cause for concern to its rector. Following the opening of Christ Church The Quinton in 1840 he perceptively notes, "At the end of two months the church is well-attended and the congregation is chiefly comprised of persons who

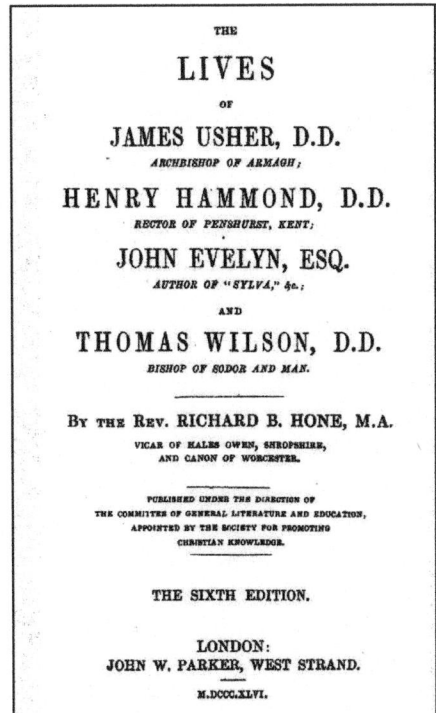

---

[64] Evelyn's son, Rev Campbell Richard Hone carried the family's cure of souls into the third generation.

[65] *Notes of Meeting of Clergy of the Archdeaconry of Worcester* (March 1857)

[66] Hone, R.B., *Notebook 1*, p 5a. NB Shenstone, W., *Ode to be performed by Dr Brettle and a chorus of Hales Owen citizens. The Instrumental Part is a Viol D'Amour*; *Elegy XXIII* DALHC

[67] Op cit p 21a

habitually neglected public worship, of those who from the distance of other churches could rarely attend and of those who had been in the habit of frequenting dissenting places."[68] Venerable Richard Brindley Hone MA died on May 5th 1881, aged 76. His funeral service was conducted by the Bishop of Worcester, with "30 clergymen and 100 of the gentry, tradesmen and working men of the parish assembled to take part in the procession."[69] He was buried in Hales Owen churchyard and there is a memorial to him in the north aisle of the church.

Under the Quinton tithe apportionments, Richard Brindley Hone, as Vicar for the time being of Hales Owen, surrendered all vicarial tithes and Easter offerings, in lieu of which he became entitled to the Small Tithes of both Ridgacre and Warley Wigorn townships.

3.11   Commutator

3.11.01   Ann Hill

Apart from Lord Lyttelton, Ann Hill was the only Quinton landowner with land commuted in the Warley Wigorn tithe apportionments under the 1836 act. Schedule C of the preamble relates to plots W7-W8 which, along with Mrs Hill's property in Ridgacre township (plots 88, 95, 198, 237-239, 242-248) amounted in total to 48 acres 35 poles, let Thomas Nicholls in 1841 and Henry Nicholls by 1844.

Baptised at St Philip's Church, Birmingham on May 28th 1770, Ann, daughter of Samuel and Elizabeth Troughton, inherited her property from her father, who died in 1782 and her brother who died in 1790. Samuel Troughton, a Birmingham japanner, had purchased his Quinton lands on a 1,000-year lease from Thomas Lyttelton in 1773. On September 15th 1797, at Polesworth Church, Warwickshire, Ann Troughton was married by licence[70] to Captain (later Lieutenant Colonel) Charles Hill of Halifax and the 50th Regiment of Foot. Widowed in 1819 when her husband died in Jamaica, after which she was in receipt of an army pension, Ann Hill was clearly a woman of property. In 1844 in the tithe apportionments, her address is given as 49 Park Road, Grosvenor Square, London. By the time she made her will, dated February 17th 1847, she was living in Connaught Terrace, Edgware Road, a prestigious address in the city of Westminster. Ann Hill died in 1854 and her Quinton property was sold in 12 lots the following year. The two Warley Wigorn plots were treated as a separate lot.

Various bequests in Ann Hill's will imply wealth and, indeed, refinement. To her cousin, Frances Bond of Polesworth, came clothes, jewels and pictures, except the portrait of Sir George Walker's family, which passed to his daughter, Harriet Elizabeth, who also received a bequest of £1,000. Ann's piano and music books were left to Frances Ann Badger of Birmingham. After a further £1,000 bequest to Charles Hewey (one of the executors to the will) and several smaller sums to family and friends, the residue of Ann Hill's estate was divided between Frances Bond and Frances Badger. The will (which was subject to a Chancery decision in 1856) also appointed Joseph Aldridge Bond and John Southerdon Burn as executors and was witnessed by George White of Middle Temple and John Edward Miller of Lincoln's Inn, further suggesting a status somewhat removed from that of her Quinton tenants.

---

[68] Hone, R.B., p44 DALHC
[69] *Worcester Journal* (14.05.1881)
[70] See Footnote 383 p 219

4   Landowners

At the time of the tithe awards, Quinton's 943 acres were in the ownership of 33 landlords and six landladies. Just 13 of these were actually resident in Quinton, the remaining 26 being absentee owners. Total holdings varied in size from William Spurrier's 161 acres spread over 33 plots to Ann White's single plot measuring only 18 poles. No less than 542 acres (57% of the total) were part of just four estates: those owned by William Spurrier, William Penn, Ferdinando Dudley Lea Smith and George William, 4th Baron Lyttelton. For all of these, their Quinton holding represented just part of their total property. Only William Penn's five areas of woodland were listed in the apportionments as being in his own occupation. Though perhaps not in the same league as Austen's proud Fitzwilliam Darcy, with his estate in Derbyshire, these four largest landowners represented a class remote from the majority of Ridgacre and Warley Wigorn townships' residents. Hopefully, however, they may have deserved a similar accolade as that given to Darcy by his housekeeper, Mrs Reynolds.

> "His father was an excellent man... and the son will be just like him – just as affable to the poor. He is the best landlord and the best master that ever lived. There is not one of his tenants or servants but what will give him a good name."[71]

The remaining 43% of Quinton was divided between 35 landowners. Of the 13 resident landowners, three held only the property in which they lived; six owned both their own homes and other plots rented out to tenants. Two lived in rented property themselves, but owned other property in which they, in turn, had tenants. Two owned garden plots, but lived in rented property. Only George Birch, with 104 acres, owned Quinton property that came anywhere near in size to that of Spurrier, Penn, Lea Smith and Lyttelton. The majority of resident Quinton landowners, eight of whose plots measured less than 36 poles, were perhaps challenged by the same concerns as Baring-Gould's fantastically-named Adonijah Saach who mismanaged his wife's property in nearby Lye Waste.

> "There's two cottages as brings in a little under 'arf a crown a week, and one is over a shillin' more, and the fifth aint got no tenant in it now. The roof be bad an' I don't see my way to repairin' of it. Reed straw is dear, about eighteenpence a bundle, an' I might want a couple of 'undred bundles for that there roof, an' the thatchin' as well; an' then the timbers be rotten, an' the carpenter would 'ave work as well; an if I let, it's but 'arf a crown a week, an' it will tek a lot of 'arf crowns to pay for the outlay."[72]

The ownership of land and property and the residential distribution of owners with vested interests, perhaps far from their own homes, gives a fascinating insight into investment in, and exploitation of, Quinton in the mid-19th century,

4.01   William Spurrier [E][73]
Total Acreage: 161 acres 1 rood 1 pole
Plot Numbers: 87, W46-W64, W66-70, W73, W92, W94-W98
Tenants: John Davenport (8.01); Joseph Davenport (8.01)

---

[71] Austen, J. (1813) *Pride and Prejudice*, Chapter 43
[72] Baring-Gould, S. (1902) *Nebo the Nailer*, Chapter 22
[73] As owner of land in Warley Wigorn township, part freehold, part copyhold. See 13.01

The largest landowner in Quinton was Birmingham lawyer, William Spurrier, born into a Walsall family in 1768. In 1795 he is listed in practice in Temple Row, Birmingham, subsequently moving to New Street and then to Paradise Street. Evidently a successful criminal lawyer, Spurrier also served as clerk to Birmingham magistrates. In the earlier years of his career, he lived in Smethwick. On June 18th 1793 at St Philip's Church, Birmingham, William Spurrier and Eleanor Boole were married by licence.[74] They subsequently had five children, three of whom pre-deceased them.

Citing earlier sources, Yates and Halverson[75] suggest that Spurrier also operated as a bounty hunter, acting as an agent provocateur and using entrapment as an agent of the Bank of England to capture forgers and coiners. Local legend attributed Spurrier's wealth to rewards paid for the capture, conviction and even execution of his victims. A contemporary witness recalled "the horror with which Mr Spurrier was regarded by a large number of his fellow townsmen. Mothers used his name to frighten their crying children into silence and it was as potent in this respect as the still more dreaded name of Bonaparte used to be during the French War."

William & Eleanor Spurrier's tombstone, Old Church Smethwick

Under the terms of his will, William Spurrier left his considerable estate to his daughter, Mary, who had married Lt Col Mortlock Studd in 1820. This included "All those my several messuages farms and lands with the appurtenances called the Four Dwellings Farm, the Lower Farm and the Ivy Farm situate in the parish of Halesowen in the Counties of Worcester and Salop or one of them now in the occupation of Joseph Davenport or his undertenants."[76] Eleanor Spurrier died in November, 1847 and William in August 1848. They were both buried at Old Church, Smethwick.

4.02   William Penn

Total Acreage: 131 acres 3 rood 18 poles
Plot Numbers: 160, 169, W9-W45
Tenants: William Johnson (8.01.05); Joseph Pearman (9.01.01)

Although William Penn was a considerable Quinton landlord, his identity remains obscure. Long-established families of Penns existed in Birmingham and throughout Worcestershire. Hales Owen poet

---

[74] See Footnote 383 p 219
[75] Yates DE & Halverson JD *The Gentry and the Clergy in Smethwick and Birmingham*, pp 58-60
[76] Prerogative Court of Canterbury Will Registers, Class PROB11, Piece 2080

William Shenstone's grandfather was William Penn of Harborough Hall. Locally, William de Penne first paid *16s of silver* annually to the Abbot of Hales Owen as rent for property in Romsley in 1378.[77] The William Penn who held Quinton land in the mid-1800s acquired his holding much more recently. Land Tax lists first record his ownership in 1798, the previous owner, from whom William Penn evidently purchased his 132 acres, being Samuel Wheatley. By 1810, the owners are listed as the executors of William Penn and by 1818, the tenant is John Johnson.[78]

Plan	Field Name	Area			Cultivation	Tithe Payable		
						Vicar		
		A	R	P		£	s	d
W33a	Road (52°27'02"N 1°59'05"W)		1	3				
W9	Plantation (52°27'34"N 1°59'05"W)		1	7	Woodland			6
W11	Pits Wood (52°27'35"N 1°59'18"W)	8	3	0	Woodland		7	0
W16	Pool Tail Plantation (52°27'21"N 1°59'11"W)	6	1	7	Woodland		5	6
W19	Feston Wood (52°27'14"N 1°59'09"W)	2	3	30	Woodland		2	6
W22	Bearlands Wood (52°27'05"N 1°59'02"W)		2	0	Woodland			6
W26	Bog Wood (52°26'54"N 1°59'09"W)	2	2	24	Woodland		2	0
		21	2	31			18	0

4.03 William Grazebrook [as trustee of the Lea Smith estate]

Total Acreage: 125 acres 1 rood; Plot Numbers: 97-102, 104, 107, 111-115, 129-141, 194, 196, 197, W1-W6;

Tenants: Thomas Coley (12.06.01); William Goode (12.06.02); Thomas Partridge (W1); William Partridge (W2); William Pritchett (4.18); Elijah Read (12.06.03); Richard Tomlinson (8.01.08), James Wragg (8.01.04)

When the barony of Dudley fell into abeyance in 1757, the senior co-heir was the head of the Lea Smith family of Hales Owen Grange. Deputy Lieutenant of the County of Worcestershire, magistrate and feofee of Hales Owen Grammar School, Ferdinando Smith was born March 26th 1779, the son of Ferdinando and Elizabeth (née Lyttelton). He rose to the rank of Lieutenant Colonel in the Worcester Militia and served with distinction in Ireland during the rebellion of 1798 and in the Peninsula War of 1808-14. Returning home, he was awarded the freedom of the City of Worcester. He married first in 1802, Eloisa Knudson, who died in 1805. Following a protracted period of widowhood, in 1830 Ferdinando married Elizabeth Grazebrook of Audnam House, Stourbridge, by whom he had two sons, Ferdinando Dudley Lea Smith and William Lea Smith. When Lt Col Ferdinando Smith died in July 1841, his son and heir was only seven years old, so the estate was managed by his brother-in-law and trustee, William Grazebrook.

William, the long-serving secretary of the Albrighton Hunt, was one of eleven children of Michael and Mary Ann Grazebrook, whose family business interests extended to coal and iron at Netherton and

---

[77] Tompkins, M. (ed) (2017) *Court Rolls of Romsley1279-1643*, p144
[78] Warley Wigorn Papers – WAAS

Hales Owen and glass at Audnam. Baptised at Kingswinford on April 7th 1791, William was still resident there in 1841, sharing his Summerhill home with his two sisters, Charlotte and Mary (both of independent means) and his farmer brother Charles. At that census William's occupation was given as glass manufacturer. Ten years later, still sharing the Summerhill residence with Mary and Charles, William was now listed as iron master, glass manufacturer and farmer of 140 acres employing four labourers. The household also employed a resident footman, cook, housemaid and kitchen maid. By 1861, William Grazebrook had moved to Park Hall Kidderminster, where he died in 1879, leaving an estate valued at £57,697 15s 8d.

The Dudley barony was restored to a descendant of Ferdinando Smith in 1916.

4.04 Aaron, Ann (Nanny), George, John White

Total Acreage: 111 acres 38 poles

(i) Aaron White
Total Acreage: 27 acres 2 roods 13 poles
Plot Numbers: 24,25, W74-W82
Tenant: Thomas White (8.01.02)

(ii) Ann (Nanny) White
Total Acreage: 18 poles
Plot Number: 31
Tenant: Benjamin Yates (12.03.11)

(iii) George White [E][79]
Total Acreage: 7 acres 1 rood 25 poles
Plot Numbers: W85-W87, W129, W170
Tenants: Charles Clay (12.04.10); Thomas Haycock (12.04.09); Thomas White (8.01.02)

(iv) John White
Total Acreage: 76 acres 22 poles
Plot Numbers: 1-5, 10, 11, 19-21, 30, 32, 34, 39-41,90-92, 96, W127, W128, W131-W134, W137-W148, W158, W184
Tenants: Jonathan Farmer (8.01.06); Samuel Hadley (12.05.03); James Male (12.11.04); Daniel Read (12.05.01); Joseph Record (12.05.02); Edward Smith (12.03.01) Thomas White (8.01.02); John Yates (12.03.10); Thomas Yeomans (12.03.02)

Aaron White inherited his Quinton property under the terms of the will of his father, Thomas White, who died in 1776, naming Pynson Wilmot, vicar of Hales Owen his executor.

I give bequeath and devise unto my loving wife Mary White all the buildings lands and premises with all and every their appurtenances mentioned in the lease granted by late Right Honourable George Lord Lyttelton… And after her decease I give bequeath and devise unto my son Aaron White all the said buildings lands and premises mentioned in the said lease for and during the whole term which shall remain unexpired in the said lease and also all my said copyhold lands buildings and premises with their and every of their appurtenances to hold to him and his heirs and assigns for ever and also all my said freehold buildings lands and premises with all and every of their appurtenances to hold to him and his heirs and assigns for ever.[80]

On February 28th 1779 at Hales Owen's Church of St John the Baptist, widower Aaron White married Nanny Rose, his first wife, Hannah Darby (whom he had married at Oldbury on December 29th 1756 and by whom he had five children – Phoebe, Thomas, Edward, Molly and Sarah) having been buried in

---

[79] As owner/occupier of freehold land in Ridgacre township. See 13.01
[80] Proved at Worcester 26.03.1776 (WAAS)

Hales Owen on November 26th 1773. Aaron and Nanny had five children – Sally and Nanny, baptised at Hales Owen on June 6th 1781, "Sally said to have been born July 1779 and Nanny said to have been born August 1780."[81] George, baptised at Hales Owen on June 8th 1783, Lucy, baptised at Hales Owen on April 17th 1791 and John, baptised at Hales Owen on July 17th 1796. Aaron White died, aged 89, in 1822 and was buried in Hales Owen on May 27th, which means that he could no longer have been a landowner at the time of the tithe award. In his will, dated July 17th 1820, he bequeathed his property to his widow, four of their children and one grandson, and two grandsons from his first marriage. The cataloguing of his Quinton holdings offers valuable detail concerning their acquisition and disposition.

I give and bequeath to my wife Nanny White and my son John White all my household furniture goods &c to be divided betwixt them as they may agree; and I give to my wife Nanny White all that house, shop and garden now in the tenure of Benjamin Yates for her own sole use and purpose... and I also give to my wife Nanny White all that messuage, farm and premises now in the occupation of Mr Chambers situate at Cakemore in that part of the Parish of Halesowen which lies in the County of Worcester except that half acre of land now lying in Upper Quinton Field and now in the holding of my son George White... I give and bequeath to my son George White the lease of the farm I rented of Lord Lyttelton for his own use and benefit; and I also give to my son George White that one acre of copyhold land I bought of Councelor Guest lying and being in the uppermost Quinton Field and also half an acre of freehold land adjoining that one acre of copyhold land which I purchased of Martin and Horn to my son George White; and also that Leasow of arable land called the Top Croft containing four acres and a half lying and being in Ridgacre to my son George White; and also those two dwelling houses, shops and gardens now in the occupation of Benjamin Clay and Thomas Haycock to my son George White; and also those three plecks of land or gardens that I enclosed from the waste and purchased of the Surveyors of the Highway to my son George White... I give and bequeath to my wife Nanny White and also to my two daughters Sally Powers and Lucy Burton and also to my two sons George White and John White and also to my grandson Joseph Powers and my other two grandsons Edward White and George White all that my messuage farm and premises called the Four Dwellings situate in the parish of Halesowen and County of Worcester and now in the occupation of George White, except that piece of land called the Top Croft heretofore disposed of to my son George White, to be equally divided amongst them... I also give and bequeath to my grandson Robert Millward all that house and garden lying in the parish of Halesowen and in the occupation of Joseph Sadler. I give and bequeath to my son John White all that farm or estate I bought of Wm Bradley of London containing about twenty acres situate at the Quinton and in the occupation of myself, my son George White, William Read, Benjamin Yates and William Jones. I also give unto my son John White all that piece of arable land called the Lower Quinton Field containing about two acres now in the occupation of George White. I also give to my son John White that Inage called Halls Inage containing about two acres lying between the top of the Lower Quinton Field and Mr Foley's land, now in the occupation of George White. And I also give that copyhold house, shop and garden situate at the Hawthorn unto my son John White and now in the occupation of Thomas Partridge. I also give to my son John White all those two copyhold leasows adjoining the aforesaid copyhold house and garden now in the occupation of George White; I also give and bequeath all those five acres of copyhold land I bought of Councelor Guest, called the Lunt and Little Inage, lying and being in the Parish of Halesowen and County of Worcester to my son John White. I also give and bequeath that little close or pleck of land lying betwixt the Widow Hayes' house & garden and Benjamin Yates & Joseph Gould's house and garden,

[81] Gregory, K.R. (ed) *Halesowen Parish Registers: Baptisms and Burial 1779-1782*

> *to my son John White. And I also give and bequeath that seat in the gallery in the Parish Church of Halesowen now occupied by James Suite at five shillings a year unto my son John White.*[82]

Under the terms of Nanny White's will made in 1826, all her property was divided equally between her daughters Sally Powers and Lucy Burton "for their entire use and purpose independent of their present or future husbands they may have."[83] On January 6th 1805 George White married Martha Penn at Bromsgrove. On January 9th 1812, their son George was born. He, however, was not baptised until February 14th 1821, also at Bromsgrove, over four years after the death of his mother. Widower George White married Catharine Humphries on July 12th 1818 at St Martin's Church, Birmingham. They had two daughters, Mary and Lucy, both baptised at Hales Owen Parish Church: Mary on February 4th 1824 and Lucy on December 10th 1830, just over two years after her mother was buried there on October 2nd 1828. John White married Sarah Connard at Bromsgrove on March 6th 1816. Their son, Thomas, was born on October 19th 1819 and baptised at Bromsgrove on April 25th 1821. George White died aged 57 and was buried at Hales Owen Parish Church on July 8th 1840, having directed in his will[84] that his property should be sold and invested for the benefit of his daughters, Mary and Lucy, with his brother, John, appointed as trustee. George White's will, however, would prove contentious and subject to a legal challenge against the trustee in 1846.

"William Burton, farmer, brought this action against John White his uncle, to recover possession of an interest in lands in Halesowen. The plaintiff claimed an interest under the will of his grandfather who died in 1822. The plaintiff claimed as heir at law of his mother, Lucy, first a fourth share of the property, by reason of her being one of the devisees; secondly one half of another portion. The will of Aaron White left a certain house to his wife Nannie; next a messuage and farm at Halesowen, now in the holding of John White; then came the point in question wherein the will left to George White the lease of a certain house, one acre of copyhold land… two other acres, a croft, two dwelling houses, and a house, shop, garden and appurtenances, occupied by Samuel Partridge; finally the will bequeathed the rest of the estate to be equally divided between the wife and the children who had issue. The plaintiff stated that these various devises of land to George White gave to him the estates for life only, and that, therefore, the estate for life was a part of the residuary estate so disposed of by the last clause in the will, which devised it to the wife and the children who had issue. Now the children who had issue at the time of the death were three: first Sally (married to one Powers); second Lucy (married to Burton); and third John who was the defendant. Each of these parties claimed one fourth; and thus the plaintiff would be entitled to have his mother's fourth share. The learned counsel was proceeding to call witnesses when Mr Whateley, for the defence, consented to a verdict for the plaintiff with liberty to move for a special case in the superior courts."[85]

---

[82] Proved at Worcester 25.09.1822 (WAAS)

[83] Proved at Worcester 15.01.1846 (WAAS)

[84] Proved at Worcester 05.03.1841 (WAAS)

[85] *Worcestershire Chronicle* 26.07.1846

A declaration made in 1857 by Benjamin Yates (12.03.01) throws further light on the family of Aaron White.

Aaron White

with whom I was intimately acquainted He often used to come to my cottage and talk with me He was married to Nanny White when I first knew him I remember her father Benjamin Rose. Aaron White had by Nanny (who was his second wife) four children Sally who married Thomas Powers, George White, Lucy who married William Burton and John White I don't remember I ever heard of any other children of Aaron White by his wife Nanny nor was she ever married otherwise than to him Sally Powers had eight or nine children some of them were born before Aaron White's death

George White was married twice By his first wife he had no children And by his second wife he had no children for several years after their marriage - He had no children till after the death of his father Aaron White. John White was married several years before his father died The present Thomas White was eldest son of John White

and was born in the lifetime of his Granfather Aaron White I believe Aaron White had four children by his first wife Thomas White Edward White and two daughters one of whom married Jones and another Millward

75

4.05   Richard Greaves

Total Acreage: 31 acres 31 poles;
Plot Numbers: 142-157;
Tenant: John Jakeman (8.01.09)

Richard Greaves acquired his Ridgacre property via his wife's inheritance. The will of her father, James Thompson, of Bradford Street, Aston, who died in 1823, devised "all that my messuage farm and lands situate at the Worlds End, Halesowen in the County of Salop, now in the possession of Thomas Hobbs... to my daughter Emma the wife of Richard Greves."[86] Both the Thompson and Greves families were Birmingham Unitarians. James and Ruth Thompson had married at Lombard Street Meeting House; the Greves' associations were with Kingswood Chapel (rebuilt after its destruction in the Priestley Riots of 1791) in Kings Norton, where they were long-established. The will of one Richard Grevis of Moseley in the Parish of Kings Norton, had been proved at the Prerogative Court of Canterbury in 1688.[87]

Richard Greves died in 1840 and was buried at Kings Norton. In 1851 Emma Greves, house and land proprietor, was living in Balsall Heath with two annuitant daughters, Ruth and Caroline and one servant. Emma Greves died in 1861 and was buried at Kingswood Chapel. Richard and Emma had seven children. Isaac, died in infancy, Emma and Ruth both died unmarried and intestate. All three were buried at Kingswood Chapel. A third daughter, Rebecca, married Unitarian minister, Rev Rees Lewis Lloyd in 1845. By 1851 Rees Lloyd was a widower, living in King Street, Kings Norton. Lloyd, in whose name a charitable trust was established following his death in 1885[88] (when he too was buried at Kingswood Chapel) and who was a correspondent of Charles Dickens,[89] subsequently married Caroline Anne, youngest daughter of Richard and Emma Greves, on August 14th 1867 at the English Episcopal Church, rue d'Aguesseau, Paris.[90] On the death of Emma Greves in 1861 the residual legatees under their grandfather's will were the three surviving of Richard's and Emma's children: Richard, Edwin and Caroline Greves, who in August 1862, sold their Ridgacre property to Robert Smart.

4.06   David, Stephen, Daniel Grainger

Total Acreage: 30 acres 2 roods

(i)   David Grainger
Total Acreage: 15 acres 8 poles
Plot Numbers: 75-80
Tenant: Richard Underhill (8.01.12)

(ii)   Stephen Grainger
Total Acreage: 10 acres 2 roods 28 poles
Plot Numbers: W113-W116, W118-W120
Tenant: James Cooper (10.01.02)

(iii)   Daniel Grainger
Total Acreage: 4 acres 3 roods 4 poles
Plot Numbers: W111, W112
Tenant: Joseph Wakeman (8.01.13)

---

[86] Prerogative Court of Canterbury Will Registers, Class PROB11, Piece 1669
[87] Prerogative Court of Canterbury Will Registers, Class PROB11, Piece 392
[88] Charity of Rev Rees Lewis Lloyd 1885-1886
[89] See Storey, G, et al (1988) *Letters of Charles Dickens* Vol 6 1850-1852, p 650
[90] Perhaps this took place in Paris as prior to the 1907 Marriage Act under English law a man was prohibited from marrying his brother's widow.

Of 1841's 16 people named David Grainger,[91] 11 were aged under 20, two lived in Scotland and one in Devon. The remaining two were both miners, one in Sedgley, the other in Wolverhampton. Neither seems a particularly likely candidate as land-owner. In 1841, a Stephen Grainger, of independent means, lived at Sweet Turf, Dudley. Head of household was Sarah Grainger (listed as independent), also resident was Julius Grainger, butcher. 10 years later Sarah (widow) and Stephen (son) Grainger, both of no stated occupation, were still living in Sweet Turf, as they were in 1861, still of no given occupation. Stephen Grainger, son of Julius and Sarah Grainger had been baptised at St Thomas's Church, Dudley on January 1st 1815 and Julius Grainger at the same church on September 13th 1812. In Cradley Heath, Rowley Regis in 1841 lived Daniel Grainger (80), independent, Sarah Grainger (60), of no stated occupation and Daniel Grainger (35), nail master.

Light is thrown on family links by the will of Daniel Grainger, "of Cradley Heath in the parish of Rowley Regis in the county of Stafford, Esquire," made on February 9th 1846. Among numerous bequests of his property, which included plots in Warley Salop rented to Joseph Wakeman (8.01.13), are those to his wife, Sarah, nephews Noel Grainger ("son of my late brother, David Grainger"), and Julius Grainger ("son of my late brother Julius"); also to Sarah Grainger ("widow of my late brother, Julius") and his grandsons George Grainger Tandy and David Grainger Ward, both of whom received shares in Dudley and West Bromwich Banking Co. Bankers returns for 1857 list the interest of representatives of Daniel Grainger in the same company.[92] Daniel Grainger's Quinton credentials are confirmed by the bequest "to my son-in-law Nathaniel Ward all my estate situate at Quinton in the parish of Hales Owen, now in the occupation of Underhill." The Ridgacre tithe apportionments list David not Daniel Grainger as Richard Underhill's landlord, suggesting that after his death, his property passed to his brother.

Daniel Grainger died in April quarter, 1848 and his will was proved at London on August 22nd of the same year.[93] The absence of any bequest to his son, Daniel, suggests the latter's death as one registered at Dudley in 1842.[94] Thus it seems that David and Daniel Grainger were brothers and Stephen their nephew.

4.07   John Birch [J][95]

Total Acreage: 23 acres 2 roods 33 poles
Plot Numbers: 116-118, 122-128, 177-180
Tenants: Thomas Haycock (12.10.02); Thomas Page (12.10.04); Thomas Partridge (12.10.03).

In addition to the 23¼ acres owned by John Birch in Ridgacre township, his property also consisted of 16 acres 3 roods 6 poles beyond Quinton in Warley Wigorn and 44 acres 17 poles in Warley Salop. This largest holding, which at the tithe apportionments Birch occupied as well as owned, also contained the dwelling where he was enumerated in the 1841 census. Most of his Warley Wigorn land (with the

---

[91] The 1841 census lists only 16 people named David Grainger, 14 named Stephen Grainger and 19 named Daniel Grainger throughout the UK.
[92] Worcester Journal 21.02.1857
[93] Prerogative Court of Canterbury Will Registers, Class PROB11, Piece 2079
[94] The deaths of two people named Daniel Grainger were registered in 1842: one in January and one in July.
[95] Juror at Amy Read Inquest. See 13.02

exception of a 10-pole plot occupied by Esther Chatwin) was rented by Thomas Nicholls as part of Hawthorn Farm. In 1841, John Birch's household consisted of himself and three servants.

John Birch's Ridgacre property encompassed Lower Ridgacre Farm, of which the tithe award also lists him as occupier. This seems unlikely, given that William Underhill (8.01.11), enumerated in 1851 as farmer of 24 acres of Lower Ridgacre was clearly farming in the same place in 1841. The unlikelihood is further compounded by the 1851 census for Warley Salop, where John Birch's successor (another John Birch) is described as farmer of 65 acres which closely resembles the 63 acres 35 poles extent of the 1844 property in Warley Salop and Warley Wigorn, without the addition of Lower Ridgacre Farm.

John Birch died in 1847 and was buried at Christ Church The Quinton on September 18th.

4.08   William King
Total Acreage: 10 acres 2 roods 36 poles
Plot Numbers: 162-168
Tenant: Joseph Wakeman (8.01.13)

Though King was not an uncommon Hales Owen surname in its earlier recorded history (the Court Rolls list Agnes, Alice, Henry, Matilda, Philip, Richard, Roger, Thomas and William King in the 13th century) and there are numerous King baptisms, marriages and burials recorded in Hales Owen parish registers in the 16th and early 17th centuries, by the mid-1800s the name had all but died out in the locality. Just two instances fall within the parameters of this study. In 1839, Mrs King was mistress of Hales Owen Sunday and Infant School;[96] on April 24th 1856, Sarah King, aged 54 of Hasbury, was buried at Hales Owen's Church of St John the Baptist. George Birch (8.01.03), who died in 1853, named George King of Elmdon, Warwickshire as one of the executors to his will. In the absence of further evidence, William King of the Ridgacre tithe award remains elusive and hidden in the shadows.

4.09   Timothy Hill
Total Acreage: 7 acres 2 roods 36 poles
Plot Numbers: 43, 188-190, 202, 204, 205, 219, 220, 223
Tenants: Richard Branton (9.01.02); Esther Cutler (12.11.03); Joseph Dixon (10.01.03); John Fox (12.11.02); John Guest (12.04.01); Benjamin Hill (12.07.01); James Partridge (12.09.01); John Taylor (12.11.04)

Though the Hill family name had evident Quinton connections in the mid-1800s – Ann Hill (3.11.01) had land commuted in Warley Wigorn, Benjamin Hill (12.07.01) was deputy constable for Ridgacre, Isaac Hill (12.12.05) was one of the township's nail-forgers, none appear to have obvious links with Timothy Hill. On December 1st 1808 a Timothy Hill was married to Esther Lowe Powell at Hales Owen Parish Church. By 1841 Esther, now widowed with two grown-up children, all of independent means, was living in Camden Hill, Birmingham. In the lack of further evidence, a link with the owner of Ridgacre plots 43, 188-190, 202, 204, 205, 219, 220, 223 is purely conjectural. However, what is known is that

---

[96] Somers, F. & K.M. (1932) p 80

a considerable portion of the property listed as belonging to Timothy Hill in the tithe award was put up for sale in 1868 and advertised in *Aris's Birmingham Gazette* on November 7th.

TO BE SOLD BY AUCTION by Messrs, Cheshire and Gibson
Shenstone Hotel, Hales Owen, Wednesday 11th November
the following highly valuable FREEHOLD PROPERTIES
situated at Beech Lanes, The Quinton.
LOT I. Tithe in the township of Ridgacre Plan 219.
The Old-established Licensed PUBLIC-HOUSE
called the Beech Tree Inn with outbuildings and appurtenances
in the occupation of Joseph Dixon, containing 29 poles.
220 Two COTTAGES and GARDENS, adjoining the last,
in the occupations of Thomas Fisher and James Male
223 Three COTTAGES and GARDENS, adjoining the last,
in the occupation of John Martin, James Faulkner and Joseph Goode
LOT 11. IN THE TOWNSHIP OF RIDGACRE, 43 HOUSE, SHOP, and GARDEN,
near to the Quinton Turnpike Gate, in the occupation of John Houghton

---

4.10   James Bissell [E][97]

Total Acreage: 7 acres 2 roods 29 poles
Plot Numbers: 44, 45, 51-53, 89
Tenants: James Cooper (10.01.02); John Hall
(12.02.02); James Price (12.02.01); William Rose
(12.02.03)

The son of Richard and Mary Bissell, James Bissell, of Webbs Green, Lapal, was baptised at Hales Owen on Christmas Day 1796. His family had acquired the land in Lapal when Thomas Bissell leased Webbs Green Farm from Sir Thomas Lyttleton in 1722.[98] By the mid-19th century, the family also owned property in Hales Owen and were established as grocers and drapers in High Street. The 1841 census shows James Bissell living at Webbs Green with his wife, Sarah and sister Charlotte, four male servants and three female servants.

Though James Bissell's occupation is not identified, it is known that the Bissell family were amongst the leading nail manufacturers in Hales Owen and that in the late 18th century Thomas Bissell had built a nail warehouse at Webbs Green adjacent to Dudley Canal.[99] That the business continued is confirmed by trade directories in the 1850s when TJS Bissell (James' nephew and heir) is listed as "Thomas JS Bissell & Co, Nail factors, Webbs Green."[100] As one of the nearest Hales Owen nail factors to Quinton, the Bissell company no doubt supplied much of the iron to the village's nail-makers, bought back their finished products and perhaps directed their custom to their High Street grocery store.

---

[97] As owner of freehold of land in Ridgacre township occupied by James Cooper. See 13.01
[98] Lyttelton Papers 605894 LB
[99] See Hunt, J. (2004) *A History of Halesowen*, p 35
[100] *Melville's Directory of Dudley and District* (1852); Billings, M (1855) *Directory and Gazetteer of the County of Worcester*

James Bissell, who had been appointed a feofee of Hales Owen Grammar School in 1818, died in 1847 and in his will[101] made five years earlier, bequeathed his household effects equally to his wife and sister. They also inherited "Red Lion Inn in the parish of Ridgacre in the county of Worcester, in the occupation of James Cooper," and the property at "The Quinton in the parish of Hales Owen, in the occupation of Samuel Dingley and his undertenants." This was plots 44 and 45 on the Ridgacre tithe map, at the apportionments occupied by James Price (12.02.01), John Hall (12.02.02) and William Rose (12.02.03). Later in the 19th century this land was sold for development and Bissell Street cut through the heart of it.   Sarah and Charlotte Bissell also inherited James Bissell's pew in Hales Owen Parish Church "for their mutual use and accommodation" for their lifetime, after which it was to pass to Thomas John Smith Bissell, James' nephew, executor and residual heir, who also inherited the Webbs Green estate.

4.11   Hales Owen Free School

Total Acreage: 4 acres 2 roods 37 poles
Plot Numbers: W122-W125
Tenant: William Pritchett (4.18)

HR Wilson - Hales Owen Free School after B Green

Hales Owen Free School was an ancient establishment. In 1652 a parliamentary inquisition directed that land and money given for charitable use in Hales Owen should be used for erecting and maintaining a free school and employing a schoolmaster. 17 feofees, who must live within a five-mile radius of the church were appointed with authority to lease out land. Their annual meetings were held on the Tuesday of Holy Week, when a bailiff to collect the rents was designated. At the time of the tithe apportionments the schoolmaster was John Lomax, who served from 1824-1863. Feofees with Quinton connections were James Bissell (4.10), Ferdinando Smith (4.03), George Hinchcliffe (13.02), TJS Bissell (4.10), Joseph Darby (4.15) – all appointed in 1818 and George Birch (8.01.03) – appointed in 1848. School hours were from 8am to 12 noon and 2pm to 5pm between Lady Day and Michaelmas and from 9am to 12noon and 1pm to 4pm between Michaelmas and Lady Day.[102] The school was closed for some months following the death of John Lomax in 1863 and re-opened in 1864 as Hales Owen Grammar School.

---

[101] Prerogative Court of Canterbury Wills Register, PROB 11: Piece 2060
[102] Lady Day = March 25th, Michaelmas = September 29th.

4.12   Edward Haden

Total Acreage: 3 acres 1 rood 13 poles
Plot Numbers: W99, W100, W102, W103
Tenant: James Yeomans (8.02.05)

Not a particularly common name in the West Midlands in the mid-1800s, the most likely candidate as James Yeomans' landlord is the Edward Haden who in 1841 was living with his wife and four children in Park Lane Tipton, where his occupation is given as agent. 10 years later the family had moved to Brewery Street, Dudley, Edward now being listed as a clerk. Yet another 10 years on, now in Dixon's Green, Dudley, Edward's occupation is further defined as clerk at iron works. Two sons were also working as clerks, William for an attorney and Charles for the railway, indicating a higher level of education than was common in Quinton in the period. The 1851 census identifies Edward Haden as born in Sedgley, perhaps making him the son of Benjamin and Rhoda Haden, who was baptised there on September 13th 1807.

4.13   Hales Owen Guardians of the Poor

Total Acreage: 3 acres 1 rood 7 poles
Plot Numbers: 161, 170-172
Tenant: Joseph Wakeman (8.01.13), 1 void property

Prior to the Poor Law Amendment Act of 1834, relief to the poor had been regulated by the Speenhamland System.[103] By this, wages were fixed according to the price of bread, with an allowance made relative to the size of a labourer's family. An additional supplement was paid out of local rates where wages were insufficient. This was a disastrous and demoralising system which confused the problem of inadequate wages with parish relief, creating a pauper underclass dependent upon handouts from parish funds. Parishes were grouped together in unions to build poorhouses, but only for the accommodation of the aged and infirm. During a national shortage of coins in the early 19th century some workhouses issued their own poor relief tokens, which shopkeepers could redeem at source.

The Poor Law Amendment Act abolished outdoor relief except for the old and sick and provided for the poor in workhouses, where conditions were deliberately harsh – designed to be less appealing than those in which the lowest-paid workers lived. Thus, the poor were compelled to work hard to

---

[103] Named after a decision by local magistrates at Speenhamland, Berkshire, May 6, 1795.

avoid the stigma of the workhouse, though even the exigencies of a nailer's life did not prevent Thomas and Sarah Haycock (12.04.09) from being declared paupers. Following the Poor Law Amendment Act most of Hales Owen parish became part of Stourbridge Poor Law Union, administered by a board of guardians who raised funds from lands under their control and were elected by rate-payers. In 1837 the overseers for Ridgacre township were George Birch (8.01.03) and Henry Nicholls (8.01.07). Joseph Wakeman (8.01.13) and Joseph Woodbridge (11.05.01) were overseers for Warley Salop, and William Pritchett (4.18) one of the overseers for Lapal township. Other overseers with Quinton interests included John Birch (4.07) and Ambrose Foley (6.03).[104] Day-to-day management of the workhouse was overseen by a master or matron, this post in Hales Owen being held in the mid-1800s by Sarah Foley.

Hales Owen Workhouse had been presented to the town by Sir Thomas Lyttelton in 1730. Just over a century later in 1838 the local Guardians sought permission to sell the building, valued at around £800, which was described as dilapidated and unfit for purpose.[105] Though the Poor Law Commission raised no objection, it noted that there might be difficulty apportioning the proceeds fairly between the townships. When the building was eventually sold the proceeds were used to provide a new house for the master at Hales Owen Free School.

4.14   John Whitehouse

Total Acreage: 1 acre;
Plot Numbers: 158, 159
Tenants: Josiah Coley (12.12.01); David Lane (12.12.02)

At the time of the tithe award, when 53-year-old John Whitehouse owned two plots in Ridgacre township, he was a tenant farmer of some 50 acres, living in Causey Green, with fields also in Langley and (mainly) Warley Wigorn. A bachelor, the census of 1841 shows his household consisting of himself, one agricultural labourer and three female servants. Ten years later, when he is described as a farmer of 35 acres employing two labourers, two of the previous three female servants are still present and are revealed to be John's nieces, 30-year-old Hannah Whitehouse, dairy maid, and 24-year-old Eliza Whitehouse, dress-maker. By 1861, the estimated size of the farm has risen to 40 acres, with Whitehouse, whose age is now given as 75, still employing two men along with Hannah Whitehouse, assisted by 12-year-old Eliza Davies as dairy maids.

John Whitehouse died on December 29th 1861 and was buried at the Parish Church of St John the Baptist, Hales Owen on January 6th 1862. Probate on his estate, valued at less than £800 was granted to his nephews George and Joseph Whitehouse, farmers of Oakham, Dudley and his niece, Hannah Whitehouse of Causey Green.

---

[104] Letter from Thomas Day, clerk to Guardians of Bromsgrove Poor Law Union to Edwin Chadwick, secretary to Poor Law Commission (6069/C/1838: MH/12/13903/233 – National Archives)
[105] Op cit

4.15   Joseph Darby

Total Acreage: 2 roods 6 poles
Plot Numbers: 37, 38
Tenants: Thomas Andrews (12.03.06);
Mary Mason (12.03.08); James Preedy
(12.03.03); John Read (12.03.07); John
Sadler (12.03.05)

In the late 18th century, nail ironmonger
Joseph Darby had taken over the nail
warehouse at Greenhill Farm, Mucklow
Hill, previously occupied by Edward
Green. Here he remained until his death

HR Wilson – Greenhill Farm c 1779 after David Parkes

aged 62 in 1838 and, like James Bissell (4.10), no doubt serviced the nail-forgers of Quinton. He was
buried at Hales Owen's Parish Church of St John the Baptist on 3rd February. In his will made just a year
earlier, he bequeathed his silver plate to his wife, Ann, the majority of his personal estate to his son,
William Joseph, land in Warley Wigorn to his daughter Amelia Wheeler and his Quinton properties to
his daughter Lucretia.

> "I devise all my freehold messuages and hereditaments at or near the Quinton in the
> township of Ridgacre in the parish of Halesowen in the County of Salop respectively now or
> late occupied by James Preedy, Benjamin Hodgetts, Samuel Mason, John Read and Thomas
> Andrews with their appurtenances and all other my freehold hereditaments near the
> Quinton aforesaid to my daughter Lucretia Isabella Darby." [106]

Despite the grant of probate on Joseph Darby's estate in April 1838, he is still named as landowner in
the tithe apportionments of 1844. The census of 1841 lists the occupiers of Green Hill as 45-year-old
farmer William Joseph Darby, his wife Ann (36) and two servants.

4.16   Sarah Hudson

Total Acreage: 1 rood 20 poles
Plot Number: W117
Tenant: Joseph Salt (12.04.15)

The most likely candidate for the ownership of this single plot is Sarah Hudson, born in Birmingham in
1801, daughter of Richard and Mary Hudson, baptised in St Martin's Church on January 4th 1802. At
the 1841 census, Sarah, of independent means, resided in Bristol Road, Edgbaston, where the
household included Catherine, Francis and Edward Hudson, also listed as independent, with one
female servant. In 1851, Sarah Hudson, annuitant, was a visitor in the home of Francis Hudson,
proprietor of houses, in Park Place, Aston Road, Aston. 10 years later, both Francis and Sarah were
listed as retired, Sarah as head of household and Francis as her cousin, at 1, Lichfield Road, Aston.
Sarah Hudson died in February 1867 and was buried at St Matthew's Church, Duddeston.

---

[106] Prerogative Court of Canterbury Wills Register, PROB 11: Piece 1893

4.17　　　Francis Taylor

Total Acreage: 26 poles;
Plot Number: 47
Tenant: John Allen (12.03.14)

According to the tithe apportionments, Francis Taylor and James Cutler (12.03.13) were joint owners of Ridgacre plot 47. This sole reference poses the question, 'Who was this absentee landlord?" Given the lack of definitive evidence, the most likely candidate appears to be Tipton-born entrepreneur Francis Taylor who, in 1841 was living with his wife, nine children and two lodgers in Park Lane, Oldbury township. At this census his occupation is given as charter master – i.e. a middle man who negotiated mining contracts and supplied the work force, taking a fee from the mine owners. By 1851 Taylor had become a farm bailiff in Bromsgrove, with his household reduced to himself, his wife and two daughters, both working as straw bonnet makers.

4.18　　　William Pritchett

Total Acreage: 19 poles
Plot Number: W121
Tenants: Stephen Armes (12.04.12);
Samuel Coles (12.04.13)

In addition to plot W121, William Pritchett is also listed as occupier of plots W4-W6, property of the Lea Smith estate, via its agent, William Grazebrook, and W122-125, property of Hales Owen Free School. That he was resident at plot W125 as the tithe award suggests is unlikely – see 12.04.14. At the censuses of both 1841

Thought to be Bogs Farmhouse in late 19th century

and 1851, Pritchett is enumerated at Bogs Farm, Lapal where, in the later census, he is described as farmer of 65 acres, employing two labourers. 12 of his 65 acres, on which he paid tithe rent to both Lord Lyttelton and Rev Richard Hone, were located in the Warley Wigorn area of Quinton.

Plan	Field Name	Area			Cultivation	Tithe Payable					
						Vicar			Imp[tor]		
		A	R	P		£	s	d	£	s	d
Property of Hales Owen Free School											
W125	House & Bdgs (52°27'48"N 2°00'42"W)			30							
W122	Lower Quinton (52°27'50"N 2°00'30"W)	1	2	14			4	3			
W123	Lower Field 52°27'50"N 2°00'38"W)	1	1	31			5	0			
W124	House Field (52°27'49"N 2°00'42"W)	1	2	2			4	0			
		4	2	37			13	3			

Plan	Field Name	Area			Cultivation	Tithe Payable					
						Vicar			Imp^tor		
		A	R	P		£	s	d	£	s	d
Property of William Grazebrook											
W6	Finches Leasow (52°27'49"N 1°59'40"W)	3	0	8	Arable		3	9		12	6
W4	Finches Leasow (52°27'46"N 1°59'48"W)	1	1	1	Pasture		5	3			
W5	Finches Leasow (52°27'48"N 1°59'46"W)	2	3	37	Pasture		12	0			
		7	1	6		1	1	0		12	6
		12	0	3		1	14	3		12	6

Born in Harborne in 1872, the son of Benjamin and Ann Pritchett, William was baptised at St Peter's Church on November 3rd. In 1841, obviously widowed,[107] William Pritchett's household consisted of himself, five children (the youngest of whom was just nine months old) and three servants: Hannah (14), John (20) Haycock and 25-year-old Ann Luckock. On April 26th 1842 at Aston Parish Church William Pritchett married Ann Luckock, some 34 years his junior. By the census of 1851, they had a 7-year-old son, Benjamin.

William Pritchett died in 1852 and was buried at St Peter's Church, Harborne on January 21st.

See also:
George Birch (8.01.03); Samuel Boulton (6.01); James Cooper (10.01. 02); Ann Cutler (12.10.01); James Cutler (12.03.13); Ambrose Foley (6.03); John Foley (12.04.04); Thomas Hall 12.04.02); Ann Hill (3.11.01); George William, Lord Lyttelton (3.10.01); Henry Foley Macdonald (11.03.01); Ann Millward (11.02.01); Sally Powers (12.01.05); Thomas Smith (11.03.02); Turnpike Commissioners (5.01); John Yates (12.03.10)

---

[107] In 1823, reporting on Hales Owen Free School, the Charity Commissioners stated that "Mrs Pritchett's husband had laid out money on the premises which have increased their annual value to about £5 5s."

5   Road transport

Though Roman occupation of Britain left a legacy of military roads intersecting the country (the nearest to Quinton being that from Gloucestershire to Yorkshire, which the Saxons named Icknield Street) subsequent highway construction and maintenance was minimal. For centuries such duties were manorial, until the 1555 Highways Act[108] fixed responsibility for the upkeep of roads upon local parishes. Under this legislation each parish was required to elect at Easter two surveyors of highways who would oversee the repair of roads within their boundaries. The surveyors would designate annually four days when every householder, cottager and labourer would be required to work daily, unpaid and supplying their own tools, for eight hours maintaining the roads, with the exorbitant penalty of 12d per day for defaulters. The Act remained in force until repealed in 1766.[109]

An increasing volume of traffic allied to a general neglect of road maintenance during the 18th century, as government failed to take the initiative and local parishes neglected their responsibilities, led to the involvement of private enterprise in the road transport system. Turnpike Trusts – companies of local people with regional responsibilities – were established to maintain given stretches of road in good order. To fund their work, trusts were empowered to issue company shares and to charge tolls. For the efficient administration of the system, toll houses were built and staffed and toll gates placed across roads, which became known as turnpike roads because tollgate keepers turned a pike or pole to admit traffic. The Birmingham and Blakedown Turnpike Commissioners held their first meeting at the Lyttelton Arms, Hagley in June 1753. Part of their responsibility was the road from Blakedown to Birmingham, via Quinton, as detailed by Act of Parliament of the same year.

> *An Act for repairing and widening several roads … in the Counties of Worcester, Stafford, Salop and Warwick respectively … the road leading from Blake Down Pool, in the parish of Kidderminster, in the said County of Worcester, through the parishes and towns of Hagley and Halesowen to the Cross of Hands near to Holloway Head, in the parish of Birmingham, in the County of Warwick … are in divers places so ruinous and deep in the winter season, that carriages cannot pass without great danger and difficulty.*[110]

Some 30 years after their appointment, the Birmingham and Blakedown Commissioners turned their attention to the route of the turnpike road at Quinton, appointing an inevitable committee, with one outsider, three local men and one village representative to take the matter further.

> *The turnpike road leading to Halesowen be continued from the turnpike gate at the Quinton across certain grounds lying behind the Black Boy and that the following gentlemen be appointed a committee to mark out the said intended road: Rev Dr Spencer, Thomas Adams, James Male, Ambrose Foley, Mr Walter Woodcock.*[111]

Biographical details of the members selected to sit on this committee are interesting. Rev Dr Spencer, in view of his legal qualification and the fact that he was the only ordained Spencer in the Worcester Diocese at the time, would appear to be Oxford graduate Benjamin Spencer, BA, MA, SCL, LLD, who in 1787 was

---

[108] 2 & 3 Philip & Mary ch.8
[109] 7 George III ch.42
[110] 26 George II ch.11
[111] Meeting of Trustees of Birmingham to Hagley Turnpike 31 May 1787

Vicar of Aston-justa-Birmingham and Rector of Hatton. Dr Spencer died in 1824. Some four years before his appointment, Birmingham iron master James Male had purchased a small farm at the top of Mucklow Hill in Hill township, and moved to *Belle Vue*, a new house which he had built there. In 1791 he was present at the Constitutional Society's dinner at Dadley's Hotel in Birmingham, to mark the French Revolution. The hotel was attacked by an irate mob which went on to burn the home of scientist and Unitarian minister, Joseph Priestley. The ensuing riots reached as far as *Belle Vue*, which was only saved by the rapid deployment of Light Horse. James Male also died in 1824, aged 75. Mr Walter Woodcock (who had a son of the same name) was the owner of a number of houses and business premises in Hagley Street and

Belle Vue from the original sketch by David Parkes 1787

Peckingham Street, Hales Owen, and is listed as surety to licensee Samuel Coley in the 1755 Alehouse Recognizances.[112] Woodcock died in 1794 and was buried in the churchyard of Hales Owen's Parish Church of St John the Baptist. Given the status and/or residence of other members of the committee, it is most likely that Thomas Adams was the owner of Cakemore House, whose daughter Ann married iron manufacturer Matthias Attwood. This would have made Adams the grandfather of celebrated political reformer, Thomas Attwood. The final committee member, Ambrose Foley (1734-1827), who lived at Quintain Green, was the owner of much of the land through which the proposed re-routed turnpike road would pass. In addition to painting Foley's portrait, David Parkes also captured him in verse:

> "His life was built upon the gospel plan.
> He knew his duty well to God and man;
> By precept, and example's pow'rful skill,
> He taught his friends their heav'nly Father's will."

Five years after the committee's appointment, the route of the turnpike road through Quinton was still on their agenda, now with action required and the means of funding specified.

> *The committee appointed to direct the improvements between the 5th milestone from*
> *Birmingham to Hagley Lane Turnpike Gate do immediately … divert the road from the end of*
> *Long Lane through the lands there in a straight line to the Black Boy so as to make the same*
> *more commodious for the public and that the said commissioners do draw upon the treasurer*
> *to the amount of £500.*[113]

Also in 1792, a parliamentary act determined that any road works were to be carried out with the minimum of disruption to users and funded by income which the tolls generated.

> *An Act for enlarging the term and powers of two Acts passed in the twenty sixth year of the*
> *reign of King George the second and the thirteenth year of the reign of his present majesty,*
> *for repairing… of the road from Blakedown Pool in the parish of Hagley and County of*

---

[112] QE 2/1/2 SA
[113] Meeting of Trustees of Birmingham to Hagley Turnpike 6 July 1792

Worcester, to the top of Smallbrooke Street, and from the Five Ways to Easy Row in Birmingham in the said County of Warwick ... be it enacted that in case the course or path of any part or parts of the said road shall be diverted, turned, or varied, so much of the old road between Birmingham and Halesowen shall, notwithstanding such deviation of road, be preserved, kept open and in repair, out of the tolls arising from this Act, by the statute duty.[114]

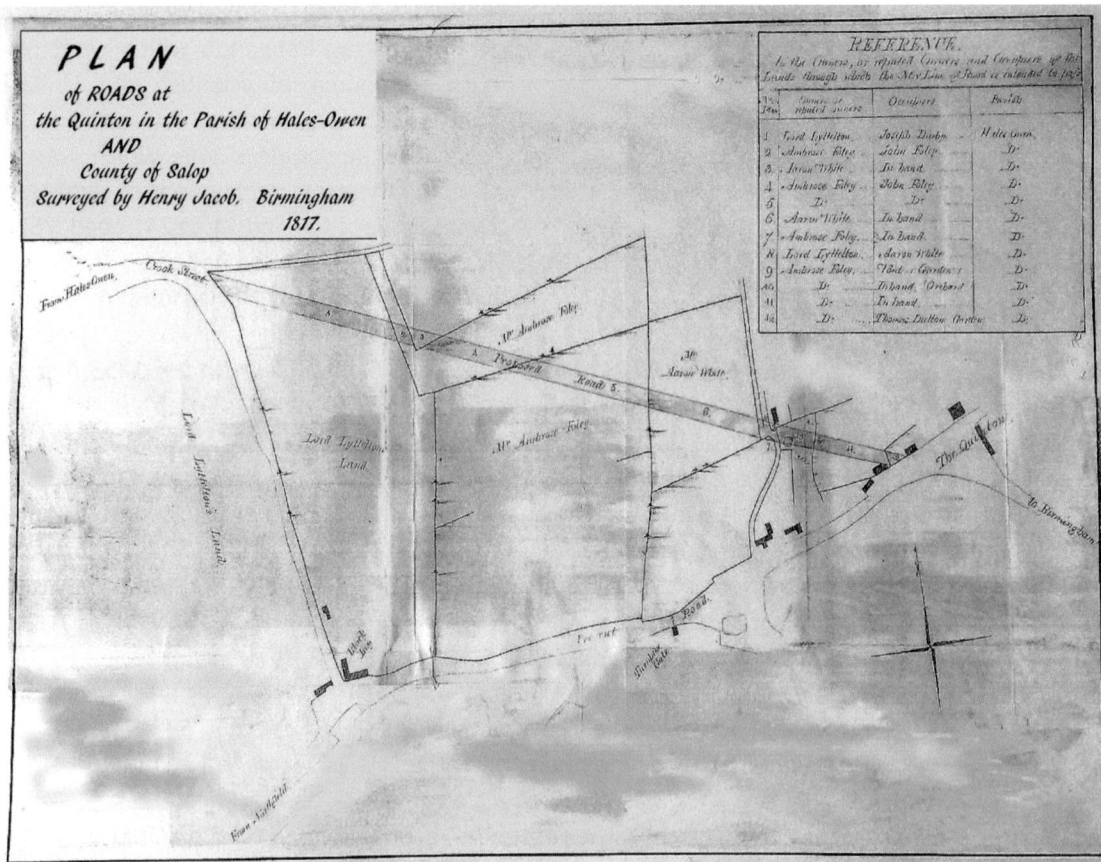

A quarter of a century would pass before the turnpike route through Quinton became that which is marked on the tithe map. The proposed route, with its list of land-owners and occupiers was surveyed by Henry Jacob in 1817 and enabled by Act of Parliament in 1818.

An Act for repairing the road from Blakedown Pool in the parish of Hagley and County of Worcester to Birmingham in the County of Warwick ... Repeals Acts of 1753 and 1792 as far as they relate to the road from Blakedown to the Cross of Hands near to Holloway Head, and thence to the top of Smallbrooke Street, and also from the Five Ways to Easy Row in Birmingham aforesaid... One full toll between the town of Birmingham and the town of Halesowen and one full toll between the said town of Halesowen and the village of Hagley in the County of Worcester... Variation of the present line of the road from the meeting house at a place called the Quinton in the parish of Halesowen in the county of Salop for the distance

---

[114] 32 George III ch.140

of 600 yards or thereabouts in a straight line ... to a place called Crock Street in the same parish ... Part of the said road from the said meeting house to the Black Boy aforesaid will be unnecessary to the continued turnpike.[115]

More than 450 separate Acts of Parliament had been required to set up individual turnpike trusts before the Turnpike Roads Act, 1773[116] enabled more rapid progress to be made. By the mid-1800s there were approximately 22,000 miles of turnpike roads, of which something like fifty percent were in good condition. The roads were controlled by nearly 8,000 toll gates and major towns were linked by a network of mail and stage coaches. So it was that by the time of the Quinton tithe maps there were in excess of 3,000 coaches travelling the turnpike roads, with more than 30,000 employees involved in operating the service they provided.

All this had to be paid for by road-users, though payment was no guarantee of comfort, as Mr Pickwick and his friends discover in Dickens' novel, which may well have been upon the shelves of such literate Quinton residents who appear in the pages of this study.

"The portmanteaus and carpet-bags have been stowed away; the coachman mounts to the box. On the outside of the coach the passengers pull their coats round their legs and their shawls over their noses. The helpers pull the horse-cloths off and away they go. They have rumbled through the streets, and jolted over the stones, and at length reach the wide and open country. The wheels skim over the hard and frosty ground: and the horses, bursting into a canter at a smart crack of the whip, step along the road as if the load behind them were but a feather at their heels. A few small houses, scattered on either side of the road, betoken the entrance to some town or village. And now the bugle plays a lively air as the coach rattles through the ill-paved streets of a country-town; the coachman, undoing the buckle which keeps his ribands together, prepares to throw them off the moment he stops. The coach twists round a sharp corner and turns into the market place; they pull up at the inn yard, where fresh horses, with cloths on are already waiting. The guard has delivered the brown paper packet he took out of the little pouch which hangs over his shoulder by a leathern strap and has seen the horses carefully put to and off they start. Shawls are pulled up, coat collars are re-adjusted, the pavement ceases, the houses disappear; and they are once again dashing along the open road, with the fresh clear air blowing in their faces. Such was the progress of Mr Pickwick and his friends by the Muggleton Telegraph to Dingley Dell; and at three o'clock that afternoon they all stood, safe and sound, upon the steps of the Blue Lion, having taken on the road quite enough of ale and brandy to enable them to bid defiance to the frost that was binding up the earth in its iron fetters, and weaving its beautiful net-work upon the trees and hedges."[117]

A variety of coaches and carts paid their dues at Quinton Toll House. Every Monday, Thursday and Saturday at 10am, the *Tantivy* coach left Stourbridge for Birmingham, whilst numerous carriers

[115] 58 George III ch.14
[116] 13 George III ch.84
[117] Dickens, C. (1837) *The Posthumous Papers of the Pickwick Club*, Chapter 28

advertised the conveyance of goods along the Turnpike Road. Pedestrians passed Quinton Toll House without charge. Riders paid 1½d for their horse, mule or donkey; those driving cattle or oxen were charged 1s 3d, whilst sheep cost only 7½d per score. Wagons cost 5d or 6d and gigs 4d or 6d according to size. A painting by W.J. Pringle, who exhibited in Birmingham from 1834 to 1843, shows the *Independent*, owned by Thomas Simpson of High Street, Stourbridge passing Quinton Gate on a return journey in 1842. This service left the *Three Crowns* Inn, Stourbridge at 9am and arrived in Birmingham in time for the 10.30am London train before returning to Stourbridge for 6pm. The service ended after the opening of the South Staffordshire Railway in 1850 and the coach was sold at auction.

An act of Queen Victoria in 1841 set ongoing legislation for the maintenance of the toll road and noted outstanding debts accruing at the very beginning of the period covered in this study, with a forecast looking to the end of the same period.

> *An Act for repairing the road from Blakedown Pool in the Parish of Hagley in the County of Worcester into the Borough of Birmingham in the County of Warwick … Whereas an Act was passed in the 58th year of the reign of His Majesty George III, intitled an Act for repairing the road from Blakedown Pool in the Parish of Hagley in the County of Worcester to Birmingham in the County of Warwick; and whereas considerable sums of money have been advanced upon the credit of the tolls authorised to be taken by the said Act, which money still remains owing … Be it enacted that this Act shall be put into execution for the purpose of more effectually improving, maintaining and keeping in repair the present Turnpike Road leading from Blakedown Pool in the Parish of Hagley to the east side of a lane or highway called Grindstone Lane in the parish of Edgbaston, within the Borough of Birmingham … And be it enacted that*

this Act shall commence on the 5 July next after the passing thereof, and shall continue in force for the term of 31 years, and from thence to the end of the session of Parliament that shall then next follow.[118]

The advent of railways in the second quarter of the 19th century triggered a decline in road transport. In the early 1840s there were an estimated 1,100 turnpike trusts; within ten years of the building of the railways nearly every trust was bankrupt. Thus, in March 1864 a parliamentary Select Committee was appointed "to inquire into the expediency and practicability of abolishing Turnpike Trusts."[119] Unsurprisingly perhaps, the committee found that "tolls are costly in collection, inconvenient to the public, and injurious as causing a serious impediment to traffic, and that the abolition thereof would be beneficial to the community."[120] The demise of the turnpike system was only a matter of time. In 1871, almost exactly at the end of the term of conditions imposed upon the Birmingham and Blakedown Commissioners, the number of trusts had reduced to 854; by 1890 there were just two.[121] The commissioners' responsibility came to an end in Quinton when they sold the Toll House to the Wesleyan Methodist Trustees, who decided to complete the transaction, having met "to consider the advisability of purchasing the Tollgate House and premises for the sum named by the Turnpike Trustees, viz. £100."[122] After serving for many years as a private residence the Toll House was eventually demolished in the 1930s. Three windows from the toll house have been incorporated into the cottage at plot 46 (11.03.02) – now 497 Ridgacre Road.

5.01   Turnpike Commissioners   Plot 58 (52°27'48"N 2°00'49"W)

Quinton Toll House and yard occupied a plot measuring 6 poles, belonging to Birmingham and Blakedown Turnpike Commissioners. At least nine collectors are known to have lived in the toll house during the mid-1800s. Obviously this meant a succession of short-stay and itinerant families passing through Quinton, who had arrived from as far away as London, Yorkshire, Monmouthshire and even Scotland. None apparently had any previous experience of toll collecting and only one continued with the role when moving on from Quinton. Common report suggests that this rapid turnover resulted from poor pay and in collectors combining the role with other occupations, often with the gatekeeper's wife actually collecting the tolls. There is scant evidence of this in Quinton and though pay evidently was poor,[123] only one of Quinton's toll collectors held two jobs.

In 1841 Quinton's toll collector was 35-year-old Benjamin Sharpe, who lived in the toll house with his wife Jane (35) and seven children. This was clearly an itinerant family as subsequent censuses would make clear. Benjamin was born in Hunslet, Yorkshire, whilst Jane was born in Scotland, as were their four older children, 13-year-old Mary (whose birthplace is specified in the 1851 census as Cothall Mills,

---

118 4 & 5 Victoria ch.101

119 *Hansard*, vol 173 c1699, 08 March 1864

120 *Hansard*, vol 182 cc462-7, 16 March 1866

121 See Woodward, E.L. (1946) *The Age of Reform*, pp576-577

122 *Quinton Wesleyan Methodist Chapel Minutes*, 11 October 1877

123 In 1847, for example, commissioners responsible for the turnpike road from Shrewsbury to Holyhead spent £4,774 1s 0½d on road repairs; £24 9s 7d on advertising and letting tolls, but only £4 6s 0d on actually collecting tolls. (Parliamentary Papers Vol 33, Reports from Commissioners 19.01 – 22.07 1847)

Fintry, Scotland), 12-year-old Anne, 10-year-old John and 7-year-old Robert. Next in line, 5-year-old Joseph was born in Wakefield, Yorkshire, whilst 3-year-old Benjamin's birth was registered in Warwick in October quarter, 1837. Sometime between Benjamin's birth and that of William, the family moved to Quinton. Both Benjamin and William were baptised at Christ Church on November 1st 1840. An eighth child, Helen, was also baptised at Christ Church on January 2nd 1842. Not long after this, the family moved on. Benjamin and Jane's ninth child, Timothy, was born in Rowley Regis in 1844, followed by Jane, born in Birmingham in 1849. In 1851 the Sharpe family (minus Mary, Anne and John) were living at the Paving Wharf in Granville Street, Birmingham, where Benjamin senior was the paving agent. Robert had become a bedstead maker and Joseph a steel toy maker. No other family member had a stated occupation. Mary and John Sharpe were both in Rowley Regis in 1851: Mary working as a servant in the home of Benjamin Laws in Newberry Lane, Oldbury and John as a stone-dresser, lodging in the Tividale home of John Humphreys.

Plot 58 - Quinton Toll House in early 20th century

The next identified Quinton Tollgate Keeper was Robert Davies who was in post in 1845. Robert was born in 1815 in Gloucester, his wife, Elizabeth was born in 1809 in Worcester; their two older children were born in Monmouthshire: Emma in 1834 and Elizabeth in 1842. Two younger children, both born in Worcestershire, were baptised at Quinton's Bethesda Primitive Methodist Chapel: William Edwin on June 11th 1845 and Levi on January 25th 1847. By 1848 this family had also moved on and in 1851 are found living in one of the courts on Communication Row in the St Thomas district of Birmingham. Robert was now employed as a labourer, Elizabeth was working as a dress-maker, daughters Emma and Elizabeth as paper box maker and button-maker respectively. The two younger children were at school.

The next Quinton Toll Collector was John Jones, who it has only been possible to identify through an entry in the baptismal register of Christ Church, where his daughter Elizabeth, named after her mother, was baptised on September 3rd 1848. Jones, like his predecessors, was only briefly in post and had moved on by 1851, by which time John Berry, his wife and nephew had moved into the toll house. 35-year-old John Berry, like the other two members of his household, from Sutton-in-Ashfield in Nottinghamshire, is listed in the census as tollgate collector and joiner. His wife, Hannah, also 35, gives her occupation as glover. Their 4-year-old nephew, Abraham Berry England, is listed as scholar. By the time of the next census the family had relocated to Shelton, Hanley, Stoke-on-Trent, where John Berry was again employed as a toll collector. Hannah was now referred to as Anne, whilst Abraham Berry (working as a carter) had lost the name England and was listed as John's son. Ten years later, still in Shelton, Anne, now a widow, was again called Hannah and was living in the home of her nephew Abraham and his family.

Like John Jones, Quinton's next known toll collector, Christopher Enoch Hill, is identifiable only through an entry in the baptismal register of Christ Church, where Christopher and his wife Ann took their son, Christopher William, for baptism on March 4th 1855. The period of his tenure is unknown, but by 1861 yet another employee of the Birmingham and Blakedown Commissioners had moved into Quinton Toll House. John Boulton was born in St Sepulchre, Middlesex in 1823, the same year as his wife, Maria, was born in Painswick, Gloucestershire. In 1851, John and Maria had been living in one of four households at 189 High Holborn, London; Maria had no stated occupation and John was working as a brass finisher. They too were birds of passage through Ridgacre township. In 1871, John, now widowed, and again working as a brass finisher, was a visitor in the home of George Gregory in Hartpury, Gloucestershire.

Christ Church The Quinton's baptismal register also provides the only evidence for the next known toll collector. On December 29th 1868, Rev C H Oldfield baptised Edward Thomas Atkin, son of Harriet and Charles Atkin, gate keeper at The Quinton, of whom no further records have been traced. By 1871, the last census at which Quinton toll was still operating, there were joint toll collectors in post: sisters Ellen (25) and Lucy (15) Pritchett. Like their predecessors they came from an itinerant family. Their father had been born in King's Norton, Worcestershire, their mother in Bishop's Castle, Shropshire, one sibling in Selly Oak, Warwickshire and another in Gospel Oak, Staffordshire. Ellen was born when her parents lived in Hagley, Worcestershire and Lucy after they had moved to Handsworth, Staffordshire. In 1861 all the family had been living together in Bolts Buildings, King Edward Road, Ladywood, Birmingham. At that census Ellen was employed as a bolt slicer and Lucy was still at school. Perhaps the move to Quinton Toll House was a bid for freedom by two independent young women? Their stay in Quinton, however was short-lived. On November 24th 1872, giving her age as 18, Lucy Pritchett married Walter Jones at Dudley and on June 1st 1873, at Cradley Heath, Ellen Pritchett married Edwin Vernals, some 9 years her junior and who, like Ellen's younger brother William, had also been born in Gospel Oak.

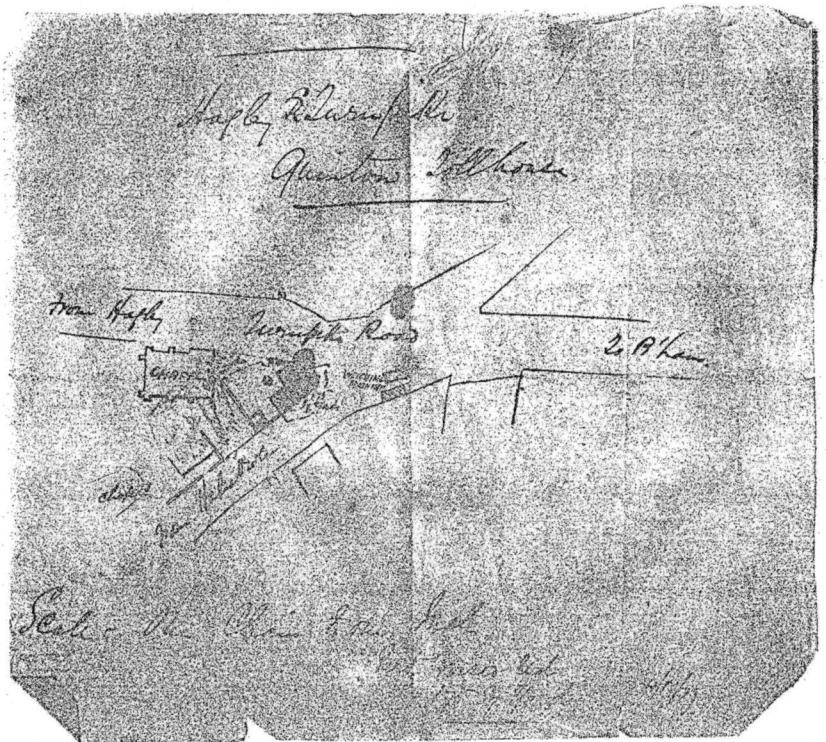

Hagley Turnpike - Quinton Tollhouse October 4th 1877, prior to the sale to the Wesleyan Methodist Chapel

6   Independent Residents

Out of Quinton's 1,047 named residents between 1841 and 1861, only 16 are identified as of independent means. These were not, as might be expected, all folk in the evening of their days, for though eight were born in the 18th century, three were only in their mid-twenties. Nor was the status necessarily lasting: two enumerated as independent in 1841 had jobs in 1851. Four owned Quinton property, either where they lived or from which they derived income. Four were farmers (or farmer's wives), placing them in the higher echelons of village society. However, for most of Quinton's independent residents, there is little evidence to suggest that they were of more than modest means. Most lived as dependents in households of which they were not the head. 10 of the 16 were female, perhaps leading lives reminiscent of the ladies of Cranford in Elizabeth Gaskell's novel.

> The ladies of Cranford… are exceedingly indifferent to each other's opinions. Indeed, each has her own individuality, not to say eccentricity, pretty strongly developed… Their dress is very independent of fashion. The materials of their clothes are, in general, good and plain… A few of the gentlefolk of Cranford were poor and had some difficulty in making both ends meet, but they were like Spartans and concealed their smart under a smiling face… We none of us spoke of money. Death was as true and as common as poverty; yet people never spoke about that, loud out in the streets. It was a word not to be mentioned to ears polite.[124]

Perhaps in the agricultural, nail-making village of factual Quinton, as in rural, fictional Cranford, neither the perceived status of its independent residents, nor the recollections of what once had been, marked them out as different from the majority of their neighbours.

6.01   Samuel Boulton   Plot 241 (52°27'49"N 1°59'48"W)

Listed in the tithe apportionments as both owner and occupier of plot 241 was Samuel Boulton. Located in Hawthorns, on the edge of Coneygre Leasow, part of Hawthorn Farm, by 1851 this house and garden on a plot measuring 16 poles was known as Hawthorn Cottage. In 1841 Samuel Bolton (aged 40) lived here with William Boulton (50) and Elizabeth Boulton (40). The relationship between these three occupants, none of whom originated from the Ridgacre Township, is not specified in the census return. The identically sized adjacent plot 240, which similarly contained a house and garden also belonged to Samuel Boulton. In the apportionments this plot was listed as void, as it also appeared to have been in 1841. However, by 1851 it had become the home of Edward Thompson and his family. (11.03.04) By this date Samuel, William and Elizabeth Boulton were no longer living in Hawthorns and plot 241 had become the home of another of Quinton's independent residents.

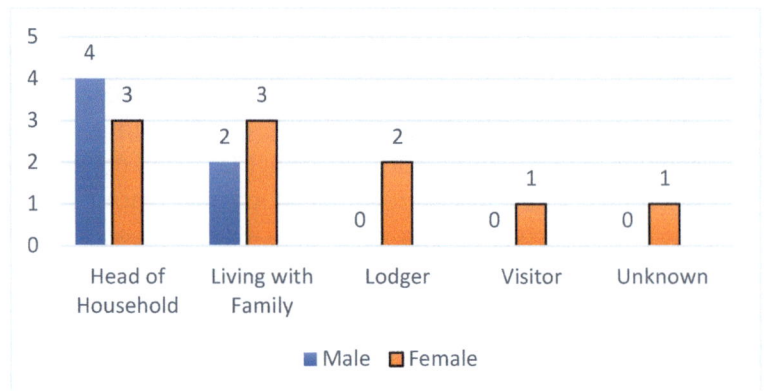

---

[124] Gaskell, E. (1851-3) *Cranford*, chapter 1

Richard Tomlinson, aged 71, gentleman, annuitant on mortgages, had retired from Windmill Farm (8.01.08) and moved with his wife Mary (58) and nephew, Richard Cooper (25)[125], who was employed as a servant, into Hawthorn Cottage. All three are listed in this census as born in Hales Owen, though in 1861 Mary Tomlinson's birthplace is shown as Warley. *Kelly's Directory* of 1850 still listed Tomlinson as the farmer of Windmill Farm, so it may be that he was newly retired in 1851. The period of his retirement, however, gave him opportunity to serve as People's Warden at Christ Church The Quinton, to which post he was elected in 1850. Richard Tomlinson died in 1854 and was buried at Christ Church on 28th August. In 1861 Mary Tomlinson, now head of the household, was still at Hawthorn Cottage, where she had been joined by her widowed niece, Matilda Penn and Matilda's two young children, Elizabeth and John. Mary Tomlinson died in 1861 and was buried at Christ Church on 30th October. Richard Cooper was no longer in Ridgacre township and may well have been the general labourer of that name, by 1861 married, with four young daughters and living in Cherry Orchard, Rowley Regis.

6.02   George Bramich

On October 2nd 1856 at Christ Church, Rev William Skilton officiated at the marriage by licence[126] of Ann Birch, daughter of George and Mary Birch (8.01.03) of Redhall (at 126 acres one of Quinton's largest farms) to George Bramich, son of farmer (of 115 acres) Thomas Bramich of Beech Lane, Harborne. The newly-weds moved into Red Hill in Ridgacre township, where they were enumerated in 1861. Their household consisted of 27-year-old George, Ann (28) and two daughters, both born in Ridgacre, Mary (3) and Annie (12 months), along with 13-year-old Mary Powell, whose occupation is given as nurse girl. Also resident was Sheffield-born Thomas Critchley (40) curate at Quinton church. The presence of the curate as lodger suggests a better-off home and possibly the influence of George Birch, who had been appointed Peoples' Warden at the beginning of Skilton's incumbency. The suggestion is substantiated by the description of George Bramich in the census as retired farmer, making him the youngest of all Quinton's independent residents. For Bramich, however, retirement and independence were apparently ephemeral. By 1871, now living in John Street, Smethwick, he was working as a store-keeper. Ten years later, still in Smethwick, but now in Rolfe Street, he appears to have descended farther down the occupational ladder, being employed as a labourer.

6.03   Ambrose Foley [E][127]

By 1844 Foley ownership of Quinton land was already well established. As far back as 1709 Hales Owen Court Rolls record the admission of John Foley to possession of lands in the manor. Following his death in 1720, the same rolls register the transference of his estate to his son, William. Though John Foley's will refers only to "my small estate" and makes bequests only of money and "my good cattle, chattels and personal estate" [128] without any mention of land, the will of William Foley, who died in 1778, defined the holding which passed to his son, Ambrose.

All that messuage or dwelling house with the outbuildings, barns, stables, gardens, orchards and appurtenances thereto belonging situate and standing at or near to the Quinton in the Parish of Hales Owen

---

[125] On February 4th 1858 Emily, daughter of Richard Cooper & Rebecca Cutler was baptised at Christ Church.

[126] See Footnote 383 p 219

[127] As owner/occupier of freehold land in Ridgacre township. See 13.01

[128] Foley, John (8.11.1720) *Last Will and Testament*, Lee Crowder Papers 383-385 LB

> *and County of Salop, and also all those several close pieces or parcels of land containing about twenty acres adjoining or lying near to the said messuage situate at or near the Quinton and lately purchased by me.*[129]

At his death in 1827, Ambrose Foley left the bulk of his Quinton estate to his nephew, also Ambrose.

> *I give and devise all the rest and remainder of my real Estate situate at Quintain Green unto my Nephew Ambrose Foley To hold to him his Heirs and Assigns for ever provided that he or they at the end of one year next after my decease pay to William Foley and John Foley Sons of John Foley the Sum of Five pounds each and so continue to pay the said sums to them each year of their respective lives and I do hereby charge and make chargeable such of the remainder of my aforesaid Quintain Estate with the payment thereof.*[130]

The respective wills of John, William and Ambrose Foley trace their changing social status. In 1720 John is described as yeoman; In 1768 William as husbandman; in 1826 Ambrose Foley as gentleman.

By the time of the tithe apportionments, the property within Ridgacre township owned by the second Ambrose Foley is listed as plots 59 (occupied jointly by John Foley and George Hall), 65-71, 73 (occupied by John Foley) and 72 (occupied by Benjamin Hadley), amounting to 16 acres 3 roods 2 poles in total. The apportionments do not show Ambrose Foley (who came from Tanworth-in-Arden Warwickshire) as occupant of any Ridgacre or Warley Wigorn houses. However, in the 1841 census for Ridgacre township Ambrose (of independent means) and Ann Foley are the final entries, following on from John and Jane Foley (12.04.04) with their place of residence given as Quinton. This, presumably, was plot 73, Monkton Farmhouse, listed in the apportionments as the residence of John Foley, who was the son of Ambrose and Mary (née Clark) who had married at Wootton Wawen on November 8th 1806. Subsequently, Ann, (previously Pugh) and Ambrose were married at St Martin's Church, Birmingham on October 12th 1826, when both were widowed. Active in the life of Quinton Parish Church, in 1845 Ambrose Foley was elected Peoples' Warden. Like his cousin John Foley (12.04.04) by 1844 Ambrose Foley was listed as joint owner-occupier of Quinton's Wesleyan Methodist Chapel. (7.01)

Rarely for any of Quinton's inhabitants in the mid-19th century, a contemporary news report reveals a dramatic incident in Ambrose Foley's life in June 1847.

> **"Accident during the Thunder Storm on Tuesday.**
> On Tuesday, during the severe thunder storm with which the town and neighbourhood were visited, several accidents of a more or less serious nature occurred. As Mr. Ambrose Foley of Quinton Green, Worcestershire, was proceeding homewards with a horse and gig, and when near the top of Monument Lane, Hagley Road, the horse took fright at a clap of thunder, and ran away. Mr. Foley was instantly thrown out of the gig, and one of the wheels went over his leg and seriously injured it. After running some distance, the horse was stopped by the policeman on the beat, and bringing it back to where Mr. Foley was lying, the constable conveyed him to the house of gentleman close by, from which he was conveyed home shortly afterwards in a car. No further damage was done."[131]

---

[129] Foley, William (25.08.1768) *Last Will and Testament*, Lee Crowder Papers 383-385 LB
[130] Foley, Ambrose (09.12.1826) *Last Will and Testament*, Lee Crowder Papers 383-385 LB
[131] *Birmingham Journal* Saturday 19.06.1847

The census of 1851 shows Ann Foley as born in King's Norton, Worcestershire. Apparently no longer of independent means, Ambrose was now returned as a farmer employing no labourers. The death of Ann Foley was registered at Stourbridge in April Quarter, 1854 and that of Ambrose Foley in October Quarter of the same year. Ann Foley was buried at Christ Church The Quinton on 12th April and Ambrose at Hales Owens Parish Church of St John the Baptist on November 29th. Ambrose's will, dated some twenty years earlier, indicates how much of William Foley's original Quinton holding now passed to the next generation and confirms the acreage recorded in the tithe apportionments.

> *My freehold property at Quinton consisting of the house now in my own occupation, two cottages and about seventeen acres of land with other appurtenances bequeathed to me by the will of my late Uncle Ambrose Foley.*[132]

FOLEY

John m Mary
d.1720

William m Anne
1698-1778   d1778
(Builder of Quintain Green)

John	Ambrose m Jane Mucklow	William m Esther Parish	Other Issue
1732-1799	1734-1827 d.1827		
	(Builder of Wesleyan Chapel)		

John m **Anne**   William m Lucy Liddell   **Ambrose** m (i) Mary Clark (ii) Ann Pugh
1771-1845 1784-1869   1776-1857   1782-1854   d1809   1782-1854

Mary m Henry Read **Thomas**   **John** m (i) **Jane** Felton[133] (ii) **Jemima**
James
b.1815   b.1831   1807-1891   1813-1847   c1818-1890

                                            Mary Ann   **Ambrose**[134] **William**[135]
                                            1845-1912   1851-1869   1856-1915

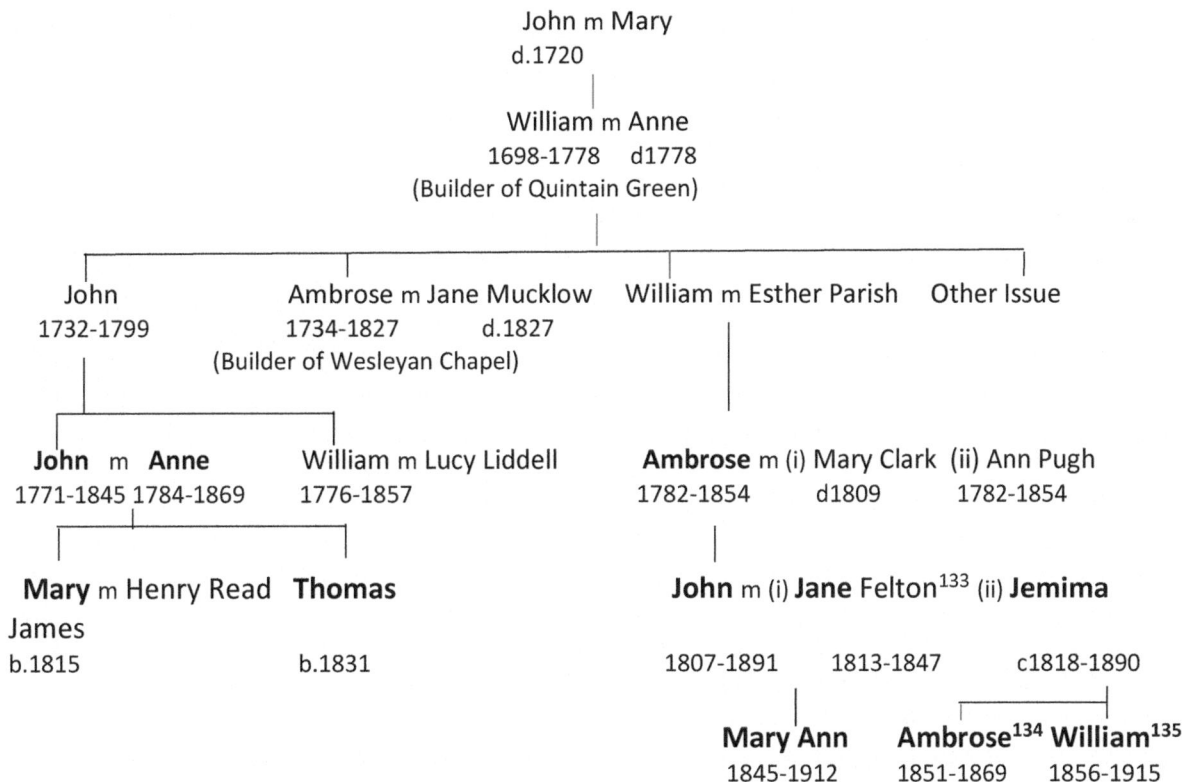

See also: Mary Ann Bass (8.05); Sarah Chambers (8.01.01); Sarah Cooper (12.05.03); Ann Cutler (12.10.01); John Davenport (8.01); Sarah Hyde (12.02.02); Mary Pitchford (12.08.01); Ann Powers, Sarah Powers (12.01.05);

---

[132] Foley, Ambrose (24.02.1834) *Last Will and Testament*, Lee Crowder Papers 383-385 LB
[133] Jane Foley was buried at The Church of St John The Baptist, Hales Owen on December 17th 1847
[134] Ambrose Foley was baptised at Christ Church The Quinton on January 4th 1852
[135] William Henry Foley was baptised at Christ Church The Quinton on June 1st 1856

7   Church and school

Religiously, the township of Ridgacre is comparatively unusual in that Methodism had gained a foothold here before the Church of England. In the small area of the tithe map were three places of worship, which between them offered eight services each Sunday. The largest of the church buildings was the Anglican *Christ Church The Quinton*. Two Methodist chapels, one Wesleyan and one Primitive, built so close to one another, that it was said that the singing in one building could be heard in the other, completed the trio of places of worship. The Wesleyan Methodist chapel had been built c1786 and both the Anglican and Primitive Methodist churches opened in 1840.

HALES OWEN CHURCH, S.W.

Before the opening of Christ Church, Quinton had no visible presence of the Established Church and no burial ground. Rites of passage ceremonies were available at the Church of St John the Baptist, Hales Owen. This was a foundation of great antiquity, the origins of which predate the Domesday Book, which records that Hales had a church with two priests. By the time of the tithe map, the four outlying daughter churches of the parish (Romsley, Oldbury, The Quinton and Cradley) to which clergy were assigned, were each in the patronage of Hales Owen's Vicar, Rev R.B. Hone, whose predecessors are traceable through an unbroken line to Richard, dictus Tinctor (i.e. Richard Dyer) de Hales and Robert de Crowle in the late 13th century.

The activity of dissenters in Hales Owen's townships was not new to the 19th century. During the 17th and 18th centuries, churchwardens regularly presented recusants to diocesan inspectors. Papists, Quakers, Anabaptists, Presbyterians and other Nonconformists appear in the *Presentments*, as, for example "Philip Duggard of Romsley for joining the Quakers and for not frequenting his church."[136] A number of townsfolk were fined for keeping conventicles in their homes and daughter churches of the parish. *"We know of nothing else at this time presentable in our parish except Oldbury Chapel which we report to be now in the possession of Presbyterians and they prevent ye reading of common prayer there."*[137] Quinton had no church to be taken over by dissenters; it did, however, have its residents who avoided the weekly services of the Established Church. *"We present Richard Parkes living in Ridgacre town for being an excommunicated person."*[138] Quinton's 19th century Parkes were all in-comers, but there were still Hadleys and Robinsons, names present 160 years earlier: *"We present George Robinson, Thomas Hadley for standing excommunicated and for not coming to church to hear divine service and sermon and for not receiving the holy sacrament"*[139]

It is, then, unsurprising that Methodism should have found fertile ground in Ridgacre township in the 18th and 19th centuries. Wesleyan Methodism, originally a reform movement within the Church of

---

[136] Parish of Hales Owen (1674-1761) *Churchwardens' Presentments*, 17.04.1676

[137] Op cit, 22.06.1708

[138] Op cit, 10.11.1684

[139] Op cit, 16.10.1682

England, with Rev John Wesley (1703-1791) as its leader, became an independent church in the late 1700s. Wesley visited Quinton six times between 1781 and 1790, developing a friendship with Ambrose and Jane Foley of Quintain Green, still a significant building (Plot 74) at the time of the Tithe Map, when Foley (1734-1827) was still a memorable figure whose influence had outlived him. Farmer, land-owner, maker of musical instruments and philanthropist, Ambrose Foley was an associate of William Shenstone (1714-63), the Hales Owen poet and David Parkes (1763-1833), the Hales Owen artist and antiquarian. Foley's influence would be crucial in the establishment of both branches of Methodism in Quinton. At Wesley's last visit on March 19th 1790, he was accompanied by Rev Joseph Benson (1748-1821), who recorded the occasion. *"After breakfast, we conducted Mr Wesley to Birmingham, calling a few minutes at Kidderminster, and about half-an-hour at Quinton, where he preached a short sermon to a few people that upon a sudden warning had come together."*[140] As Wesley's *Journal* references to Quinton congregations suggest larger numbers, Benson's "few people" is significant and, given the size of the township in 1790, likely to be more accurate.

Ambrose Foley by H.R. Wilson (1981) after David Parkes

Quinton Wesleyan Society clearly did not merit a high profile in the Birmingham Wesleyan Circuit of which it was a part and was frequently neglected by the preachers appointed to lead worship there. Between 1838 and 1865, Brothers Beynon, Boulton, Hewitt, Jackson, Wilson, Wesley, Johnson and Goodall were all reported to the Local Preachers' Meeting for failing to arrive for their Quinton appointments.[141] Similarly, the Society did not accord a high profile to its own heritage. The chair which John Wesley had used as his open-air pulpit when preaching in Quinton (which presumably came Quintain Green) was placed in the chapel vestry until it became unfit for purpose. Acquired by an unnamed entrepreneur, in exchange for 2s 6d given to a member of the Society in poor circumstances, it was refurbished and shipped to USA. There it took pride of place in a new church until both were destroyed by fire.[142]

The visible presence of Wesleyan Methodism in Quinton can, then, be traced to the 1770s. Half a century later, it was followed by the arrival of Primitive Methodism, a breakaway movement from the parent body, which began in the early 1800s with open-air meetings at Mow Cop, on the Staffordshire-Cheshire border. Its founders were Hugh Bourne (1772-1852) and William Clowes (1780-1851), both of whom would visit Quinton. However, it was William Stringer from Darlaston who, in Autumn 1820, first brought Primitive Methodism to the township when he *"took his stand under a beech tree and commenced singing, 'My soul's full of glory, which inspires my tongue.' The people flocked together because it was to them a strange thing. The word he preached came in power; many were much*

---

[140] Benson, J. (ed) (1809-13) *The Works of Rev John Wesley* in 17 volumes (*Journal*: 19.03.1790 – footnote)
[141] *Birmingham Local Preachers' Minute Book* (1823-1949) 18.05.1838, 08.03.1844, 17.09.1847, 13.12.1850, 17.03.1854, 16.03.1855, 16.12.1864, 16.06.1865
[142] Hackwood, F.W. (1915) *Oldbury and Round About*, p 118

Head of Hugh Bourne c 1875 from Durngate Street Primitive Methodist Church, Dorchester, Dorset

affected and made a start in the way to heaven."[143] 16 years later, Stringer's visit was followed by the first of a number made by Hugh Bourne, who also preached with great power. *"His subject of discourse was 'The wrath of the Lamb' and he gave extraordinary effect to his denunciations and warnings by the fervency of his spirit and the animation of his gestures."*[144] Such was the impression made by Bourne that his visits were clearly recalled 50 years later by Joseph Price whose memory provided the above quotation, and Henry Dingley, with whose parents, Samuel and Sarah, Bourne lodged (and who himself was baptised at Quinton's Bethesda Primitive Methodist Chapel on February 27th 1859). *"I remember the aged divine by his big-collared coat, the breeches he wore, his thick, black-ribbed, home-knitted worsted stockings and his low-bucked boots."*[145] Between the visits of Stringer and Bourne much had happened within Quinton Primitive Methodism, leading up to the opening of Bethesda Chapel in 1840, and it is this denomination that gives the clearest picture of the religious life of Ridgacre township prior to the drawing of the tithe map.

On May 4th 1826, the following petition was addressed to the Bishop of Worcester:

We the undersigned do hereby certify Your Lordship that a certain Room situate at Quinton in the Parish of Hales Owen in the County of Worcester,[146] and is now occupied by Saml. Chatwin is intended to be used as a place of Public Worship by a congregation of Protestants and we request that the same may be registered in Your Lordship's Court according to the Law in this case made and provided.
> *Witness our hands*
> *Ambrose Foley, Saml. Chatwin, David Wood,*
> *James Hall, Thomas Beswick, William Priddy, Thos. Foster.[147]*

The authorisation was registered in the Consistory Court of Worcester by John Clifton, the Deputy Registrar, on June 2nd 1826. It has been implied that this was the beginning of an Anglican presence in Quinton.[148] The 1688 Toleration Act granted to Protestant Nonconformists the freedom to worship in public buildings or rooms that had been registered for that purpose by the diocesan bishop. As buildings of the Church of England were exempt from the requirements, and the term 'congregation of Protestants' would normally refer to dissenters, of whom Primitive Methodists were a good

---

[143] Chambers, J. (1842), p 23

[144] McKechnie, C. (1892) *The Life of Hugh Bourne*, p 302

[145] Op cit, p 302

[146] In 1826 Hales Owen, and therefore Quinton, were in the County of Shropshire.

[147] Records of Ecclesiastical Parish of Christ Church Quinton (1826) EP 72/17/1 LB

[148] See Bunting, T.W. (1990) *The Story of a Parish: The Quinton 1840-1990*, p 2; Rosser, A.N. (1998) pp 15,43 – Rosser, however, re-evaluated the evidence in an article published in *Quinton Oracle* N° 50 (May 2011) p 41

example, and as Ambrose Foley, Samuel Chatwin and James Hall were known Methodists, it is most unlikely that this petition had anything to do with Anglican worship. Furthermore, in the following year Quinton was officially recognised as one of the 35 preaching places of the Darlaston Circuit. The 15 members of the new society are listed among the 995 circuit members: Samuel Chatwin (Leader); Richard Winward; S. Harris; James Hall; A.M. Mason; S. Coley; Sarah Haycock; S. Mason; Richard Holloway; B. Hall; S. Golds; Wm Haycock; P. Haycock; D. Cutler; Ann Haycock. Their meeting place was Monckton Farm, where Samuel Chatwin, *"a very excellent and eminent Christian gentleman,"*[149] had a barn converted to a chapel accommodating 110 people, a bold statement of faith in the future in a society of 15 within a small village community. Worship in Chatwin's 'chapel' is graphically described. *"There was a stall in the barn for small cattle, which was cleaned out on the Saturday night, and in this stall our Sunday-school children were huddled together on Sundays morning, while preaching service was being conducted in the barn."*[150]

Tombstone of Samuel Chatwin Quinton churchyard

The early years of Quinton Primitive Methodism did not proceed smoothly. *"Our preachers were much persecuted; they were pelted with rotten eggs and other things; the windows of their place of worship were broken, and at one time there was scarcely a whole pane left; and their services were frequently disturbed by bands of music."*[151] To deal with this Quinton mob, the Darlaston Circuit took decisive steps, resolving that *"the society at Quinton print handbills and 2 guineas reward shall be offered to any person who shall impeach on the persons who have persecuted that society."*[152]

Samuel Chatwin's farmhouse and barn – early home of Quinton's Primitive Methodists by H.R. Wilson

---

[149] Pugh, P. (1869) *Primitive Methodist Magazine*, p 303
[150] McKechnie, C. (1892) p 302 [Tithe Map Plot 73]
[151] Flesher, J. (1850) *Primitive Methodist Magazine*, p 324
[152] *Darlaston Primitive Methodist Circuit Minutes* (05.04.1827) WLHC

Such then was Ridgacre township's religious background to the three places of worship present in 1844. On March 30th 1851, according to the ecclesiastical census returns, the almost unbelievable number of 1,003 people availed themselves of these facilities.

As non-religious bodies gradually took responsibility for such traditional social functions as poor relief, the church's role in education was jealously guarded. The *National Society for Promoting the Education of the Poor in the Principles of the Established Church*, which favoured the monitorial system, whereby knowledge was cascaded from master to monitor to a group of pupils, using the Bible as textbook and offering instruction in the '3Rs,' Geography and General Knowledge was formed in 1811. In the previous year, the *British and Foreign School Society* had emerged from the Royal Lancasterian Society, founded by Quaker Joseph Lancaster, whose curriculum, omitting the catechism and advocating non-denominational religious instruction, was favoured by nonconformists. State intervention in education found its first significant focus in 1833 with a parliamentary grant of £20,000 for the education of the children of the poorer classes, to be distributed by either the National or British Societies. The 1844 Factory Act required children between the ages of 8 and 13 to spend six half-days each week in school. Quinton tithe map residents during the mid-1800s included ten school teachers. No scholars were listed in 1841, 69 in 1851 and 65 in 1861. Though education is generally regarded as becoming compulsory following the 1870 Act, it was not until 1902 that it was brought under municipal control. As a result of this, many Nonconformists feared that Anglican teaching would predominate and consequently refused to pay the portion of their rates dedicated to education. Consequently, many suffered distraint of their property, as would be the case in Quinton. (See page 117.)

Within the space of six years (1840-1845) Quinton acquired two churches, a school, a parson and a schoolmaster to complement the visiting Wesleyan Methodist and resident Primitive Methodist preachers who already ministered to its spiritual and educational needs. One wonders what this largely agricultural and nail-making village made of these new leaders who had come amongst them. What were their expectations of their new neighbours? Perhaps they hoped for pillars of society who would broaden their horizons and relieve their poverty such as those who enriched another, albeit very different, community in Oliver Goldsmith's poem *The Deserted Village*.
First the parson:
  "A man he was to all the country dear, And passing rich with forty pounds a year...
  Unpractis'd he to fawn, or seek for power, By doctrines fashion'd to the varying hour;
  For other aims his heart had learn'd to prize, More skilled to raise the wretched than to rise.
  His house was known to all the vagrant train, He chid their wanderings, but reliev'd their pain...
  And in his duty prompt at every call, He watch'd and wept, he pray'd and felt, for all...
  At church, with meek and unaffected grace, His looks adorn'd the venerable place;
  Truth from his lips prevail'd with double sway, And fools, whom came to scoff, remain'd to pray."

Then the schoolmaster:
  "There, in his noisy mansion, skill'd to rule, The village master taught his little school;
  A man severe he was, and stern to view; I knew him well, and every truant knew;
  Well had the boding tremblers earn'd to trace The day's disasters in his morning face...
  Yet he was kind; or if severe in aught, The love he bore to learning was in fault;
  The village all declar'd how much he knew; 'Twas certain he could write, and cypher too...

While words of learned length and thundering sound Amaz'd the gazing rustics all around,
And still they gaz'd, and still the wonder grew, That one small head could carry all he knew."[153]

Was a copy of this poem on the shelves of Rev William Skilton's study or in the schoolhouse? Was it included amongst the books which farmer and church warden George Birch mentioned in his will in 1853? Perhaps even, this popular verse which sealed Oliver Goldsmith's reputation as a poet may have been found in the cottages of those villagers who could read. Though Goldsmith's Auburn, "loveliest village of the plain" was clearly not Quinton, dark and wicked place of the heights, perhaps the hopes and dreams of its inhabitants and the aspirations and ambitions of its perpetual curate and successive schoolmasters and mistresses really did resonate with the exemplars of Goldsmith's *Deserted Village*.

7.01   Wesleyan Methodist Chapel   Plot 56 (52°27'49"N 2°00'53"W)

On Saturday 24th March 1781, John Wesley, the founder of Methodism, recorded in his *Journal*, "I was invited to preach at Quinton, five miles from Birmingham. I preached there at noon in the open air, to a serious and attentive congregation. Some of them appeared to be very deeply affected. Who knows but it may continue?" Wesley had come in response to an invitation from Ambrose Foley "of Quintain Green, in the Parish of Hales Owen and County of Salop, Gentleman,"[154] three years earlier.

March 18th 1778

Rev. Sir,
Having long waited for an opportunity of conveying a line to you, blessed be God! the time is now come; and as 'I am a man that have seen affliction by the rod of His wrath,' have engaged myself for some years past in frequently reading your sermons to a considerable company who wish well to your labours of love; and as they are but some of them but babes in Christ, an instructive lesson might (with the Divine blessing) greatly establish their faith and much good be done to others. If you have an hour or two to spare, my house, which is a good one, and my heart which is a bad one, are both open to you. Pardon, dear Sir and Rev Father in Christ, the importunate request of your humble servant,
Ambrose Foley.[155]

How Foley and Wesley had met is uncertain, but as Foley was in the habit of journeying to London, it seems likely that he heard Wesley preach there. As a result of his introduction to Methodism, Foley had built in his garden a grotto or hermit house, where Quinton's farm labourers and nailers could meet to hear Wesley's sermons read. By Easter Sunday 1785, when Wesley made his third visit to the village, his *Journal* notes, "Notice had been given of my preaching at Quinton at noon. As the house would not hold the people, I was constrained, cold as it was, to preach abroad."[156] To accommodate these eager crowds, Foley had a preaching house, built on his estate. (Early Methodist preaching houses were, as their name suggests, places for preaching and were not designed to supplant the sacramental role of the parish church. Hales Owen diarist David Parkes writes of Foley that "*according*

---

[153] Goldsmith, Oliver (1770) *The Deserted Village*, lines 141-180, 195-216
[154] Foley, Ambrose (09.12.1826) LB
[155] Cited by Hackwood, F. (1915 p 116
[156] Curnock, N. (ed) (1938) *The Journal of the Rev. John Wesley*, Vol VII, 26.03.1785

to the rule adopted by Mr Wesley, he regularly attended the service of the Parish Church."[157]) On his next visit on March 21st 1786, Wesley was able to record, *"At three in the afternoon, I preached at Quinton in the new Preaching House."* Thus, the building date of 1780 given in the 1851 ecclesiastical census return is clearly inaccurate.

The congregation which met in Foley's preaching house during the early 19th century held determined views. Following Wesley's death in 1791, disagreements arose concerning the relationship between Methodism and the Church of England, particularly with regard to access to the sacraments (baptism and holy communion). The Methodist Conference of 1795 produced a *Plan of Pacification* under which the sacraments were not be administered in any chapel except where a majority of trustees, leaders and stewards allowed it and Conference permission (often delegated to superintendent ministers)

Ambrose Foley's Preaching House – built c1785

was given. This was to cause division in Birmingham with some societies breaking away. "The Quinton Society, 'Church Methodists' to a man, separated themselves bodily, and their pulpit was supplied in turn by Messrs Whitehouse, Bourne and Longmore... The Quinton Society maintained their separation for more than thirty years."[158] That links with the parish church continued to be valued beyond this period is seen in Enoch Read, signatory to Quinton Wesleyan Methodists' 1851 ecclesiastical census return, a nailer who lived at the centre of the village, who took all seven of his children to Christ Church for baptism. (12.03.07)

Ambrose Foley's Chapel remained his personal property, part of his estate mentioned in his will at his death in 1827.

> *I give and devise to Richard Longmore and Thomas Floyd, Preachers of the Gospel and to my said godson, Henry Foley Macdonald a part of my estate at Quintain Green (that is to say) my Chapel or Schoolroom.*[159]

Longmore and Floyd were by this date the local preachers, who preached alternately in Quinton Chapel. By 1844 John and Ambrose Foley (nephews of the first Ambrose) were listed as owner-occupiers of the chapel which accommodated a congregation of 100 and occupied a plot of land measuring 1 rood 1 pole.

Let, in 1846, on a twenty-one-year lease to the Birmingham West Wesleyan Methodist Circuit, this chapel was thus linked with nine others, including Cherry Street in the centre of Birmingham. In the same year, the circuit preachers directed that "enquiry be made into the case of Quinton in order to

---

[157] Parkes, David, *Diary* (Summary for 1786)
[158] Sheldon, W.C. (1903) *Early Methodism in Birmingham*, p 47
[159] Foley, Ambrose (09.12.1826) LB

9

Census of Great Britain, 1851.

(13 and 14 Victoriæ, cap. 58).

A RETURN

OF THE SEVERAL PARTICULARS TO BE INQUIRED INTO RESPECTING THE UNDERMENTIONED

PLACE OF PUBLIC RELIGIOUS WORSHIP.

[N.B.—A similar Return will be obtained from the Clergy of the Church of England, and also from the Ministers of every other Religious Denomination throughout Great Britain.]

I	II			III	IV	V	VI	VII			VIII			IX
Name or Title of Place of Worship	Where Situate; specifying the			Religious Denomination	When Erected	Whether a Separate and Entire Building	Whether used exclusively as a Place of Worship (Except for a Sunday School)	Space available for Public Worship			Estimated Number of Persons attending Divine Service on Sunday, March 30, 1851			REMARKS
	Parish, or Place	District	County					Number of Sittings already Provided		Free Space or Standing Room for	Morning	Afternoon	Evening	
								Free Sittings	Other Sittings					
	(1)	(2)	(3)					(4)	(5)					
Wesleyan Methodist	Quinton Haubridge Ridmore Union	Worcester-shire		Wesleyan Methodist	October 1780	Yes	Nbe cropt Worship Yes	Free	No		General Congregation 40 Sunday Scholars 40 TOTAL.. 80	Afternoon 40 40 80	63 63 63	
											Average Number of Attendants during months (See Instruction VIII) General Congregation Sunday Scholars 40 40 TOTAL.. 80	40 40 80	63 63 63	

I certify the foregoing to be a true and correct Return to the best of my belief. Witness my hand this 31st day of March 1851.

x (Signature) ...... Enoch Read

(Official Character) 1

(Address by Post) Enoch Read Quinton Worcestershire of the above-named Place of Worship

The particulars to be inserted in Divisions I. to VI. inclusive

ascertain if Bro. Floyd be under the necessity of preaching in that chapel every fortnight."[160] Evidently not satisfied with the answer they decided that Floyd should take his Quinton appointments in rotation with other preachers. Further light is shed in Barr's comment that Floyd "seems to have grown weary in well-doing and surrendered for a money consideration the bequest to which he apparently had a legal claim, although he did not continue his pulpit services."[161] During the 1840s the average circuit membership was 1,706 of whom just 11 were members at Quinton Chapel, where a morning Sunday School complemented services at 3pm and 6pm. In 1851 Quinton Wesleyans raised 13s 11d in class ticket money towards a circuit total of £177.14.11d. and the ecclesiastical census reported a congregation of 103 with 40 Sunday School scholars on March 30th.

When the lease of 1846 had almost expired, Cherry Street Circuit considered buying Quinton Chapel, which was offered to them for £285. Ways and means of raising the money were investigated and Quinton Methodists pledged to do their part toward raising the required sum. However, negotiations failed, and Alfred Hodge,[162] the principal fund-raiser, was directed to return to the donors the money which had been collected, and a new arrangement was made to lease the chapel at an annual rental of £8. Hodge, however, proved less eager to pay back the money raised than he had been to collect it. In September 1871, circuit officials resolved that "Mr Butler be employed to obtain from Mr Hodge the amount paid to him by the Quinton friends as a subscription towards the erection of a new chapel."[163] Even so, it was September 1873 before the total amount of £19 9s 9d was eventually recovered. The Quinton members now decided that a new chapel was needed and undertook to raise £300 towards the estimated £600 cost. Ambrose Foley's Chapel was demolished in June 1877 and a new chapel opened in 1878, by which time Quinton Methodists had raised £244 10s towards their promised £300.

7.02 Christ Church The Quinton   Plot 50 (52°27'46"N 2°00'33"W)

On Wednesday 18th July 1838, this announcement appeared in the *Wolverhampton Chronicle*:

"Hagley Park will be thrown open to the public for a Bazaar early in August as the claims of her Majesty upon the attendance of Lady Lyttelton[164] will allow her Ladyship's presence. The object of the bazaar is to raise funds for the erection of a new church in the Parish of Hales Owen, one of the many excellent objects by which the pious and indefatigable Vicar, Rev R.B. Hone, is endeavouring to promote the welfare of his extensive parish. The site will be at The Quinton, near the fifth milestone from Birmingham, where there is a large and scattered population, not only two miles from Hales Owen Church, but virtually severed from it by a steep hill.

The bazaar raised £800 and a number of the wealthier Quinton farmers also made contributions: George Birch (Redhall Farm): £40; Henry Nicholls (Hawthorn Farm): £5; Richard Tomlinson (Windmill

---

[160] *Birmingham West Wesleyan Methodist Local Preachers' Meeting Minutes* (09.01.1846) LB
[161] Barr, D. (1890) *Village Methodism: How Methodism came to Quinton* in Christian Miscellany, pp 464-466
[162] Could this be Alfred Hodge, attorney's clerk of Balsall Heath Road Birmingham, whose wife gave her occupation in the 1861 census as *Wesleyan Local Preacher*?
[163] *Birmingham West Wesleyan Methodist Circuit Quarterly Meeting Minutes* (25.09.1871) LB
[164] Lady Sarah Lyttelton (1787-1870), widow of the 3rd Baron who had died in 1837, was Lady of the Bedchamber to Queen Victoria. Her son, George, 4th Baron Lyttelton, did not marry until 1839.

Farm): £10; Joseph Wakeman (Warley Farm): £2.10.0d. With the exception of Joseph Wakeman who died during the period, all these donors were rewarded by being appointed Church Wardens during the first decade of Christ Church's existence. In addition to that from the farmers, a donation of £1 to the building fund was received from James Adams of the Holly Bush Inn, who did not become a Church Warden.

Approximately 10 acres of land, for buildings and glebe, were given by Lord Lyttelton; Richard Charles Hussey (1806-87) who had joined his more famous partner Thomas Rickman in 1835 in practice at 45 Anne Street,[165] Birmingham, was appointed architect and locally-hewn stone from The Rough, a quarry adjacent to the Turnpike Road near the sixth milestone from Birmingham, with red stone quarried in Hasbury, Hales Owen were the chosen building materials. On a wet and windy day in July 1839, at a ceremony truncated because of the weather, the foundation stone was laid, appropriately, by Lord Lyttelton. Amazingly, Rev Richard Brindley Hone's prayer survives (unique amongst his notebook entries) from this ceremony. That the prayer must have been prepared in advance of the service is suggested by the absence of any reference to the challenging climatic conditions of the occasion, as Hone would surely have found opportunity to invoke the mercies of God despite the weather had his words been truly extempore. The florid language of the early Victorian age – a mixture of adoration, invocation, religious cliché and informing the Almighty what was happening in Quinton on July 7th 1839 – offers a fascinating and valuable insight into what worshippers in the established church may have heard when their priest departed from the liturgy of the Prayer Book.

"Eternal God, mighty in power, glorious in holiness and majesty incomprehensible, whom the Heaven of Heavens cannot contain, much less the walls of temples made with hands, who yet has been pleased graciously to promise thine especial presence even wherever two or three are gathered together in thy name, we beseech thee to prosper the work which we this day commence. We desire to erect a house to be set apart for thy worship, like a holy temple in which prayer may be offered to thee and thy praise declared and thy truth preached, and we lay the foundation stone in the name of the Great Jehovah, the Holy, Holy, Holy Lord God of Hosts, the Father, the Son and the Holy Ghost, three persons and one God. O let thy blessing attend the work, let thy providence order all things concerning it for good and when the building of wood and stone is finished, may many, many

Quinton Church.

THE

FOUNDATION STONE

of the NEW CHURCH intended to be erected at the QUINTON, in the Parish of Hales-Owen, will be laid by

The Right Hon. Lord Lyttelton,

On FRIDAY NEXT, 19th JULY, 1839.

Those Parishioners and Friends who are willing to join the Procession, are requested to assemble near the Quinton Gate at *Eleven o'Clock*, in order to receive LORD LYTTELTON, and accompany him to the site.

SEATS WILL BE PROVIDED FOR LADIES.

THE FOLLOWING HYMN WILL BE SUNG ON THE OCCASION.

Thus saith the high and lofty One,
Inhabiting eternity ;
" Earth is my footstool, heaven my throne,
What temple will ye build for me ?"

Yet mortals, bound by time and space,
May plead thy faithful promise, Lord,
To bless and hallow every place,
Where they thy holy Name record.

Here, then, where none hath stood before
A House of Prayer to Thee we build ;
May it, till seasons change no more,
Be with thy grace and glory filled.

From age to age, thy Gospel here,
Its line, its health, its power impart,
Be preach'd to every listening ear,
And sown in every fruitful heart.

So, as the heavenly Church above,
When Saints their course on earth review,
Thousands may tell, with joy and love,
That here their souls were born anew.

To the Parishioners.

My Dear Friends,

I regret to be obliged to give you so short a notice of this important and interesting event, but I only heard a few days ago that it would be agreeable to Lord Lyttelton to lay the Foundation Stone next week, and it was not before yesterday that it could be arranged to comply with his Lordship's wishes.

Believe me Yours faithfully,

Vicarage, Hales-Owen,
July 12th. 1839.

R. B. HONE.

HARRIS, PRINTER, HALES-OWEN.

---

[165] Anne Street later became Colmore Row.

living stones be here added to thy spiritual house, that it may grow and be enlarged. May the light of thy truth shine within and around it, may multitudes bless thy name for having put it into the hearts of thy servants to arise and build. And, O Lord, look down in mercy upon this whole parish; pour out thy grace upon its inhabitants in larger measure, also purify, strengthen and bless thy church in this land and let the time speedily arrive when thy people may be no longer broken into many flocks, but when peace shall flourish and unity prevail and there shall be one fold as there is one shepherd. Hear us, O Lord, for Jesus Christ's sake. Amen."[166]

Christ Church The Quinton, photographed April 2017

Christ Church The Quinton, "a small neat erection, in the early English style of architecture,"[167] was consecrated by Rt Rev Dr Robert Carr, Bishop of Worcester on September 18th 1840, when the sermon was preached by Rev Richard Hone. Despite the generosity of Lord Lyttelton and the gifts of local benefactors, the required estimate of £2,066 had not been raised, delaying the building of the planned spire. The church was consecrated for marriages in December 1841. In the same year, by Order of the Queen in Council,[168] the existing Hales Owen Parish was divided into five districts: Hales Owen Borough, Romsley, Oldbury, The Quinton (townships, albeit re-named, within the ancient parish boundary) and Cradley (beyond its borders). In the mid-1800s Christ Church offered two services each Sunday, one at 10.30am and one at 3.00pm.

By the time of the tithe map, the plot occupied by church and church yard (shared with the neighbouring school) measured 1 acre 9 poles. Established as a perpetual curacy[169] in the gift of Rev Hone, Christ Church was reported as having a general congregation of 295 and 89 Sunday Scholars on census day, March 30th 1851. Remarks appended to the return by the incumbent, Rev William Skilton, repeat the *Wolverhampton Chronicle*'s assessment of 13 years earlier that this was a scattered parish, with the population living up to two miles distant from the church. Obviously, pew rents, which should have brought in an income on 204 of the available 605 sittings, had been an issue of some contention. (See following page.) Nevertheless, the congregation looked beyond its parish boundaries at least to one Birmingham hospital for the work it supported. "At the Weekly Board of the Queen's Hospital held on Friday last, a donation of £1 was presented by Rev W.H. Skilton, being part of the collection at Christ Church The Quinton held at the 'Fare-Day'."[170]

---

[166] Hone, R.B. "Prayer at the laying of the foundation stone, Christ Church, 19.07.1839," DALHC
[167] Billings, M. (1855)
[168] August 11th 1841
[169] Christ Church became a rectory in 1866 during the time of the second incumbent, Rev Christopher Oldfield.
[170] *Birmingham Aris's Gazette* (April 16th 1855)

Census of Great Britain, 1851,
(13 and 14 Victoriæ, Cap. 53.)

A RETURN

Of the several Particulars to be inquired into respecting the undermentioned CHURCH or CHAPEL in England, belonging to the United Church of England and Ireland.

[A similar Return (*mutatis mutandis*,) will be obtained with respect to Churches belonging to the Established Church in Scotland, and the Episcopal Church there, and also from Roman Catholic Priests, and from the Ministers of every other Religious Denomination throughout Great Britain, with respect to their Places of Worship.]

	NAME and DESCRIPTION of CHURCH or CHAPEL.
I.	Christ Church, being the Church of a District Parish.

	WHERE SITUATED.	Parish, Ecclesiastical Division or District, Township or Place	Superintendent Registrar's District	County and Diocese
II.		Township of Hedgyt any of the 4 Townships shut from the District	Stourbridge	Worcester

	WHEN CONSECRATED OR LICENSED	Under what Circumstances CONSECRATED or LICENSED
III.	September 18, 1840	As an additional Church.

In the case of a CHURCH or CHAPEL CONSECRATED or LICENSED since the 1st January, 1800; state

	HOW OR BY WHOM ERECTED	COST, how Defrayed	
IV.	By Private Benefaction or Subscription	By Parliamentary Grant................	
		„ Parochial Rate	
		„ Private Benefaction, or Subscription, or from other Sources...... }	2066
		Total Cost......£	2066

V.			VI.	
HOW ENDOWED.			**SPACE AVAILABLE FOR PUBLIC WORSHIP**	

	£		£		
Land...............		Pew Rents	12.10.	Free Sittings	401
Tithe (Rent Charge)	84.	Fees	10.	Other Sittings	204
Glebe........	15.	Dues...............			
Other permanent Endowment.... }	45.12.6	Easter Offerings		Total Sittings...	605
		Other Sources			

VII.	Estimated Number of Persons attending Divine Service on Sunday, March 30, 1851.				AVERAGE NUMBER OF ATTENDANTS during 12 Months next preceding March 30, 1851. (See Instruction VII.)			
		Morning	Afternoon	Evening		Morning	Afternoon	Evening
	General Congregation }	95	200	✗	General Congregation }	80 to 90	80 to 90	✗
	Sunday Scholars	51	38		Sunday Scholars	65	65	
	Total..	146	238		Total...	145 to 155	145 to 155	

VIII.	REMARKS	✗ In consequence of a question having been raised, under peculiar circumstances as to rights of payment, the expense from Pew Rents is rendered almost nil; ✗✗ the population of the District is spread over a considerable area, chiefly inhabiting groups of Cottages, at various distances to an extent of 2 miles from the Church.

I certify the foregoing to be a true and correct Return to the best of my belief.

Witness my hand this *Thirty first* day of *March* 1851.

IX. (Signature) W. R. Skilton

(Official Character) Perpetual Curate of the above named District Parish Church

(Address by Post) The Quinton Parsonage, near Birmingham.

7.03   Glebe Land   Plots 36, 48 (52°27'41"N 2°00'42"W; 52°27'44"N 2°00'38"W)

In addition to the 1 acre 9 poles of land on which the church, churchyard, school and parsonage stood, in 1840 Lord Lyttelton also donated a further 7 acres 2 roods 7 poles as glebe land, i.e. land assigned to the church as part of its income. This was made up of Big Leasow (Plot 48 – 6 acres 2 roods) designated in the tithe apportionments as pasture and a garden (Plot 36 – seven poles). Presumably this had previously been part of Lower Quinton Farm owned by Lord Lyttelton and let to Thomas White (8.01.02). Initially, the burial ground was limited to the churchyard, that is the area immediately surrounding the church building. This was consecrated along with the church in September 1840, with the first interment taking place the following November, when 45-year-old Esther Wood of Hill township was buried. The second burial, in January 1841, was of 25-year-old Charles Fox of Ridgacre. It is evident, then, that from the time of its consecration the facilities offered by Christ Church extended way beyond the township in which it was located. Though Ridgacre, closely followed by Warley Wigorn, provided by far the greatest number of burials in the period upon which this survey focuses, the dead of ten other areas were also brought to Christ Church for burial.

Burials 1840 - 1851

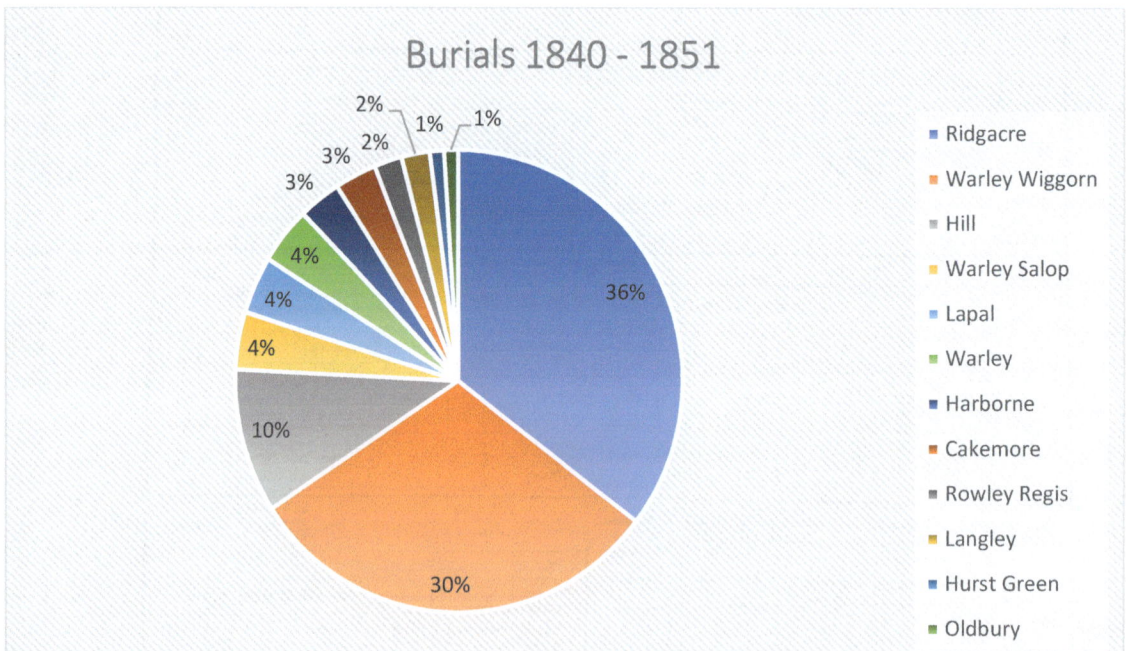

Pie chart legend: Ridgacre 36%, Warley Wiggorn 30%, Hill 10%, Warley Salop 4%, Lapal 4%, Warley 4%, Harborne 3%, Cakemore 3%, Rowley Regis 2%, Langley 2%, Hurst Green 1%, Oldbury 1%.

By 1889, after 1,415 burials, the churchyard was full and was closed by an Order in Council dated February 19th. To address this problem in September 1889 1acre 9 poles of Glebe land (from plot 48) was sold to Alexander Macomb Chance of Edgbaston for of £158.10s.[171] The following year it became necessary to clarify the identity of the purchaser(s). "Whereas although the aforesaid £158.10s are expressed to have been paid by Alexander Maycomb Chance, the same were in fact paid by him and the said Arthur Albright in equal shares and the piece of land which became vested in the said Alexander Maycomb Chance was acquired by him on behalf of himself and the said Arthur Albright."[172]

---

[171] Conveyance: Rev[d] Aaron Lewis Manby to Alexander Macomb Chance Esq[re] (10.09.1889)
[172] Indenture: Arthur Albright, Alexander Macomb Chance and 10 others (06.12.1890)

The purpose of the purchase by Chance and Albright was: "For providing a new Burial Ground for the parish of Quinton, one half of which Burial Ground (namely that provided by the said Alexander Maycomb Chance) should be consecrated and the other half of which (namely that provided by the said Arthur Albright) should remain unconsecrated."[173] A letter from the Secretary of State at the Home Department confirms that official approval of the site as a burial ground had been given.[174] On August 23rd 1890 Chance conveyed his half of the plot to the Ecclesiastical Commissioners for England and a week later it was consecrated by the Bishop of Worcester for use by members of the parish. Similarly, on December 6th 1890, Albright conveyed to a board of trustees[175] "an unconsecrated portion of the Burial Ground for the burial of all persons whomsoever for the burial of whom therein application has been made."[176] Simply expressed, the consecrated half of the new Burial Ground was available to all people residing within the parish, but particularly adherents of the Church of England, whilst the unconsecrated ground was for the use of Nonconformists from the parish and beyond.

By the beginning of the 20th century the amount of Glebe Land had been reduced by 1.018 acres for the new Burial Ground and 1.027 acres occupied by the New Inns Beer House at the south west corner of the plot.[177] Further encroachments had also been made by extensions to the National School in 1852, 1864, 1871 and 1893 and the building the Parish Hall in 1934. In September 1923, brewers Mitchells and Butlers purchased (for £844) a plot of land adjacent to the New Inns for use as a bowling green and pleasure garden, with a view to enabling the existing use as a beer house[178] to be extended to a full licence.[179] Between June 1931 and April 1934 four plots at the south of the Glebe Land, between the New Inns and Stoney Lane and fronting Meadow Road and what was then called Ridgacre Lane, were leased on 99-year terms to housing developers.[180] The remaining and greatly reduced area of Big Leasow, by then known as Rectory Field, was swallowed up by new school buildings in 1961 and 1971, and thus the Glebe Land donated by Lord Lyttelton in 1840 was finally surrendered.

---

[173] Indenture: Arthur Albright, Alexander Macomb Chance and 10 others (06.12.1890)

[174] Whitehall 376[D]/[3] to Reverend A.L. Manby (20.08.1890)

[175] The original trustees were William Arthur Albright, George Stacey Albright, John William Wilson, Arthur Godlee. Robert Gee, William Green, Rev George Middleton (Governor of Bourne College), Thomas James Alden, George Henry Robbins and Samuel Round.

[176] Indenture: Arthur Albright, Alexander Macomb Chance and 10 others (06.12.1890)

[177] OS Map Worcestershire Sheet V; Warwickshire Sheet XIII Second Edition 1904

[178] A beer house was not licensed to sell spirits.

[179] Correspondence re Quinton Glebe sale from Holbeche & Son, Land Agents & Surveyors, Smythe, Etches & Co, Solicitors, Queen Anne's Bounty Office to Rev W.A. Rowlands (08.02.1923 – 01.09.1923)

[180] 1,065 square yards to the east of New Inns for one substantial detached dwelling (Rev Alfred Ernest Palmer to Mr Douglas Harold Brindley,17.10.1932); 1,080 square yards to the east of land demised to DH Brindley for one substantial detached dwelling (Rev Alfred Ernest Palmer to Mr Arthur Vernon Crowley, 31.03.1934); 1,397 square yards to the east of land demised to AV Crowley for one pair of substantial semi-detached dwellings (Rev Alfred Ernest Palmer to Mr William Thompson Yates, 24.04.1934); 6,484 square yards to the west of Stoney Lane (and to the east of that subsequently leased to WT Yates) for 11 detached/semi-detached dwellings (Rev Alfred Ernest Palmer to RH Bridge, 04.06.1931). The two substantial detached dwellings which fronted Ridgacre Lane (now Ridgacre Road West) remain. The pair of substantial semi-detached dwellings which also fronted Ridgacre Lane and the 11 detached/semi-detached dwellings which fronted Stoney Lane were casualties of the construction of Quinton Expressway in 1964.

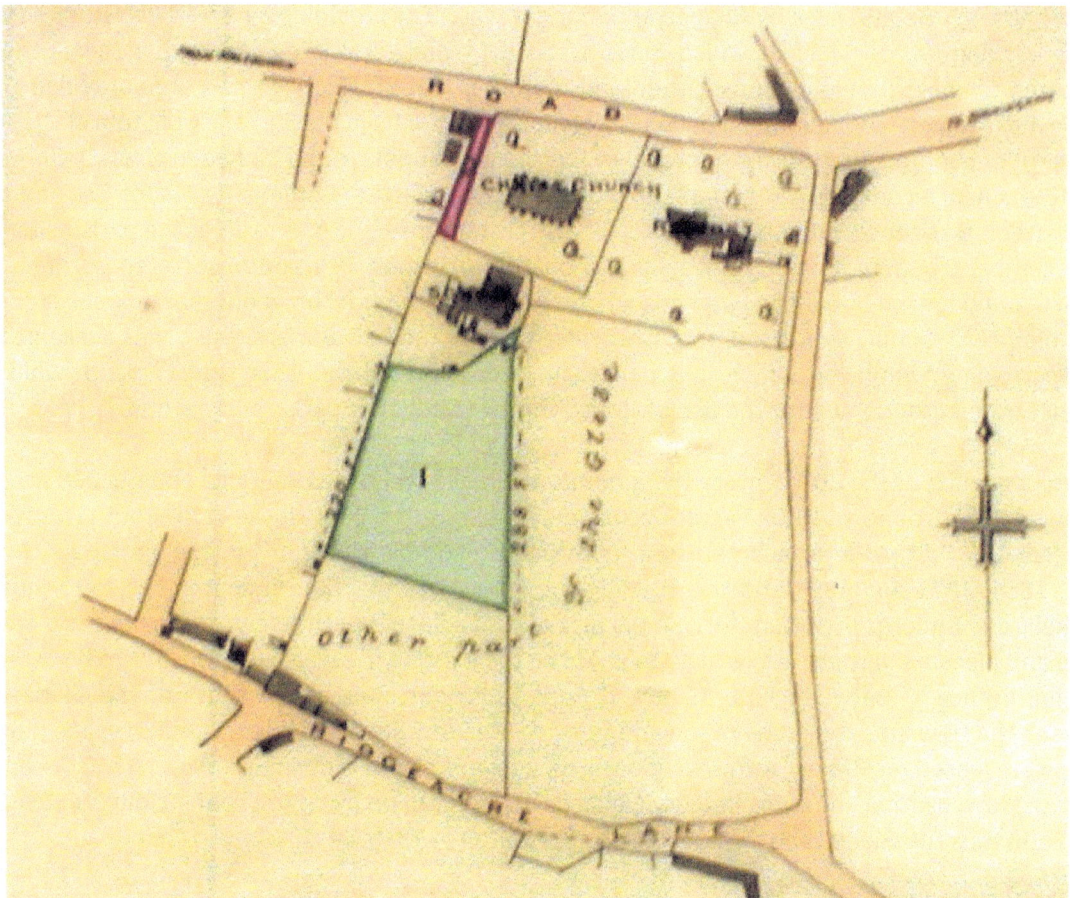

New Burial Ground numbered 1, coloured green; access numbered 2, coloured pink

7.04   Bethesda Primitive Methodist Chapel   Plot 57 (52°27'48"N 2°00'51"W)

Less than one month after the consecration of Christ Church, Bethesda Primitive Methodist Chapel was opened just behind the Wesleyan Chapel on a plot of Lord Lyttelton's land, measuring 18 poles, which was mistakenly listed in the tithe apportionments as a house, shop and garden occupied by James Hall. Services here were held at 11am, 3pm and 6pm and attracted by census Sunday, 30th March 1851, an adult congregation of 214, with 222 scholars in the Sunday School. Part of the Birmingham East Circuit for the first 27 years of its life, Bethesda was served by 16 circuit ministers during the mid-1800s. Amongst the 26 signatures in the baptismal register in this period were those of 14 laymen, with only James Hall (12.04.03) living on the tithe map. A distinguished visitor to Bethesda in 1845 was William Clowes, President of the Primitive Methodist Conference. "On Sunday November 16th Mr Clowes preached two sermons at Quinton, and though the day was very unfavourable, yet the congregations and collections were good. Mr Clowes, with his usual zeal and energy, brought down upon us the Divine Glory, so that every heart seemed to be filled."[181] Whilst at Quinton Clowes baptised two babies – one from Crock Street and one from Webb's Green.

---

[181] Flesher, J. (ed) (1846) *Primitive Methodist Magazine*, p 31

PRESENTATION ADDRESS,

FROM THE TEACHERS & SENIOR SCHOLARS

OF THE

PRIMITIVE METHODIST SUNDAY SCHOOL, QUINTON,

TO THEIR

Highly-Esteemed and Beloved Superintendent,

MR. JOHN CHAMBERS.

DEAR SIR,--

Deeply interesting as all our Annual Easter Festivals have hitherto been to us, as Teachers of the Quinton Primitive Methodist Sabbath School, we feel this to be one of unusual interest, since we have chosen it as a favourable opportunity of giving you a public Demonstration of our high appreciation of your much-esteemed and invaluable services as our honoured Superintendent, during a period of more than twenty-five years. In so doing we feel it to be our duty to offer up to Almighty God our grateful acknowledgements and sincere thanks for His great and continued mercy, in sparing your life, and preserving your health, thereby permitting you to attend to your Sabbath School duties in a manner, which, for regularity and punctuality, is highly creditable to yourself, and worthy of the immitation of your Fellow-Teachers.

In reviewing the origin of our School we do not fail to recognize the hand of Divine Providence as signally displayed in the event of your connecting yourself with it just at the time when the need and importance of an efficient Superintendent was so deeply felt by a few devoted Teachers, who were anxious to establish a Sunday School at Quinton. They had, to the utmost of their ability, struggled with opposing influences, and were fearing they should be compelled to give up the attempt. It was at that important crisis when God, in His all-wise Providence, directed you to come and join the feeble few, and enter at once upon the important and responsible duties of a Superintendent. Those duties you have continued to discharge to your own honour, to the satisfaction of your Fellow-Teachers, and to the good and welfare of the rising youth.

We still look upon the event as an era in the history of our School, and upon you as having the honour of first establishing and organizing a Sunday School at Quinton, upon a systematic and proper basis.

After the lapse of more than a quarter of a century, it is highly gratifying to us to be able to say, that the very high opinion we at first formed of your qualifications has been more than confirmed by experience. We should like to say more in reference to your abilities, but fearing you would consider us too enlogistic, we forbear. Yet we cannot forbear making some allusion to the success, which, through the blessing of God, has attended your labours in connection with your Fellow-Teachers. They have not, indeed, been in vain. Very many have been the pleasing and encouraging instances which have come under our notice, which we regard as a decided testimony to the co-operation of the Holy Spirit with your successful endeavours; and we believe many have, under God, through your efforts, been prepared to depart this life in peace. It is our further pleasure to know that a goodly number are at present with us in society; and we feel persuaded that many who have left the School, still retain the impressions and remain under the influence they received therein, which influence, we feel assured, will continue to be felt by future generations.

It is a deep conviction of the pleasing facts here referred to, that has prompted us to express in a humble manner our sensibility of your worth, by a small presentation, which we hope will meet your willing acceptance; and believe us when we say it is the offering of sincerity and disinterestedness. You will, we doubt not, be pleased to hear that the senior scholars have most cordially joined and nobly assisted us in procuring the testimonial, which consists of Dr. Kitto's Pictorial Bible, in two quarto volumes, in half-morocco, with gilt edges; an Electro Silver Inkstand; a sterling Silver Pencil Case, set with a Topaz stone, with the initials of your name engraved thereon; a Ruby-pointed Gold Pen; and a small Ebony Ruler. We feel it to be our duty to acknowledge, that our choice in the selection of the above has been directed by the following very important facts, namely:—As it has been your pleasure to sustain, and honourably discharge the important duties of a Bible Class Teacher ever since you united yourself with the School, we have chosen the above-named Bible, a work highly valued by the learned of all Christian denominations, and one which will render you invaluable aid and assistance in the future discharge of your important duties; at the same time that it will remain as a memorial of the many delightful and happy hours you have spent with your class. And in consideration of the scholar-like and business-like manner in which you have managed and conducted the affairs of the School as Secretary and Treasurer during the same length of time, we have chosen the afore-named Inkstand and Pencil Case, as an appropriate and useful part of our testimonial; the Inkstand has an inscription engraved thereon, which will tell to future generations of the high and honourable position in which you are placed this day. The Ruler we have added as forming a necessary appendage to the Inkstand, and at the same time we view it as being somewhat emblematical of that straightforward, unbending, and undeviating line of conduct it has ever been your aim to pursue in connection with the duties of the School.

There is, however, one very pleasing feature connected with our testimonial which we cannot possibly pass over—it is not a *farewell* testimonial. Our present enjoyment is not lessened by the expectation of being compelled in a few hours to utter that bosom-harrowing word, Farewell! But while we have the delightful recollections of the past, and the enjoyment of the present, we have the heart-cheering hope of enjoying many long and profitable years of your future life; for we humbly and sincerely pray, that the God of Sunday Schools will be pleased to bless you with a continuation of all those mercies he has so liberally and bountifully bestowed upon you in years that are past, and that your valuable life may be spared to a good and honourable old age. And then when you have finished your labour of love, and your Heavenly Father is about to call you hence; and those who have been called away by death from among us to their rest in Heaven, shall be foremost in the throng of the redeemed, waiting to administer unto you an abundant entrance among the saints in light; then, and not till then, do we expect to say *Farewell.*

And now, dear Sir, we conclude by praying, that the choicest of Heaven's blessings may rest upon you, and upon your dear family; that the School may continue to prosper under your care; and that at last each teacher and each scholar, with their parents, may have the happiness of meeting you and your family at God's right hand. Amen.

Your's most affectionately,

In behalf of the Teachers and Senior Scholars,

SAMUEL DINGLEY, JUN.

EASTER MONDAY, 1857.

10

Census of Great Britain, 1851.

(18 and 14 Victoriæ, cap. 53).

A RETURN

OF THE SEVERAL PARTICULARS TO BE INQUIRED INTO RESPECTING THE UNDERMENTIONED

PLACE OF PUBLIC RELIGIOUS WORSHIP.

[N.B.—A similar Return will be obtained from the Clergy of the Church of England, and also from the Ministers of every other Religious Denomination throughout Great Britain.]

I. Name or Title of Place of Worship	II. Where Situate; specifying the		III. Religious Denomination	IV. When Erected	V. Whether a Separate and Entire Building	VI. Whether used exclusively as a Place of Worship (Except for a Sunday School)	VII. Space available for Public Worship			VIII. Estimated Number of Persons attending Divine Service on Sunday, March 30, 1851			IX. REMARKS
	Parish, or Place (1)	District (2) / County (3)					Number of Sittings already Provided			Morning / Afternoon / Evening			
							Free Sittings (4)	Other Sittings (5)					
Bethesda Chapel	Quinta	Chirk, near Oswestry Union	Primitive Methodist	1840	Yes.	Yes.	150	84		General Congregation 53 / 64 / 97	Sunday Scholars 101 / 91 / —		
										TOTAL.. 154 / 155 / 97			
							Free Space or Standing Room for			Average Number of Attendants during 6 months (See Instruction VIII.)			
										General Congregation 65 / /	Sunday Scholars 135 / /		
										TOTAL.. 200.			

I certify the foregoing to be a true and correct Return to the best of my belief. Witness my hand this 7th day of April 1851.

x (Signature) .... John Chwrkel

(Official Character) Trustee

(Address by Post) John Chwrkel

Quinton nr Birmingham

of the above-named Place of Worship.

The particulars to be inserted in Divisions I. to VI. inclusive, and in IX., may be written either along or across the columns, as may be more convenient.

114

18 45 November 16th No. 12	Anne Daughter of	John & Sarah	Evans	Crock Street	Nailer	William Clowes
18 45 November 16th No. 13	Charles Son of	William & Anne	Powell	Webbs Green Cottage	Labourer	William Clowes
18 46						

Quinton Primitive Methodist Baptismal Register 1841-1955

John Chambers, trustee and Sunday School Superintendent, recipient of the effusive address shown on page 113, who completed the 1851 census return, lived just beyond the tithe map to the west of the village centre. A native of London and a managing warehouseman for a company producing edge tools, Chambers obviously ranked higher on the social scale than Enoch Read, his Wesleyan nail-forger counterpart, an interesting comment on the view that 19th century Methodism generally included skilled workers amongst the Wesleyans and unskilled workers with the Primitives. John Chambers was responsible for the following account of the origins of the Bethesda Chapel.

"On April 1, 1835, a meeting was held for the purpose of taking the necessary steps for erecting a chapel. We commenced subscribing our mites till our subscriptions amounted to five pounds seven shillings and two-pence. This money was collected on the condition that if the way did not fully open to buy land and build a chapel, the money subscribed should be returned. Our speculation was begun and carried on in faith but governed by honesty. Many unavailing attempts were made to secure land, but to no purpose. We kept on praying for the Lord to open our way, and we occupied the old place till April 11, 1840, when our way began to open. The lord of the manor being minded to dispose of some of his cottages, one of them was purchased by Mr James Hall, one of our local preachers, and he let us have as much land out of his garden, at two shillings a yard, as suited our purpose.

"On Monday, June 20, 1840, the foundation stone was laid, on which occasion a sermon was preached by one of our ministers, from the following words: 'The God of heaven he will prosper us, therefore we his servants will arise and build.' Nehemiah ii.20. Under this sermon our faith rose into strong confidence, which was never lost. At the close we collected five pounds nine shillings and one penny. The building rose gradually amidst much opposition and conflict, till on November 8, 1840 the chapel was ready for opening. Mr S. Tillotson preached morning and afternoon, and Mr Davies, Baptist minister, in the evening; on which day more than eleven pounds were collected. We commenced our opening service, by all the scholars being collected in the old chapel, the hymn books being delivered to the scholars, we sung and prayed, then moved in solemn procession from the old to the new place, bearing our pulpit bible along with us. It is impossible to describe the mingled feelings attendant upon that procession. Some wept aloud for sorrow at leaving the old place others wept and rejoiced aloud at the prospect of opening the new one. Since the opening our society and congregations have much increased. Nearly all the pews are let and the cause is very encouraging."

Though no known illustration exists of Bethesda Chapel, Chambers adds a graphic word picture to the above account. "The chapel is built with good brick, slated with blue slates. It is thirty-two feet in length, and twenty-four in width; and under the gallery there is a kitchen and parlour; also a workshop adjoining, with other appurtenances; the whole cost was three hundred and one pounds sixteen shillings and four-pence half-penny. It is galleried in front besides an extra gallery, which holds sixty Sunday scholars."[182] The strange living accommodation incorporated into Bethesda, which led a later writer to describe it as "in its internal arrangements and purposes about the greatest curiosity I have yet met in my rambles in the district,"[183] was let for over 40 years at a rental of 1s 8d per week, providing the Society with a regular income. It was eventually sold for £70, on being replaced by College Road Primitive Methodist Chapel in 1888.

7.05   National School   Plot 50 (52°27'46"N 2°00'33"W)

Occupying the same plot (measuring 1 acre 9 poles) on the tithe map as the church and churchyard, was Quinton National School (originally one single room which could be divided by a screen) and

schoolmaster's house. However, Anglican interest in education within the township had begun prior to the presence of these two buildings. Following the vacating of Samuel Chatwin's barn for their new chapel, Quinton Primitive Methodists noted, with some mixed feelings, of the Anglican presence that "the Church rents our old place for a Sunday and day school."[184]

The Minute Book of the Vestry and Annual Parish Meeting of Christ Church records the opening of a Sunday School with 45 children in March 1841. A month later, on April 22nd, this establishment was placed on a more official footing with its affiliation to the *National Society for Promoting the Education of the Poor in the Principles of the Established Church*, with Rev R.B. Hone as sole manager. By a deed dated February 22nd 1842, Lord Lyttelton conveyed to the Perpetual Curate and Church Wardens of Christ Church the land on which the school would be built. The date of March 1846, which has been suggested[185] for the opening of the school,

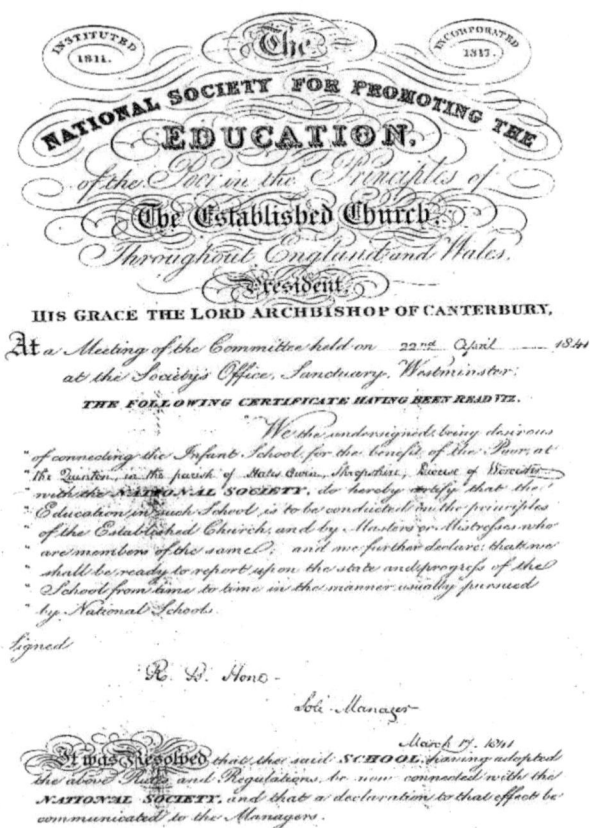

---

[182] Chambers, J. (1842) p 24
[183] M.J.N. *The Rambler* in Middleton, G., (1888) p 27
[184] Chambers, J. (1842) p 24
[185] Bunting, T. (1990) p 11

seems unlikely as the building is clearly shown in 1844 on the tithe map and a schoolmaster was in post in 1845, though then living in Hill Quarter.[186] The Statement of Accounts for the building of the school, dated March 25th 1846, was more likely to have been produced to show that the required £455 13s 10d had now been raised. This statement once again indicates the contributions made by Quinton farmers. Three, who had sponsored the building of Christ Church (George Birch – Redhall; Henry Nicholls – Hawthorn; Richard Tomlinson – Windmill) again donated. For the building of the school Richard Underhill of Tinker's Farm and John Jakeman of Mockbeggar Farm also joined the subscribers. Following the lead given by James Adams of the Holly Bush in the Christ Church appeal, the Holly Bush Club contributed 5s towards the building of the school. A notable absentee from the list once again was John Foley of Monckton Farm. This may well suggest a dissenter's objection to Anglican bias in religious education in National Schools, which was still present in Ridgacre township over half a century later. In 1902, Quinton Primitive Methodists wrote to the Prime Minister voicing their objections to the religious clauses of the new Education Act and in the following year a number of them were fined for refusing to pay the education rate.[187]

ERECTION OF THE SCHOOL AT THE QUINTON, IN THE PARISH OF HALES-OWEN.

STATEMENT OF ACCOUNTS.
(*March 25th, 1846.*)

	£	s.	d.		£	s.	d.
Lord Lyttelton, -	40	0	0	Brought forward	£237	15	0
An Anonymous Benefactor,	100	0	0	Mr. John Hodgetts, -	1	0	0
Rev. R. B. Hone, -	10	0	0	Mr. Ward, -	5	0	0
Rev Hugh Matthie, .	3	10	0	Miss Susanna Crawley,	1	0	0
Rev. J. R. Peake, -	5	0	0	Mr. & Mrs. Severne, -	5	0	0
Rev. B W. Savile, -	5	0	0	Miss Hone,		10	0
Mrs. Smith, (*The Grange,*)	5	0	0	A Card, (Mrs. Garbett's)		10	0
A Friend, (*Per Mr. B. Best,*)	25	0	0	J. E. Piercy, Esq. -	5	0	0
Mr Davenport, -	5	0	0	Per Mr. Frith, .		10	0
Mr. Darby, -	5	0	0	Card (*Miss Birch's*) -		17	0
Mr. F. Carter, -	5	0	0	Holly Bush Club,		5	0
Mr. Pixell, -	5	0	0	Black Heath Club, -		3	6
Mr. John Birch, -	5	0	0	The Lords of the Treasury	54	0	0
Mr. R. Tomlinson, -	5	0	0	National Society,	40	0	0
Mr. George Birch, -	5	0	0	Ditto, Second Grant, -	10	0	0
Mr. John Jakeman, -	1	0	0	Diocesan Board, -	25	0	0
Mr. R. Underhill,		5	0	Ditto, Second Grant,	10	0	0
A Friend, -	5	0	0	Collections after Sermons } July, 1841.	26	6	7
Miss Adams, (*Cakemore*)	1	0	0	Committee of Council on } Education	10	0	0
Mr. H. Nichols, -	1	0	0	Balance paid by the } "Anonymous Subscriber,"	22	16	9
Mr Smout, -	1	0	0				
	£237	15	0		£455	13	10

The Treasurer, (the Rev. R. B. Hone,) in account with the Quinton Schools.

Various Contributions as above,	455	13	10	Fittings of temporary School } Rooms,	7	12	0
				Conveyance of Site, -	14	6	2
				Payments to Contractor,	347	15	4
				Well Sinker, -	28	5	2
				Bricks for Well, Stove, &c.	22	15	2
				Architect, -	35	0	0
	£455	13	10		£455	13	10

The Treasurer hopes shortly to print a Balance Sheet of the Quinton Church Accounts. Some Subscriptions are still unpaid.

(*Harris, Typ.*)

At the opening of Quinton National School, the salary of the master was set at £20 per annum, with such extra fees (which given the nature of Quinton's population were presumably negligible) as he was able to collect. Learning was checked by inspection. A report in 1847 found standards of teaching and discipline to be unsatisfactory,[188] perhaps the result of the rapid turnover of staff. At least four masters were separately in post during a single decade in the mid-1800s. Christ Church Baptismal Register records the baptism, on February 2nd 1845, of Emma Ann, daughter of Henry and Marianne Searle, with Henry's occupation being given as Master of Quinton School. The same register for November 5th 1848, records the baptism of Sarah Maria, daughter of Edward Augustus and Maria Gray, of the School House, The Quinton. *Kelly's Directory* of 1850 lists Edward Gray, master; Maria Gray, mistress of the National School, Quinton. By the census of 1851, the residents of the School House had changed again with the arrival of the Bayley family. Head of the household was 60-year-old John Bloomer Bayley,

---

[186] *Christ Church The Quinton Baptismal Register* (02.02.1845) LB
[187] *Quinton Primitive Methodist Quarterly Meeting Minutes* (07.06.1902; 07.03.1903) LB
[188] See Rosser, A.N. (1998) p 125

Quinton National School buildings on plot 50 were extended several times during the 19th century, renamed Quinton Church of England School in 1908 and demolished in 1971.

school master, who lived with his wife Mary Ann (46) school mistress, sons William Standbridge (19), apprentice glazier and Clinton Hill (10), scholar, and daughter Jane (18) of no stated occupation. *Billing's Directory* of 1855 records that the master and mistress of the National School were Mr & Mrs J.H. Huxley. Following this, two teachers (Miss W. and Miss Finch[189]) served the school, prior to the long-term appointment of Quinton-born Aaron Millward (11.02.01), who was in post at the 1861 census and remained until his death in 1888. Quinton's appreciation of his service is recorded on a memorial cross in the churchyard.

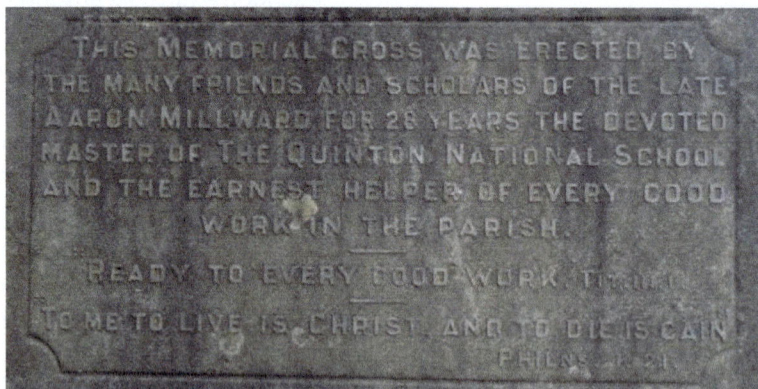

THIS MEMORIAL CROSS WAS ERECTED BY THE MANY FRIENDS AND SCHOLARS OF THE LATE AARON MILLWARD FOR 26 YEARS THE DEVOTED MASTER OF THE QUINTON NATIONAL SCHOOL AND THE EARNEST HELPER OF EVERY GOOD WORK IN THE PARISH.

READY TO EVERY GOOD WORK TITUS III
TO ME TO LIVE IS CHRIST AND TO DIE IS GAIN
PHILAS I 21

7.06   Parsonage   Plot 49 (52°27'45"N 2°00'32"W)

On a plot measuring 1 acre 2 poles, part of Lord Lyttelton's gift, Quinton Parsonage was built in 1841-2 at a cost of £1,000 to a design by Richard Charles Hussey, who specified that it be "in every respect and particular executed in the best and most workmanlike with materials of the best quality."[190] £400 of the required sum came from the bazaar which had been held at Hagley Hall in August 1838, £250 from Queen Anne's Bounty[191] and the remainder from local subscriptions. The house was extended in 1863 and demolished in 1964.

---

[189] Oldfield, Christopher (1866) *A Pastoral Memorandum* cited by Bunting, T. (1990) p 12

[190] Notes to the architect's plans for the parsonage, Shrewsbury Record Office, cited by Rosser, A.N. (1990)

[191] Established in 1704 to augment the livings of poorer clergy, Queen Anne's Bounty was funded from the first year's incomes of clergy newly-appointed to a benefice and from their tithes in subsequent years. Paid to the Pope before the Reformation these funds were afterwards transferred to the Crown. Between 1809 and 1820 available monies were supplemented by parliamentary grants and from 1810 parishes worth less than £50pa were entitled to apply for assistance. The status of Quinton parish is thus illuminated.

Quinton Rectory by Beatrice May Phillips, 1963

The first resident was Rev William Robert Skilton, MA, who was appointed to Quinton in 1842. Unlike his patron, Rev R.B. Hone, Skilton's more lowly status as Perpetual Curate did not qualify him for an entry amongst the gentry or clergy in Cassey's or Melville's *Directories* of the period. Kelly's and Billing's *Directories*, however, do rectify the omission. Born in Edmonton, Middlesex in 1798, Skilton had been awarded his MA at St John's College, Cambridge in 1828. Prior to his arrival in Quinton he had the cure of souls at Walton-on-the-Hill, Surrey where, at the 1841 census, resident with him at the rectory were his wife Maria (born in Dagenham, Essex in 1798) their 14-year-old son, William James, two lodgers, three servants, one visitor and eight pupils between the ages of nine and 15. Shortly after their arrival in Quinton, a daughter, Elizabeth Frances, was born and was baptised by her father at Christ Church on October 2nd 1842.

Present at Quinton Parsonage in 1851 were William and Maria, their 21-year old daughter Sarah Maria, who had been born in Middlesex, Elizabeth Frances and Skilton's sister-in-law, Catherine Biggs, who had been one of the lodgers present in the rectory at Walton-on-the-Hill 10 years earlier. Also present on that occasion had been Esther Humphrey (born 1812, Newdigate, Surrey) one of the two house servants. Evidently Esther accompanied the family on their move to Quinton and was still with them 10 years later. The 1851 household was completed by a second servant, Mary Chinn (30) from Atherstone who, at the previous census had been employed as a domestic servant at Eliza Lewis's Ladies School, Long Street, Atherstone. William and Maria's son, now Rev William James Skilton, was, in 1851, curate at neighbouring Harborne. On May 25th 1853, at Christ Church, Skilton married his daughter Sarah Maria to Joseph Tarn, who had been one of his resident pupils at Walton-on-the-Hill. Four years later, Rev William Skilton left his Quinton appointment and the following year Maria died at Islington. Obviously at the move from Quinton, the Skiltons were unable to accommodate Esther Humphrey who, by 1861 had returned to her native Surrey where she was an inmate at Reigate Union Workhouse. By 1871 she was living with an aunt in Horley.

119

At the census of 1861, Skilton, "clergyman of the Church of England – out of office," was living in Richmond Terrace, Islington, with his daughter Elizabeth and his sister-in-law, Catherine Biggs ("property: railway shares") both of whom had been with him at Ridgacre, and one household servant. 10 years later, at a different Islington address, Elizabeth Skilton and Catherine Biggs were still part of Rev Skilton's household, now joined by another sister-in-law and two household servants. These later homes, like Quinton Parsonage, thus presented an ideal dramatis personae for a sentimental novelette with a clergyman surrounded by admiring and ministering female relatives and other dependants.

Rev William Robert Skilton died on April 15th 1877 at his home in Hungerford Road, Holloway, leaving an estate valued at under £5,000, a not inconsiderable sum for a perpetual curate. His executors were his son, Rev William James Skilton, now Rector of Romford, Essex and his son-in-law, Joseph Tarn of Brunswick Square, St Pancras, Gentleman.[192]

Rev Christopher Oldfield

Skilton's successor in Quinton was Rev Christopher Holroyd Oldfield, born in York in 1821. Educated at St Peter's School, York and Christ's College, Cambridge, where he was awarded his BA in 1850, Oldfield was ordained deacon in Peterborough Cathedral in 1849. Curacies in Wellingborough, Northamptonshire and Brighton, Sussex preceded his appointment as perpetual curate of Quinton in 1857. The following year he returned to St Nicholas Church, Brighton, where he was married to Elizabeth Charlotte Bevan of the same town. At the 1861 census, Christopher and Elizabeth Oldfield were living in Quinton Parsonage with two children, Christopher, born in 1859 in Brighton and baptised at Christ Church The Quinton on August 14th 1859, and Dora, born in 1860 in Quinton, where she was baptised on October 7th 1860. The household was completed by three servants: 42-year-old Sarah James from Hales Owen, cook; 26-year-old Ellen Barber from Caxton, Lincolnshire, nurse maid; 17-year-old Lois Turner from Brighton, housemaid.

In 1861, the perpetual curacy of Quinton was elevated to a rectory, meaning that Christopher Oldfield would no longer be responsible to the rector of Hales Owen and would himself become the recipient of the relevant tithes. Oldfield remained in post in Quinton until his retirement in 1885 to Wivelsfield, Essex, where he died in 1903, his wife having pre-deceased him in 1895. Oldfield's estate, rather more than that of Rev William Skilton, was valued at £6,468 4s 7d. The 28-year incumbency of Rev Christopher Oldfield remains the longest to date of any perpetual curate/rector of Quinton. The insights of his notebook (see, for example, chapter 10 *Innkeepers* on the evils of alcohol) continue to shed a fascinating light on his view of his parish as a dark and wicked place in the mid-1800s.

---

[192] England & Wales, National Probate Calendar (Index of Wills and Administrations), 1858-1966

8   Farms and Farming

Though by the mid-1800s the period of agricultural unrest was largely over, memories of earlier rick burnings were not easily forgotten. The Tithe Commutation Act had replaced payment in kind by rent charges, which still applied to tenant farmers, for not until 1891 did they become the responsibility of land owners. Payments made to landlords, impropriators of great tithes and clergy cut into profits and demanded that farm labour should remain cheaply available. This in turn discouraged expenditure on mechanisation, which consequently was relatively slow to modernise the pattern of farming. The ever-increasing population, which resulted in more mouths to feed, emphasised the need for home-produced food. Following the repeal of the Corn Laws in 1846 more and more previously open land was enclosed and cultivated, leading to the disappearance of the vast majority of open fields, evidence of which is clearly visible on the Quinton tithe map (e.g. plots 1-4,6, W130, W146-W148).

The agricultural picture of Worcestershire in 1854 was captured by a Board of Trade survey[193] of 7,113 occupants of over two acres, which in Quinton would have included 13 named farms (varying in size between 15 and 140 acres) glebe land and holdings of two inn-keepers and a cattle dealer. Though the survey was regarded with some suspicion as a potential means of increasing taxation, 90% of those surveyed in Worcestershire returned the schedules. It was recognised that the "return for livestock is necessarily imperfect as many persons possess cattle who do not occupy land, but purchase food for consumption by their cattle on their own premises or send their cattle out to tack, paying for their keep by the week or season."[194] Though the general picture for Worcestershire was of "a green countryside of small farms, well stocked with cattle and sheep," it was also noted that along the northern edge of the county (including Stourbridge Union of which Quinton was a part) "one could find more striking evidence of the urban influence on land use, a run-down farming area of tiny milk and vegetable holdings."[195] All three comments throw light on the likely state of Quinton's farms.

In the early 1790s the Board of Agriculture instituted a series of county surveys into the state of farming, with a view to identifying means for its improvement. Worcestershire was revisited in 1813 and a detailed portrait of Warley Wigorn's Brand Hall Farm included in William Pitt's report. Though just beyond the Quinton boundary, Brand Hall is close enough geographically, geologically and economically to offer reliable insight into the farms of its near neighbours. It is clear that crops other than those identified in the preambles to the tithe apportionments of Ridgacre and Warley Wigorn townships featured in the local farming cycle. a

> "Brant Hall in the hamlet of Warley Wigorn, in the parish of Hales Owen, Richard Miller tenant on lease. The soil moist clay loam on brashy rock, part lighter loam on clay, some peat bog, now drained, the whole elevated and inclining to cold. Harvest later by a month than the fertile parts of the county. Some of the hills or swells from 7 to 800 feet above sea level. Generally mown to grass and well stocked with sheep and cattle: the former of the Leicester, the latter of the long horn breed. 20 or more (cows) in the dairy. 80 breeding ewes. 7 horses do the business of the farm, including a hackney and breeding mare. Horses black and brown but not heavy, about 15½ hands, employed at all leisure times in drawing muck from

---

[193] Dodd, JP (1979) *Worcestershire Agriculture in the Mid-Nineteenth Century: An analysis of the 1854 Returns*
[194] Op cit, pp 7-8
[195] Op cit, p 24

Birmingham, the distance 6 miles; several hundred tons drawn in a year. This farm by industry and perseverance has been greatly improved and is producing good crops and well supporting a large stock… Mr Miller sows wheat about half upon summer fallow and the other half upon vetch fallow, 2½ bushels per acre or 3 bushels (if late sown) produce 20 to 30 bushels per acre… With respect to barley, from hard tillage and on some moist loam from want of drainage, the average is not more than 20 bushels per acre, but in the well-managed enclosures and after turnips, much more. Oats are grown but in smaller proportion and sometimes sown upon the ploughing of grasslands. Mr Miller generally grows thus from 35-40 bushels per acre; the oats are succeeded by potatoes or winter vetches… Upon Brant Hall estate Mr Miller has executed hollow drains in almost every field. This method has answered extremely well by rendering sound and wholesome a farm formerly cold and springy and which from being sterile and unproductive, now yields good crops of grain or excellent pasture for sheep and cattle."[196]

In Quinton, some 118 out of its total population of 1,047 between 1841 and 1861, were employed in agriculture, ranging from the townships' gentry to farm labourers, generally numbered, like their nail-making brothers and sisters, among the most consistently depressed class of 19th century England.

8.01.01   Four Dwellings Farm

Plan	Field Name	Area			Cultivation	Tithe Payable					
						Vicar			Imp[tor]		
		A	R	P		£	s	d	£	s	d
W67	Four Dwellings Farmhouse (52°27'16"N 2°00'12"W	2	2	15			11	0			
W56	Wall yard, buildings (52°27'06"N 2°00'12"W)		3	27			2	0			
W94	Ivy House, farm & c (52°27'46"N 2°00'27"W)		3	5							
W46	The Warms (52°27'08"N 1°59'42"W)	10	0	26	Arable		10	0	1	11	6
W47	Holly Croft (52°27'04"N 1°59'48"W)	6	3	29	Arable		6	3	1	1	0
W50	Third Leasow (52°27'07"N 1°59'56"W)	8	0	30	Arable		8	0	1	5	2
W58a	Holly Leasow (52°27'06"N 2°00'16"W)	4	0	25	Arable		4	6		15	0
W61	Little White Close (52°27'05"N 2°00'30"W)	5	0	12	Arable		4	10			
W62	Gorsy Piece (52°27'08"N 2°00'18"W)	5	2	24	Arable		5	9	1	3	9
W63	Ten Acres (52°27'11"N 2°00'27"W)	8	0	27	Arable		7	4	1	14	0
W64	Well Close (52°27'14"N 2°00'23"W)	5	3	18	Arable		5	6	1	5	6
W69	Massy Leasow (52°27'24"N 2°00'14"W)	4	3	39	Arable		4	0	1	1	0
W70	Dunn (52°27'23"N 2°00'22"W)	13	0	3	Arable		12	4	2	8	6
W95	Broad Leasow (52°27'45"N 2°00'22"W)	7	3	4	Arable		6	6	1	7	0
W96	Ox Leasow (52°27'42"N 2°00'18"W)	4	2	26	Arable		3	2		10	0
W96a	Windmill Leasow (52°27'43"N 2°00'14"W)	2	2	23	Arable		2	0		9	0
W97	Great B'ham Piece (52°27'45"N 2°00'21"W)	3	3	24	Arable		3	0		14	1
W98	Little B'ham Piece (52°27'46"N 2°00'23"W)	2	2	11	Arable		2	0		9	0

---

[196] Pitt, W (1813) *General View of the Agriculture of the County of Worcester*, pp 30, 77, 86, 194

Plan	Field Name	Area			Cultivation	Tithe Payable				
						Vicar			Imp^{tor}	
		A	R	P		£	s	d	£	s	d
W48	Holly Croft (52°26'59"N 1°59'47"W)	1	3	28	Pasture		3	6			
W49	Little Meadow (52°26'58"N 1°59'56"W)	2	1	33	Pasture		6	0			
W51	Broad Meadow (52°27'02"N 2°00'02"W)	4	2	24	Pasture		12	3			
W52	Half Close (52°27'07"N 2°00'04"W)	5	3	18	Pasture		14	6			
W53	Half Close (52°27'11"N 2°00'06"W)	1	3	29	Pasture		3	0			
W54	Upper Leasow (52°27'11"N 2°00'11"W)	5	0	2	Pasture		14	6			
W55	Dun Leasow (52°27'11"N 2°00'19"W)	4	0	19	Pasture		11	2			
W57	Barn Leasow (52°27'05"N 2°00'07"W)	3	0	12	Pasture		8	2			
W58	Lower Leasow (52°27'03"N 2°00'11"W)	2	1	36	Pasture		5	9			
W59	Low^r Long Meadow (52°26'59"N 2°00'14"W)	4	0	0	Pasture		12	6			
W60	Up^r Long Meadow (52°27'01"N 2°00'29"W)	5	2	0	Pasture		14	0			
W66	Mary's Leasow (52°27'14"N2°00'16"W)	3	3	15	Pasture		8	4			
W68	Harp Leasow (52°27'17"N 2°00'06"W)	4	1	29	Pasture		10	4			
W73	Dwellings Meadow (52°27'18"N 2°00'27"W)	5	2	14	Pasture		12	6			
W92	House Meadow (52°27'45"N 2°00'27"W)	5	1	34	Pasture		12	4			
		158	1	31		12	7	0	15	14	6

Four Dwellings, the largest of Quinton's farms, both in acreage and number of employees, lay entirely within the township of Warley Wigorn, with six of its 30 fields separated from the bulk of the holding by Lower Quinton Farm. Warley Wigorn tithe apportionments and censuses of 1841 – 1861 confirm that the tenant was Joseph Davenport, who leased the land from William Spurrier. (4.01) However, Ridgacre tithe apportionments list John Davenport as occupier of plot 87 (52°27'48"N 2°00'23"W), *Meadow*, pasture measuring 2 acres 1 rood 11 poles, also rented from William Spurrier, which attracted 5s tithe rent payable to the Vicar of Hales Owen. Though separated from plot W98 only by the turnpike road, plot 87 was not named as part of Four Dwellings farm. Davenport's total holding included both Four Dwellings and Ivy House farmhouses: the first where he lived and the second let to under-tenants. Once two discrete farms, in the 20th century they were again treated separately, the area of Ivy House Farm being unmistakably identified as plots W92 and W95-W98 in a conveyance of December 1909.[197]

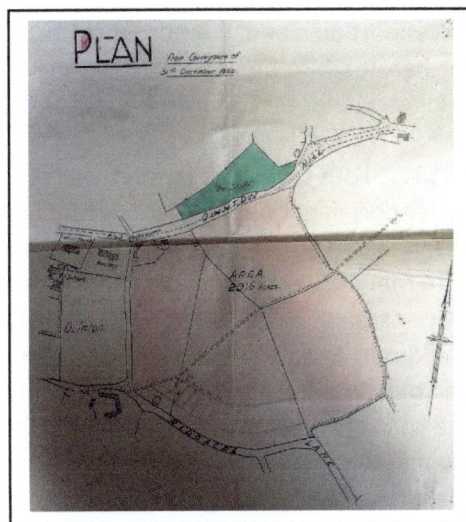

[197] Conveyance: Edward Fairfax Studd to Trustees Of the Birmingham Freehold Land Society: All that farm and lands known as The Ivy House Farm situate in the Parish of Halesowen in the County of Worcester (with the exception of a piece of pasture land in Ridgacre known The Stuff containing 2 acres 1 rood and 4 perches or thereabouts) containing in the whole by admeasurement 29½ acres or thereabouts. (31.12.1909) QLHS

On October 1st 1782, at Bromsgrove, John Davenport married Bridget Smith. Their son, Joseph, was baptised at Northfield on February 8th 1796. That John Davenport [E][198] was established at Four Dwellings by 1826 is confirmed by an advertisement in the *Birmingham Chronicle*.

> A most desirable and pleasant country residence to be let at Lady Day next situate at The Quinton adjoining the Turnpike road… consisting of a Hall, two Parlours, Dining Room, Kitchen, Brewhouse, two Cellars, four Chambers and three Attics, with Kitchen Garden and Pleasure Ground, Stabling, Gig-house, Piggeries and other Appurtenances. It is eminently situated upon a dry, healthy spot, commanding a most beautiful and extensive prospect and is calculated for the residence of a genteel family. For further particulars apply to John Davenport, Four Dwellings, Warley Wigorn, near The Quinton aforesaid.[199]

Ten years later, on June 12th 1836, the *Worcester Journal* announced the marriage "at Himbleton, by the Rev Mr Vernon, Joseph Davenport of Quinton near Birmingham, to Jane daughter of Mr Chambers of the former place." When a subscription towards a new organ in Hales Owen Parish Church was opened in 1840, a donation of 10/- from Mr Davenport was one of three contributions from Quinton.[200]

At the 1841 census John, Bridget, Joseph and Jane Davenport were all resident at plot W67, with Joseph listed as a farmer and John of independent means. Two agricultural labourers, 20-year-old John Davenport and 15-year old James Davenport (whom the next census would reveal to be Joseph's nephew, born in Combe Lovett, Worcestershire) also lived at the farm. Later that year, Bridget Davenport died and was buried at Christ Church on December 6th. The family were of sufficient status for her death to be announced in the press: "Sincerely regretted by her family and friends, aged 89, Bridget wife of Mr John Davenport of Quinton near Halesowen."[201]

In 1841, Four Dwellings farmhouse returned a large household. In addition to the six members of the Davenport family were eight further residents. 25-year-old merchant, John Robinson and his wife Susan (25), were both born within the county. By 1851 they lived in Ravenhurst Street, Deritend, Aston, with their three children and a female servant. John's occupation was given as nail merchant, his birthplace as Dudley, and Susan's as Droitwich. As their eldest child was born in Birmingham in 1843, John and Susan Robinson had clearly left Four Dwellings by that date. Sarah Chambers, also 25 years old and of independent means, was most likely Jane Davenport's sister. William Bennett (20), born outside the county and employed as an agricultural labourer at Four Dwellings in 1841 appears to have been plying the same trade 10 years later, then living with his wife, Hannah, at Wythall Heath, Kings Norton. His birthplace is then given as Bidford, Warwickshire. 15-year-old Isaac Willis, also born outside the county and an agricultural labourer, in 1851 may well have been agricultural labourer Isaac Wallis, living with his sister, wife and two children in Badgworth, Gloucestershire, where he was born. Four Dwellings' final agricultural labourer in 1841 was 25-year-old Richard Yates, born within the county.

---

[198] As owner/occupier of freehold land in Ridgacre township. See 13.01
[199] *Birmingham Chronicle* (02.03.1826) – the description matches that of Ivy House (12.04.11)
[200] Hone, R.B. pp 35-38 DALHC (The organ cost an estimated £330.)
[201] *Worcestershire Chronicle* (15.12.1841)

He too was one of Quinton's temporary residents. By 1851, still working as an agricultural labourer, he appears to have been living with his wife and five children in Timberhouses Lane, Bromsgrove. His birthplace is revealed as Alvechurch. The remaining two members of the 1841 household were female servants Jane Dyer (12) and Jane Hynett (20). Ten years later Jane Dyer was still working as a servant, then in the home of coach harness plater John Oakes in Lee Bank Road, Edgbaston. The death of a Jane Hinett was registered at Dudley in October quarter, 1847. John Davenport died on March 30th 1844 and was buried at Christ Church The Quinton six days later. His death, like that of his late wife, was also announced in the press.[202]

The 1851 census reveals that Joseph Davenport was born in Northfield and Jane in Droitwich. He is described as farmer of 154 acres employing eight labourers, of whom six are listed at Four Dwellings farmhouse. Still present from 10 years previously was James Davenport; the other five were new arrivals. Widower George Pollard (40), born in Warwick, William Andrews (27) and John Gould (19) both born in Hales Owen, with William Hall (18) and Richard Hall (10), both born in Frankley, had all left Four Dwellings 10 years later. Only one female servant served the household in 1951: 17-year-old Emma Millward, daughter of Robert and Ann Millward (11.02.01). On July 25th 1852, Mary Millward, daughter of Emma, servant of Quinton, was baptised at Hales Owen Parish Church. The household was completed by 6-year-old James Davenport, nephew, listed as born in Dudley and still at school. In December 1852, another Davenport death was announced in the press. "December 17th, in her 29th year, sincerely regretted by her relatives and friends, Jane the beloved wife of Mr Joseph Davenport of the Quinton, near Halesowen."[203] Jane Davenport was buried at Christ Church on December 23rd 1852, when her age was entered into the register as 38. The 1841 census had listed her as 20, the 1851 census as 35. Just over three years later, the marriage of Joseph Davenport and Mary Ann Roper was registered at West Bromwich in January quarter 1856.

By 1861 Four Dwellings farm was listed as 165 acres upon which Joseph Davenport employed seven men and two boys. His household consisted of himself, his 32-year-old wife, Mary, his 17-year-old nephew, James Davenport, now working as a shepherd, along with his 7-year-old niece, Clara Walters from Bilston. The resident servants all had specific roles. Ann Darby (18) from Oldbury was house maid; Amelia Stokes (21) from West Bromwich, dairy maid; John Holden (20) from Oxfordshire, cowman; Thomas Perkins (14) from Northfield, under cowman and Thomas Rookes (21) from Rosscommon, Ireland, agricultural labourer.

John Davenport died aged 83 in 1879 and was buried at Christ Church on February 18th. His personal estate was valued at under £800.[204] His widow continued to manage the farm until 1884, after which it remained in the hands of William Clay until World War I. Following this, Birmingham City Council intervened. "Smallholdings for ex-servicemen: The Council having considered the provisions of the draft Birmingham Corporation Bill, approved the purchase of... Windmill and Ridgacre Farms Quinton (143 acres) at £80 per acre and the Four Dwellings Farm, Quinton (131 acres) for the sum of £8,580."[205]

---

[202] *Birmingham Journal* (13.04.1844)
[203] *Worcester Journal* (23.12.1852)
[204] Proved at Worcester (24.05.1879)
[205] *Birmingham Mail* (10.12.1918)

Four Dwellings Farm photographed 1940s

8.01.02　Lower Quinton Farm

Plan	Field Name	Area			Cultivation	Tithe Payable	
						Vicar	Imp^{tor}
		A	R	P		£　s　d	£　s　d
Property of Lord Lyttelton							
W91	House, Bdgs &c (52°27'39"N 2°00'31"W)	1	0	37			
27	Part of Foldyard (52°27'39"N 2°00'33"W)			26			
120	Farm House (52°27'34"N 1°59'56"W)			38			
22	Marl Pit (52°27'37"N 2°00'43"W)			26			
64	Foredrove (52°27'53"N 2°01'00"W)		1	8			
W135	Road (52°27'56"N 2°01'57"W)		1	0			
15	Jack Clerk's Meadow (52°27'43"N 2°01'25"W)	1	1	12	Arable	10	
16	Further Mancroft (52°27'45"N 2°01'20"W)	7	0	35	Arable	6　0	
17	Four Acres (52°27'41"N 2°01'11"W)	4	0	5	Arable	2　8	
23	Far Rough Meadow (52°27'34"N 2°00'44"W)	3	2	24	Arable	3　5	
42	Hither Mancroft (52°27'45"N 2°01'04"W)	4	0	36	Arable	2　9	
103	Taylor's Close (52°27'36"N 1°59'582W)	1	0	0	Arable	1　5	
105	Windmill Piece (52°27'39"N 2°00'09"W)	2	2	3	Arable	2　9	
106	Bonfire Leasow (52°27'36"N 2°00'15"W)	3	3	28	Arable	3　0	
108	Taylor's Croft (52°27'35"N 2°00'07"W)	4	0	1	Arable	4　0	
121	Dafodil Leasow (52°27'33"N 1°59'54"W)	2	1	27	Arable	2　0	
192	Lower Leasow (52°27'32"N 1°59'49"W)	1	3	28	Arable	1　9	
195	Bridge Leasow (52°27'35"N 1°59'47"W)	4	1	16	Arable	4　0	
W83	Furth' Green Croft (52°27'27"N 2°00'22"W)	5	3	11	Arable	10　0	
W84	Hither Green Croft (52°27'29"N 2°00'20"W)	3	3	9	Arable	3　6	
W88	Upper Meadow (52°27'38"N 2°00'25"W)	2	2	30	Arable	3　6	

Plan	Field Name	Area			Cultivation	Tithe Payable			
						Vicar		Imp^{tor}	
		A	R	P		£ s d		£ s d	
W136	Duncemoor Wood (52°28'05"N 2°01'03"W)	13	1	13	Arable	17 0			
6	Part Quinton Field (52°27'54"N 2°01'19"W)	2	0	0	Pasture	5 0			
18	Mancroft Meadow (52°27'40"N 2°00'57"W)	1	3	33	Pasture	5 0			
26	Rough Meadow (52°27'38"N 2°00'36"W)	7	2	10	Pasture	1 0 2			
28	The Close (52°27'40"N 2°00'43"W)		3	36	Pasture	8			
109	The Park (52°27'35"N 2°00'03"W)	3	1	2	Pasture	9 3			
110	Little Leasow (52°27'32"N 2°00'00"W)	1	1	5	Pasture	3 0			
119	The Meadow (52°27'33"N 1°59'57"W)	2	1	33	Pasture	6 4			
191	Gosty Leasow (52°27'33"N 1°59'45"W)	3	0	33	Pasture	7 6			
193	Upper Leasow (52°27'34"N 1°59'54"W)	2	1	34	Pasture	6 0			
W89	Big Meadow (52°27'38"N 2°00'30"W)	5	3	29	Pasture	1 4 6			
		99	2	28		7 16 0			
Property of Aaron White									
W75	Dwelling Big Meadow Rough (52°27'20"N 2°00'32"W)		1	7					
W76	House, bdgs & c (52°27'19"N 2°00'27"W)			33					
W78	Pound Close (52°27'26"N 2°00'25"W)	2	0	9	Arable	2 0		7 6	
W80	Long Meadow (52°27'29"N 2°00'33"W)	3	0	13	Arable	3 0		11 0	
W81	Coneybury (52°27'31"N 2°00'30"W)	3	3	29	Arable	2 6		15 0	
W82	Swans Field (52°27'31"N 2°00'27"W)	4	3	20	Arable	3 6		16 0	
24	Up^r Golds Meadow (52°27'31"N 2°00'42"W)	2	1	10	Pasture	4 4			
25	Lw^r Golds Meadow (52°27'26"N 2°00'39"W)	2	0	3	Pasture	3 8			
W74	Dwellings Big M'w (52°27'21"N 2°00'31"W)	4	2	27	Pasture	12 0			
W77	Pigsty Meadow (52°27'21"N 2°00'28"W)	3	0	3	Pasture	9 6			
W79	Little Meadow (52°27'23"N 2°00'31"W)	1	0	19	Pasture	3 0			
		23	1	0		1 15 6		2 9 6	
Property of George White									
W129	In Lower Horseletts (52°27'54"N 2°01'39"W)		3	36	Arable	6		4 0	
W85	Top Croft (52°27'36"N 2°00'19"W)	4	2	4	Pasture	11 6			
W130	In Up^r Quinton F'ld (52°27'54"N 2°01'21"W)	1	1	24	Pasture	3 0			
		6	3	24		15 0		4 0	
Property of John White									
3	Cotterill's Innage (52°27'59"N 2°01'24"W)	4	2	24	Arable	3 0		16 6	
W148	Little Innage (52°27'59"N 2°01'28"W)	1	0	16	Arable	1 0		4 0	
W127	In Milestone Piece (52°27'49"N 2°00'59"W)			13	Pasture	3			
W128	In Milestone Piece (52°27'49"N 2°01.03"W)			24	Pasture	6			
W131	In 1st Quinton Field (52°27'52"N 2°01'05"W)			36	Pasture	6			
W132	In 1st Quinton Field (52°27'56"N 2°01'08"W)		3	26	Pasture	2 0			
W133	In 1st Quinton Field (52°27'55"N 2°01'03"W)	1	0	25	Pasture	3 6			

Plan	Field Name	Area			Cultivation	Tithe Payable					
						Vicar			Imp[tor]		
		A	R	P		£	s	d	£	s	d
W134	In First Innage (52°27'57"N 2°01'08"W)			37	Pasture			6			
W146	The Lunt (52°28'04"N 2°01"33"W)	4	1	27	Pasture		10	0			
W147	Noble's Innage (52°28'01"N 2°01'29"W)	1	2	7	Pasture		3	6			
		9	3	11		1	18	3	1	0	6
		139	2	23		12	4	9	3	14	0

Unlike Four Dwellings Farm, Lower Quinton Farm was divided between the townships of Ridgacre and Warley Wigorn. With the bulk of its land concentrated around the farmhouse and resembling an inverted L, the farm also included five plots at the western edge of the map, near the village centre, with a number of strips in Quinton Field in the north west corner of the map. Cotterill's Innage, bequeathed to Henry Foley Macdonald by Ambrose Foley, by 1844 belonged to John White and was the only Ridgacre field on Lower Quinton Farm to attract a tithe payment to Lord Lyttelton. The anomaly of Quinton's division between two townships is seen in the farmhouse (W91) and yard (27) where the house lay in Warley Wigorn and the adjoining foldyard in Ridgacre. Lower Quinton's farmhouse survived until the 1960s as Pax Hall. Lower Quinton Farm also housed a second farmhouse (120) available for sub-letting.[206] The 1841 census shows Lower Quinton farmer as George White; by the time of the tithe awards he has been replaced by Thomas White, who remains the occupant

Pax Hall shortly before demolition.

in 1851 and 1861. A significant proportion of the farm was family-owned. Plots W74-W82 assigned to Aaron White in the tithe award (even though he had been dead for over 20 years) had once been part of Four Dwellings Farm. (8.01.01)

---

[206] The occupancy of the house at plot 120 is uncertain. In 1841 eight households were not associated with plots: Sarah Gatesfield (8.02.03), George Williams (11.06.01), John Read (12.03.04), Mary James (12.04.07), Richard Ancon (8.02.01), Francis Hall (8.02.02), Edward Breton (11.01.01) and Joseph Butler (12.10.07). The last four were enumerated consecutively immediately after plot 217. The most likely occupant in 1851 seems to be James Pearman (9.01.01), enumerated immediately after Thomas White. With the Ridgacre/Warley Wigorn boundary cutting through Lower Quinton farmyard, an enumerator's inadvertent transposition of a resident from one township to another would not be surprising.

.

The Whites, however, were not new arrivals in Quinton, having appeared in various official returns throughout the late 17th, 18th and early 19th centuries. Admitted to feoffment of Ridgacre land within the manor of Hales Owen in 1671, various members of the family regularly appear in the Manor Suit Rolls, Warley Wigorn and Ridgacre Land Tax lists. Aaron White was regularly assessed at 12s 4d during the 1780s, though this had increased to £4 7s 0¾d by 1798 and fallen back to £1 8s 11¾d in 1822.[207] Apart from the arable and livestock which Lower Quinton Farm supported, there is evidence that Aaron White husbanded his land in other ways. At an auction at Hagley's Lyttelton Arms on October 29th 1810, included in ten lots of timber "standing upon lands near Hales Owen," was Lot IV – 12 Ash, 4 Beech, upon Mr Aaron White's Farm at Ridgacre.[208]

The 1841 household, for so large a farm, was meagre, consisting of 20-year-old farmer George White, two female servants: Mary Mander (30) and Mary Lawrence (13), and two agricultural labourers: Edwin Millard (15) James Furnes (13), all born within the county. By 1845 George White had left Lower Quinton Farm and been replaced by Thomas White, the son of John and Sarah White. On June 5th 1844 Thomas White (25) was married by licence to 19-year-old Maria, daughter of farmer John Hodgetts, at Christ Church.[209] Unusually for Quinton at this period, all of the principals at this marriage were able to sign their names. Between 1845 and 1851 three of Thomas and Maria's children were baptised at Christ Church: John Hodgetts (July 12th 1845), Lucy (January 17th 1849) and Thomas (March 12th 1851), and one (Ann-Maria) was buried there on January 31st 1847, during her father's term of office as Vicar's Warden. Shortly after this, on September 12th 1847, at the Chapel of St Michael, Bartley Green, Anne Maria White, daughter of farmer Thomas and Maria White, of Quinton, Harborne, was baptised – a very rapid recycling of forenames for this, the only one of Thomas and Maria's children not baptised at Christ Church The Quinton.

In 1845 the sale of part of Lower Quinton Farm was advertised. This consisted of that portion of the tithe award in the name of Aaron White, assessed at a total of 27 acres 2 roods 13 poles, some 4 acres 1 rood 3 poles greater than the tithe calculation. As in Aaron White's will the land is called Four Dwellings. Though otherwise surrounded by Lower Quinton farm, White's land also bordered plots W70 and W73 of Four Dwellings Farm.

> Freehold estate in Warley Wigorn and Ridgacre to be sold by auction at the Red Lion Inn, Perry Hill near Halesowen, on Friday 17th October 1845. All that freehold estate called or known by the name of the Four Dwellings, situate near to the Quinton in the hamlet of Warley Wigorn and in the township of Ridgacre now in the occupation of Mr John White.[210]

In 1851, the White household consisted of Thomas (32), Maria (26), Ann (4), Lucy (3) and Thomas (2 months). John Hodgetts White was not listed. Five servants were also present: Hannah Garner (16) from Hill Top, nurse to baby Thomas; Maria Smith (22), dairy maid from Bromsgrove; William Gibbs (29), waggoner from Church Honey Court; Andrew Allen (16) stable boy from Hanbury; Joseph Coal (18), cowman from Worcester. In 1861 Gibbs, Allen and Coal were all still working as agricultural

---

[207] E.G mss 705.1090; 4600/507; 4600/870 WAAS
[208] *Worcester Journal* (25.10. 1810)
[209] See Footnote 383 p 219
[210] *Aris's Birmingham Gazette* (06.10.1845)

labourers: William Gibbs, now married, but not living with his wife, [211] lodging in Bell Lane, Stourbridge; Andrew Allen with his own household in Crowle; Joseph Coal, returned to his family home at Tibberton. Hannah Garner had married James Walters at Christ Church on January 4th 1857 and in by 1861 was living in Bristnall Fields, Warley Wigorn. Maria Smith has not been positively identified. [212]

Thomas White in 1861 was returned in the census as farmer of 150 acres employing four men and four boys. Present in the farmhouse were his wife, Maria, eldest son, John, employed on the farm, eldest daughter, Lucy, employed at home and Thomas, who had been a baby at the previous census, now at school. Four more children had been born to Thomas and Maria during the past decade, all of whom had been baptised at Christ Church: Eliza (March 6th 1853), Edward (March 12th 1856), Frederick (March 2nd 1858) and George (November 11th 1859). The household was completed by 23-year-old dairymaid Elizabeth Butler, 15-year-old carter William Rutland and visitor 16-year-old office clerk Alfred Powers from Birmingham. Alfred Powers was the son of landed proprietor Joseph Powers, who was the grandson of Aaron and Nanny White and thus a relative of Thomas White. Lower Quinton Farm's tenancy by the White family ended in 1872 after the following press announcement.

> Messrs Cheshire & Gibson have received instructions from the Rt Hon Lord Lyttelton to offer for sale by auction at the Great Western Hotel, Birmingham, on Tuesday 20th June, the following highly valuable freehold estates and accommodation lands situate at the Quinton in the townships of Ridgacre and Warley Wigorn with all the mines and minerals therein and thereunder and the farmhouse and homestead known as the Lower Quinton Farm in the occupation of Thomas White as yearly tenant. The whole of the above lots are freehold and tithe free and within two and a half miles of the boundary of the City of Birmingham. The lands are elevated, commanding extensive views over the Lickey and Clent Hills, are rapidly improving in value, and well adapted for the erection of suburban residences.[213]

In the detailed inventory of eight lots which followed, Lot 3 – Lower Quinton Farmhouse and surrounding land totalling some 21 acres was described as bounded by lands belonging to Mr Alfred Powers and the executors of John White.

8.01.03   Redhall Farm

Plot	Field Name	Area			Cultivation	Tithe Payable		
						Vicar		
		A	R	P		£	s	d
209	Farm House, Yard (52°27'38"N 1°59'08"W)	1	2	13				
176	L^r Hannah Green (52°27'26"N 1°59'35"W)	5	0	39	Arable		5	6
182	Lunt Leasow (52°27'29"N 1°59'35"W)	3	0	37	Arable		2	2

[211] On February 17th 1856 William Gibbs of Warley Wigorn married Elizabeth Meredith of Ridgacre at Christ Church The Quinton.

[212] Of the two possible candidates, born in Bromsgrove and of the right age, one was a nail-maker, boarded in the home of James Mole in Strand, Bromsgrove; the other, a screw-maker lodged at 94 High Street, Kinver.

[213] *Birmingham Daily Post* (15.06.1872)

Plot	Field Name	Area			Cultivation	Tithe Payable Vicar		
		A	R	P		£	s	d
183	Field (52°27′29″N 1°59′29″W)	1	3	12	Arable		1	2
184	World's End L'ow (52°27′26″N 1°59′26″W)	7	0	12	Arable		4	10
185	Ewe's Well L'ow (52°27′30″N 1°59′26″W)	5	3	33	Arable		4	0
186	Pit's Wood L'ow (52°27′34″N 1°59′26″W)	4	1	10	Arable		3	0
187	The Sling (52°27′37″N 1°59′35″W)	3	3	32	Arable		4	0
200	The Muttons (52°27′43″N 1°59′38″W)	3	2	34	Arable		2	6
203	Great Ox Leasow (52°27′41″N 1°59′32″W)	7	3	27	Arable		5	0
207	Ox Leasow (52°27′40″N 1°59′22″W)	7	1	2	Arable		16	0
212	Great Wood L'ow (52°27′44″N 1°59′07″W)	5	1	3	Arable		10	6
213	2nd Wood Leasow (52°27′46″N 1°59′13″W)	4	1	20	Arable		3	2
224	Upper Tolly L'ow (52°27′51″N 1°59′14″W)	3	2	10	Arable		2	4
225	Square Leasow (52°27′47″N 1°59′26″W)	4	2	3	Arable		3	0
173	World's End Meadow (52°27′22″N 1°59′28″W)	3	2	21	Pasture		4	10
181	Big Leasow (52°27′34″N 1°59′35″W)	7	1	38	Pasture		14	0
199	Aldridge Meadow (52°27′44″N 1°59′44″W)	4	2	2	Pasture		11	0
206	Two Hill Leasow (52°27′44″N 1°59′27″W)	5	0	36	Pasture		13	0
208	Little Meadow (52°27′36″N 1°59′17″W)	2	3	18	Pasture		6	3
210	House Meadow (52°27′38″N 1°59′03″W)	4	1	22	Pasture		12	0
211	Barn Close (52°27′41″N 1°59′14″W)	3	1	26	Pasture		9	1
226	Smart's Leasow (52°27′48″N 1°59′26″W)	1	2	18	Pasture		3	2
227	Smart's Piece (52°27′49″N 1°59′19″W)	1	0	4	Pasture		2	0
231	Road Leasow (52°27′51″N 1°59′20″W)		1	7	Pasture			
		104	0	39		7	0	6
Property of Lord Lyttelton								
214	Redhill Piece (52°27′51″N 1°59′03″W)	17	2	2	Arable		18	0
236	Redhill Piece (52°27′50″N 1°59′12″W)	4	3	30	Arable		5	0
		22	1	32		1	3	0
		126	2	31		8	3	6

Hales Owen Abbey's Grange Farm within Ridgacre township, Redhall (Radewell, Radewelle, Radwall, Radwalle, Redhill, Rudall, Rudhall, Rudhalle – the derivation of which is thought to be 'red spring') Farm was self-evidently an ancient establishment. It is listed in *Taxatio Ecclesiastica* (1291) as measuring 1 carucate worth 10s. This was a grant by Pope Nicholas IV to King Edward I of one tenth of the revenue of English benefices for a period of six years to defray the cost of an expedition to the Holy Land. Grange farms, which were at first worked by lay brothers of the abbey or by paid grange keepers, were eventually let out on long leases. Early in the 15th century Radewell was included in a 60-year lease to the Vicar of Kidderminster. In 1499, when the total rent paid by tenants of Hales Owen Abbey was

£136 9s 10d, Radewell Grange's contribution amounted to £2 13s 8d.[214] Also during the reign of King Henry VII, Bishop Lyttelton notes, Radewelle was let for 4 marks. In 1522 the Abbot issued a 60-year lease to William and Jane Grene of Radwalle Grange for Nether Radwall pasture. In October 1706, the accounts of the Lyttelton estate record a payment received from John Birch for the surrender of a house and land in Ridgacre. Throughout the 18th century the names of John, George and Thomas Birch in Ridgacre Suit Rolls, Land Taxes and Lyttelton rent accounts sometimes specifically cite Redall.[215]

Redhall Farmhouse photographed in 1930s

Owner of this Ridgacre farm (listed in contemporary *Kelly's* and *Cassey's Directories* as *Redhill* Farm) in the mid-1800s was George Birch. [E,J][216] With the exception of two plots, which he rented from Lord Lyttelton, all of the land farmed by Birch on this tithe map was his own and attracted tithe rent to the Vicar of Hales Owen. Like all Ridgacre farmers, George Birch paid more in tithe rental for pasture land (2s.2d per acre on average) than for arable (1s per acre). Birch was fortunate, however, in that his payments were made only to the Vicar as those farmers who paid rental to Lord Lyttelton as Impropriator of the Great Tithes paid anything between twice and six times as much for the same plot of land to Lyttelton than to the Vicar.

Aged 48 at the census of 1841, George Birch, who was born at Redhall, lived with his wife Mary (35), whom he had married at Hales Owen Parish Church on October 7th 1828. Their son, George, had been baptised at Hales Owen on March 14th 1840 and buried there six days later. Elysa Beach (23) assisted in the farm house, whilst John Hemus (38), William Watkins (35), Charles Watkins (18) and Joseph Reynolds (17), all born within the county, lived in as farm labourers. On the appointment of Rev William Skilton as Perpetual Curate of Quinton in 1842, George Birch was elected (on the proposal of Henry Foley Macdonald) as the first Peoples' Warden. Interestingly, in the list of subscribers to Hales Owen Church's organ fund, it is Mrs Birch of Redhall who contributed 10s, the only Ridgacre lady in the list.[217]

By the census of 1851, two farm servants - Richard Styles (27) and Thomas Corbett (26) both of South Lyttelton lived at Redhall Farm, as did house servant Mary Simmons (20) and Martha Aston (71), employed as a monthly nurse! These two female servants both came from Lapworth. None of Redhall's resident servants remained long in Ridgacre. By 1851, Joseph Reynolds was a farm labourer at Yardley

---

[214] Hales Owen Abbey Rent Roll 1500
[215] Ms 351484 LB
[216] As owner/occupier of freehold land in Ridgacre township. See 13.01 and Juror at Amy Read Inquest. See 13.02
[217] Hone, R.B., pp 35-38 DALHC

and had moved on to Sare Hole by 1861. Neither William Watkins nor Richard Styles stayed with agriculture, Watkins becoming a labourer for the parish of Oldbury (1861) and Styles a labourer in a Smethwick ironworks (1881). Unskilled work was clearly transferable. In 1851, in addition to George and Mary Birch, four children were included in Redhall Farm's census return. Ann (19) and Elizabeth (16), who had not been listed in 1841, along with two younger children. Hannah (9) and Thomas (1 month) had both been baptised at Christ Church The Quinton, Hannah on September 11th 1841 and Thomas on April 16th 1851. On October 2nd 1856 at Christ Church, Ann Birch, married George Bramich, son of Thomas Bramich of Beech Lane, Harborne. (6.02) On February 17th of the following year, also at Christ Church, Elizabeth Birch married miller William Avery of Alvechurch.

George Birch died in 1853 and in his will[218] appointed three trustees to administer the estate, *"all my freehold lands, buildings, messuages and hereditaments situated at or near to Redhall in the Parish of Hales Owen,"* until Thomas George Wyrley Birch came of age. He left to his wife £30 and *"all the wine, liquor and housekeeping stores which shall belong to us at the time of my death,"* plus an annuity of £250, terminating should she re-marry. Mary was also able to choose for her lifetime's use items from among his books, pictures, plate and household furniture, all of which was held in trust for Thomas, who was specifically left *"my silver tankard, marked with the name George Birch."* His daughter Hannah received *"my other silver tankard marked with the name John Birch."* Provision was made for any other children who may have been living at the time of his death. The trustees were directed to repair and improve all land and buildings on any part of the estate and to out-lease where necessary, but were forbidden to sell or mortgage the Redhall lands unless Thomas should die before the age of 21. They were also given power to acquire additional land in England and Wales. This clause was enacted when in 1872 (having attained his majority) Thomas purchased 3 acres 20 poles of land fronting the lane from Harborne to Perry Hill, with an estimated rental value of £14. This was in addition to *The Return of Worcestershire Landowners (1873)* calculation of George Birch's estate at 176 acres 2 roods 8 poles with a gross estimated rental of £609.10s. In 1875, Thomas George Wyrley Birch completed the purchase of Lower Ridgacre Farm (8.11) from Mark Barker, one of the trustees of his father's will.

After George Birch's death, Redhall farm was rented out to a series of tenants, beginning with Thomas Oakley. Described as a 'landed proprietor' in the 1861 census, Mary Birch (who died in 1884) was living in Perry Hill with Hannah and Thomas. The following year, in the church where she had been baptised, Hannah Birch married the family's resident groom Henry Oakley, from Beoley near Redditch. Never again residing in Ridgacre, Thomas George Wyrley Birch, whom subsequent censuses identify as 'living on his own means,' died in 1908. Under the terms of his will, his widow Emma, with their four children as her trustees, became tenant for life of Redhall Farm. It was she who finally sold it for £18,000 in 1933 to building contractor John White for housing development, ending both the Birch family's ownership of the land and its agricultural use. The Redhall name is commemorated in Redhall Road at the extreme north-north-east of the ancient farm.

---

[218] Prerogative Court of Canterbury Will Registers, Class PROB11, Piece 2182

8.01.04 (Upper) Ridgacre Farm

Plan	Field Name	Area			Cultivation	Tithe Payable					
						Vicar			Imp^{tor}		
		A	R	P		£	s	d	£	s	d
113	Farm House, Bdgs (52°27'25"N 2°00'10"W)	1	1	37							
114	Lane (52°27'22"N 2°00'07"W)		1	30							
129	Yell Leasow (52°27'22"N 1°59'58"W)	2	2	2	Arable		2	0		13	0
130	Up^r Ridgacre Field (52°27'18"N 2°00'03"W)	6	0	7	Arable		6	0	1	4	0
131	Low^r Ridgacre Field (52°27'13"N 2°00'03"W)	7	2	29	Arable		8	0	1	9	0
132	Old Meadow (52°27'13"N 1°59'58"W)	4	1	31	Arable		7	9			
133	Smooth Moor (52°27'10"N 1°59'47"W)	4	1	29	Arable		3	0		13	1
134	Big Rye Hill (52°27'15"N 1°59'54"W)	6	3	19	Arable		4	4	1	3	3
136	Rushy Piece (52°27'20"N 1°59'57"W)	2	3	18	Arable		2	6		14	6
137	Little Rye Hill (52°27'18"N 1°59'56"W)	4	0	38	Arable		2	8		14	8
138	Brickkiln Leasow (52°27'26"N 1°59'42"W)	8	0	5	Arable		5	6	1	3	6
139	Broad Leasow (52°27'26"N 1°59'38"W)	6	1	23	Arable		4	4		18	6
140	Piece behind Powells (52°27'21"N 1°59'38"W)	4	3	19	Arable		3	8		14	6
107	Far Meadow (52°27'33"N 2°00'12"W)	4	0	37	Pasture		8	8			
111	Old House Meadow (52°27'29"N 2°00'11"W)	5	0	35	Pasture		10	7			
115	Ridgacre Meadow (52°27'25"N 2°00'06"W)	6	3	25	Pasture		17	7			
135	The Sling (52°27'19"N 1°59'58"W)	2	2	16	Pasture		5	1			
141	The Warms (52°27'15"N 1°59'43"W)	3	3	29	Pasture		8	4			
		83	0	29		5	0	0	9	8	0

19th century sketches of (Upper) Ridgacre Farm – artist unknown

James Wragg (*Ragg* in the tithe apportionments) leased his mixed acreage farm from the trustees of the estate of Ferdinando Smith. Tithe rents were payable on all of his fields to the Vicar of Hales Owen, and additionally on all his arable except *Old Meadow* to Lord Lyttelton.

On January 23rd 1746, Ferdinando, son of William and Ann Smith of Ridgacre, was baptised at Hales Owen Parish Church. His mother was the eldest sister and co-heir of Ferdinando Lea 11th Lord Dudley. On her brother's death in 1757, Ann Smith inherited Hales Owen Grange, subsequently styling herself Baroness Dudley. Her elevation naturally also raised her husband, who in the 1766 Manor Suit Roll for Ridgacre is listed along with his son, as William Smith, gent, and Ferdinando Smith, gent. Ann Smith, Baroness Dudley, died in 1762 and William Smith in 1784. His will makes clear the terms under which he had inherited. "I William Smith of ye Grange in ye Parish of Halesowen in the County of Salop make this my last will & testament in manner & form following. That is to Say I give to my daughter Frances Smith & to her heirs for ever six hundred pounds given at my disposal to any child or children that were living at my death in ye marriage writings settled on my wife…"[219] A codicil to the will, proved at Worcester on June 15th 1784, refers to Smith's estate at the Authorn (Hawthorns) in the parish of Hales Owen. Ann and William Smith's son, Ferdinando, died in 1794 and was buried at Hales Owen Parish Church on January 13th. His estate was inherited by his son, another Ferdinando. The 1822 Land Tax for Ridgacre lists property owned by F. Smith Esq and occupied by Thomas Padmore [E],[220] assessed at £2 9s 11½d. When this Ferdinando Smith died in 1841 and was buried at Hales Owen on July 27th, his estate was inherited by his seven-year-old son, Ferdinando Lea Smith (4.03), which is the point at which James Wragg [J][221] enters the narrative.

On May 28th 1835, at St Philip's Church, Birmingham, James Wragg of Alton Derbyshire, married Fanny, daughter of Thomas and Mary Padmore of Ridgacre. James' and Fanny's son, Abraham, born on July 23rd 1836, was baptised at St Philip's on August 12th 1836. The entry in the register gives the family's address as Bull Street, Birmingham and James' occupation as butcher. Thomas Padmore died aged 72 in 1839 and was buried at Hales Owen Parish Church on March 29th. By the census of 1841 James, Fanny and Abraham Wragg were living at Ridgacre Farm, where James had replaced his father-in-law as tenant-farmer. Also present were Mary's two brothers, James and John who, like their sister, had been baptised at Hales Owen: James on September 29th 1793, Fanny (Frances) on April 24th 1895 and John on August 2nd 1801. The final resident member of the Padmore family, 12-year-old Joseph, was the son of John and Rebecca Padmore, and was baptised at Hales Owen on July 26th 1829. James Timmins (20) and Ann Foulkes (25), both born outside the county, completed the household.

In 1851, James Wragg was listed as farmer of 85 acres in Ridgacre. Joseph Padmore was working at nearby Howley Grange Farm in Lapal township. James Timmins and Ann Foulkes had also moved on. A new house servant was Elysa Barrett (20), who ten years earlier had been living in the Bartley Green home of nail-maker Sarah Barrett, presumably her grandmother. Abraham was at school, James and John Padmore were listed as labourers. James Wragg, by then resident in Windsor Street, Aston, died in 1854 and was buried at St Paul's Church, Birmingham on May 5th. James Padmore, resident at the same address, died in 1856 and was buried at St Paul's Church on December 28th. By 1861, Fanny and Abraham Wragg had moved to neighbouring Francis Street, Aston, where both were working as cow keepers. John Padmore, still an agricultural labourer, was a boarder in the home of Thomas Farmer in

[219] Ms 351841 LB
[220] As owner/occupier of freehold land in Ridgacre township. See 13.01
[221] Juror at Amy Read Inquest. See 13.02

Long Lane, Hill township. It seems, then, that in a comparatively short time from occupying one of Quinton's largest farms, the Wragg and Padmore families had moved markedly down the social scale.

A reverse social journey brought the Wraggs' replacement to Upper Quinton Farm. By 1854 39-year-old David Deeley, a native of Cakemore, who had been working as an agricultural labourer in Upper Penn, Staffordshire, had moved to Quinton with his large family: wife Mary (35), daughters Ann (11), Mary (9), Sarah (7) and sons Jesse (5) and Charles (2). Shortly after their arrival, David was born, followed by Thirza in 1857, Josiah in 1858 and Fanny in 1860. All these, plus David and Mary's six-month-old granddaughter, Rose, were living in Quinton at the census of 1861, at which David Deeley was described as farmer of 85 acres employing two men.

Like Four Dwellings and Windmill Farms, Ridgacre Farm was purchased by Birmingham City Council under its smallholdings for servicemen scheme. By a conveyance dated November 26th 1924, "All and singular the lands farms and hereditaments situate at Quinton in the City of Birmingham and known as Windmill Farm and Ridgacre Farm as then in the occupation of H. Birch Barker and William Merris respectively, which contained in the whole together 143 acres 1 rood and 19 poles or thereabouts"[222] were transferred from Rt Hon Ferdinando Dudley William Lea Smith, Baron Dudley to the Lord Mayor, Aldermen and Citizens of City of Birmingham for the sum of £11,471 12s 0d. Farming continued for another 20 years on the land until December 1944 when the entire contents of the farm were sold at auction, by the final occupant, T. Merris "who is leaving in consequence of the Corporation requiring his farm,"[223] when it was eventually developed as housing by H. Dare and Son, Builders.

8.01.05   Worlds End Farm

Plan	Field Name	Area			Cultivation	Tithe Payable					
						Vicar			Imp^{tor}		
		A	R	P		£	s	d	£	s	d
W33	House, garden (52°27'05"N 1°59'19"W)	1	0	11							
169	Old Road (52°27'14"N 1°59'18"W)		1	17							
W33b	Road (52°27'04"N 1°59'12"W)		1	19							
W23	Up^r Bears Land (pt) (52°27'03"N 1°59'03"W)	2	0	0	Arable		1	6		6	0
W25	Low^r Bears Land (52°26'58"N 1°59'03"W)	2	0	0	Arable		1	6		6	0
W29	Swale Well Leasow (52°26'58"N 1°59'24"W)	4	0	9	Arable		2	0		10	0
W31	The Hill (52°26'00"N 1°59'12"W)	6	0	35	Arable		3	0		14	0
W35	1st Gorsty Leasow (52°27'12"N 1°59'19"W)	4	2	2	Arable		2	6		9	0
W36	2nd Gorsty Leasow (52°27'13"N 1°59'23"W)	4	2	4	Arable		2	6		9	6
W37	Common Go (52°27'04"N 1°59'28"W)	1	3	38	Arable		1	0			
W38	Garden Pleck (52°27'05"N 1°59'23"W)		3	37	Arable			6		2	0
W41	Big Well Leasow (52°27'01"N 1°59'27"W)	4	3	10	Arable		3	0		12	0

---

[222] Contained in *Abstract of the Title of Messrs H. Dare and Son Ltd to land and premises known as Windmill Farm Quinton in the City of Birmingham*, 1937. QLHS
[223] *Birmingham Daily Post*, (08.12.1944)

Plan	Field Name	Area			Cultivation	Tithe Payable			
						Vicar		Imp[tor]	
		A	R	P		£ s d		£ s d	
W42	Days Hill (52°27'02"N 1°59'29"W)	4	0	2	Arable	2 6		9 0	
W44	Square Leasow (52°26'59"N 1°59'36"W)	2	2	16	Arable	2 0		6 0	
160	Pleck (52°27'17"N 1°59'23"W)	1	1	2	Pasture	2 6			
W24	Bears Land (52°27'02"N 1°59'05"W)	3	1	22	Pasture	6 0			
W27	Little Hill (52°26'57"N 1°59'08"W)	3	2	1	Pasture	7 0			
W28	Big Meadow (52°26'56"N 1°59'19"W)	4	2	6	Pasture	9 2			
W30	Flat Piece (52°27'02"N 1°59'17"W)	3	2	14	Pasture	6 0			
W32	Shop Leasow (52°27'04"N 1°59'15"W)	8	1	8	Pasture	5 0			
W34	Peter's Piece (52°27'06"N 1°59'14"W)	1	2	4	Pasture	2 6			
W39	The Brake (52°27'03"N 1°59'24"W)	1	2	0	Pasture	1 7			
W40	Little Meadow (52°27'01"N 1°59'24"W)	1	0	8	Pasture	2 0			
W43	Long Meadow (52°26'56"N 1°59'40"W)	4	3	15	Pasture	10 0			
W45	Three Cornered Piece (52°27'02"N 1°59'33"W)	1	2	0	Pasture	2 6			
		74	2	0		3 16 3		4 3 0	

Both the Ridgacre and Warley Wigorn tithe awards list William Johnson as occupier and William Penn as owner of the 25 plots which constituted Worlds End Farm. Of these just two lay within Ridgacre township. Johnson occupation of this land was not new; Warley Wigorn land tax had assessed John Johnson at £3 15s 10d in 1816 and Mary Johnson at the same amount in 1830.[224] At the 1841 census William Johnson, whose age was given as 40, occupied the farm, along with Phoebe (30) and Hannah (20) Johnson, Mary Maccabe (3) and agricultural labourers William Woodcock (20) and Thomas Rose (15). None of these were listed as born within the county.

Ten years later, William and Phoebe were the only members of the Johnson family still at World's End. They were now revealed to be brother and sister, William born in Solihull and Phoebe in Moseley. William is listed as farmer of 70 acres employing one labourer and Phoebe as house servant. Hannah Johnson, daughter of John Johnson, farmer, married John Hodgetts at St Martin's Church, Birmingham on March 3rd 1844. Both gave their address as Lancaster Street, Birmingham. In 1851 they were living in Court Oak Road, Harborne. William Woodcock, still working as a labourer, was living with his mother in Moseley, Kings Norton; Mary Maccabe and Thomas Rose have not been traced. Two new servants were resident at the farm in 1851: 23-year-old Eliza Partridge, from Northfield, assisting Phoebe Johnson as a house servant and 17-year-old Edward Hodgetts from Kings Norton, farm servant, presumably the one labourer employed by William Johnson. Also present as a visitor on census night, was 35-year-old Mary Ann Bass, annuitant, from, Leicestershire.[225]

---

[224] Warley Wigorn Papers – WAAS
[225] The 1841 census lists three Leicestershire-born contenders of the right name and age. The most likely would be Mary Ann Bass, daughter of veterinary surgeon Thomas Bass of Hinckley.

By 1861 William Johnson had retired and was living as a visitor in the home of farmer James Clayton in Hopwood, Alvechurch, where Phoebe Johnson was employed as housekeeper. At this point Worlds End Farm disappears from the census records, coinciding with the confused status of Warley Wigorn. In 1861 the township was enumerated, as it had been in the previous two censuses in Worcestershire; 1871 saw it moved to Staffordshire, returning to Worcestershire in 1881, when the only household listed at Wards (sic) End was that of Thomas Putt, cow-keeper. Interestingly, John Whitehouse, listed in the 1861 census as an engine fitter and in 1871 as an engineer, living in Worlds End, Quinton, appears with an identical address in a Kelly's *Directory* of 1868 in the list of farmers.[226]

Worlds End Farm
c1934

However, by the 1881 census, in the Wards End district of Ridgacre, within "those isolated and detached or inconveniently situated parts of the Hamlet of Warley Wigorn which lie to the south of the road leading from Hales Owen to Birmingham,"[227] were two farmers, William Hayward and Edward Hadley – neither with named properties. By 1901, then occupied by James Payne, Worlds End Farm once again appeared in the census, with entries following in trade directories throughout the first half of the 20th century. The absence of any census entries in 1861-1871 may perhaps be explained by the increasing size of neighbouring Four Dwellings Farm which had grown from its 158 acres at the tithe award to 279 acres in 1871, presumably by absorbing parcels of adjacent farms such as Worlds End.

8.01.06   Hagg Farm

Plan	Field Name	Area			Cultivation	Tithe Payable					
						Vicar			Imp[tor]		
		A	R	P		£	s	d	£	s	d
W142	House, bdgs, garden (52°28'14"N 2°00'03"W)			38							
5	Foredrove (52°27'58"N 2°01'23"W)		1	12							
39	Barn & yard (52°27'42"N 2°00'51"W)			28							
32	Garden (52°27'40"N 2°00'48"W)		3	15							
4	In the First Innage (52°27'56"N 2°01'20"W)	2	1	18	Arable	2	4		12	0	
W137	Wood Leasow (52°27'58"N 2°01'05"W)	3	0	3	Arable	2	6		10	6	
W138	Middle Close (52°28'03"N 2°01'09"W)	3	1	37	Arable	3	0		12	6	
W139	The Hill (52°28'07"N 2°01'13"W)	3	2	3	Arable	3	0		13	0	
W141	Old Meadow (52°28'14"N 2°00'57"W)		2	18	Arable	2	6		7	0	

[226] Kelly, E.R. (1868) *Post Office Directory of Birmingham, Staffordshire, Warwickshire and Worcestershire*
[227] Description of Enumeration District, 1881 Census

Plan	Field Name	Area			Cultivation	Tithe Payable			
						Vicar		Imp[tor]	
		A	R	P		£ s d		£ s d	
W158	The Lunt (52°28'07"N 2°01'39"W)	3	2	5	Arable	3 0		13 0	
1	In Nobles Innage (52°28'02"N 2°01'30"W)	1	2	27	Pasture	3 0			
2	New Innage (52°28'02"N 2°01'18"W)	2	3	0	Pasture	5 6			
10	In 1st Quinton Field (52°27'57"N 2°01'05"W)	1	2	8	Pasture	3 0			
11	In 1st Quinton Field (52°27'50"N 2°01'02"W)		1	11	Pasture	9			
19	Low[r] Cutler's L'sow (52°27'36"N 2°01'01"W)	3	2	29	Pasture	5 0			
20	Mid Cutler's L'sow (52°27'36"N 2°00'56"W)	3	1	20	Pasture	4 10			
21	Little Cutler's L'sow (52°27'38"N 2°00'47"W)		3	26	Pasture	1 2			
40	Cutler's Meadow (52°27'40"N 2°00'54"W)	4	0	36	Pasture	9 4			
92	The Hill (52°27'47"N 2°00'04"W)	2	1	17	Pasture	4 8			
96	The Long Hills (52°27'45"N 2°00'05"W)	3	1	14	Pasture	6 8			
W140	Little Meadow (52°28'09"N 2°01'03"W)	1	1	10	Pasture	3 6			
W143	Cart Leasow (52°28'14"N 2°01'09"W)	2	0	21	Pasture	3 6			
W144	Orchard (52°28'12"N 2°00'04"W)		2	18	Pasture	1 6			
W145	House Piece (52°28'09"N 2°01'14"W)	2	3	5	Pasture	5 0			
W184	Higgins Close (52°28'17"N 2°01'08"W)	6	1	30	Pasture	1 0 4			
		55	1	29		4 14 1		3 8 0	

The 55 acres of Hagg Farm (almost equally divided between the townships of Ridgacre and Warley Wigorn) rented by Jonathan Farmer at the tithe award in 1845 belonged to John White, who had been admitted to them at the Manor Court of June 15th 1830. "Whereas on 3rd September 1794, Aaron White of that part of the parish of Halesowen which lies in the County of Worcester, was admitted tenant to two closes called the Lunts, containing by estimation six acres, and two parcels of land in Tomwell Field, containing by estimation three acres, and one parcel of land, containing by estimation one acre lying in Horslett Field, all within the Manor of Warley Wigorn, And whereas Aaron White by his will bearing date 17th July 1820, gave to his son John White all those five acres of copyhold land bought of Counsellor Guest, called the Lunt and the Innage in the Parish of Halesowen and County of Worcester, Now be it remembered that on 15th day of June in the year of our Lord 1830, John White came before me, William Henry Lord Lyttelton, now Lord of the Manor of Warley Wigorn, out of court and prayed to be admitted tenant of the five acres of copyhold land devised to him by the will of his father, Whereupon I, William Henry Lord Lyttelton, have granted to John White the lands and premises aforesaid…"[228] The Guest family, from whom Aaron White bought the land, are traceable to the 18th century. At a court of 1737, ownership passed from one Richard Guest to another. "Richard Guest gent, late one of the customary tenants of this Manor, who held of the Lord by copy of court roll, two closes called the Lunts, two parcels of land in Tomwell Field and one parcel of land in Horslett Field within this Manor, died since the last Court and Richard Guest the son prayed to be admitted tenant to the said lands which descend to him upon the death of his father…"[229] The elder Richard Guest, had been

---

[228] Warley Wigorn Court Rolls, 15.06.1830 WAAS
[229] Op cit, 02.09.1737 WAAS

admitted to the property in 1723,[230] on the death of his father Nicholas, who had purchased the land in 1705[231] from William King, who in his turn had inherited from his brother, John in 1698.[232]

Jonathan Farmer had taken up the tenancy between 1836 when Benjamin Woodhouse [E][233] rented the farm, and 1841 when he appeared in the Warley Wigorn census. 30-year-old Jonathan Farmer lived at Hagg Farm with his wife Harriet (30), daughter Angelina (7) and sons Jonathan (4) and Philip (2). The household was completed by 15-year-old John Mole, employed as an agricultural labourer. Jonathan Farmer had married Harriet Phillips at St Philip's Church Birmingham on November 18th 1833. The register shows that he was literate, she was not. Their three children had all been baptised at Hales Owen Parish Church: Angelina on March 12th 1834, Jonathan on May 28th 1837 and Philip on March 31st 1839. In 1834 the family's address was recorded as Quinton, in 1837 as Corn Hill, Dudley and in 1839 as within the borough. Two more children were born to Jonathan and Harriet during their stay in Quinton, both baptised at Christ Church: Elizabeth on November 7th 1841 and Harriet on January 21st 1844. By 1851 Jonathan Farmer had left Hagg Farm and moved to the larger (82 acres) Hoole Farm in Kings Norton, with three more children, all born in Elmley Lovett, added to his family.

At the census of 1851, Hagg Farm was occupied by 21-year-old James Hadley from Harborne, farmer of 30 acres and Samuel Slim (18) agricultural labourer from Rowley Regis. This was also a short-term tenancy, as Hagg Farm was put up for sale in 1857. "Near the Quinton Toll Gate, By order of the representatives of the late Mr White – All that desirable estate called the Hagg Farm, with the farm house, buildings and premises thereto belonging, and the several fields of arable, meadow and pasture land containing in the whole 38a 1r 25p all freehold, except 4a 1r 22p in the occupation of Mr George Lees and Mr Thomas White."[234] By 1861 James Hadley had given up farming and become a publican in Rubery Lane, Kings Norton, where he lived with his housekeeper and her two children; Samuel Slim had also changed trades, having become a nail-maker in Sycamore Lane, Warley Wigorn.

Hagg Farm does not appear in the 1861 census; however, Kelly's *Directory*[235] names Joseph Hacket at Hagg in its list of farmers for 1868. By 1871, Thomas Sabin from Lapworth and his wife Matilda are resident at Hagg Farm, his occupation given as farm labourer. Ten years earlier, they had been living in Tabernacle Street, Oldbury, where Thomas and his three sons worked as carters. That the farm continued into the 20th century is shown by its charming depiction by local artist H.R. Wilson (1911-2006).

---

[230] Warley Wigorn Court Rolls 10.05.1723 WAAS
[231] Op cit, 01.05.1705 WAAS
[232] Op cit, 07.02.1698 WAAS
[233] As occupier of freehold land in Ridgacre township. See 13.01
[234] *Wolverhampton Chronicle* 03.06.1857 (Hagg Farm was the 1st of 10 lots of White property to be sold at the Hen and Chickens Hotel, New Street, Birmingham on June 4th 1857.
[235] Kelly, E.R. (1868)

8.01.07   Hawthorn Farm

Plan	Field Name	Area			Cultivation	Tithe Payable		
						Vicar		
		A	R	P		£	s	d
243	Farm House & Bdgs (52°27'48"N 1°59'57"W)		3	24				
237	Upper Sawpit Leasow (52°27'52"N 1°59'36"W)	3	1	10	Arable		3	8
238	Lower Sawpit Leasow (52°27'52"N 1°59'43"W)	4	1	2	Arable		3	0
242	Pleck (52°27'48"N 1°59'51"W)		1	3	Arable			3
245	Hither Leys (52°27'53"N 1°59'59"W)	2	1	28	Arable		1	8
247	Little Leys (52°27'53"N 2°00'05"W)	2	0	28	Arable		1	6
248	Top of the Meadow (52°27'55"N 2°00'09"W)	2	3	21	Arable		2	0
W8	Upper Redhill (52°27'50"N 1°59'32"W)	2	2	31	Arable		3	0
88	Great Hill (52°27'48"N 2°00'14"W)	7	2	10	Pasture		15	0
95	Shop Close (52°27'47"N 1°59'582W)	1	2	27	Pasture		3	8
198	Roundabout (52°27'45"N 1°59'50"W)	2	1	20	Pasture		6	2
239	Coneygre Leasow (52°27'53"N 1°59'49"W)	4	1	5	Pasture		11	4
244	Barn Close (52°27'53"N 1°59'55"W)	3	2	34	Pasture		10	0
246	Home Meadow (52°27'51"N 2°00'05"W)	3	0	20	Pasture		3	0
W7	Lower Redhill (52°27'50"N 1°59'36"W)	6	2	12	Pasture	1	4	6
		48	0	35		4	8	9

At the tithe awards of 1844-1845, the Nicholls family held 81 acres 2 roods 3 poles of mixed farming in the townships of Ridgacre, Warley Wigorn and Warley Salop. Land in Ridgacre was in the name of Henry Nicholls [E,J];[236] that in Warley Wigorn and Warley Salop in the name of Thomas Nicholls [E].[237] Some 48 acres, property of Ann Hill, lay in Quinton, the remainder, in Warley Salop and a swathe of Warley Wigorn sandwiched within it, the property of Ann Hill, H.J.B. Galton (3.05) and John Birch (4.07).

The ownership journey of Hawthorn Farm from the Lord of the Manor to Ann Hill, on a 1000-year lease, began in May 1773 when "Thomas Lyttelton conveys to Samuel Troughton and his trustee Joseph Troughton a certain maize farm, lands and premises situate in the parish of Halesowen in the county of Worcester and Salop or one of them."[238] Samuel Troughton, plater and japanner of Edmund Street, Birmingham, died in 1782, leaving his estate to his children Samuel and Ann, who married Captain Charles Hill at Polesworth, Warwickshire in 1797. (3.11.01) Her marriage settlement, reciting the will of Samuel Troughton, refers to freehold land in the parish of Halesowen, and specifically to Hawthorn Farm.[239] By the following year, Samuel Nicholls, occupying Troughton property, is recorded paying land tax of 5s 6d in Warley Wigorn and £2 6s 3¼d in Ridgacre.[240] The family's continuing Ridgacre presence

---

[236] As owner/occupier of freehold house and land in Ridgacre township. See 13.01. Juror at Amy Read Inquest. See 13.02
[237] As owner/occupier of freehold house and land in Ridgacre township.
[238] Ms 9273 LB
[239] Galton Papers 3101/A/B/7/13 LB
[240] Op cit

is confirmed by the registers of Hales Owen Parish Church where 26-year-old John Nicholls of Ridgacre was buried on June 16th 1813, 75-year-old John Nicholls on September 26th 1815 and 23-year-old Ann Nicholls on January 29th 1819. Even more specific were the burial records of 67-year-old Ann Nicholls of Hawthorn on June 28th 1826 and 78-year-old Samuel Nicholls of Hawthorn on October 9th 1829.

At the census of 1841, Hawthorn Farm was held by Thomas Nicholls (55) and his wife Elizabeth (60) Also present at the farmhouse were Henry Nicholls (40), his wife, Rebecca (20) who came from Birmingham, and their baby daughter, Ann, who had been baptised at Christ Church on January 3rd. On October 22nd 1839, at St Philip's Church, Birmingham, Henry Nicholls, son of farmer Samuel Nicholls of Hales Owen had married Rebecca Moore, daughter of Francis Moore, hair-dresser of Edmund Street Birmingham. The witnesses were Sarah and Thomas Hill. The 1841 Hawthorn Farm household included three servants: Henry Essex (15), Joseph Record (13) and Hannah Hall (12).

The Hawthorn Farm by W. Nicholls – who exhibited at the Royal Birmingham Society of Artists in the last quarter of the 19th century – whether he was related to the Hawthorn Nicholls family is unknown

In 1843 the tranquillity of this pastoral idyll was shattered, when Hawthorn Farm became the scene, and Hannah Hall the victim, of a violent crime. On Thursday 1st June at the Public Office, Hales Owen, Thomas Hall on behalf of Hannah Hall his daughter, brought a charge against William Knight for assault with intent to commit rape. The statements of both Hannah and Thomas Hall and of Benjamin Hill, the arresting officer, have survived.[241]

---

[241] QR 388/72 SA

Hannah Hall

For the last two years I have been in the Service of Mr Henry Nicholls of Hawthorn Farm in the Parish of Hales Owen in the County of Salop and the prisoner William Knight is waggoner for Mr Nicholls. He came there last Michaelmas. Between one and two o'clock yesterday afternoon my master sent me into one of his fields to pick squitch and the prisoner was carting manure into the same field. The prisoner took me and shewed me where I was to begin and as I was stooping to pick the squitch I heard somebody coming up behind me and on my looking back the prisoner caught hold of me and tried to take liberties with me. He put his hands and attempted to pull my clothes up and wrestled with me. I resisted him and told him there was a man coming and that if he was not quiet, I would hoot. The prisoner said he didn't care and became more violent and struggled with me and threw me down on my face and afterward turned me upon my back. He then pulled up my clothes as far as he could and exposed my person. I hooted "Murder" several times and struggled to get away but the prisoner lay himself on me and kept me down by force and said "Damn you I'll feel you before I leave you" and attempted to force my legs apart and was unbuttoning his trousers when my father came up and released me from him. After the prisoner threw me down, I hooted as loud as I was able. I was much exhausted from my struggling with the prisoner and my forehead was bruised and swollen from the fall. I cried out "Murder" several times. There was no other person working in the field."

Thomas Hall

The witness Hannah Hall is my daughter and is nearly 14 years old. I was yesterday employed in getting gravel for the roads near the field of Mr Nicholls where my daughter was at work. I was returning from my dinner about two o'clock in the afternoon when I heard the cries of "Murder, Murder" several times. I went to the field and saw my daughter lying on the ground struggling to get away from the prisoner who was lying across her body. As soon as I got up to them, I struck the prisoner with my fist and knocked him off my daughter and released her. My daughter's clothes were turned up and half her person exposed. The prisoner did not see me until after I struck him. He was lying across my daughter and kept her down by main force and with his right hand was attempting to separate her legs which were crossed. My daughter was crying and was much exhausted from the violence of the prisoner's conduct. Her bonnet was crushed and her hair hanging about her face. After I struck the prisoner on the side of his head, he bled a good deal and lay on the ground for two or three minutes. When he got up, I said to him "You villain, I'll punish you, I'll have the law on you for this." And the prisoner replied "You have punished me already, you've took the law into your own hands." I then took my daughter to Hales Owen and obtained a warrant against the prisoner and gave it to Benjamin Hill the constable. I was about 100 yards distant when I first heard my daughter hoot Murder.

Benjamin Hill[242]

I am a Parochial Constable for Ridgacre in the Parish of Hales Owen and apprehended the prisoner on this charge. I accused him of assaulting Hannah Hall and he did not deny the charge but told me he should have loosed her if her father had not come up. As I was bringing him to the Lockup at Hales Owen the prisoner asked if I thought Thomas Hall would be willing to make it up and said he would give him a sovereign to do so and asked me to make Hall that offer for him. The place where the assault took place is about 400 yards from the turnpike road and almost as far from any house.

---

[242] The only adult Benjamin Hill living in Ridgacre in 1841 was a whitesmith at plot 188. (12.07.01)

25-year-old William Knight was committed for trial before the County Sheriff, Sir Andrew Vincent Corbet, at Shrewsbury Quarter Session on Monday 26th June 1843. There he was found guilty and sentenced to two months in prison.[243]

Thomas Nicholls died, aged 65 and was buried at Christ Church on January 28th 1848. By 1851, Henry Nicholls (who had succeeded Thomas White as Vicar's Warden in 1847) had assumed the tenancy of Hawthorn Farm and increased his acreage to sixty and his children to five. Like their elder sister, the four new arrivals had all been baptised at Christ Church: William (January 7th 1844), Mary (January 4th 1846), Rebecca (July 2nd 1848) and Henry (November 13th 1850). Elizabeth Nicholls, of no occupation, was now head of her own household in Warley Wigorn. She died in 1853 and was buried at Christ Church on January 24th. None of the three servants from 1841 remained at the farm. Henry Essex, now working as a nail-forger, was lodging at plot 93 in the home of Joseph Harris (12.05.04); Joseph Record had returned to his family home at plot 91, where he also was working at the nail forge (12.05.02); listed as sick, Hannah Hall, 22-year-old nailer of Quinton, was one of the 255 inmates of Stourbridge Union Workhouse at Wordsley. Three new servants lived at Hawthorn Farm: Etty Hall (17) who ten years earlier resided at Ivy House (12.04.11) with her parents Thomas and Ann Hall and seven siblings; Mary Hunt (12) who may have been enumerated twice (12.10.06) and Thomas Leek (17) from Hampton Lucy, listed as house servant rather than one of the two labourers employed on the farm.

Following the death of Ann Hill, Hawthorn Farm was sold on July 12th 1855 in 12 lots at an auction held at the Hen and Chickens Hotel, New Street, Birmingham.[244] The settlement of the estate proved complicated, with disputes over ownership reverting to the will of Samuel Troughton and, like Dickens' famous contemporary fiction of Jarndyce v Jarndyce,[245] was subject to judgment in Chancery. The sale resulted in the splitting up of the farm and the end of its association with the Nicholls family. Henry Nicholls died in 1860, and his family in 1861 are found in Icknield Street, Birmingham, where Rebecca is working as a dress-maker. Their eldest daughter, Ann, is a warehouse woman, Mary is a paper-box maker, William a chaser (metal-engraver) and Henry a silversmith. Daughter, Rebecca has no stated occupation, Joseph is just seven years old and a seventh child, Sarah, was born in Birmingham in 1858.

Hawthorn Farm in 1861, reduced to 20 acres, was occupied by John and Hannah Wood and their 11 children, the eight eldest of whom were all baptised at Hales Owen Parish Church. William (November 21st 1841), John (December 25th 1842), Alfred (January 7th 1846), Henry (June 7th 1848), Joseph (April 28th 1850), Hannah (March 3rd 1852), Emma (April 26th 1854) and Charles (January 16th 1856). The five eldest sons were all employed on the farm; Hannah, Emma and Charles were at school. Eliza (3), Fanny (2) and Thomas (6 months) had all been born since the family's arrival in Ridgacre township and baptised at Christ Church: Eliza on February 8th 1858, Fanny on June 6th 1859 and Thomas on November 4th 1860. His arrival at Hawthorn Farm was obviously an upward step for John Wood, who had previously been employed as a gardener, living in Manor Lane in Lapal township. Clearly the move was also a success, as he was still at Hawthorn Farm, now expanded to 61 acres, in 1881. His daughter, Emma, married Thomas George Wyrley Birch of Redhall Farm (8.03).

---

[243] Calendar of Prisoners, Shropshire 1657342 1786 – 1849/7 SA
[244] Sale Catalogue Hawthorn Farm, 1855 SC/47 LB
[245] Dickens, C. (1852-1853) *Bleak House*

8.01.08　　　Windmill Farm

Plan	Field Name	Area			Cultivation	Tithe Payable					
						Vicar			Imp[tor]		
		A	R	P		£	s	d	£	s	d
101	Farm House (52°27′38″N 1°59′56″W)		2	22							
97	Mill Field (52°27′42″N 2°00′10″W)	5	1	19	Arable		4	10		17	0
99	Bottom Piece (52°27′44″N 1°59′57″W)	3	0	38	Arable		4	6		11	9
104	Rickyard Piece (52°27′39″N 2°00′04″W)	5	1	2	Arable		4	8		17	3
194	Cow Leasow (52°27′37″N 1°59′51″W)	3	3	37	Arable		5	6		13	0
98	Middle Piece (52°27′44″N 2°00′02″W)	5	1	38	Pasture		15	6			
100	Barn Piece (52°27′40″N 1°59′55″W)	1		24	Pasture		4	10			
102	Rump Piece (52°27′37″N 1°59′56″W)	1	1	30	Pasture		3	0			
196	Daleday Math (52°27′39″N 1°59′42″W)	1	3	28	Pasture		5	2			
197	The Meadow (52°27′41″N 1°59′49″W)	6	1	22	Pasture		18	0			
		35	2	20		3	6	0	2	19	0

The name Windmill Farm suggests the previous existence of a mill, as do two named plots on the tithe maps – Windmill Piece (105) and Windmill Leasow (W96a). In his study of regional windmills, McKenna states that Quinton's mill, most probably a post mill,[246] was the last known of Birmingham's windmills. Not shown on any 18th century maps, it was apparently demolished before 1772.[247] The most likely site for the mill was either of the higher elevation plots 105 or W96a, the first in Ridgacre township, the second in Warley Wigorn. Though adjacent to Windmill Farm, neither of these plots were part of it, Windmill Piece belonging to Lower Quinton Farm and Windmill Leasow to Four Dwellings Farm.

The property of the estate of Ferdinando Smith, Windmill Farm in the tithe award was occupied by Richard Tomlinson [E,J],[248] who had been there for at least 20 years, Ridgacre Land Tax for 1822, recording "Owner: F Smith Esq, Occupier: R^d Tomlinson; Amount: £1 10s 9d."[249] Aged 60 at the census of 1841, Tomlinson lived with Mary (40) and Sarah (20) Tomlinson. Four live-in servants completed the household: George Vaughan (20), Ellen Read (15), John (28) and Anne (30) Goode.

On November 8th 1847 at Christ Church, George Vaughan married Eliza, daughter of blacksmith William Jones; both bride and groom gave their address as Warley Wigorn. By 1851 they were living in Parkhouse Lane, Oldbury; George now employed as a puddler in an iron works. On June 26th 1848, also at Christ Church, Ellen Read married blacksmith George Greenup. (12.11.01) In 1851, John and Hannah Goode, with three children born in Hales Owen, were living in Holt Lane, Cakemore. John's birthplace now identified as Harborne and Hannah's as Warley Wigorn. Both were working as nail-forgers. Sarah Tomlinson has not been positively identified after the census 0f 1841. Still listed as the farmer of

---

[246] A post mill is one mounted on a vertical post, around which it rotates, bringing the sails into the wind.

[247] McKenna, J. (1986) *Windmills of Birmingham and the Black Country*, pp 8-9

[248] As owner/occupier of freehold house and land in Ridgacre township. See 13.01. Juror at Amy Read Inquest. See 13.02

[249] Ms 351841 LB

Windmill Farm in *Kelly's Directory* of 1850, the year in which he was elected People's Warden at Christ Church, by 1851, Richard with Mary Tomlinson, now described as annuitants on mortgage, had moved into Hawthorn Cottage. (6.01) By this date, Windmill Farm, now listed as 40 acres, was run by Joseph Tomlinson (48) from Wilmcote, his wife Mary (47) from Cotwall End, with the help of two servants: Ann Fellows (16) from Gornal Wood and John Conley (43) from Pershore. Ten years later all had changed again. Joseph and Mary Tomlinson had removed to Hatherton, Staffordshire, where Joseph was employed as a game keeper; John Conley had become a gardener in the household of landed proprietor, Elizabeth Chillingworth, in Astley, Worcestershire. Ann Fellow has not been positively identified after 1851.

Although Windmill Farm is not named in the 1861 census, the enumerator's route indicates that James Pearman, farmer of 43 acres, employing two 2 men, was the tenant. This is confirmed in the 1871 census, which identifies Pearman as the occupant of Windmill Farm, where his son, another James, had taken over from him ten years later. At the tithe apportionments of 1845, Joseph Pearman was tenant of 41 acres of Warley Wigorn land, belonging to William Penn, where, in 1851, James Pearman carried on his business as cattle dealer. (9.01.01)

Later in the 19th century, a suicide and attempted double murder on the site triggered a description of Windmill Farm. "In the rural district lying between Halesowen and Harborne... Windmill Farm, situate in the township of Ridgacre, and near the village of Quinton, Worcestershire... about half a mile from the village, approached by a long lane leading from the Hagley Road on the Birmingham side of Quinton. The house is an ordinary homestead, substantial and comfortable but not excessive."[250]

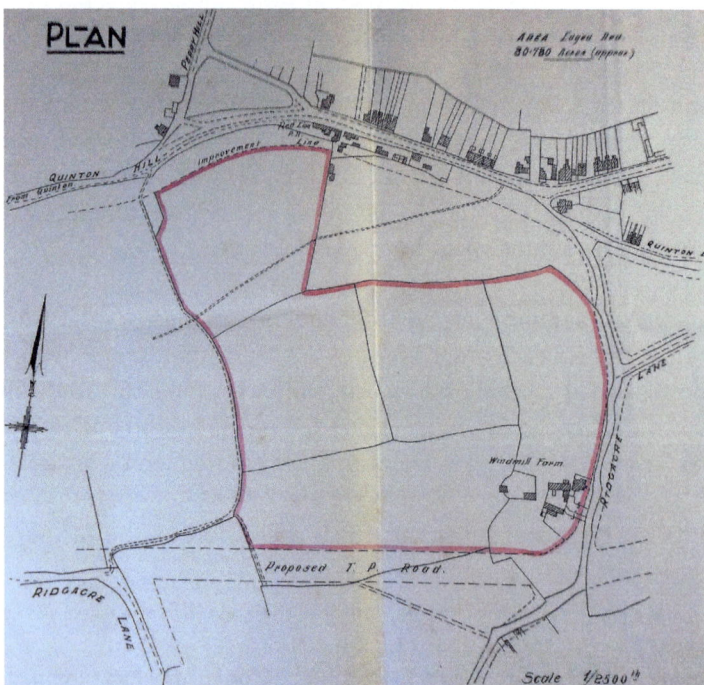

Like Four Dwellings and Ridgacre Farms, Windmill Farm was purchased by Birmingham City Council under its smallholdings for servicemen scheme. By a conveyance dated November 26th 1924, "All and singular the lands farms and hereditaments situate at Quinton in the City of Birmingham and known as Windmill Farm as then in the occupation of H. Birch Barker" were transferred from Rt Hon Ferdinando Dudley William Lea Smith, Baron Dudley to the Lord Mayor, Aldermen and Citizens of City of Birmingham. On December 14th 1934, title passed to H. Dare & Son Ltd, specifically "all that farm

---

[250] *Lichfield Mercury* (11.09.1886)

house stabling and other buildings and premises erected standing and being thereon or on some part thereof known as 'Windmill Farm' which said pieces of land and premises were for the better description thereof delineated and edged pink respectively in the plan annexed thereto."[251]

8.01.09   Mockbeggar Farm

Plan	Field Name	Area			Cultivation	Tithe Payable
						Vicar
		A	R	P		£ s d
156	House & Garden (52°27'14"N 1°59'28"W)		1	19		
142	Long Leasow (52°27'14"N 1°59'39"W)	1	3	12	Arable	1 4
143	Little Leasow (52°27'10"N 1°59'40"W)	1	1	9	Arable	1 0
144	Spring Leasow (52°27'14"N 1°59'36"W)	1	3	31	Arable	1 4
146	Well Leasow (52°27'04"N 1°59'33"W)	1	1	6	Arable	1 0
147	Clover Leasow (52°27'05"N 1°59'32"W)	2	1	19	Arable	1 8
149	Five Acres (52°27'08"N 1°59'32"W)	1	2	2	Arable	1 0
145	Broad Leasow (52°27'08"N 1°59'36"W)	2	0	27	Pasture	4 6
148	Head Piece (52°27'10"N 1°59'28"W)	2	3	33	Pasture	5 6
150	Brickkiln Piece (52°27'11"N 1°5931"W)	1	2	23	Pasture	2 6
151	Plant Leasow (52°27'12"N 1°59'33"W)	1	2	6	Pasture	3 0
152	Garden Leasow (52°27'14"N 1°59'29"W)	3	2	25	Pasture	4 6
153	Jones's Leasow (52°27'14"N 1°59'35"W)	1	2	27	Pasture	1 10
154	World's End Leasow (52°27'14"N 1°59'32"W)	3	2	15	Pasture	6 8
155	Big Meadow (52°27'19"N 1°59'27"W)	2	0	31	Pasture	4 4
157	The Croft (52°27'18"N 1°59'26"W)		3	26	Pasture	1 10
		30	3	31		2 2 0

Mockbeggar Farm remains something of an enigma. Absent from earlier OS maps, it appears as Mopbeggar on the 1887 edition,[252] which does not identify a Worlds End Farm. Its isolated location was graphically described: "the cartway to Mockbeggar Farm passed through a marshy valley and here could be seen at times the Jack o'Lantern, otherwise Will o'the Wisp."[253] Coined by Nicholas Breton[254] in the early 17th century, "mock-beggar" usually referred to a house that had an appearance of wealth but was deserted or occupied by poor or miserly inhabitants. Mock-beggars were also included in a lengthy list of spirits, fairies and other fantastic beasts (which included hobbits – cf J.R.R. Tolkien and dobbies cf J.K. Rowling) in the mid-19th century *Denham Tracts*,[255] which may also fit with Presterne's reference to will o'the wisps encountered along the route to Quinton's Mockbeggar Farm.

[251] Contained in *Abstract of the Title of Messrs H. Dare and Son Ltd to land and premises known as Windmill Farm Quinton in the City of Birmingham*, 1937. QLHS
[252] Worcestershire Sheet V SW; Staffordshire Sheet LXXII SW
[253] Presterne, T. (1913) *Harborne Once Upon a Time*, p45
[254] Prolific English writer (?1555-1626), best known for *Englands Helicon* (1600)
[255] A series of 54 pamphlets collected between 1846-1859 by Michael Denham, edited by James Hardy (1892)

The best match to the OS location of Mopbeggar Farm and Mockbeggar Farm in *Around World's End*,[256] is the property of Richard Greaves, held at the tithe award by John Jakeman, [E][257] born at Spernall in Worcestershire. Aged 50 at the census of 1841, John Jakeman shared his home with Elizabeth (80) and Susanna (60) Jakeman and servants Edward (16) and Sarah (14) Barton, who came from Kings Norton. Elizabeth Jakeman died aged 94 and was buried at Christ Church on January 22nd 1847; Susanna Jakeman died aged 72 and was interred at Christ Church on October 6th 1848. In 1851 only Sarah Barton, unmarried at 24, remained in the household with John Jakeman. Edward Barton, now married, was working as a gardener and living with his wife, two children and mother- and father-in-law in Belbroughton, Worcestershire. On December 9th 1852, widower John Jakeman married widow Sarah Hill (née Deeley) at Christ Church The Quinton. At the census of 1861, Jakeman is still listed as farmer of 30 acres. (12.12.05) John Jakeman died in 1869 and was buried at Christ Church on November 12th. By 1871, the farm was in the occupation of 28-year-old William Clay who, at the previous census had been living in the Warley Wigorn home of his parents and working as a nail-maker.

On August 14th 1862, at an auction at the Hen and Chickens Hotel, Birmingham, the farm was sold by Richard Greaves' three surviving children, Richard, Emma and Caroline, to Robert Smart for £2210. The solicitor's abstract of title, commencing with the will of James Thompson continues the Mockbeggar mystery. In Thompson's will the farm is described as "situate at World End." (4.05) The 1862 title then proceeds to refer to it as "all that messuage, tenement or farmhouse with the barn, stables and buildings called the Worlds End Farm… in the occupation of John Jakeman."[258] Then follows a schedule of 16 plots (equal to the number of plots in the tithe award to Greaves/Jakeman) totalling roughly the same acreage (30a 13p compared with 30a 3r 31p of the tithe award) but with field names which bear no resemblance to those held by John Jakeman, or indeed by William Johnson in the actual Worlds End Farm. The accuracy of the Abstract is further called into question by its recording of the death of Rebecca Lloyd (Greves) in April 1844, more than 12 months before she married Rees Lewis Lloyd! (4.05)

Having remained in the ownership of Robert Smart and his heirs since 1862, the land was sold in 1935 for £9000 to Worlds End Farm Estate Ltd, which went into liquidation three years later, at which point it was acquired by Birmingham estate agent D.W.A Barton for building development. The attached plan, drawn on a west-east orientation, gives the field names used in 1862, but fits exactly to the land owned by Richard Greaves and occupied by John Jakeman in 1844.

---

[256] Birmingham Public Libraries (n.d.) *Around World's End: Some notes on the Quinton Area*
[257] As owner/occupier of freehold house and land in Ridgacre township. See 13.01.
[258] *Abstract of Title to freehold property known as Worlds End Farm Quinton 1938*, QLHS

8.01.10 Monckton Farm [Also known as Quinton Green Farm]

Plan	Field Name	Area			Cultivation	Tithe Payable					
						Vicar			Imp^{tor}		
		A	R	P		£	s	d	£	s	d
Property of Ambrose Foley											
73	Farm House & Bdgs (52°27'50"N 2°00'44"W)			20							
59	Garden (52°27'50"N 2°00'48"W)			20							
68	Lt Wood Leasow (52°27'58"N 2°00'55"W)	1	3	6	Arable		1	6		7	3
69	Big Wood Leasow (52°27'58"N 2°00'49"W)	2	3	19	Arable		2	0		10	6
70	Big Middle Leasow (52°27'55"N 2°00'48"W)	2	2	0	Arable		2	8		9	9
65	Little Meadow (52°27'55"N 2°01'01"W)	1	0	19	Pasture		3	6			
66	Church Leasow (52°27'52"N 2°00'58"W)	3	0	18	Pasture		9	5			
67	Lt Middle Leasow (52°27'55"N 2°00'54"W)	1	2	0	Pasture		4	6			
71	Barn Close (52°27'53"N 2°00'48"W)	3	0	18	Pasture		9	5			
		16	**1**	**0**		**1**	**13**	**0**	**1**	**7**	**6**
Property of John Foley											
62	Garden (52°27'50"N 2°00'54"W)			4							
12	King's Leasow (52°27'50"N 2°01'18"W)	3	1	0	Arable		3	6		12	6
8	In The Field (52°27'52"N 2°01'20"W)		2	17	Pasture		1	2			
9	In The Field (52°27'52"N 2°01'17"W)	2	0	13	Pasture		4	0			
13	Lower Meadow (52°27'48"N 2°01'17"W)	2	2	11	Pasture		6	10			
54	Top Meadow (52°27'48"N2°00'04"W)	1	3	3	Pasture		3	6			
		10	**1**	**8**			**19**	**0**		**12**	**6**
		26	**2**	**8**		**2**	**12**	**0**	**2**	**0**	**0**

Foley presence in Quinton is noted from the early 18th century, when Hales Owen Court Rolls record the admission of John Foley to land in the manor. On his death in 1720, his land passed to his son, William,[259] under the terms of whose will his son, Ambrose, inherited in 1778.

> *In the name of God Amen. I William Foley of the Quinton in the parish of Halesowen in the County of Salop, husbandman, being in sound mind make this my last will and testament… I give and devise unto my son Ambrose Foley all that my messuage or dwelling house with the outbuildings, barns, stables, gardens, orchards and other appurtenances, situate at or near the Quinton and now in the possession of Joseph Smith… And also, all those several parcels of land containing about twenty acres lying near to the said messuage and lately purchased by me from William Lowe… Also, I give and devise all those my enclosed and common field lands now in my own possession lying in and near to a common field called the Quinton Field, which I some time ago purchased from Joseph Shelburn, unto my said son William Foley… Also, I give and bequeath unto my son John Foley to whom as my heir at law all my copyhold messuages, lands and premises situate at or near the Quinton will descend, my wagon and all the horses of which I shall die possessed.[260]*

---

[259] May 23rd 1709 LB 3033/252230, 252232, 252227
[260] Will of William Foley, proved at Worcester March 9th 1778, Lee Crowder Papers, LB

At the death of John Foley in 1799, future inheritance was clearly defined. "Court Baron of The Right Honourable William Henry Lord Lyttelton, 22nd April 1799, before Samuel Baker, Deputy of Wilson Aylesbury Roberts Esquire, Steward... The Homage present that John Foley late one of the customary Tenants of this Manor died since the last Court and that on his death a heriot fell to the Lord according to custom for which the Lord hath received satisfaction... The Homage further present that John Foley at a Court Leet and Court Baron held 26th April 1779 duly surrendered the said promise unto his brother Ambrose Foley... and immediately after his decease unto his brother William Foley... and after his decease unto his nephew John Foley... and after his decease unto his nephew William Foley... and after his decease unto his nephew Ambrose Foley his heirs and assigns for ever. And that the said Ambrose Foley the brother, the first Tenant for Life, ought to be admitted Tenant to the said premises, whereupon at this Court the Lord by his Deputy Steward hath granted to Ambrose Foley the said messuages or tenements, lands and premises with the appurtenances. And the said Ambrose Foley is hereof admitted Tenant and agreed with the Lord for a fine and did his homage." [261] On the death of Ambrose Foley in 1827, the next devisee, John Foley was admitted to the property.

The Ridgacre tithe award does not distinguish in either occupier or landowner between John Foley the uncle and John Foley the nephew. As John Foley the uncle lived at plot 55 and at the time of his death in 1845 had crops to sell, it seems logical that he also occupied the adjoining 1 acre 3 roods 3 poles plot 54, Top Meadow, which also adjoined Monckton Farm. John Foley was also the owner of plots 81-84 and 86, leased to James Cooper (10.01.02), the 1 rood 2 poles void plot 85 (52°27'47"N 2°00'27"W) – a garden and a house in ruins, and (jointly with Ambrose Foley) the Wesleyan Methodist Chapel (7.01) and the cottage at plot 63 occupied by John Mason (12.01.04). Following the death of John Foley, William Foley the next devisee was admitted in 1847. (See 12.04.04 and Foley family tree 6.03)

At the census of 1841 John (34) and Jane (28) Foley were the sole occupants of Monckton Farmhouse. On April 25th 1838, at St Martin's Church, Birmingham, John Foley had married Jane Felton, of Temple Row, Birmingham, daughter of victualler Thomas Felton. One of the witnesses was Susannah Foley, whose burial, aged 34, was recorded at Christ Church The Quinton on July 25th 1842. In 1841 Susanna Foley (30) was enumerated as a female servant in the household of Sarah Jones, Powk Lane, Rowley Regis. Jane Foley died, aged 36, and was buried at Hales Owen Parish Church on December 17th 1847. On November 14th 1850, John Foley returned to St Martin's Church, Birmingham to marry Jemima James, 29-year-old daughter of miller John James. Both bride and groom gave their address as Moor Street. The 1851 census places John's birthplace at Tamworth, Worcestershire and Jemima's at Bredon, Worcestershire. No labourers are employed at the farm, which is listed at Quinton Green. Also present was six-year-old Mary Ann Foley, John's daughter from his first marriage, who had been baptised at St Peter's Church, Harborne on July 7th 1844. Two children were subsequently born to John and Jemima, both baptised at Christ Church: Ambrose (January 4th 1852) and William (June 1st 1856).

In 1861 the five previous members of the Foley family are still present. Jemima's birthplace is given as Himbleton, Gloucestershire (it is actually in Worcestershire) and John is described as farmer of 40 acres employing one man. The household is completed by the one man, namely 18-year-old Alfred Watson, carter, from Northfield. There is a discrepancy of some 14 acres between the 26 recorded in the tithe

---

[261] Hales Owen Court Rolls April 22nd 1799

apportionments and the 40 attributed in the census. It seems likely that this may be accounted for by the disappearance of Tinkers Farm by 1861, perhaps partly replaced by the 20 acres farmed by Amos Goode. Tinkers Farmhouse re-appears in 1871, but is listed as uninhabited. The absorption of some of the land of Tinkers Farm into Monckton Farm would seem to be confirmed by William Foley's 1909 purchase of "all that messuage or tenement with the barn, stable, cow-house, outbuildings, fold yard and garden and several parcels of arable meadow and pasture land thereto belonging containing together 15 acres or thereabouts then and for some time since occupied and enjoyed, known as Tinkers Farm, situate in the parish of Halesowen in the county of Worcester."[262]

The Foley family continued its occupation of Monckton Farm until the early 20th century, when they began to sell off parcels of land for development. In 1915 William Foley paid £203 to Viscount Cobham, Lord of the Manor of Hales Owen for the enfranchisement of 25 acres i.e. "All those messuages buildings, garden closes, pieces or parcels of land situate at The Quinton and as stated in the tithe apportionment in the township of Ridgacre in the parish of Halesowen, but now (by alteration of boundaries) partly in the parish of Quinton in the City of Birmingham and partly in the township of Warley in the Urban District of Oldbury." [263] The plots concerned were then listed by their 1844 names: 8 In the Field, 9 In the Field, 12 Kings Leasow, 13 Lower Meadow, 54 Top Meadow, 62 Garden – all of which in 1844 had been part of Monckton Farm; 81 Meadow, 82 Middle Leasow, 82 Lower Leasow, 84 Top Leasow, 86 Slough Leasow – all in 1844 the property of John Foley, but rented to James Cooper of Red Lion Inn; 55 house, buildings & garden – in 1844 occupied by John Foley the uncle; 85 site of houses – in 1844 a void property. None of the plot sizes had varied since the tithe apportionments. Less than two months later, William Foley sold some of his Quinton land to Birmingham Corporation.[264]

Monckton Farmhouse & barn photographed in early 20th century

William Foley died on June 30th 1929, having two years earlier sold more of his Quinton land to brewers, Mitchells & Butlers. The piecemeal dispersal of Monckton Farm was continued by his widow.

---

[262] Abstract of Title of Messrs L & G Rudge to property fronting Kingsway, Quinton (1938) QLHS
[263] Ms 3033/ February 27th 1915 LB
[264] Conveyance of Freehold Land at Quinton – William Foley to Birmingham Corporation, April 20th 1915

8.01.11   Lower Ridgacre Farm

Plot	Field Name	Area			Cultivation	Tithe Payable					
						Vicar			Imp^{tor}		
		A	R	P		£	s	d	£	s	d
117	House, bdgs (52°27'28"N 2°00'00"W)		1	16							
116	Garden (52°27'29"N 2°00'00"W)			15							
118	Garden (52°27'29"N 1°59'59"W)			23							
180	Old Lane (52°27'30"N 1°59'41"W)		1	12							
123	Pit Leasow (52°27'28"N 1°59'54"W)	1	3	8	Arable		1	2		5	6
127	Fog Leasow (52°27'25"N 1°59'52"W)	3	2	11	Arable		2	7		9	6
122	Mid Meadow (52°27'29"N 1°59'56"W)	1	1	31	Pasture		2	6			
124	Upper Meadow (52°27'28"N 1°59'58"W)	1	3	39	Pasture		4	0			
125	2ndCow Leasow (52°27'26"N 1°59'59"W)	2	0	27	Pasture		5	10			
126	Cow Leasow (52°27'25"N 1°59'58"W)	1	3	20	Pasture		5	0			
128	Clover Leasow (52°27'22"N 1°59'58"W)	3	0	2	Pasture		7	6			
177	Lunt Coppy (52°27'29"N 1°59'40"W)	3	0	34	Pasture		6	0			
178	Wood Leasow (52°27'28"N 1°59'47"W)	1	2	20	Pasture		3	0			
179	Long Leasow (52°27'30"N 1°59'48"W)	2	0	15	Pasture		3	5			
		23	2	33		2	1	0		15	0

Though the tithe award lists John Birch as occupier as well as owner of the above mixed-use plots, this seems unlikely, given that William Underhill, enumerated in 1851 as farmer of 24 acres of Lower Ridgacre was clearly farming in the same place in 1841. John Birch, in 1841, was enumerated at his own farm in Warley Salop. (4.07) At the same census, William and Diana Underhill (both aged 35) lived with their daughters Mary (11), Amelia (9) and Anne (6). The household was completed by 65-year-old Mary Willis.

William Underhill, son of Joseph and Ann, was baptised at St Mary's Church, Moseley on May 5th 1805. On November 18th 1830 at the Church of St Peter & St Paul, Aston, William married Diana Willis. Their daughter, Amelia, was baptised at Hales Owen Parish Church of St John the Baptist on November 11th, 1831; Ann was baptised at St Peter's Church, Harborne on December 20th 1834. It is unclear, then, from this succession of movements, at what point they arrived at Lower Ridgacre. The 1851 census revealed three Worcestershire births: William in (Kings) Norton, Diana in Abbots Morton, Amelia in Hales Owen; and one in Staffordshire: Ann in Harborne. Mary Willis and Mary Underhill were no longer present, but 78-year-old retired farmer Joseph Underhill, also born in Norton was visiting. Ann Underhill died, aged 21 in 1856 and was buried at Christ Church The Quinton on November 22nd. Hers is one of the rare burials from this period marked with an extant headstone. Joseph Underhill also died in 1856 and was buried at St Nicholas' Church, Kings Norton on December 24th. By 1861, only William ("farmer of 24 acres"), Diana and Amelia were still present at Lower Ridgacre Farm. Census records indicate that William Underhill continued to farm there for the next 20 years, presumably until his death, registered at Birmingham in July Quarter 1881. Diana Underhill died six years later, her death also being registered at Birmingham, in July Quarter 1887.

The sale of Lower Ridgacre Farm was advertised in 1874. "An estate of 16 acres 2 roods and 23 poles with a farm house and homestead, situated in the township of Ridgacre on the road leading from the Hagley Turnpike Road to Harborne. Also, three fields of excellent pasture land situated close thereto, containing 7 acres 5 poles, the whole in the occupation of Mr William Underhill."[265] The purchaser was George Birch of Redhall Farm (8.01.03). His acquisition remained part of Birch property 60 years later at the disposal of the Redhall estate.[266] However, the final conveyance of the land in 1938 for development by Whites (Quinton) Estates Ltd, gives Lower Ridgacre Farm its own identity. "All that farm land and premises known as Lower Ridgacre Farm having frontages to Ridgacre Lane, Higgins Lane and Worlds End Lane Quinton, in the City of Birmingham and containing in the whole 23acres 2roods 28poles or thereabouts, delineated and described on the plan and thereon coloured pink."[267]

The friend of sinners was her friend;
Trusting in him she met her end;
Nor in the judgement shall she fear,
There shall her friend as Judge appear.

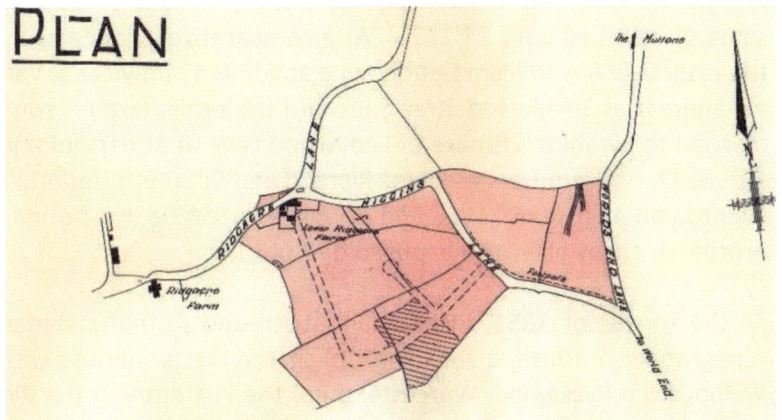

8.01.12   Tinker's Farm

Plan	Field Name	Area			Cultivation	Tithe Payable					
						Vicar			Imp[tor]		
		A	R	P		£	s	d	£	s	d
75	Farm buildings (52°27'53"N 2°00'36"W)		2	0							
77	Far High Leasow (52°27'58"N 2°00'36"W)	3	1	26	Arable		5	0		12	10
78	Far Middle Leasow (52°27'59"N 2°00'29"W)	2	3	13	Arable		3	0		11	10
79	Near Mid Leasow (52°27'56"N 2°00'27"W)	2	3	30	Arable		3	4		12	4
76	Near High Leasow (52°27'55"N 2°00'36"W)	3	0	19	Pasture		11	5			
80	Meadow (52°28'01"N 2°00'25"W)	2	1	0	Pasture		5	9			
		15	0	8		1	8	6	1	17	0

[265] *Worcestershire Chronicle* (04.07.1874)

[266] Second Part of First Schedule: Abstract of Title to Redhall Farm Quinton of: i John White (1933); ii Douglas James (1934); iii. John White & Mrs K.M. Orcott (1935) QLHS

[267] Abstract of Title to Lower Ridgacre Farm, Quinton in the City of Birmingham (1938) QLHS

Comprising just five fields (three of arable and two of pasture), totalling some 15 acres, the smallest of the Quinton farms was Tinker's, which poses an interesting question of etymology. Pointing out that there were also Tinkers and Lower Tinkers farms in Frankley (part of the Lyttelton manor), Hackwood suggests that the name is a corruption of Synekar, "an occupant in the centuries of long ago."[268] Romsley Court Rolls identify a John le Synekere, brought before the court for trespass in Uffmoor in November 1311[269] and the *Lyttelton Charters* record the grant of a cottage to Richard Synekar of Arley in 1362.[270] Neither convince regarding the Ridgacre name, though the possibility of one who engraves figures or designs on dies is more attractive than a repairer of pots and kettles![271]

Tinker's Farm, the sole Ridgacre township property of David Grainger, was occupied at the tithe award by Richard Underhill [J][272], who was already tenant at the census of 1841, the only other resident at that point being Anne Underhill. Their respective ages were given as 25 and 20. Richard, son of William and Nancy Underhill, was baptised at Oldbury on June 9th 1811; his sister, Anne was baptised at the same place on January 2nd 1820. At a comparatively young age, Richard Underhill obviously earned the respect of Rev William Skilton, who appointed him Vicar's Warden at Christ Church in 1843. Giving his address as Smallwood Street, Richard Underhill, farmer, son of William Underhill, publican, was married to Elizabeth Elsmore of Ladywood Lane at St Bartholomew's Church Edgbaston, on October 13th 1847., William Henry, son of Richard and Elizabeth Underhill was baptised at Christ Church The Quinton on August 16th 1848 and on July 9th 1850 he was buried there, some three months after his brother Anthony had been baptised on April 17th.

At the census of 1851, Richard, Elizabeth and Anthony Underhill (born respectively in Oldbury, Albrighton in Shropshire and Quinton) shared the farmhouse with 22-year-old farm labourer William Philpot from Packwood, Worcestershire, the last entry in the Ridgacre census. Surprisingly, Richard Underhill is described in the census notes as employing three men and farming 40 acres. Anne Underhill had returned to live with her now widowed father and sister in Union Street, West Bromwich. Tinker's Farm is not mentioned in the 1861 census and is described as uninhabited in 1871. The likelihood is that, for a time at least, its land was absorbed into Monckton Farm (8.01.10). The Underhill family left Quinton early in the 1850s. Their son, Ernest was born in Quinton, but baptised in Smethwick on September 19th 1852. The 1861 census lists Richard Underhill as farmer of 50 acres, living at Oldbury Road, Smethwick, with Elizabeth, Anthony, Ernest and two younger sons, Andrew and Maurice, both born in Smethwick. William Philpot presumably left Ridgacre around the same time as his employer, as in 1861 he was working as a milkman, living in Warner Street, Deritend, with his wife and five children, the eldest of whom was baptised at St Andrews Church, Bordesley on February 26th 1854,

In the early 20th century, Tinkers Farm reappeared in various *Kelly's Directories* as the address of Charles Powell, Tinker's Farm, Monckton Road, Quinton.[273] Acquired by William Foley in 1909, the land

---

[268] Hackwood, F.W. (1915) p14

[269] Tompkins, M. (2017) *Court Rolls of Romsley 1279-1642*, p50

[270] Jeayes, I. H. (1893) *Descriptive Catalogue of the Charters & Muniments of the Lyttelton Family*, 169

[271] The respective occupational definitions of syneker and tinker.

[272] Juror at Amy Read Inquest. See 13.02

[273] E.g. *Kelly's Directory of Birmingham With Its Suburbs* (1902)

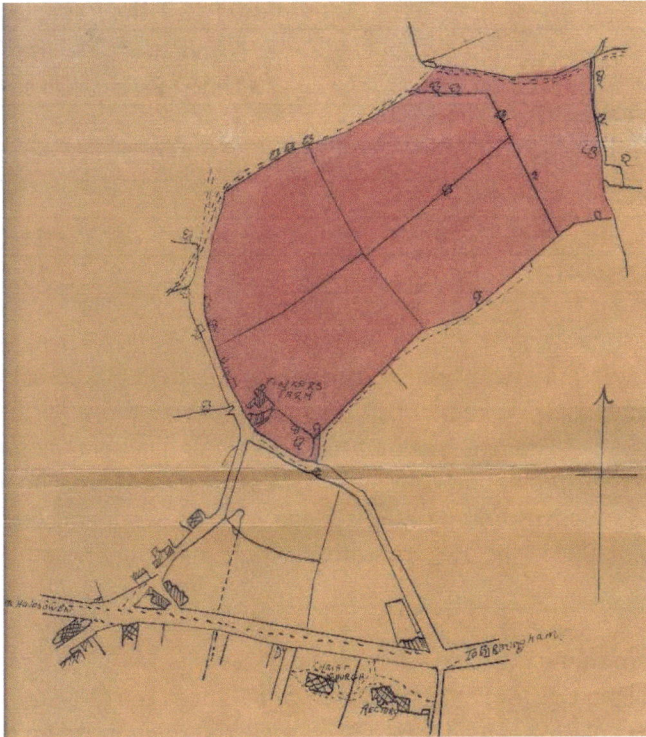

was finally sold for residential development some 30 years later, its description still matching that of the tithe award in 1844: "All that messuage or tenement with barn, stable, cow house, outbuildings fold yard and garden thereto belonging… fronting to Tinker's Lane and Monckton Road and also all those 5 pieces of arable meadow and pasture land containing 15 acres or thereabouts, known as Tinkers Farm situate and lying in the parish of Halesowen in the county of Worcester, delineated and coloured red in the plan."[274]

8.01.13   Detached Portion of Warley Farm

Plan	Field Name	Area			Cultivation	Tithe Payable					
						Vicar			Imp[tor]		
		A	R	P		£	s	d	£	s	d
Property of William King											
163	House & garden (52°27'12"N 1°59'17"W)			37							
165	Peter's Piece (52°27'08"N 1°59'13"W)	1	3	0	Arable		1	9		4	6
166	Wood Leasow (52°27'12"N 1°59'13"W)	1	1	23	Arable		1	4		3	0
162	Little Meadow (52°27'16"N 1°59'17"W)	1	2	12	Pasture		3	1			
164	Well Leasow (52°27'11"N 1°59'17"W)	1	0	19	Pasture		2	2			
167	Wood Leasow (52°27'16"N 1°59'15"W)	2	0	19	Pasture		4	2			
168	Holly Meadow (52°27'19"N 1°59'17"W)	2	2	6	Pasture		5	0			
		10	**2**	**36**			**17**	**6**		**7**	**6**
Property of Hales Owen Guardians of the Poor											
161	Parish Ground (52°27'14"N 1°59'22"W)	1	1	14	Pasture		2	8			
170	Potatoe Leasow (52°27'17"N 1°59'21"W)		3	30	Pasture		2	0			
172	Orchard (52°27'19"N 1°59'24"W)		3	0	Pasture		1	4			
		3	**0**	**4**			**6**	**0**			

---

[274] Abstract of the Title of Messrs L. & G. Rudge to property fronting Kingsway, Quinton (1938) QLHS

Plan	Field Name	Area			Cultivation	Tithe Payable				
						Vicar			Imp[tor]	
		A	R	P		£	s	d	£ s d
Property of Daniel Grainger										
W112	Pool Meadow (52°28'01"N 2°00'18"W)	3	0	18	Arable		2	6	11 0
W111	Great Hall Piece (52°27'59"N 2°00'13"W)	1	2	26	Pasture		5	0	
		4	3	4			7	6	11 0
		18	2	4		1	11	0	18 6

Although the Warley Wigorn plots were reasonably close to the principal site of Warley Farm, the Ridgacre plots, in the south east of Quinton, were less conveniently situated. The bulk (30 acres) of Warley Farm, occupied at the tithe awards by Joseph Wakeman [J][275], lay north of Hawthorn Farm in Warley Salop. Of this, some 20 acres were Daniel Grainger's property, the remainder belonging to Wakeman, who lived at Beech Lanes. Though the tithe apportionments list Wakeman as the occupant of the house and garden at Ridgacre plot 163, census enumerations place Joseph, Mary and David Wakeman in 1841-1861 at Warley Salop plot 066. Plot 163, therefore would have been sub-let. (12.12.04)

At the 1841 census, 70-year-old Joseph Wakeman ran the farm with the aid of his wife Mary (55), sons David (20) and Timothy (15), male servant William Cox (64) and female servant Frances Lea (20). *Kelly's Directory* of 1850 lists Wakeman as *farmer, Holly Bush,* an address not particularly relevant to any of his holdings. Joseph Wakeman died, aged 84, in 1850 and was buried at St Nicholas' Church, Kings Norton on August 20th. Less than four months later, Timothy Wakeman died, aged 26, and was buried in St Nicholas' churchyard on December 9th. The 1851 census lists Mary Wakeman (70), born in Rowley Regis, as farmer of 50 acres, employing one man. Also resident were agricultural labourers David Wakeman (30), born in Hales Owen, William Cox (74), now identified as Mary Wakeman's brother, also born in Rowley Regis, and Francis Lea (31), from Alvechurch. Still in the management of the Wakeman family ten years later, the 1861 census then names the holding as Warley Farm.

See also: James Cooper (10.01.02) 31 acres; Joseph Dixon (10.01.03) 3 acres;
William Pritchett (4.18) 12 acres; Glebe (7.03) 6 acres

8.02   Farm Labourers

There is a considerable discrepancy between the number of agricultural labourers enumerated in the Quinton censuses and the number of labourers Quinton farmers returned as employed on their farms. Even assuming that all the labourers working on Quinton farms resided in Quinton, then the census returns reveal that no more than 61% of the village's named agricultural labourers between 1841 and 1861 were necessary for the working of Quinton's 12/13 farms. No doubt some made the short journey to the farms of neighbouring townships, whilst others may have grandiosely described working on their own cottage plots as agricultural labour.

---

[275] Juror at Amy Read Inquest. See 13.02

Agricultural Labourers

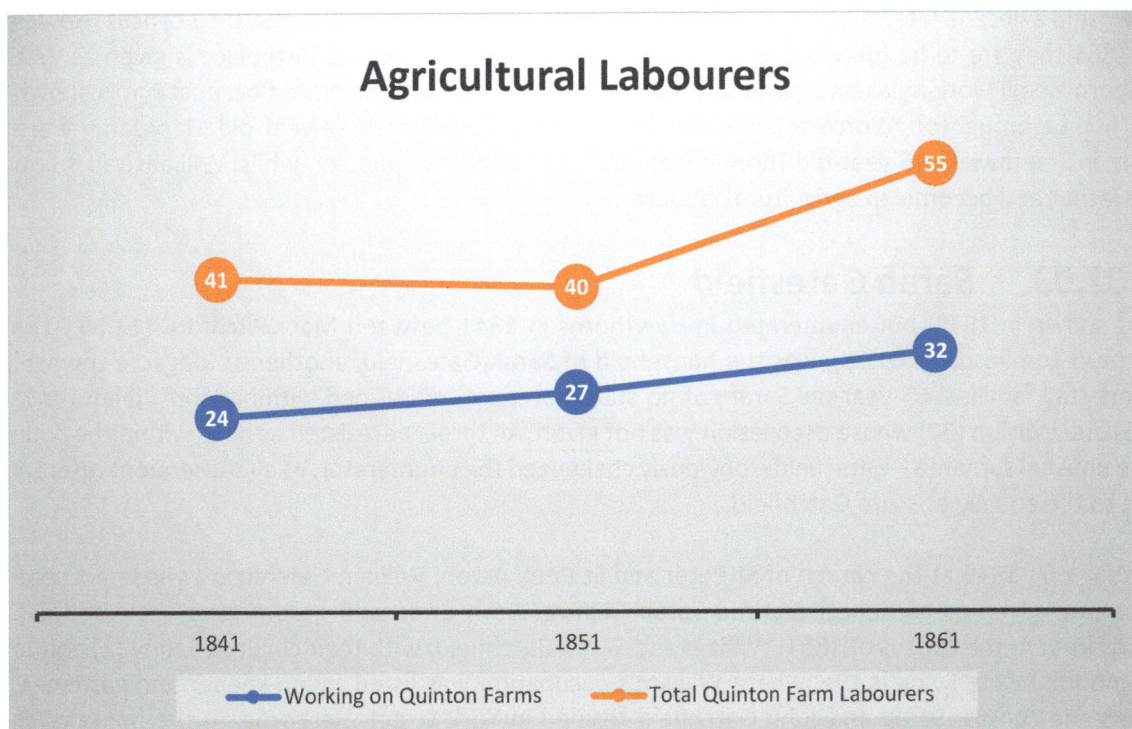

Chart: Agricultural Labourers. Data points for "Working on Quinton Farms" (blue): 1841 = 24, 1851 = 27, 1861 = 32. "Total Quinton Farm Labourers" (orange): 1841 = 41, 1851 = 40, 1861 = 55.

8.02.01   Richard Ancon

Not shown in 1844, but enumerated in the census of 1841 immediately before Joseph Butler (12.10.07) was the household of Richard Ancon in Beech Lanes. 35-year-old labourer Richard, who was not born in the county lived with his wife, Mary (35), of no stated occupation, and children Anne (11) and John (6). Richard and Mary's second daughter, Jane, was baptised at Hales Owen Parish Church on August 28th 1842. One of Ridgacre township's itinerant families, the Ancons had moved on by 1846, the year in which Richard Ancon died. His burial at Christ Church The Quinton on 18th November gives his address as Warley Wigorn. The 1851 census sheds further light on this. Now living in Londonderry, Warley Wigorn, Mary Ancon is head of a household which consists of her children Anne (like her mother now working as a nailer), John (a glass-polisher), and scholars, eight-year-old Jane and four-year-old Thomas, born since the previous census. The birthplace of Mary and her three older children is listed as Warley Salop, and that of Thomas as Warley Wigorn. Mary's 1851 household was completed by two lodgers: 47-year-old agricultural labourer John Miner from St John's, Worcester and 22-year-old nailer Emma Hadley from Warley Wigorn.

8.02.02   Francis Hall

The third Beech Lanes household not shown in the tithe apportionments of 1844 but enumerated in 1841 between plots 217 and 216 was that of labourer Francis Hall, which appeared immediately after the listing of Joseph Butler. (12.10.07) Aged 30 at the time of the census, Francis Hall lived with his wife, Mary (26) and children, Anne (6), John (4) and Joseph (1). All three were baptised at Hales Owen Parish Church: Anne on September 28th 1834, John on September 24th 1837 and Joseph on May 10th 1840. Apart from Mary, all were shown as born within the county. No longer present in Ridgacre township a decade later, Francis Hall and his family have not been traced in the 1851 census. However, in 1861 they are to be found living in Cape, Smethwick. Francis, whose birthplace is given as Warley Wigorn is still working as an agricultural labourer; Mary, still with no stated occupation, is shown as born in Belbroughton, Worcestershire. Twin sons and a daughter (three-year-old Mary Jane) were all born in Smethwick. 16-year-old Thomas was employed as an iron puddler, whilst William had followed his father and become an agricultural labourer.

8.02.03   Sarah Gatesfield

Not shown in 1844, but enumerated in Hawthorns in 1841 between Mary Pitchford (12.08.01) and Richard Tomlinson (8.01.08), was the household of Sarah Gatesfield, another of Ridgacre township's short-stay families. 65-year-old Sarah, of no stated occupation, resided with her sons, labourer John (45) and William (30) whose occupation was not given. All three were listed as born within the county. The unusual surname – Gatesfield – obviously challenged the enumerator, as all subsequent references are to the equally obscure Gatchfield.

On June 6th 1849 at the church of St Peter and St Paul, Aston, William Gatchfield (whose occupation was now given as gardener) married Sarah Chance. Both bride and groom gave their address as Harborne. At the census of 1851, William and Sarah Gatchfield, with their children Fanny (1) and John (2 months) were living in Lye, where William's occupation was listed as inn-keeper and gardener. At the same census, Sarah and John Gatchfield resided in York Street, Harborne, in the home of their son/brother-in-law, Isaac Greaves and his wife, Mary. John still worked as an agricultural labourer. This census gives the birthplace of Sarah, John and William Gatchfield as Hales Owen.

8.02.04   Joseph Haycock   Plot 34 (52°27'40"N 2°00'46"W)

By 1851, labourer Joseph Haycock had succeeded James Male (12.11.04) as the occupant of the 15 poles plot 34, property of John White, in Lower Quinton. Haycock, whose age was given here as 59, though the censuses of both 1841 and 1861 indicate that this was ten years out, lived here with his wife, Susana (53) and mother-in-law, Mary Mason (85). Ten years earlier, Joseph and Susana Haycock, whose ages were both then given as 40, were enumerated in Spies Lane in Hill township, at which time Joseph was already working as a labourer and Susana had no stated occupation. At that census Mary Mason was head of the household at one of the cottages on plot 37, where she was also listed as occupant in the tithe apportionments. (12.03.08) Shortly after the 1851 census, Mary Mason died and was buried at Christ Church on September 7th 1851.

Still resident in Quinton in 1861, when his age apparently remained at 59 and his occupation as agricultural labourer, Joseph Haycock now lived with his wife (of no stated occupation) and his 81-year-old father, Thomas Haycock, dealer in iron. Ten years earlier Thomas Haycock had lived with his son and daughter-in-law, Thomas and Elizabeth Haycock and farm labourer brother, Charles Haycock, at plot W87. (12.04.09) Thomas Haycock died, aged 85 and was buried at Christ Church on March 22nd 1865.

8.02.05   James Yeomans   **Plot W99** (52°27'18"N 1°59'35"W)

The Worlds End area of Warley Wigorn in Quinton included just two dwellings: plot W33 – Worlds End Farmhouse (8.01.05), and the 31 poles plot W99 with house, shop and garden. Resident James Yeomans, agricultural labourer, was also listed as the occupier of three fields of pasture (plots W100, W102 and W103) comprising an entire enclave of Warley Wigorn within Ridgacre township, all the property of Edward Haden. Big Meadow (W100 - 52°27'17"N 1°59'35") at 1 acre 3 roods 8 poles, Spring Meadow (W102 - 52°27'15"N 1°59'38"W) at 2 roods 16 poles and Shop Leasow (W103 - 52°27'17"N 1°59'36"W) at 2 roods 38 poles brought the total of James Yeomans' holding to 3 acres 1 rood 13poles. The three fields attracted a total Small Tithe of 10s 6d payable to the Vicar of Hales Owen.[276] This clearly sets James Yeomans apart from the remainder of Quinton's agricultural labourers.

Aged 25 at the census of 1841, James Yeomans was born in Kings Norton. He lived at plot W99 with his 20-year-old wife, Emma, born in Hales Owen and two children, Eliza (2) and Emma (2 months). Presumably the family had only recently arrived in Warley Wigorn as (the next census reveals) Eliza had been born In Smethwick. Emma Yeomans was baptised at Christ Church The Quinton on May 2nd 1841, as was her younger brother James on October 1st 1843. The birth of James and Emma's next child, Mary Ann, was registered in Kings Norton in April Quarter, 1846, by which time the family had presumably continued their upwardly mobile journey. In 1851, James and Emma Yeomans, now with six children, were living in Lapal, where James is described as a farmer of 18 acres. Plot W99 was void at this census: the enumerator recorded the property immediately following Worlds End Farm as "one house unoccupied."

See also:

Charles Clay (12.04.10); Josiah Coley (12.12.01); James Cutler (12.03.13); Charles Dutton (11.02.02); John Elliman (12.12.06, Joseph Fox (11.05.01); George Gee (11.05.02); Joseph Goode/Preedy (12.03.03); James Greaves (12.13.01); John Greaves (12.06.01); Joseph Greaves (12.13.01); Owen Greaves (12.13.01); Benjamin Hadley (12.04.05); Charles Hadley, (12.08.01),Enoch Hadley (12.12.02); Frederick Hadley (12.10.05); James Harris (12.13.02); Charles Haycock (12.10.01); John Haycock (12.08.01); Thomas Haycock (12.10.02); William Haycock (12.08.01); Joseph Hill (12.06.03); John Houghton (12.06.01); Henry Hunt (12.10.06); Thomas Irons (12.03.03), John Jacques (12.10.01); William Jones (12.04.03); David Lane (12.12.02); David Mills (12.06.03); George Mills (12.06.03); Isaac Partridge (12.13.02); James Preedy (12.03.03); Henry Read (11.01.04); James Rose (12.02.03); Charles Sadler (12.05.05); Richard Salter (12.10.01); Benjamin Standley (11.04.01), John Thompson (11.03.04); Edward Westwood (12.01.06); Benjamin Yates (12.03.11); John Yates (12.03.10); Joseph Yates (12.03.10); William Yates (12.03.11); David Yeomans (12.03.02), Thomas Yeomans (12.03.02)

---

[276] Big Meadow: 6s; Spring Meadow: 2s; Shop Leasow: 2s 6d.

9   Dealers and Traders

The comment attributed to Napoleon[277] that England was a nation of shopkeepers was not borne out in mid-19th century Quinton. Nor is there any evidence to suggest that either of the shops placed by Disraeli in Mowbray suburbs in his exactly contemporaneous novel were replicated in the townships of Ridgacre or Warley Wigorn.

> "The bright and lively shops were crowded and groups of purchasers were gathered round the stalls, that by the aid of glaring lamps and flaunting lanterns, displayed their wares. A jolly-looking woman, who was presiding at a stall which, though considerably thinned by previous purchasers, still offered many temptations to many who could not afford to purchase…
>
> "A crowd of women and girls assembled before the door of a still closed shop… The door of Mr Diggs' shop opened. The rush was like the advance into the pit of a theatre when the drama existed; pushing, squeezing, fighting, tearing, shrieking."[278]

Indeed, Quinton apparently had no shops in the recognised sense of the word in the mid-19th century. Only 12 out of its estimated population of 1,047 were engaged in trade and of these, only one was active across two censuses. None owned the premises from which they operated, all but three were heads of household.

In 1841 two provisions dealers were identified in the census, one operating from his father's Beech Tree Inn and the other from the house and nail-shop shared by three households. Only one provisions dealer is listed in 1851 who, now aged 77 had changed his occupation from nail-maker. In 1861, William Yates (12.03.11) farm labourer turned publican and shopkeeper, and Mary Read, a newcomer to the Quinton area of Ridgacre township, huckster and shopkeeper, were the only residents fulfilling that role. Dealers in livestock included one horse-dealer in 1841 and another in 1851, with Amos Goode, another in-comer to Ridgacre township offering the service in 1861. One cattle dealer plied his trade in the Warley Wigorn area of Quinton in 1851, with James Cooper, landlord of Red Lion Inn (10.01.02) also dealing in cattle in 1861. From 1841, presumably to the death of the proprietor in 1854, Quinton residents would have been able to purchase vegetables from a village nursery. Finally, in 1861, Thomas Haycock, who had moved within Quinton from Warley Wigorn to Ridgacre and in 1841 had been a nail-forger, in 1851 a pauper – formerly nailer, had become a dealer in iron, perhaps suggestive of a grandiose term for scrap-metal merchant. This distinct lack of service-providers strongly indicates self-sufficiency, at least in terms of food supplies, in this largely agricultural and nail-making community.

9.01.01   James Pearman   Plot 120 [?] (52°27'34"N 1°59'56"W)

Listed in Warley Wigorn tithe apportionments as the occupier of just over 40 acres of land, the property of William Penn (4.02), was Joseph Pearman, father of James. The latter's occupations would fluctuate during half-a-century through dealer, cattle dealer, commercial traveller, farmer, farmer and corn merchant and finally, gentleman. None of Joseph's nine plots in 1844, which attracted tithe payments of £5 14s 6d in addition to rent, included a dwelling.

---

[277] There is no evidence that Napoleon ever used the phrase, which was coined by the revolutionary Bertrand Barère de Vieuzac in a 1794 speech: "Let Pitt then boast of his victory to his nation of shopkeepers."
[278] Disraeli, B. (1845) *Sybil*, Book II, chapter IX; Book III, Chapter III

Plan	Field Name	Area			Cultivation	Tithe Payable					
						Vicar			Imp[tor]		
		A	R	P		£	s	d	£	s	d
W10	Big Piece (In) (52°27'33"N 1°59'05"W)	2	2	10	Pasture		6	0			
W12	Upper Moor (52°27'31"N 1°59'15"W)	6	3	20	Pasture		13	0			
W13	Lower Moor (52°27'24"N 1°59'16"W)	4	0	4	Pasture		10	0			
W14	Middle Moor (52°27'25"N 1°59'09"W)	6	1	32	Pasture		14	6			
W15	In Big Piece (52°27'29"N 1°59'03"W)	5	1	29	Pasture		12	6			
W17	In Wheat Field (52°27'15"N 1°58'00"W)	1	2	27	Pasture		3	0			
W18	Lower Feston[279] (52°27'17"N 1°59'09"W)	5	1	23	Arable		4	6		16	5
W20	Upper Feston (52°27'10"N 1°59'06"W)	7	1	4	Arable		6	0	1	2	1
W21	In Off Leasow (52°27'10"N 1°59'02"W)	1	2	22	Arable		1	6		5	0
		41	1	11		3	11	0	2	3	6

Born in Birmingham in 1813, the son of Joseph and Mary Pearman, James was baptised at St Martin's in the Bull Ring on January 1st 1820. At the census of 1841, he was living with his parents at Tennal Hall, Harborne, one of the parish's most important houses, where his father's occupation was given as grazier and James was listed as dealer. On April 13th 1850, at St George's Church, Birmingham, James Matthias Pearman married Elizabeth Todd. By the census of 1851, James and his household were established in the Quinton area of Warley Wigorn, where they were enumerated immediately following Thomas White at Lower Quinton Farm. (8.01.02) James Pearman's occupation was now given as cattle dealer. The 27 acres of pasture which he rented would have fed (according to 21st century standards) a comparatively small herd of around 15 animals, with the three fields of arable contributing to winter feed.[280] However, 19th century standards were less exacting and figures for average density of livestock in Worcestershire in 1854 suggest that Pearman's herd could have been anything up to eight times that number.[281] Forty years earlier at neighbouring Brandhall Farm, Richard Miller pastured 20 or more long-horned cows, seven horses, 80 breeding ewes (averaging four lambs to three ewes) and an unspecified number of hogs on 148 acres.[282]

In 1851 Elizabeth Pearman (whom the census reveals was also born in Birmingham) had no stated occupation and the couple had a 3-week old daughter, Mary. Their household was completed by 50-year-old nurse Elizabeth Hawksford from Birmingham and two general servants: 23-year-old Mary Ann Smith from Kings Norton and 20-year-old Joseph Douglass from Bromsgrove. In 1841 Douglass was living with his parents and two older brothers in Callow Brook Lane, Bromsgrove, where his father was an agricultural labourer and his mother a nail-maker. Still working for James Pearman in 1861, but now described as carter, Joseph Douglass continued his upwardly mobile journey and by 1871 had become a farmer of 30 acres in Muttons in Ridgacre township. For a family of three to afford an equivalent number of live-in servants places the Pearmans amongst the more affluent of Quinton's residents.

---

[279] Feston: French = scallop, which does indeed suggest the shape of both fields W18 & W20.
[280] Data supplied by Natural Resources Conservation Service accessed 17.08.2018
[281] Dodd, JP (1979) p 10
[282] Pitt, W (1813) pp219, 227,239,245

Six weeks after the census, on May 14th 1851, Mary Esther Pearman was baptised at Christ Church The Quinton, where her father's occupation was recorded as farmer. The following year (on October 13th 1852) Mary's brother James was also baptised at Christ Church: James senior's occupation was this time recorded as dealer. Two years later, on February 9th 1854, another son was born to James Matthias and Elizabeth. However, Michael Pearman was baptised on March 13th 1854 at St Philip's Church, Birmingham, where his father's occupation was given as commercial traveller and his address as Bull Street, Birmingham. For their fourth child's baptism James and Elizabeth returned to Christ Church where Emily Pearman was taken on July 25th 1858. James' occupation was once again listed as farmer. This was confirmed by the 1861 census when the family was enumerated in Ridgacre township, where James Pearman was described as a farmer of 43 acres employing two men. This clearly did not include the three resident servants: Joseph Douglass, housemaid, 23-year-old Mary Lloyd from Tipton and nurse girl, 16-year-old Sarah Hunt, daughter of Henry and Ann Hunt of Red Hill. (12.10.06) The 1871 census identified James Pearman's farm as Windmill Farm, (8.01.08) to which the family had evidently removed by the time of Emily's baptism in 1858, when their address was given as Ridgacre.

Described as farmer and corn merchant in 1881, James Matthias Pearman, gentleman of Grosvenor Road, Harborne, died in March 1892, with effects valued at £522. He was buried on March 19th at St Peter's Church, Harborne. Probate was granted to his son, Michael Pearman, farmer. The 1891 census, however, shows Michael Pearman, farmer's son and helper on his uncle's farm, as resident at Tennal Hall, Harborne, returning the family story to its location of half-a-century earlier. Elizabeth Pearman survived for another 19 years. Her death, aged 88 is recorded at Kings Norton in April Quarter, 1911.

9.01.02   Richard Branton   [J][283]   Plot 220 (52°27'52"N 1°59'07"W)

Living and working adjacent to the turnpike road near Ridgacre township's eastern extremity was nurseryman Richard Hunter Branton who rented from Timothy Hill a house and garden at plot 220, measuring 20 poles and from Lord Lyttelton at plot 221 (52°27'51"N 1°59'07"W) a further garden measuring 16 poles. Here he carried on his trade as a nurseryman. Aged 66 at the time of the tithe map, Branton, a bachelor of Red Hill, shared his home with Hannah Stokes (65), a widow of Beech Lanes, returned on both the census of 1841 and 1851 as house servant. Richard Branton died in 1854 and was buried at Christ Church on February 7th. This presumably ended a nurseryman's presence in Ridgacre, further reducing the township's service industries. In 1861, plot 220 was occupied by a family of agricultural labourers. Following Richard Branton's death Hannah Stokes left Ridgacre. At the census of 1861 she was enumerated lodging at the home of greengrocer Zechariah Parkes in Ledsum Street, Ladywood, Birmingham, where she was described as formerly gardener's wife. Hannah died in Ladywood, aged 82 and her funeral was held at Christ Church The Quinton on October 6th 1861.

See also:

Dealer in iron:	Thomas Haycock (8.02.03; 12.04.09)
Horse dealers:	Edward Smith (12.03.01); James Gould (12.04.15)
Provisions dealer:	John Clews (12.01.02); Joseph Dixon (10.01.03)
	Benjamin Westwood (12.01.06)

---

[283] Juror at Amy Read Inquest. See 13.02

10   Inn-keepers

In the mid-19th century Ridgacre township was home to three inns. All were listed in the *Hales Owen Alehouse Recognizances*[284] of 1822, when the licensee of the Holly Bush was Elizabeth Hall; James Cooper already kept the Red Lion and John Bridge was landlord of the Beech Tree. Sureties were guaranteed respectively by Hales Owen victuallers Reuben Parsons, Joseph Cooper and Aaron Rose. Clearly, the presence of inns and ale houses in Quinton far predates 1822. In the 13th century various members of the Green family of Ridgacre appear in Hales Owen Court Rolls and it may well be that Radulphus de Grene, who on February 1st 1270 was fined 1d along with 19 other offenders for selling weak beer,[285] was one of them.

Though Quinton's three inns survived long enough to be photographed, their exteriors offer no clue as to their interiors. Hopefully they were more appealing to their customers than the doleful Wessex inn visited by Jude Fawley and Arabella Donn in Thomas Hardy's last novel.

> "They entered an inn of an inferior class and looked round the room, at the picture of Samson and Delilah which hung on the wall, at the circular beer-stains on the table and at the spittoons underfoot filled with sawdust. The whole aspect of the scene had a depressing effect. Jude by this time wished he was out of such an uncongenial atmosphere, but he ordered beer which was promptly brought. Arabella tasted it. 'Ugh!' she said. 'Adulterated – I can't touch it!' She mentioned three or four ingredients that she detected in the liquor beyond malt and hops. Nevertheless, she drank her share, and they went on their way."[286]

Caricaturist George Cruikshank's prints such as *The Bottle* and *The Drunkard's Children*, drawn in the 1840s, show alcohol as a chief cause of crime and breakdown of family life, a view supported in Quinton by Rev C.H. Oldfield, who in 1862 wrote to the licensees. "You are the only people who, as a class, neglect your church; your houses are places most watched by the police, and to which the greatest misery is traced; those who most frequent your houses have less happiness than those who avoid them." The plaintive rider is added to this note: "I issued this privately to the publicans but never heard that it did good or affected anyone."[287]

In most villages and townships, for those not attracted by church or chapel, the inn was the only alternative as a meeting-place for the community. It was largely as a result of this simple fact that drunkenness constituted one of the major evils of working-class life in the mid-1800s. Life was hard and for many workers drink, followed by the oblivion which it could induce, was the only relief from the unremitting cycle of work and sleep.

10.01.01   James Adams   Holly Bush - Plot 234 (52°27'49"N 1°59'26"W)

Marked by the site of present-day Hollybush Grove, on a plot of land belonging to John Birch (4.07) and measuring 2 roods 8 poles, making it the largest of Ridgacre Townships three inn yards, stood the *Holly Bush* inn which between 1841 and 1861 had at least three tenants.

---

[284] *Shropshire Alehouse Recognizances* (1822) Shropshire Record Office E 2/1/6
[285] Amphlet, J. (1910) p4
[286] Hardy, T. (1895) *Jude the Obscure*, Part 1-vii
[287] Christ Church The Quinton, *Minutes of Vestry & Annual Parish Meetings 1842-1914*, EP72/5/2/1 LB

The Inn keeper in 1841 was 50-year-old James Adams from Blackheath He is listed in *Bentley's Directory* for that year as victualler, Holly Bush, Red Hill. The census reveals that his family consisted of his wife Jane (60) and sons George (18) and Alfred (16), all in-comers to the township. The household was completed by local girl Mary Hall (19). Jane Adams died in 1844 and was buried at Christ Church on September 11th. *Kelly's Directory* of 1850 lists James Adams as beer retailer, Gosty Hill and keeper of the British Arms, Overend, Cradley. The 1851 census enumerated James Adams in Gorsty Hill in Hales Owen's Hill township, where his housekeeper was his 49-year-old sister-in-law, Hannah Adams from Barking, Essex. James Adams died in 1855 and, like his wife, was buried at Christ Church on May 31st.

Licensed victualler of the Holly Bush in Red Hill in 1851 was 26-year-old Joseph Cox from Alvechurch in Worcestershire. Ten years earlier, he had been living with his parents and two siblings in Woodside, Dudley. At that census Joseph had no stated occupation. His 1851 household consisted of himself, his wife Jane (35), a servant, Mary Ann Lane (18) and 5-year-old visitor, Richard Beck, all of whom were born in Tipton. During their stay in Quinton, Joseph and Jane Cox brought two children for baptism at Christ Church: Elizabeth on February 11th 1852 and Alfred Albert on July 3rd 1853. By 1861, Joseph, now working as a labourer, Jane and their 8-year-old daughter, Elizabeth, were resident in Mount Pleasant, Wedgwood, Staffordshire.

The Holly Bush licensee in 1861 was 37-year-old George Downing who had been born in Harborne. His household was completed by 25-year-old housekeeper, Mary Bashford from Edgbaston. Downing's arrival at the Holly Bush had been just a short journey: in 1851 he had been living in Beech Lanes, Harborne where he worked for his blacksmith father, Paul. George's career as a licensee appears to have been a short interlude, as at his marriage to Mary Bashford at Birmingham's Parish Church of St Martin's in the Bull Ring on April 19th 1863, his occupation is given as blacksmith. Paul Downing died in 1870 and at the census of 1871, George Downing had returned to take over the Beech Lanes smithy.

10.01.02   James Cooper [E][288]   Red Lion - Plot 89 (52°27'49"N 2°00'06"W)

Evidently a long-term inn-keeper, James Cooper (who was baptised, son of Richard and Sarah, at Hales Owen Parish Church on November 10th 1799) was named at the Red Lion in the *Alehouse Recognizances* of 1822.[289] Listed in the 1841 census as farmer, in *Kelly's Directory* of 1850 as "Red Lion, butcher and farmer" and in the 1851 census as farmer of 16 acres and victualler, Cooper was evidently something of an entrepreneur. Situated at the bend of the turnpike road near its centre point on the tithe map, the Red Lion inn, stable yard and garden occupied a plot measuring 29 poles, leased from James Bissell. (4.10) Cooper's 31 acres of mixed farming – nearly twice the declared amount of the 1851 census – were leased from James Bissell, John Foley and Stephen Grainger, attracting tithe payments to both the Vicar of Hales Owen and Lord Lyttelton.

Plan	Field Name	Area			Cultivation	Tithe Payable					
						Vicar			Imp^{tor}		
		A	R	P		£	s	d	£	s	d
Property of James Bissell											
51	Up^r Stony Cross (52°27'47"N 2°00'49"W)	3	0	12	Arable		4	6		12	6
52	Lower Stony Cross (52°27'46"N 2°00'45"W)	2	1	13	Pasture		8	6			
53	Lt Stony Cross (52°27'46"N 2°00'54"W)	1	2	13	Pasture		6	0			
		6	3	38			19	0		12	6
Property of John Foley											
82	Middle Leasow (52°27'53"N 2°00'27"W)	4	2	10	Arable		8	2		19	9
83	Lower Leasow (52°27'52"N 2°00'30"W)	2	0	8	Arable		3	6		8	0
84	Top Leasow (52°27'50"N 2°00'28"W)	2	0	30	Arable		4	2		8	7
86	Slough Leasow (52°27'51"N 2°00'25"W)	4	0	13	Arable		7	0		16	2
81	Meadow (52°27'56"N 2°00'20"W)	1	1	12	Pasture		4	2			
		14	0	33		1	7	0	2	12	6
Property of Stephen Grainger											
W113	Big Piece (52°27'57"N 2°00'16"W)	2	2	35	Not stated		3	0		9	6
W114	Little Piece (52°27'57"N 2°00'12"W)	1	2	29	Not stated		1	6			
W115	Long Meadow (52°27'58"N 2°00'18"W)	1	2	23	Not stated		6	0			
W116	Near Piece (52°27'54"N 2°00'15"W)	2	0	33	Not stated		2	3		8	6
W118	The Pleck (52°27'50"N 2°00'16"W)		2	11	Not stated		1	9			
W119	House, garden (52°27'49"N 2°00'15"W)			39							
W120	Roundabout (52°27'51"N 2°00'10"W)	1	0	18	Not stated		4	0			
		10	0	18			18	6		18	0
		31	1	9		2	4	6	4	3	0

In addition to the land which he rented, Cooper, a native of Warley Wigorn, owned the house, shop and garden at the 21 poles plot 93, which he rented out to nail forger Joseph Harris. [(12.05.04)

---

288 As occupier of land in Ridgacre township valued at £50 a year. See 13.01
289 E 2/1/6 SA

At the census of 1841, Cooper (then aged 42) lived with his wife Letitia (43), who was born in Hales Owen, and nephew/servant James Cooper (12) also from Hales Owen. George Hall (25)[290] and Alice Green (18) completed the household. Ten years later, the three members of the Cooper family were still present. George Hall had returned to his parents' home in Warley Salop, where he was working as a carter. Two new servants had moved in to the Red Lion: 20-year old Jane Hall, born in Ridgacre

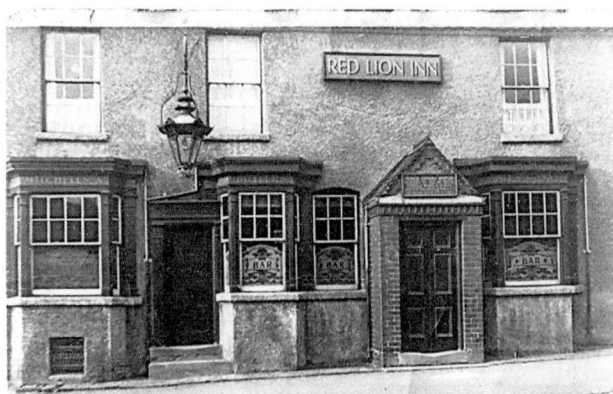
Red Lion Inn photographed in mid-20th Century

(12.04.11) and 25-year-old John Blick from Northfield. In 1841 Blick had been working as a butcher in Market Square, Worcester and in 1861 had returned to his birthplace, where he lived at Blackmore Corner and was employed as a machine man. James Cooper, elected People's Warden at Christ Church The Quinton in 1851, died in 1853 and was buried at Christ Church on December 23rd. Less than two years later, on July 16th 1855, Letitia Cooper married inn-keeper William Bishton at St Thomas's Church, Dudley, suggestive of a networking of local licensed victuallers. This marriage, however, proved short-lived: the death of Letitia Bishton was registered at Dudley in January quarter 1860.

In 1861, the Red Lion inn remained under the management of the Cooper family. James Cooper's nephew, the younger James, had become landlord and was described as victualler and cattle-dealer. On May 26th 1851 James Cooper had married Elizabeth Clark in her birthplace, Rowley Regis. By 1861 they had five children: 8-year-old Joseph (baptised at Hales Owen Parish Church on May 16th 1853); 6-year-old James; 4-year-old Henry (baptised at Christ Church on August 2nd 1857, when his father's occupation was given as butcher); 2-year-old Mary (baptised at Christ Church on May 1st 1859, when James was described as farmer) and 2-month-old Sarah (baptised at Christ Church on April 7th 1861, when her father was again described as butcher). At the 1861 census the live-in servants were 14-year-old Faith Williams from Netherton, employed as a nurse maid and 16-year-old Thomas Warwood, employed as a carter (presumably meaning that he was employed more on the farm than at the inn) who ten years earlier had been living with his parents and three siblings in Red Hill, Kings Norton.

10.01.03   Joseph Dixon   Beech Tree - Plot 219 (52°27'52"N 1°59'05"W)

The Beech Tree Inn, on a plot measuring 29 poles, the property of Timothy Hill, (4.09) was managed in 1841 by 75-year-old licensed victualler, Joseph Dixon. He lived with his wife Mary (70) who originated from Elmdon, son Joseph (36) born in Solihull, daughter-in-law Mary Ann (31) from Derbyshire, and grandchildren Ann (5), John (2) and Mary (10 months), all born in Ridgacre. The younger Joseph's occupation was given as dealer in provisions. Behind the inn, Dixon rented a garden, measuring 21 poles at plot 218, from Lord Lyttelton. (3.10.01) A little distance from the Beech Tree, to the south of the lane leading to Harborne, Dixon also rented from Timothy Hill two fields of pasture where, presumably, he grazed livestock and for which he paid tithe rent to the Vicar of Hales Owen.

---

[290] Could this be the George Hall listed in Ridgacre tithe apportionments as occupier of a garden at plot 59 (52°27'50"N 2°00'48"W), the property of John Foley?

Plan	Field Name	Area			Cultivation	Tithe Payable		
						Vicar		
		A	R	P		£	s	d
218	Garden (52°27'51"N 1°59'05"W)			21				
202	Close (52°27'43"N 1°59'33"W)	1	2	19	Pasture		5	6
204	Close (52°27'43"N 1°59'28"W)	1	1	18	Pasture		4	6
		3	**0**	**18**			**10**	**0**

Joseph Dixon senior's time at the Beech Tree had obviously been protracted: he is listed as licensee in the *Alehouse Recognizances* of 1828.[291] His tenure, however, came to an end in 1842 when, in the October quarter, his death was registered at Stourbridge. By the census of 1851, the Beech Tree was in the hands of the next generation: the second Joseph Dixon, spelt Dickson in *Kelly's Directory* of 1850 and no longer described as dealer in provisions but as licensed victualler. All other members of the family who had been present ten years earlier were still listed. Four more children had been born to Joseph and Mary Ann in the intervening period: Joseph (7), Elysa (5), and twins Emilia and William (3). Apart from the twins, all of the Dixon children, the eldest of whom was now 15, were listed as scholars.

Ten years on Joseph was still licensee of the Beech Tree. His mother had died in 1855 – her death was registered at Stourbridge in the October quarter. Still at home with their parents were Mary (20) now working as a bar maid; Joseph (18) a labourer on the road; Eliza (15) and Emily (13) both scholars. John Dixon (22) was now lodging in the household of William Johnson in Lower Bebington, Cheshire, where he was working as a labourer. Ann and William have not been traced. The Beech Tree household was completed by lodger Thomas O'Bryan (38) from Ireland who, like Joseph Dixon junior, was employed as a labourer on the road.

Beech Tree Inn photographed in early 20th century

See also: Glebe Land (7.03); Thomas Andrews (12.03.06)

---

[291] E 2/1/6 SA

11   Skilled workers

Life for the skilled worker in the mid-1800s, though by no means easy was, according to George Eliot's somewhat idyllic account in *Adam Bede*, far less uncouth, deprived and wearisome than the life of the nail-forger who made up the majority of Quinton's workers. The particular artisan Eliot described is a woodworker, representative of the 16 named carpenters, joiners, cabinet-makers and wood-turners in Quinton in the mid-1800s, which makes workers in wood the largest skilled worker group present in the village.

> "The sound of tools to a clever workman who loves his work is like the tentative sounds of the orchestra to a violinist who has to bear his part in the overture. All passion becomes strength when it has an outlet from the narrow limits of our personal lot in the labour of our right arm, the cunning of our right hand, or the still, creative activity of our thought. It had cost Adam Bede a great deal of trouble, and work in over-hours, to know what he knew over and above the secrets of his handicraft and the nature of the materials he worked with, which was made easy to him by inborn inherited faculty. Such men as he are reared here and there in every generation of our peasant artisans. Their lives have no discernible echo beyond the neighbourhood where they dwelt, but you are almost sure to find there some good piece of road, some building, some improvement in farming practice with which their names are associated by one or two generations after them. Their employers were the richer for them, the work of their hands has worn well and the work of their brains has guided well the hands of other men. They are men of trust and when they die before the work is all out of them, the master who employed them says, "Where shall I find another like that?"[292]

In addition to woodworkers, Quinton's skilled workers in the mid-1800s included workers in metal throughout its stages of production and manufacture from the raw material to the finished product – puddler,[293] brass-founder, crank-iron-forger,[294] blacksmith, whitesmith,[295] file-cutter and grinder, screw-wrench-filer, steel-pin-maker and gun-finisher. Also amongst exponents of the heavier manual skills were wheelwrights and two coal-miners, both of whom were heads of households which included nail-makers. (12.01.02, 12.02.03) Clothing trades were represented by tailors, dressmakers, a glover and shoemakers, the latter in the 1841 census designated cordwainers.[296] The list was completed by two stonemasons, an apprentice glazier and one worker in the jewellery trade. Altogether, there were 55 named skilled workers in Quinton in the years between the censuses of 1841 and 1861. This relatively small number compared with 274 nail makers and 118 farmers and agricultural workers is a clear indicator of the village's social status at the time. Some 20% of these skilled workers lived in family-owned property. Unlike their nail-forger neighbours, no skilled worker head of household had put any of their children under the age of twelve to work. Of those skilled workers where any church affiliation is traceable, all were connected with the Parish Church rather than Quinton's Methodist

---

[292] Eliot, G. (1859) *Adam Bede*, chapter 19

[293] A highly-skilled worker who removed the carbon from molten pig iron in a reverberatory furnace by stirring it with rods which were consumed in the process

[294] A worker who forged iron by the use of a hand-cranked blower

[295] A tinsmith; one who polishes finished metal goods as distinct from one who forges them.

[296] Cordwain from the Spanish town of Cordoba where leather much used for shoes during the Middle Ages was made. Hence cordwainer, a worker in cordwain – a shoemaker.

chapels. Also setting them apart from the nail-making community, where younger members of the family learned from the example of their parents and older siblings, Quinton's skilled workers included formalised relationships of employer and apprentice. All of Quinton's skilled workers fall within the final three groupings (7, 8 & 9) of the HISCO codes of occupation (see page 15): i.e. "Production and related workers... engaged in the extraction of minerals... manufacturing processes... those who handle materials, operate equipment and perform labouring tasks requiring primary physical effort."[297]

Quinton's skilled workers blurred the boundaries between post-Industrial Revolution work-places and ancient cottage industries. Some, like their nail-making cousins (who toiled in their own workshop, or that of a neighbour) were home-based; the workdays of others were clearly passed in factory or mine, in company with (perhaps large numbers of) other employees pursuing the same or similar trades. It has been argued that the impact of moving from the inherited skills of a cottage industry into the rote labour of a mechanised factory environment tended to de-skill the previously highly skilled worker.[298] However, the assumed pre-existing skill level is retained for the definition of Quinton's skilled workers in the mid-19th century.

11.01 Cordwainer

11.01.01   Edward Breton

Not included in the tithe apportionments, but enumerated at the census of 1841 in the Beech Lanes area of Ridgacre township, between the households of Francis Hall (8.02.02) and James Milner (11.04.01) was the household of cordwainer, 80-year-old Edward Breton. The only other occupant was Mary Breton, also aged 80, but of no stated occupation. Edward was born within the county; Mary was not. This couple remain enigmatic, as no further details concerning them have been positively verified. It is possible that they were the Edward Brueton and Mary Watton who married at King's Norton's Church of the Ascension on May 24th 1793. There is no record of them in the 1851 census, it being most probable that both were deceased by that date.

See also: John Allen (12.03.14); Joseph Grosvenor (12.01.01); James Male (12.11.04)

11.02 Tailor

11.02.01   Ann Millward   **Plot 29** (52°27'38"N 2°00'43"W)

The widow of Robert Millward [E][299](who died aged 56 in August 1841 and was buried at Christ Church), Ann or Hannah Millward,[300] some ten years younger than her husband, was the owner-occupier of a house and garden in Lower Quinton on a plot measuring 25 poles on the edge of Thomas White's *Rough Meadow*. Interestingly, the tithe map does not mark a building on plot 29. However, the

---

[297] Mandemakers, K., Muurling, S., Maas, I., van de Putte, B., Zijdeman, R.L., Lambert, P., van Leeuwen, M.H.D., van Poppel, F., Miles, A. (2013) *HSN Standardized, HISCO-coded and classified Occupational Titles,* IISG

[298] Aminzade, R. & Hodson, R. (1982) *Social Mobility in a Mid-Nineteenth Century French City*, p453

[299] As owner of freehold house in Ridgacre township. See 13.01

[300] Only the tithe apportionments list her as Ann; in census returns she is Hannah.

statutory declaration made in 1857 by Benjamin Yates (12.03.10) indicates the existence of the cottage which had previously been occupied by William Newbold. Unlike her late husband who worked as a tailor, Hannah Millward had no stated occupation. In 1841, five children completed the family: Frederick Howard (16) and Mary (10), Emma (7), Ann (baptised at Hales Owen Parish Church on July 2nd 1836) and Aaron Millward (2). The family originally migrated to Ridgacre township: Ann came from Alvechurch, Frederick (Hannah's son from a previous relationship?) was born in Frankley, and the younger children were born in Quinton.

By 1851, Emma Millward was working as a general servant for Joseph Davenport at Four Dwellings Farm. (8.01.01) Frederick (still unmarried) had followed in his father's footsteps and become a tailor, Mary (also unmarried) gave her occupation as dress-maker, Anne was listed as a servant and Aaron as a scholar. During the following decade three members of the household married. On May 25th 1851 Mary Millward married widowed cabinet-maker William Milton at Christ Church[301] and on July 20th 1851, also at Christ Church, Frederick Howard married Harriet Wheeler, daughter of Benjamin and Hannah Wheeler of Lower Quinton (12.03.12). Frederick, still working as a tailor, and Harriet made their home in Long Lane in Hill township. Six years later, on July 5th 1857, Ann Millward married wheelwright John Milner at St Bartholomew's Church, Birmingham. Both bride and groom gave their address as Coleshill Street, Birmingham. John Milner was the son of James and Mary Milner of Beech Lanes (11.04.01) By 1861 Ann and John Milner, now with a 3-year-old daughter, Anne (who had been baptised at Christ Church on April 11th 1858) had returned to Ridgacre, where John remained a wheelwright and Ann gave her occupation as dressmaker. Robert and Hannah's youngest child, Aaron Millward, who according to Rev Christopher Oldfield, also trained as a tailor,[302] changed occupation to become master of Quinton National School. (7.05) On April 2nd 1861 at Christ Church Aaron Millward married Sarah Cooper from Hampshire. Five days later the census recorded them, along with Sarah's father plumber Jonathan Cooper, resident at Quinton's schoolhouse.

11.02.02   William Dutton

Apparently arriving in Quinton in the year after the tithe map was drawn and enumerated in Red Hill in 1851 between the households of George Gee (11.05.02) and Joseph Butler (12.10.07) was 31-year-old tailor William Dutton. The other three members of his family were his wife Mary (age 28) and sons 3-year-old Henry and 1-year-old Thomas. Ten years earlier, William Dutton, then unmarried and, like his father, a tailor, had been living with his parents and four siblings in Northfield. Though the 1851 census lists all members of the Ridgacre Dutton family as born in the township, this is corrected in 1861 when William, Mary and their six children were living in Beech Lanes. Now all the children are listed as born in Ridgacre, but William's birthplace is given as Northfield and Mary's as Belbroughton. William is still working as a tailor and Mary still has no stated occupation. The eldest son, 16-year-old Charles (who in 1851 was living in Northfield with his grandparents William and Sarah Dutton) is working as a carter/agricultural labourer. Henry is employed as a cabinet-maker. The births of all six Dutton children had been registered in Stourbridge: Charles in October quarter 1845; Henry in July quarter 1847;

---

[301] William and Mary's children were baptised at Christ Church: Emma on March 7th 1852and William on March 31st 1854
[302] See Bunting T.W. & Taylor, B.J. (2005) *The Story of a Parish: The Quinton 1840-1990* p 17

Thomas in January quarter 1850; Owen in April quarter 1852; Frederick in October quarter 1856 and James in July quarter 1860.[303]

See also:
Dressmaker: Sarah Smith (11.03.03); Elizabeth Thompson (11.03.04); Caroline Clay (12.04.10); Kezia Grosvenor (12.01.01); Ann Price (12.02.01)
Glover: Hannah Berry (5.01)

11.03 Woodworker

11.03.01   Henry Foley Macdonald [E,J][304]   Plot 74 (52°27'49"N 2°00'47"W)

Plot 74 *Quintain Green* (completed 1772, demolished c1940) c 1920

Henry Foley Macdonald inherited the part of *Quintain Green,* a plot measuring 1 rood 28 poles, which he occupied, through the will of his godfather, Ambrose Foley, who died in 1827.

> *I give and devise to my said Godson Henry Foley Macdonald during the term of his natural life, a part of my said dwelling house and premises at Quintain Green (that is to say): the best parlour, the little parlour and pantry, the lodging room and the room over the little parlour, together with the antechamber, ante-hall and the front court facing the Turnpike Road, together with the dial garden and orchard and the music shop, the use of the well brewhouse and fish pool and all conveniences and passages thereto belonging... Also all my tools and effects in my music shop, together with my library.[305]*

---

[303] England & Wales Civil Registration Birth Index 1837-1915
[304] As owner/occupier of freehold house and land in Ridgacre township. See 13.01. Juror at Amy Read Inquest. See 13.02
[305] Foley, Ambrose (09.12.1826) LB

Though this bequest came to Macdonald only for his lifetime, he became a considerable freehold landowner under other clauses of Foley's will. His Quinton estate included Cotterill's Innage, plot 3 on the tithe map, by which time it was owned by John White, part of Lower Quinton Farm (8.01.02). In addition, came The Cottages, then held by Sarah Hyde (12.02.02); two gardens with tenements, then occupied by Henry Allen and Joseph Bastable;[306] the piece of land, measuring just 2 poles, opposite plot 74 with the Hermitage, where the earliest Methodist meetings in Quinton were held (plot W126 - 52°27'48"N 2°00'46"W). The land, with tenements (plot 56), on which Quinton's first Wesleyan Chapel was built (7.01) would revert to Macdonald's lawful heirs after the death of the last surviving trustee. (Macdonald obviously surrendered this right as the tithe apportionments show the owners of plot 56 as John and Ambrose Foley.) Beyond Quinton, by Foley's will, Macdonald also inherited in Birmingham's Edgbaston Street, Ladywell Chapel – three tenements and gardens at the bottom of Glasshouse Court in perpetuity and one front house and garden at the top of Glasshouse Court for his lifetime. After numerous other bequests, the residue of Foley's estate was bequeathed to his wife, Jane (who predeceased him) and his godson, Henry Foley Macdonald, who together with Foley's nephew, Ambrose, were appointed his executors.

Carpenter, joiner and cabinet-maker, Henry Foley Macdonald, who merited an entry in *Kelly's Directory* (1850), was apparently born in Quinton. There is, however, confusion over the year of his birth. Christ Church The Quinton's burial register indicates that he was born in 1794, the 1851 census suggests 1795, the 1841 census suggests 1801. The baptism of Henry Foley Macdonald is recorded at Hales Owen Parish Church on June 10th 1803, with the note "said to be 9 years old on the 11th day of April last." On July 11th 1825 at Sedgley, Staffordshire, Henry Foley Macdonald married Sarah Cooksey, whose early death was announced in the *Worcester Journal*, July 29th 1830: "On the 26th inst in her 35th year, Sarah, wife of Mr Henry Foley Macdonald of Quinton in the parish of Hales Owen." Exactly four months earlier *Aris's Birmingham Gazette* of March 29th had announced the death of Henry and Sarah's infant son: "On Monday aged 3 years and months, Ambrose son of Mr Henry Foley Macdonald of Quinton Green, near Hales Owen, Salop." Ambrose and Sarah were both buried at Hales Owen, on March 29th and July 29th respectively. On August 29th 1830, Isabella Macdonald, who had been baptised at Hales Owen Parish Church on July 27th 1830, followed her mother and brother to interment in Hales Owen churchyard. On September 15th 1834, Hales Owen parish register records the baptism of Linnaeus Augustus Macdonald, illegitimate son of Henry Foley Macdonald and Mary Cooksey. On January 1st 1836 at Sedgley, Macdonald married Linnaeus' mother, presumably a relative of his first wife.[307] At the census of 1841, Macdonald occupied *Quintain Green* with his 35-year-old wife, Mary and children Henry Foley (13), Lucius (sic) Augustus (7), Horace Foley (5), Lavinia (3) and Maurice (2). Henry junior (who had been baptised at Hales Owen on August 31st 1828), therefore was the sole survivor of Sarah's children, with Mary Jane being the mother of the other children. Horace Foley Macdonald was baptised at Hales Owen Parish Church on July 6th 1836.

---

[306] One of the two aforementioned parcels of land is presumably plot 60, rented to Benjamin Westwood (12.01.06) in the tithe apportionments.

[307] If Sarah (baptised March 1st 1796) and Mary (baptised March 20th 1807) were the daughters of Arden and Mary Cooksey, of Brierley Hill, Staffordshire as seems likely, then the marriage was illegal, under *The Marriage Act 1835* (5&6 Will.4 c.54), which prohibited marriages between brother-in-law and sister-in-law.

Before the 1851 census the deaths of Lucius and Lavinia were announced. The *Worcester Journal* of July 14th 1842 carried the following announcement: "July 2nd of scarlet fever, aged 8 years, Linnaeus Augustus, third son of Mr Henry Foley Macdonald of Quinton Green, near Hales Owen, Salop." Tragically, four months later, *Aris's Birmingham Gazette* carried the new of Lavinia's death: "After a severe illness of two days caused by her clothing taking fire, aged 5 years, Lavinia Macdonald, second daughter of Mr Henry Foley Macdonald of Quinton Green, near Hales Owen, Salop."[308] Linnaeus and Lavinia were both buried at Christ Church: on July 9th 1842 and November 13th 1842 respectively.

The 1851 census for the Macdonald household, when Henry senior employed two men in his business, lists the presence on census night of a visitor: agent, Thomas Hickling Joicey (or Joney?) from Birmingham, whose age is indecipherable. It also indicates that 15-year-old Horace Foley Macdonald was now working as a carpenter, whilst 12-year-old Maurice was still at school. Two further children, also listed as scholars, had been born: Olivia in 1841 and Lavinia Isabella, who had been baptised at Christ Church on July 7th 1844. The re-use of the name of a child who had died for a subsequent child in the same family, was not uncommon in the 19th century. Sadly, the second Lavinia Isabella also died before reaching adulthood and was buried at Christ Church on May 1st 1859. Henry Foley Macdonald junior had left Quinton by 1851 and was living and working as a draper's assistant in the home of Thomas Jones in Bull Street, Birmingham. By 1861, now married and with three children, Henry had moved to Grant Street in Birmingham's St Thomas district. However, over the next decade he maintained a melancholic link with Quinton, bringing four of his infant children for burial in the family grave at Christ Church: 8-week-old Anabella Maria on April 15th 1859; twins Annie Abella, aged 4 months on April 9th 1862 and Minnie Amelia, aged 5 months on May 7th 1862; 10-month-old Ernest William on March 3rd 1867.

Though in 1840, Henry Foley Macdonald was the subject of a writ for non-payment of debt to one John Bott,[309] the importance of the Macdonald family within the little Quinton community in the mid-1800s is indicated in a number of ways. Death announcements in both Birmingham and county press suggest a status which few other Quintonians would have attained. First to be listed at the 1841 census, at which he was enumerator for both Lapal and Illey townships, in 1851 Henry Foley Macdonald was enumerator for Ridgacre. This role was taken over in 1871 by his son, Henry, though no longer resident in Quinton. In February 1844 Henry Foley Macdonald had commissioned attorney Charles Best of Lee, Pinson and Best, Newhall Street, Birmingham to draw up his will. This lengthy document identifies none of his property beyond the usual generic household goods, furniture, plate, linen and china, which were left to his wife. Everything else was placed into the hands of trustee, Thomas Eyre, with the direction that all freehold property be sold, the proceeds invested in government securities, and the interest paid to Mary Macdonald, as long as she did not remarry. She had the responsibility of maintaining and educating their surviving children during their minorities. When they came of age, the children would receive their share of the accrued capital. The will is an interesting indicator of generational change. In 1826, Ambrose Foley's will opened with the words "In the name of God, Amen" and continued "I Ambrose Foley … being of sound and disposing mind, memory and understanding

---

[308] If the description of Lavinia as Henry Foley Macdonald's second daughter is correct, then an elder child remains unidentified.
[309] Lee Crowder Papers LB

(praised be God for the same) and calling to mind the uncertainty of this life…" Macdonald's will[310] has no such divine attribution or intimation of mortality.

Henry Foley Macdonald died in 1853 and was buried at Christ Church on April 18th. His will was proved at London on 24th October 1853 by Mary Jane Macdonald, the executrix. Under the terms of Ambrose Foley's will the Macdonald family had to vacate Quintain Green and by 1861, none remained in Ridgacre township. Henry's widow, Mary, who gave her birthplace as Bridgnorth and was listed as proprietor of land and houses, had moved into the Quinton area of Warley Wigorn, along with her children, Horace, still working as a carpenter, and Olivia, of no stated occupation. Maurice had died, aged 19 and was buried at Christ Church on June 4th 1858. Mary Macdonald lived on until 1880 and was buried at Christ Church on November 16th.

11.03.02 Thomas Smith [E,J][311]   Plot 46 (52°27'43"N 2°00'45"W)

Traditionally known as the *Nailer's Cottage* (ironical as neither of the families living there in 1844 were nail-makers) and one of only three extant buildings shown on the tithe map, is 497 Ridgacre Road West. Prior to the arrival of Thomas Smith, however, the plot was occupied by a number of nail-makers. In 1727 when Joseph Hadley, yeoman of Lapal, purchased the property for £26 5s, the occupants were nailer Thomas Cutler and Mary his wife. Ten years later when Joseph Hadley died, his will defined his intention regarding the property. "I give and bequeath unto Hannah Moore, Joseph Moore, Mary Moore, George Moore and William Moore my grandchildren fifty shillings apiece as the money shall become due by the rent of the said house, nail shop and backside wherein Thomas Cutler now dwells. My will and desire is that the said buildings shall be kept in moderate tenantable repair and not go to ruin. When the money above mentioned is fully paid then my will and desire is as my granddaughter Ann Bardon shall have the said house and backside and half the nail shop as the said Thomas Cutler hath now in his occupation to have hold and enjoy to her for ever."[312] Just three years later nailer Gabriel Bardon and Ann his wife, acting jointly with Hannah Moore, sold the property to nailer William Cutler of Northfield. Another change of ownership occurred in 1757 when, for a consideration of £25, labourer George Hawkesford of Lapal took an interest in "Two dwelling houses or tenements wherein one Thomas Cutler and Joseph Pearson heretofore did and one William Parsons and Thomas Hall now do inhabit with the nail shops, yards, gardens, ground and backsides to the same dwelling houses or tenements belonging, at a place called The Quinton."[313] Three years later, with the price increasing to £28 and the same tenants in residence, the property was sold on again to Hales Owen pig merchant William Taylor. In 1807, by which time Joseph Glaze and John Cutler were now the tenants, joiner and cabinet-maker, William Taylor, grandson of the aforementioned William, sold plot 46 to wood cutters Thomas Smith of Warley Wigorn and Edward Smith of Frankley, for £100. In 1844 the house, shop and garden occupied a plot measuring 1 rood 6 poles.

Thomas Smith was born in Illey and baptised at Hales Owen's Parish Church on October 16th 1774. In due course, like many Quinton residents, Thomas chose a Birmingham church when he married Mary

[310] Probate 11 Will Registers Piece 2179 Vol 15 Quire 701-750 (1853) Prerogative Court of Canterbury

[311] As owner/occupier of freehold house in Ridgacre township. See 13.01. Juror at Amy Read Inquest. See 13.02

[312] BA 4715 October 27th 1737 (WAAS)

[313] BA 4715 July 22nd 1757 (WAAS)

Allen from Langley Green at St Martin's in the Bullring on July 6th 1800. At least seven children resulted from this marriage: Phoebe (1801), James (1803), John (1804), George (1809), Edward (1811), David (1816) and Jesse (1819). At the census of 1841 one household at plot 46 consisted of Thomas, Mary and Jesse Smith. Thomas was described as a wood-turner, Jesse (who had been baptised at Hales Owen Parish Church on April 11th 1819, when his father was described as a wood-cutter) as a carpenter and Mary had no stated occupation. By 1851, the household had reduced to Mary, with Thomas still working as a wood-turner and employing his son, David, whose household was listed separately at both censuses and in the tithe apportionment. Jesse Smith, still a carpenter, was now married and with his wife, Sarah, and three young children, lived In Bennett Street, Birmingham. Thomas Smith died, aged 84, on March 2nd 1859 and was buried six days later at Christ Church. Still in Ridgacre township in 1861, Mary Smith now lived with her widowed daughter, Phoebe Lees, both working as tally makers. Mary died later that year and was buried at Christ Church on October 26th.

Plot 46 (497 Ridgacre Road West) before and after 21st century restoration

11.03.03   David Smith   Plot 46 (52°27'43"N 2°00'45"W)

The second household on Thomas Smith's 1 rood 6 poles plot in Lower Quinton was that of his son, David. In 1841, wood-turner David Smith (whose age is given as 25, confirmed by his baptism at Hales Owen Parish Church on July 25th 1815) lived with his wife Sarah (25), of no stated employment and daughters Mary (2), baptised at Hales Owen Parish Church on January 6th 1839, and Fanny (4 months). Though his father was not accorded the distinction, David Smith was listed among the Hales Owen traders in *Kelly's Directory* of 1850 as *Smith, David, turner, Quinton*. By the following year Sarah Smith was listed as one of Quinton's several dress-makers and two more children had been added to the household: Henry (5) and Kate (2), who had been baptised at Christ Church on September 3rd 1848. All the children, with the exception of Kate, were listed as scholars, whereas in the nail-making community, the older two would most probably have been working at the hearth for several years. However, more enlightened treatment was no guarantee of improved infant mortality, as Kate Smith died at the age of 4 and was buried at Christ Church on June 17th 1852. Less than two years later, David Smith died and, like his daughter, was interred at Christ Church, on March 12th 1854. The following

February, at St Edburgha's Church, Yardley, David's widow, Sarah Smith, née Williams,[314] married Ridgacre bachelor William Yates and at the census of 1861 was living, along with her children Fanny and Henry at plot 31 in Lower Quinton. (12.03.11)

Recent restoration removing the 20th century concrete render, revealed that the cottage is of much coarser construction than many of its 1844 neighbours,[315] suggesting its greater age. It appears originally to have been a single storey building, perhaps dating from the early 18th century, with the second storey being a later addition. The construction is a mixture of brick, stone and hand-cut timbers. It is likely that some of the materials were re-cycled from earlier buildings, the stones being mixed in both shape and size. Some of the larger, rectangular, flat-faced stones have obviously been dressed; others show signs of carved decoration.[316]

11.03.04   Edward Thompson   Plot 240 (52°27'49"N 1°59'46"W)

One of three locations listed in 1851 as Hawthorn Cottage, this 16-pole plot, property of Samuel Boulton, was void in the tithe apportionments and, apparently, in 1841. However, by 1851 it was the home of a Harborne family, headed by 50-year-old carpenter Edward Thompson. His household consisted of his wife, Hannah (56), schoolboy son, John (11) and two lodgers, also from Harborne, Edward's brothers-in-law, James (59) and Joseph (44) Whitehouse. Hannah Thompson had no stated occupation, James Whitehouse was working as a gardener and Joseph Whitehouse as a lapidary.[317] Such an occupation, unique in Quinton in the mid-19th century, suggests that Whitehouse was most likely employed in Birmingham's Jewellery Quarter, where factories detached from domestic facilities had become a feature by the 1850s.[318] Financially, this would favour Whitehouse over Quinton's other skilled workers, as workers in the Jewellery Quarter were estimated as the best paid of Birmingham's artisans.[319] The downside, however, came from detrimental effects of the working environment. "That some owe their complaints and, too frequently, their deaths to their employment, there is not the slightest question… at 45 when a peculiar fatality begins to attend these men… Workshops ill-constructed for the supply of air for breathing… where the air is loaded with dust… an excess of death from lung disease, including phthisis."[320] Joseph Whitehouse, who died of phthisis aged 50, and was buried at St Peter's Church, Harborne on 23rd November 1855, exemplifies Heslop's concern.

---

[314] If Sarah was the Sarah Williams who married David Smith at St Bartholomew's Church, Edgbaston on February 15th 1836, then February 19th 1855 was her second marriage in a Birmingham church.

[315] See photographs at 12.03.03, 12.03.10, 12.03.14

[316] Inspections by archaeologists Tim Cornah, April 2017 and Mike Hodder, December 2017

[317] An artificer who cuts, polishes or engraves precious stones (OED)

[318] See Cattell, Ely & Jones (2002) The Birmingham Jewellery Quarter, p 4

[319] See Wright, J.S. (1866) The Jewellery and Gilt Toy Trades in Timmins, S. The Resources, Products and Industries of Birmingham and the Midland Hardware District, p 458

[320] Heslop, T.P. (1866) pp 693, 697-8

In 1861, still in Hawthorns, Edward Thompson continued to work as a carpenter, Hannah still had no stated occupation, John had become an agricultural labourer, as had his uncle, James Whitehouse. The family had now been joined by Edward and Hannah's 36-year-old daughter, Elizabeth, a dress-maker. Twenty years earlier on census night, Hannah Thompson, of independent means, had been living in Nine Leasows, Harborne, with her two daughters, Elizabeth (15) and Hannah (7). Edward's whereabouts in 1841 have not been identified.

See also:

Cabinet-maker:	William Milton (11.02.01); Henry Dutton (11.02.02); Joseph Field (12.03.01); Edward Williams (12.04.14)
Carpenter:	John Gibbs (11.05.01); William Robinson (12.04.08); Thomas Page, William Page (12.10.04); John Birch (12.11.02)
Joiner:	John Berry (5.01)

11.04 Wheelwright

11.04.01   James Milner [J][321]   Plot 216 (52°27'52"N 1°58'57"W)

Occupying the last plot alongside the turnpike road in Beech Lanes, was wheelwright James Milner. The tithe apportionments indicate that in addition to the house and garden on plot 216 (measuring 20 poles) Milner was also the tenant of the adjacent garden plot 215 (52°27'52"N 1°58'56"W), measuring 23 poles). Both plots were the property of Lord Lyttelton. In 1841, 35-year-old James Milner, who hailed from Ludlow, Shropshire, occupied the properties with his wife, Mary (30) who came from Stottesdon, Shropshire, and their children, John (5), James (3), Anne (2) and Mary (3months). Shortly after the census, on May 2nd 1841, Mary was baptised at Christ Church The Quinton, as was her younger sister, Emma, on August 4th 1844. Milner's 1841 household was completed by 20-year-old Anne Jones, of no stated occupation and 15-year-old apprentice John Haynes. In the fourth quarter of 1848, the birth of Edward Milner was registered at King's Norton, suggesting that the family had left plot 216. Certainly by 1851, they had re-located to Harborne township, though still within Beech Lanes. Milner's business obviously prospered, as by then he is listed as blacksmith and wheelwright, employing three men and a boy – presumably, his son John, described as blacksmith's son in the 1851 census. However, at his marriage in 1857 and on the census of 1861, John Milner's occupation is given as wheelwright. (11.02.01)

By 1851, plot 216 was no longer occupied by a wheelwright, but by 66-year-old labourer and carter Benjamin Standley (Stanley). His household included his wife, Catherine (62), son-in-law, file-cutter Thomas Partridge (40) and grandson 7-year-old William Partridge. (12.04.02; 12.10.03) Ten years earlier, Benjamin and Catherine had been living in Lightwoods, Warley Salop, with their son, daughter-in-law and two grand-children. Benjamin Standley was buried at Christ Church on February 10th 1856 and Catherine Stanley on March 21st 1858.

See also: William Evans (12.10.07)

---

[321] Juror at Amy Read Inquest. See 13.02

11.05 Metalworker

11.05.01   Joseph Woodbridge   Plot 217 (52°27'52"N 1°59'03"W)

The 1844 occupancy of this Beech Lanes plot by Joseph Woodbridge appears to be an anomalous interlude, interrupting the tenure of the Fox family. Described in the tithe apportionments as house, blacksmith's shop and garden, plot 217, the property of Lord Lyttelton, at the turnpike road's eastern extremity in the township, measured 2 roods 35 poles. At the 1841 census, Joseph Woodbridge, who gave his age as 80 and his occupation as farmer, was enumerated in Lightwoods, Warley Salop, where his household also consisted of Frederick (35) and Harriet (30) Woodbridge. Shortly after the tithe map was drawn, Joseph Woodbridge died and was buried at Northfield's St Laurence Church on December 4th 1844, as was Frederick Woodbridge on October 1st 1848.

The Ridgacre enumerator's route in 1841 suggests that the occupants of plot 217 were 69-year-old blacksmith Thomas Fox and 21-year-old Joseph Fox, of no stated occupation. On December 11th 1842, at St Nicholas' Church, Kings Norton, blacksmith Joseph Fox married Charlotte Maria Collins. The witnesses at the wedding were Thomas and Ann Haycock, perhaps Joseph's neighbours from nearby plot 233? None of the principals were able to sign their name. The death of Thomas Fox is recorded at Stourbridge in October quarter, 1843.

By 1851, blacksmith Joseph Fox is head of this Beech Lanes household. He and Charlotte Maria (whose birth-place is given as Tibberton, Gloucestershire) now have three daughters – Maria (whose birth was registered at Stourbridge in April quarter 1842), Matilda (Stourbridge, January, 1849) and Tabitha (Stourbridge, January, 1851). Bizarrely, Henry Foley Macdonald, the Ridgacre enumerator, has recorded Tabitha as Fatabetha, which could be an affectionate nickname for a chubby baby named Tabitha! Another daughter, Amelia, whose death before her second birthday was registered at Stourbridge in January quarter, 1848, had been baptised at Christ Church on July 14th 1846. The household was completed by 35-year old lodger, John Gibbs, a carpenter who, ten years earlier had been living in Bretforton, Worcestershire. Joseph Fox and family, with the addition of three more children: 8-year-old Joseph (who had been baptised at Christ Church on March 15th 1853), 5-year-old Esther and 2-year-old Rosanna, were still in Beech Lanes in 1861. Daughters Maria and Matilda were now working as nail-makers but Joseph was no longer listed as a blacksmith having become an agricultural labourer.

11.05.02   George Gee

Not shown in the tithe apportionments but enumerated in the census of 1851 immediately after the household of Joseph Fox, as the first entry for Red Hill, was the household of labourer and carter George Gee. 49-year-old George, from Wootton Wawen, Worcestershire, lived here with his 40-year-old wife, Elysa from Belbroughton and seven children: Esther (20), Robert (14), Ann (9), Selena (7), Farmer (6), Charles (3) and 1-year-old Elysa, who had been baptised at Christ Church on September 20th 1849. At some point the family had apparently lived in Harborne where Esther was born. The two oldest children were both working, Robert as a labourer and Esther as a steel pin maker.

Steel pin making, established in Birmingham by the Ryland family in the mid-18th century was originally done by hand. An American patent of 1824 allowed manufacture to be mechanised, ultimately with a complete pin produced in one process. Esther Gee made steel pins during the transitional period, described by Charlotte Elizabeth Tonna, in very different tones from that in which Eliot pictured her carpenter: "winding slender wire which being passed through a machine by steam power is drawn out... straightening the coiled wire which they cut into lengths and point... spin, by a very exact monotonous process some wire into spiral shape which is subsequently cut into rings forming heads for the pins... pick out one with the pointed head of the wires and passing it up the shank... fix it at the blunt end and holding the pin obliquely under a small hammer turn it round, until with four or five smart strokes it is properly secured in place."[322] By 1866, it was estimated that more than 1000 workers were employed in the Birmingham pin trade.[323]

In 1841 George Gee and his family had been living in Warley Salop; in 1861 they were still in Ridgacre township, but with their address now given as Beech Lanes. Charles had died aged eight and been buried at Christ Church on March 23rd 1856. George was now described as an agricultural labourer, Ann as a servant of all work, Farmer as a harness boy, George (who was not present in 1851) as a striker at the smithy, Elysa was at school, and there were now two younger daughters, Mary (5) and Ellen (3). Esther, Robert and Selena were no longer in the family home. The marriage of Esther Gee and Josiah Moore of Warley Wigorn was celebrated at Christ Church on May 10th 1852. By 1861, Robert Gee, now working as a chemical labourer, lived with his wife and young daughter in Hill Top, Warley Salop. Selena Gee was a house servant at John Hite's farm in Tanworth-in-Arden, Warwickshire.

See also:

Blacksmith:	Thomas Fox (12.10.02)
Brass-founder:	Joseph Partridge (12.05.07)
Crank-iron-forger:	David Deeley (12.12.06)
File-cutter:	Thomas Partridge (12.10.03), Edward Butler (12.10.07)
File-grinder:	Joseph Mason (12.01.04)
Gun-finisher:	Joseph Butler (12.10.07)
Iron-bedstead-maker:	Campbell Woodward (12.12.07)
Puddler:	Edward Fox (12.10.02)
Screw-wrench-filer:	John Fox, Joseph Fox (12.11.02)
Whitesmith:	Benjamin Hill, John Hill, Benjamin Hill (12.07.01)

11.06 Stonemason

11.06.01   George Williams

Not shown in the tithe apportionments but enumerated in 1841 between the household of John Foley at plot 73 in Quinton and John Hall at plot 45 in Horse Pool Row, was the large household of stonemason George Williams. With 40-year-old George as the only resident with a stated occupation,

---

[322] Tonna, CE (1843-1844) *The Wrongs of Woman – The Little Pinheaders*, pp 449-450

[323] Timmins, S (1866) *The Resources, Products and Industries of Birmingham and the Midland Hardware District*, p 603

lived his 35-year-old wife Phoebe and eight children. These were: John (13), Mary Ann (11) Manuel (8) Emily and Emender[324] (6), Sarah and William (4), and Isabella (1). Presumably Emily and Emender, Sarah and William were two sets of twins. All are listed as born within the county, which the next census further reveals to be in Hales Owen for the parents and older children and in Ridgacre for Sarah, William and Isabella. John, Mary Ann and (E)Manuel were all baptised at Hales Owen Parish Church, on October 12th 1828, April 25th 1830 and May 12th 1833 respectively. The register also indicates the family's itinerancy: in 1828 their address is given as borough, in 1830 as Lapal and in 1833, Moor Street. By the time of the next census, the Williams family had removed from Ridgacre township to Lapal, where George was still working as a stonemason, with Phoebe, Emily and Emender at the nail-forge. Three more children (9-year-old George, 5-year-old Thirza and 2-year old Prudence) had been born since the last census, and four of George and Phoebe's older children (John, Mary Ann, Manuel and Sarah) were no longer listed. On August 26th 1849 at St Martin's Church, Birmingham, with her brother John as one of the witnesses, Mary Ann Williams married brick-layer George Ryley. John Williams could write his name, his sister could not. Both bride and groom give their address as Moor Street, suggesting that the Williams family had already returned to Lapal. The death of an Emanuel Williams was recorded in the January quarter 1847 in Birmingham. In 1851, John Williams, now like his father working as a stonemason, along with his nail-maker wife, Elizabeth, lodged in the home of Thomas Cole in Waterfall Lane, Rowley Regis. Sarah Williams has not been positively traced after 1841.

See also: Enoch Read (12.03.01)

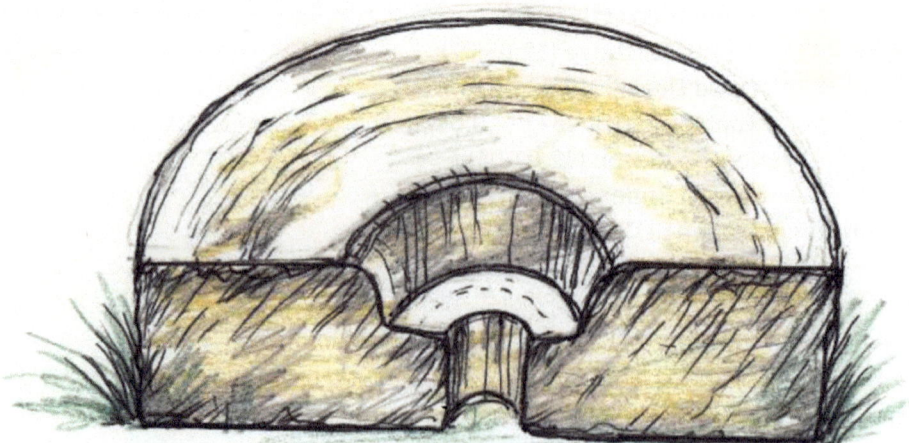

Part of the 52" diameter stone which held Quinton Toll Gate sketched in a local field in 1960 by HR Wilson.

---

[324] In an attempt to decipher this unusual name, the transcriber of the 1851 census has opted for "America."

12   Nail-forgers

As we have already seen, nail-making was the most prolific of Quinton's trades in the mid-19th century. It was also one of the most ancient. Evidence of nail-forgers in Ridgacre township is apparent in the reign of King Henry VIII, when in 1525-6, Hales Owen's Churchwardens' accounts name John Banners: *Reyseyvid of Willia' Hadley of money y^t was of a Nale made at Jhon Banners of Rugeacur: iiij marks.*"[325] Ten years later, Banners' sepulchre in Hales Owen Parish Church would cost 6s 8d.[326] However, that debt and nail-making were long-standing partners is suggested by a will of 1588 in which Edward Pepwall, nail-maker of Handsworth, left property to the value of £10 13s 1d, with debts considerably exceeding his assets, totalling £32 3s 4d, included amongst which were his obligations to a fellow nail-maker: *"By bill dated 3 June 29 Eliz. to Richard Greene of Ridgater, Salop, nailer: £1."*[327]

As the later history of nail-making shows, debt and poverty continued to be one of the hallmarks of the trade, which was reckoned one of the most poorly paid of iron manufactures throughout the 18th and 19th centuries. Certainly, Quinton's nail forgers had fallen on hard times by 1844. Though wages had always been low and working hours excessive, the trade remained popular as it could be carried out with the minimum of capital equipment in small shops attached to cottages. Many workers eked out a living by combining the job of nail forger with that of agricultural labourer or similar. The privations of the nail trade served to produce communities of uncouth, heavy-drinkers, sullen and exhausted through overwork. The success, in such places as Quinton, of Methodism with its emphasis on sobriety and cleanliness, was largely a reaction to the excesses of the cottage workers, many of whom themselves joined the growing movement. At the very least three of Quinton's nail-forgers were office holders in the local Methodist Chapels.

Following the decline of the American market and the introduction both of machine-made nails and Belgian imports, the price of nails slumped and life for the nail forgers became even harder in the mid-nineteenth century. This was compounded by the corruption of the industry, organised by nail factors or foggers who both sold iron rod to the nail forgers and bought back the finished product. Payment was frequently made in tokens which could be spent only at the fogger's own "tommy" shop or public house. A number of nail factors are listed in Hales Owen directories of the mid-nineteenth century, the most convenient for Quinton being Thomas Bissell of Webb's Green and Joseph Darby of Greenhill.

The miserable lot and appalling conditions under which the region's nail-makers laboured and lived throughout the 19th century frequently resulted in protest. Perhaps a number of Quinton's nail-forgers were so incensed by the privations which they suffered, or wearied by the poverty of their lives, that they joined with other Hales Owen nailers in 1842, in a protest march to Dudley, which caused such disturbance that the Riot Act was read, the nailers dispersed by a troop of cavalry with drawn swords, and detachments of Enniskillen Dragoons and Worcestershire Yeomanry deployed to prevent further disorder. Unrest, however, continued throughout the 1860s. A ten-week strike at the end of the decade was called to protest about the starvation wages upon which nail-making families had to exist. An indication of the extent of involvement in and sympathy for this action is seen in the Relief Fund established in Hales Owen which distributed over eight hundred loaves a week to over three hundred

---

[325] Somers, F. (1953 Part II, p 53 (NB 1 mark = 13s 4d or ⅔ £1)
[326] Op cit, p 69
[327] *Transactions of Midlands Record Society* (1889) Vol iii, 13

families of striking nailers. For those who spent their strength in the nail-shops, there would be no reward or respite when working days were done. Thomas and Sarah Haycock, nailers of Quinton at the 1841 census, had by 1851 become *"paupers — formerly nailers."*

Much has been written about the lives of 19th century nailers.[328] The following description of a nailer's cottage is by Levett Nokes, who focused upon the nail-makers of Bromsgrove.

"The wrought nail-maker's home is generally a house of misery and poverty. Their houses contain some two and some three rooms – one down and one or two upstairs; where there are two up-stairs they are very small, as the downstairs room generally ranges about twelve feet square. In bad times two or three families live and sleep in the same house. The writer knew of a case where a young woman and her child slept in the pantry and two families slept upstairs. Men, women and children have to work in the nail shop, which has access to the house, and very much helps to degrade the home, not only in their work, but other things, such as the keeping of rabbits, pigeons and fowls, which roost in the shop, and there are some who have them sit in the house, which makes the place look more like an out-house in a farm-yard than a home. In the summer time, the keeping of fowls is part of a great many nail-makers' living, as they sit the hens on duck-eggs, and keep the ducks, when they are hatched, from fourteen to twenty-eight days, and sometimes there is one hundred or more to be stored in the house and shop, beside the fowl sitting still on." [329]

How far this description resonates with the Quinton nailers' homes we are now to visit is, of course, a matter for conjecture, though there is no reason to doubt its comparability. 274 nail-makers, whose ages ranged from 6 to 86 and who were spread across some 85 households, have been identified in Quinton between 1841 and 1861. However, this must be regarded as the minimum number present, as the 1841 census enumerators rarely recorded occupations other than of heads of households. Only 23 dwellings in the relevant Ridgacre and Warley Wigorn tithe apportionments are described as containing "house and shop," raising the question of where the nail-makers in the remaining 62 households worked. The answer is supplied by Elihu Burritt, American Consul who explored the trade and economy of the Black Country in the 1860s. "The nail-maker utilizes every square foot of space at and around his forge. If he and his wife or daughter are the only members of his family to use it, he often lets one or two stalls to his neighbours for 8d each per week. That is, he lets a neighbour heat his rod in the same fire and make nails on the other side of the forge."[330]

Beginning at New Road, the route we follow around the nail-makers' cottages takes us from the north west of the tithe map, ending in Worlds End at the south east. It will become clear from the frequent changes of occupation of the township's inhabitants revealed in this Ridgacre profile that nail-making was not necessarily regarded as a job for life.

----

[328] Examples from fact are: Nokes, L. (1884) *The Mysteries of the Wrought Nail Trade Revealed*; Sherard, R.H. (1897) *The White Slaves of England*; and from fiction: Murray, D.C. (1896) *A Capful O'Nails*; Baring-Gould, S. (1902) *Nebo the Nailer*, and several of the novels of Young, F.B., particularly (1937) *They Seek a Country*.
[329] Nokes, L. (1884) pp 10-11
[330] Burritt, E. (1868) *Walks in the Black Country and its Green Borderland*, p 230

Accommodation of Quinton Nail-makers 1841-1861

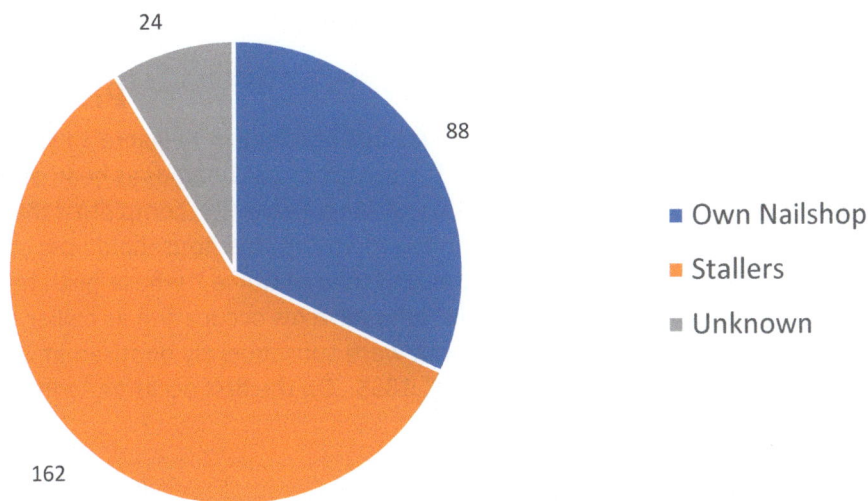

Pie chart with values: 88 (Own Nailshop, blue), 162 (Stallers, orange), 24 (Unknown, grey)

- Own Nailshop
- Stallers
- Unknown

NB: 'Unknown' indicates households identified by census enumerators, but not listed in tithe apportionments.

12.01 New Road

12.01.01 John Grosvenor [E][331]   **Plot 7** (52°27′53″N 2°01′21″W)

At the western extremity of the tithe map, adjoining the boundary with Hill township and bordered by a foredrove,[332] the turnpike road and a small enclave of Warley Wigorn, was a dwelling identified in successive censuses and by different enumerators as "Grosvenor's," "Grosvenor's Buildings" and "Grosvenor's Houses."[333] The censuses of 1841 and 1851 indicate that on this substantial plot were actually three households. Unique within Ridgacre township, and a rarity within the wider nail-making community, was nail-forger John Grosvenor, owner of the 1 rood 34 poles plot on which a house, nailshop and garden was located. At the census of 1841, John Grosvenor (60) and his daughters Harriet (25) and Kezia (15) were all returned as nail-forgers. His wife, Elizabeth (60), had no stated occupation, whilst his elder son, Joseph (36), was described as a cordwainer and his younger son, William (20), as a brick-layer. Though both John and Elizabeth were local people, they had obviously travelled, as Joseph had been born in Norwich. By 1851 John Grosvenor was registered as blind; Harriet was no longer at home; Joseph and Kezia, still unmarried, now gave their occupations respectively as shoemaker and dressmaker. Sarah Grosvenor, John and Elizabeth's seven-year-old granddaughter completed this household. Sarah, who was baptised at Hales Owen on June 1st 1848, was the daughter of William and Emma Grosvenor who, with four other children, occupied a separate household on plot 7. (12.01.03) Elizabeth Grosvenor died in 1857 and was buried at Christ Church on June 10th, John

---

[331] As owner/occupier of freehold house in Ridgacre township. See 13.01

[332] This lane, approximately opposite modern-day Victoria Avenue, led towards Jonathan Farmer's Hagg(e) Farm in the township of Warley Wigorn.

[333] E.g. 1851 – Henry Foley Macdonald; 1861 – Thomas White; 1891 – Horace Foley Macdonald

Grosvenor died aged 93 and was buried at Christ Church on May 5th 1873. Kezia, who in the tithe map decade had variously given her occupation as nail-forger and dressmaker, continued the alternations, returning her occupation as nail-maker in 1861 and seamstress in 1871. 20 years later she was retired and living as head of her own household in Lower Quinton.

12.01.02   James Hunt   Plot 7 (52°27'53"N 2°01'21"W)

The apportionments list James Hunt (who was not resident in Ridgacre township in either 1841 or 1851) as occupier of the second household. The census of 1841 names as head of household provisions dealer John Clews (25), with Sarah Clews (35) and Mary Evans (79) completing the family unit. By 1851, the Clews family was no longer living within the township, the household now consisting of John (31) and Harriett (32) Taylor with Jemima Milton (2) "child at nurse," whose birth had been registered in Birmingham in the January Quarter of 1849. John gave his occupation as collier, whilst Harriett was a nail-forger. Two of John and Harriet's children were subsequently baptised at Christ Church: Thomas on September 29th 1851 and Kezia on July 13th 1855. On the first occasion John gave his occupation as miner and on the second, labourer.

12.01.03   Thomas Morton   Plot 7 (52°27'53"N 2°01'21"W)

Not shown in 1844 but enumerated in the censuses of 1841 and 1851 contiguous with the residents of plot 7 was (in 1841) the household of labourer Thomas Morton (20), Sarah (19) and their children, Mary Anne (2) and Thomas (1), who, ten years later had left the township. In 1851, William Grosvenor, still a brick-layer, who had married Emma Parkes from Harborne, at Christ Church on October 1st 1843, who gave her occupation as nail-forger, with their four children, Lavinia (10), John (6), Ada Matilda (3) all listed as scholars, and Jane Elizabeth (1), with Agnes Coley (8), a visitor present on census night, had established their own household in Grosvenor's Buildings. Lavinia, Sarah (12.01.01), John and Ada Grosvenor were all baptised at Hales Owen on June 1st 1848. Jane was baptised there on April 28th 1850, when the family's residence was given as Hill township. William and Emma's son, Thomas, who lived only six days, was baptised at Christ Church The Quinton on November 13th 1855, and buried there on November 16th. William Grosvenor survived into the 1900s and was buried at Christ Church on December 28th 1900. Emma Grosvenor was buried at Christ Church on January 23rd 1904.

12.01.04   John Mason   Plot 63 (52°27'50"N 2°00'56"W)

Unlike his 50-year-old wife, Susannah, who came from Staffordshire, John Mason (aged 40 at the 1841 census) was born in Hales Owen. Husband and wife were both nail-forgers; their 20-year-old son, Joseph, gave his occupation as grinder. The plot of land occupied by their home, nail shop and garden, in a row of three cottages north of the turnpike road and east of a foredrove leading to Hagg Farm, measured 22 poles and was the property of John and Ambrose Foley. A John Mason had occupied this cottage 15 years earlier and was mentioned in the will of John and Ambrose Foley's uncle:

> *I give and devise one tenement and premises let to John Mason to Richard Longmore, Thomas Floyd and Henry Foley Macdonald.*[334]

---

[334] Foley, Ambrose (09.12.1826) LB

By 1851, Joseph Mason (baptised at Hales Owen's Church of St John the Baptist on May 13th 1821) was still working as a file-grinder, but now living with his own family in New England in Hill township. John and Susannah Mason, still nail-makers, had moved to plot W121 and plot 63 had new occupants. Nail-forgers Henry (36) and Mary (36) Read had, at the previous census, been living in Long Lane in Hill township. Their household was competed by three lodgers, all of whom were listed as nail forgers.

The first of these was George Woods (23) who had moved on by 1861, and as a 13-year old had been living with his father and six siblings in Spies Lane in Hill township. The second lodger, Ann Foley, was actually Mary Read's mother (identified as such in 1861) and widow of John Foley. (12.04.05) Though of no stated occupation in 1841, it is unsurprising that ten years later Ann Foley should be working as a nail forger, as the annuity left to her husband under the terms of Ambrose Foley's will would have ceased with John Foley's death in 1845. The third lodger, named by the enumerator as nail-maker 20-year-old Thomas Coley, was presumably Thomas Foley, Ann's son and Mary Read's brother. (12.04.04) Still in Ridgacre township in 1861, Henry Read had become an agricultural labourer, Mary Read a huckster's shop keeper and Ann Foley again had no stated occupation. Ann Foley died in 1869 and was buried at Christ Church on 31st July.

12.01.05   Sally Powers   Plot 61 (52°27'50"N 2°00'53"W)

Not used for nail-making in 1841, the house and garden at plot 61, measuring 20 poles and the property of Lord Lyttelton, adjacent to the Turnpike Road, was occupied by Sally (55) and Anne (25) Powers, both of independent means. Sally Powers, the daughter of Aaron and Nanny White (4.04) and the widow of Thomas Powers, was the owner of the house and garden at plot 33, let to Joseph Goode and John Yates (12.03.09, 12.03.10), from which she derived income. Anne Powers died in June 1847 and was buried at Christ Church. Sarah Powers made a will on March 1st 1850, by which time she was living in the parish of Northfield.

In a lengthy testament, Sally divided her considerable estate between her eight surviving children: sons George, William, John and Edward Powers, and daughters Mary Hollington, Rebecca Thomas, Emma Green and Sally Russell. Following her death on 27.11.1853, the progressing of Sally's estate gives a clue as to the legal processes of the mid-19th century. Her will was proved at the Prerogative Court of Canterbury on 20.12.1853, but the estate, the details of which survive and are shown below, was not settled until 11.01.1858.

27.11.1853			
Cash in house	142.00.00	Probate	10.00.00
Personal property	15.00.00	Funeral expenses	14.01.10
Rents due at death	19.00.00	Estate administration	549.17.00
Bonds etc. due at death	57.00.00	Debts	29.13.05
Real estate	1811.08.00		
Total at death	**2044.08.00**		**603.12.03**
Balance at death	**1440.15.09**		
11.01.1858			
Brought forward	1440.15.09		
Rents from real estate	202.02.10	Property repairs	**9.04.03**

Interest on bonds	7.15.10		
4% interest on £1440.15.09	179.19.06		
Total at settlement	**1830.13.11**[335]		**9.04.03**
Total estate	**1821.09.08**		
Duty paid			18.04.06
Final balance	**1803.05.02**		

By the census of 1851, plot 61 had moved down the social scale from its previous moneyed occupants to the more usual Ridgacre township residents: nail-makers, in this case Phoebe (62) and her daughter, Emma (22) Guest. Also present was Emma's 2-year-old son, Thomas, who had been baptised at Christ Church The Quinton on March 4th 1849, where he was labelled Illegitimate. Phoebe was the widow of John Guest, listed in the apportionments as occupant of plot 43, but who had not been in the township at the 1841 census. Phoebe Guest died in 1851 and was buried at Christ Church on December 21st. Two days later, Emma Guest was married there to Joseph Sadler (12.05.05) by Rev William Skilton. Could the bride also have been the Emma Guest who, at the 1841 census was lodging with Thomas and Mary Ann Partridge? (12.10.03) After less than four years of marriage, Emma Sadler died in 1855 and was buried at Christ Church on September 9th. The following year, on August 2nd at Hales Owen Parish Church, Joseph married spinster Rosannah Siviter. At the census of 1861 they were still living in Ridgacre township and, along with 12-year-old Thomas (listed as Guest in 1851, but now called Sadler and acknowledged as Joseph's son) were all nail-makers.

12.01.06   Benjamin Westwood   Plot 60 (52°27'50"N 2°00'51"W)

In the 20th century the building on the Westwood family's plot 60 served as a cottage and a shop, then as two cottages, before finally being demolished ahead of the closure of the *King's Highway* in 2007.

Henry Foley Macdonald was the landlord of the plot measuring 20 poles where, in 1841, 67-year-old Benjamin Westwood, who originated from Rowley Regis, worked as a nail-forger. Also present were his wife, Elizabeth (67), who was born in Alcester, Worcestershire, and their daughter, Prudence (25),

---

[335] Messrs Hayes & Wright, solicitors of Hales Owen actually miscalculated this figure to £1831.13.11d in the Residuary Account presented to the Inland Revenue Commissioner in January 1858.

born in Hales Owen, neither of whom had any stated occupation. On May 19th 1847, Prudence Westwood was married to widower Thomas Knight, carrier of Hales Owen at Quinton Parish Church and had therefore left her parents' home by the census of 1851. Then she was returned as living with her husband and two children in Church Street, Hales Owen, seemingly in improved circumstances as the census also records that the household had two resident servants.

By 1851, Prudence's unmarried brother, Edward, who at 37 worked as a farm labourer, was at home. Like his father, Edward had been born in Rowley Regis. He is recorded in the census as deaf and dumb, the only Quinton resident to be so listed. Benjamin, now aged 77 had changed his occupation from nail-forger to provisions dealer, which is confirmed by *Kelly's Directory* for 1850, where he is listed as a shopkeeper. Once again Elizabeth had no stated occupation. The Westwood family evidently left Ridgacre township shortly after the 1851 census and all three appear to have died in the mid-1850s.

12.01.07   Benjamin Clay   Plot 74 (52°27'49"N 2°00'47"W)

At the census of 1841, nail-forger Benjamin Clay, his wife and three children lodged with Joseph and Elizabeth Goode in Lower Quinton. (12.03.09.) By the time the tithe map was drawn in 1844, the Clay family had moved into a house, shop and garden, property of Henry Foley Macdonald, on this large plot, measuring 1 rood 28 poles, north of the turnpike road near the village centre. Plot 74, which consisted of three separate households, had been inherited by Macdonald under the terms of Ambrose Foley's will. (11.03.01) In 1841, the enumerator's route suggests that the portion subsequently occupied by Benjamin Clay, was the household of nail-forgers George (27) and Susannah (26) Woodward and their sons, Benjamin (7) and Thomas (3), all of whom had been born in Hales Owen. By 1851 the Woodward family were working as nailers at New England, Long Lane in Hill township.

The three households of plot 74 were irregularly addressed by the enumerator (Henry Foley Macdonald) in 1851. His own household was listed as Quinton Green; that of Benjamin Clay as New Road; that of James Robinson (12.04.06) as Quinton. Could it be that Macdonald wished to establish a distinct social hierarchy which placed him above his neighbours? That John Foley of Monckton Farm, who lived at Plot 73 (8.01.10) is also listed under Quinton Green would seem to support the suggestion.

In 1851, now at plot 74, Benjamin Clay (35) worked as a labourer on the turnpike road, while his wife Sarah (35), son William (15), and daughter Myra (13) – baptised at Hales Owen Parish Church on November 4th 1835 and April 1st 1838 respectively – were nail-makers. Two younger children, Joseph (7) and Anne (10)[336] both baptised at Christ Church The Quinton on May 9th 1844, were at school. Ten years later, Benjamin still worked on the road, Sarah as a nailer, William had become a farm worker and Joseph a nail-maker. Three months before the census, Anne Clay married George Deeley in Edgbaston Parish Church, with witnesses William Clay and E. Rose who, unlike the other three principals was unable to sign her name. Could this have been Ann Clay's near neighbour Eliza Rose of Horse Pool Row? (12.02.03.) It would be in the Smethwick home of Ann and George Deeley that Sarah Clay lodged,[337] following Benjamin's death and burial at Christ Church on November 11th 1872.

---

[336] See 12.01.07

[337] Still head of her own Ridgacre household in 1881, by the census of 1891 Sally Clay ("living on own means") had moved to lodge with her daughter Ann and her husband, George Deeley, in Bearwood Road, Smethwick.

12.02 Horse Pool Row

12.02.01   James Price   Plot 44 (52°27'46"N 2°01'55"W)

Though no James Price is listed in either the census of 1841 or 1851, living in the right place at both dates was Joseph Price, enumerated immediately following John Hall and William Rose at plot 45, which was adjacent to plot 44 on the tithe map. It may safely be assumed, therefore, given the known inaccuracies of the early records, that James and Joseph Price are one and the same person. The property of James Bissell, plot 44 measured 1 rood 1 pole and its house, shop and garden were occupied in 1841 by nail-forgers Joseph Price (aged 30) and his wife Ann (30) along with their children Elizabeth (7) and Joseph (3), both of whom had been baptised at Hales Owen Parish Church of St John the Baptist: Elizabeth on January 12th 1834 and Joseph on April 1st 1838. Elizabeth Price died aged 10 and was buried at Hales Owen Parish Church on May 5th 1844.

By the census of 1851 Joseph had joined his parents at the nail forge and three more children, each of whom had been baptised at Bethesda Primitive Methodist Chapel, Quinton, had been born. 9-year-old Ann (baptised on September 9th 1842 – only the second baptism in the chapel[338]), was already at work at the hearth, whilst 7-year-old John (April 8th 1844) and 4-year-old Emma (September 9th 1846) were both listed as scholars. Two visitors were present in March 1851, Joseph Price's brother-in-law, David Smith (26), whose occupation was given as labourer at chemical works, and his wife Mary (21).

Still living in Ridgacre township in 1861, Joseph Price was now listed as Methodist preacher: Nail Maker. Ann Price and the four children still at home (Joseph, Ann, John, Emma) were also all nail-makers. A fifth child, Jason born in 1852 and baptised at Bethesda on February 8th, was at school. The two older children were both married at Christ Church in 1864; Joseph, described in the register as a horse-nail forger, to Laura Horton of The Quinton on March 25th and Ann, who gave her occupation as dressmaker to Walter Horton of The Hawthorns on December 12th. On both occasions, their father had also specified his occupation as horse-nail forger. Sadly, the younger Joseph died in June 1867 and was buried at Christ Church. Ten years later, Jason Price, now married to Elizabeth and with a one-year old son, Joseph William (baptised at Bethesda Primitive Methodist Chapel on January 5th 1869), also gives his occupation as horse-nail maker.

Jason Price epitomises Ridgacre township's later generation nail-maker who breaks away from the trade and indeed from the village of his birth. In 1881, living in Leicester[339] with an increasing family (two sons and two daughters were born there) Jason's occupation is Clerk: Bible Depository. At the next three censuses, living at various addresses in Smethwick, Jason and Elizabeth had produced four more children and Jason's occupation had moved from Commercial (1891) through Insurance Agent (1901) to Office Clerk (1911).

---

[338] The first, on 19.12.1841, was William, son of David and Phoebe Payne, who were not listed in the tithe apportionments.

[339] The 1881 census inaccurately gives Jason Price's birthplace as Quinton, Northamptonshire. The enumerator was most likely unaware of the existence of Quinton, Worcestershire!

Quinton Nail-makers changing occupation 1841-1861

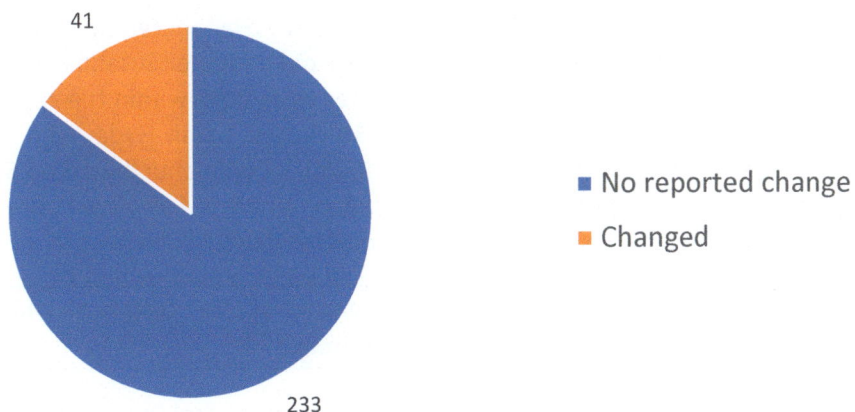

41

233

- No reported change
- Changed

Occupations to/from which Quinton Nail-makers changed 1841-1861

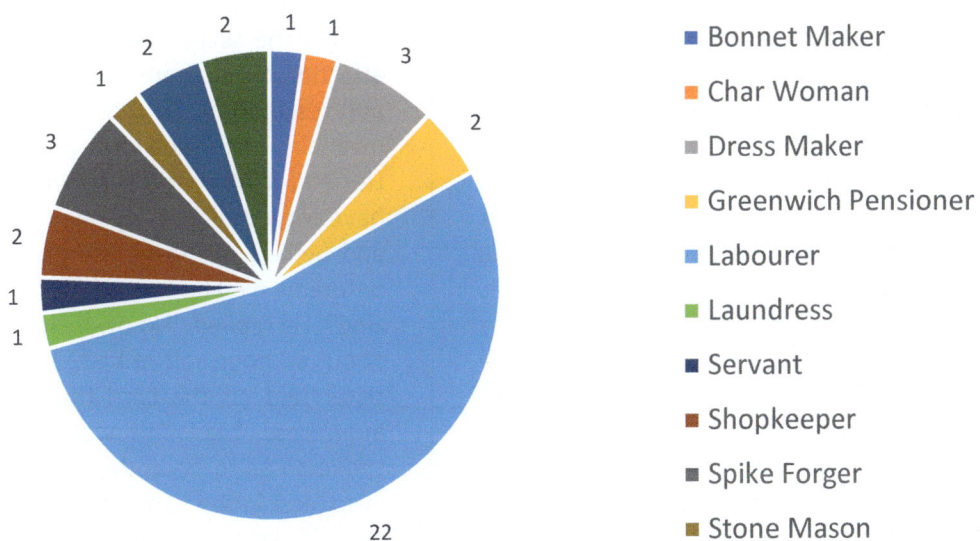

2 1 1
2   3
1
3   2
2
1
1
22

- Bonnet Maker
- Char Woman
- Dress Maker
- Greenwich Pensioner
- Labourer
- Laundress
- Servant
- Shopkeeper
- Spike Forger
- Stone Mason

12.02.02 John Hall   Plot 45 (52°27′44″N 2°00′53″W)

At the 1841 census nail-forger John Hall, the 29-year-old son of James Hall (12.04.03), resided with his wife Ann(e) (40) in a cottage, the property of James Bissell, in Horse Pool Road. A somewhat larger plot than most nail-forgers' homes, this site, which measured 1 rood 1 pole, also accommodated the separate household of William Rose. (12.02.03.) John and Ann Hall shared their home with Sarah Hyde (85) and William and Jane Southall and their eight-year-old daughter Susanna. William (25) and Jane (20) were both nailers; neither they nor their daughter were born within the county; and the family had left Ridgacre township by the time of the 1851 census. Sarah Hyde, who is described as 'of independent means,' died in 1841 and was buried in Hales Owen churchyard on September 4th. Her stay in Ridgacre had evidently been of a longer duration. Ambrose Foley's will, drawn some 15 years before the 1841 census, identifies Sarah Hyde as a local resident.

> *"I give and devise to my Godson Henry Foley Macdonald all that Tenement and Premises with the appurtenances in the holding of Sarah Hyde called the Cottages."* [340]

Nail-forger John Hall, like his father, was a Primitive Methodist Local Preacher. His early death at the age of 38 was recorded in the *Primitive Methodist Magazine*[341] in less enthusiastic tones – 'he was not, as some say, talented, but he was useful' – than that of his father 18 years later.

"John Hall resided at Quinton, his native village, about five miles west of Birmingham. Its inhabitants were noted for wickedness when the Primitive Methodists first missioned it. Yet, in the midst of all, the Lord owned his word, and John Hall was a member of the first class that was formed. He was brought to the Lord about the year 1831; and he had the pleasure of seeing the cause of God in his native place prosper from its commencement to the close of his life. For this he lived, and prayed, and laboured; for he knew that his labour was not in vain in the Lord. He was a local preacher about ten years. Generally, his appointments lay from five to ten miles away from his home, along country lanes; but in all kinds of weather he attended them. He was not, as some say, talented, but he was useful, and by every society was respected. He did not keep a journal, but we believe some souls were saved by his ministry. He was a class-leader and was much respected by his class. He was a Sunday-school teacher; and when not planned to preach, he was diligently engaged in the school. He was a chapel-steward for 10 years.

"In November last, he took a severe cold, which brought on a consumption, and though every effort was made to relieve him, the disease baffled the skill of the physician. He bore his affliction throughout with Christian fortitude and resignation. To those who visited him he invariably expressed strong confidence in God. He said, 'I know the Lord will not leave me; I have served him in my health and I love him, and he will not leave me now.' A few hours before he died he was asked, 'Are you happy in God?' He replied, 'I know he is my Saviour;' and about an hour before he breathed his last, his sister said, 'Is the Lord thy portion?' and he answered, 'Yes.' This was the last word he spoke so as to be understood. In the Lord he lived, and in the Lord he died, March 6th 1850, aged 38 years.

---

[340] Foley, Ambrose (09.12.1826)
[341] Flesher, J. (1850) pp325-326

"On Sabbath evening last, his funeral sermon was preached in Quinton chapel, and the crowds that attended and the tears that were shed, showed that he had been greatly respected in his life, and was lamented at his death. He has left a widow, a father and a mother, sisters and many friends to mourn their loss, but their loss is his infinite gain."

John Hall was buried in Christ Church graveyard on March 11th 1850.

Still operating the nail forge after her husband's death, Ann Hall, by the census of 1851, was assisted by Bilston-born nail-forger Harriett Payne (24) who, with her children, three-year-old Sarah, two-year-old Julia-Ann (both born in Birmingham) and two-month-old Charles (born in Quinton) now lodged at the cottage. On census night, Harriett's husband, chemical works labourer William Payne from Pershore, was resident at Icknield Chemical Works in Icknield Square, Birmingham.[342] Sarah, Julia and Charles Payne were all baptised at Quinton's Bethesda Chapel on March 22nd 1851. By 1861 all of the residents of this cottage had left Ridgacre township and the Payne family, now with two more children were re-united in Ladywood, Birmingham.

12.02.03   William Rose   Plot 45 (52°27'44"N 2°00'53"W)

Aged 33 at the 1841 census, William Rose lived with his wife Sarah (23) and children John (7), Thomas (5), Eliza (18 months) and Lavinia (9 months), occupying a house, nail-shop and garden, the property of James Bissell on the same Horse Pool Road plot as John Hall. (12.02.02) On October 11th 1833, William Rose had married Sarah Robinson at Hales Owen Parish Church. In 1841, 9-year-old Ann Robinson was part of their household. (12.03.05) Subsequently three further children were born to William and Sarah: Edwin (1845), William (1847) and James (1850). The three elder children were all baptised at Hales Owen's Parish Church of St John the Baptist: John on March 9th 1834, Thomas on February 12th 1837 and Eliza on November 11th 1839. By the time Lavinia was born, Quinton's Christ Church had been dedicated, and she was baptised there on March 7th 1841. No baptisms have been traced for the next two children, Edwin and William, but James was baptised at Quinton's Primitive Methodist Bethesda Chapel on March 10th 1850. This raises the interesting question of whether the Rose family had undergone some period of religious turmoil during the 1840s.

By 1851, Sarah Rose (who had been the family's sole nail-forger) had been replaced at the hearth by her three older children. Lavinia, Edwin and William were returned as scholars and James was still a baby. Like John Taylor (12.01.01), William Rose senior, who came from Hagley, was a miner. The

---

[342] Though Kelly's *Directories* of the period list numerous chemical works in Birmingham, there are none called Icknield Chemical Works, nor by another name at this address.

nearest large-scale colliery to Quinton was *Old Hawne* Pit which had opened in Hales Owen sometime in the 1820s. Did John Taylor and William Rose work there, or perhaps at one of the dozens of small pits which had been sunk at the end of the eighteenth century on the exposed coalfield to the north of the town?

The Rose family is one of Ridgacre township's minority families living in the same cottage at the census of 1841, the compilation of the tithe map and the 1851 census. Indeed, the family were still present a decade later, though by then they had suffered two deaths: Lavinia, aged 14, in 1856 and her mother, Sarah, aged 39 in 1857. Both were buried at Christ Church. By 1861 Thomas and Edwin were no longer at home and John had established his own household with his wife Jane and three children, Joseph (6), Sarah (3), who had been baptised at Christ Church on May 2nd 1858, and Leviniah (12 months), presumably named in memory of her aunt. Though James had become an agricultural labourer, his sister Eliza, brother John and sister-in-law Jane maintained the nail forge. Ten years later, though Jane Rose continued as a nail-maker, John had left the forge for a career in electro-plating.

12.03 Lower Quinton

12.03.01   Edward Smith   Plot 41 (52°27'43"N 2°00'51"W)

Not a nail-maker's household in 1841, 30-year-old Edward Smith, the listed occupant of this house and garden in the tithe apportionments, is described as "dealer," and was apparently, a horse-dealer. Edward was the son of Thomas Smith, wood-turner of plot 46. (11.03.02) He lived with his wife Harriet (33), their children Betsy (11), Thomas (9) and Joseph (6) and with 16-year-old labourer William Payne. Thomas and Joseph Smith had both been baptised at the Parish Church of St John the Baptist, Hales Owen: Thomas on January 17th 1834 and Joseph on February 22nd 1837. The Smith family were all born in Hales Owen; their lodger came from within the county. Together they part-occupied Plot 41 sandwiched between Hither Mancroft to the north and Cutler's Meadow to the south near the village centre. Their plot measured 1 rood 17 poles, was the property of John White and was shared with the family of farm labourer Thomas Yeomans. (12.03.02.)

By the census of 1851 Edward Smith, now a widower, and his three children had left Ridgacre and settled in Warley Salop. Also by this time, plot 41 had become a nail-making household. This occurred through the removal of an established Ridgacre family who, in 1841, had been resident at plot 112. (12.06.03) At some point in the decade, Elijah and Sarah Read moved from Upper Ridgacre to Lower Quinton where, in 1851, their household included six children and three lodgers. From Elijah (53) through his wife Sarah (45) and their children David (19), Reuben (14), Elijah (13), Mary Ann (11), Enoch (9) to Amy (6) all were nail-forgers. Thus, Amy Read is the youngest recorded of Quinton's nail-makers from 1841-1861. Though Christ Church had been consecrated in 1840, Enoch had been baptised at Hales Owen Parish Church on April 24th 1842 and Amy on September 28th 1845, as their older sister, Mary Ann had been on December 1st 1839. The three lodgers, Joseph (20), Harriet (23) and John (1) Yeomans, were actually Elijah and Sarah's daughter, son-in-law and grandson. Both Joseph and Harriet gave their occupations as nail-forgers. On March 24th 1850, Harriet Read had married Joseph Yeomans at Christ Church and on April 1st 1850 their son John (whom the register notes was born on March 1st)

was baptised at Bethesda Primitive Methodist Chapel. This family obviously took full advantage of the religious diversity available to them.

Still in the family home in 1861, parents Elijah and Sarah Read were still nail-making, as were their son Elijah and daughters Amy and Mary-Ann (now married to cabinet-maker, Joseph Field). Also still at home, Enoch Read was now employed as a mason. Head of his own household in Spies Lane in Hill township, David Read and his wife Hannah both worked as nail-makers. Reuben Read had given up the nail trade and was lodging in Ladywood, Birmingham, where he worked as a labourer. Joseph, Harriet and John Yeomans (plus five more children) were living in Warley Wigorn, where Harriet and John both worked as nail-makers, though Joseph had joined the growing number of phosphorous workers.

12.03.02   Thomas Yeomans   Plot 41 (52°27'43"N 2°00'51"W)

Like the adjacent household of Edward Smith, Thomas Yeoman's cottage did not include any nail-makers in 1841. Yeomans, who was the brother of Sarah Smith (sister-in-law of Edward Smith (12.03.01) was 34 years old at the time of the census and a labourer. His family consisted of his wife Anne (32), sons David (16), also a labourer, George (11), Thomas (2), and daughters Mary (14) and Sarah, who had been baptised at Hales Owen Parish Church on May 10th 1835. The baptism of David Yeomans on February 27th 1825 at Church Honeybourne, Worcestershire, suggests the family's place of origin (though Anne Yeomans was born in Kings Norton). The baptism of Thomas Sardinia Yeomans at Hales Owen on December 31st 1838, reveals that his middle name was also his father's.[343]

Mary Yeomans died in March 1842 and was buried at Christ Church. Completing the 1841 household were Mary Ann (11) and Sarah (5) Smith. If these two residents were children of Edward and Harriet Smith next door, then Mary Ann[344] and Betsy Smith would have been another of Quinton's sets of twins. By 1851, the surviving members of the Yeomans family had moved to Icknield Port Road, Birmingham, where Thomas and George now gave their occupations as chemical works labourers,[345] whilst David was a German silver smelter.

Following the removal of the Yeomans family, their home on plot 41 became a nail-forger's household. Joseph Hall, aged 29, who, ten years earlier, the eldest of eight children, had been working as a nail-maker and living at his parents' home in Warley Wigorn, was now married. He and his wife Lucy (24), also a nail-forger, had three children, Sarah (3), Thomas (1) and Ann Maria (3 months). Joseph and Lucy were another of Quinton's nail-making families whose religious allegiance fluctuated. Thomas was baptised at Christ Church on December 2nd 1849; Ann Maria was baptised at Bethesda Primitive

---

[343] It is interesting to speculate as to the origin of Yeomans' exotic name, which the census enumerators carefully avoid! Perhaps it reflects the prominence of Sardinia during the Napoleonic Wars which were raging at the time of Thomas senior's birth around 1807. In 1792, the Kingdom of Sardinia had joined the First Coalition against the French Republic, but was beaten in 1796 by Napoleon. Two years later Charles Emmanuel IV was forced to abdicate and leave the Italian mainland for his island kingdom of Sardinia, which stayed out of French control for the rest of the war.
[344] On September 29th 1850 at Christ Church Mary Ann Smith married David Huston of Warley Wigorn.
[345] Presumably, given their address, Thomas and George Yeomans were employed at the same chemical works as Harriet Payne's husband, William - 12.02.02.

Methodist Chapel on September 21st 1851; a further daughter, Emily was taken to Christ Church for baptism on February 1st 1857. This family also proved to be somewhat migratory. By 1861 they had left the township for Perry Hill in Warley Wigorn. Joseph had abandoned nail-making for labouring; Lucy had no stated occupation; Thomas had died in 1858 and was buried at Christ Church on November 23rd. In 1871, back in Ridgacre at Hawthorns, Joseph was a builder's labourer, whilst Lucy, Sarah and Ann Maria were all working at the nail forge.

12.03.03 James Preedy   Plot 38 (52°27'42"N 2°00'50"W)

[Prady in Tithe Apportionments]

Still a substantial building in the mid-20th century, the house on plot 38 (measuring 36 poles) was the property of Joseph Darby (4.15), identified in the will of his father, also Joseph Darby, nail-monger of Hill township, in 1837. Amongst various parcels of property is included a "freehold messuage and other hereditaments at or near the Quinton in the township of Ridgacre occupied by James Preedy."[346]

Plot 38, photographed in mid-20th century

At the census of 1841, farm labourer James Preedy (50), a native of Droitwich, his wife Sarah (50), daughter Sarah (25), both nail-forgers, sons James (20), employed as a brick-layer, and Benjamin (10), daughter-in-law Lucy (19) and grandson Joseph (1) lived at plot 38 near the heart of the village. James and Benjamin had both been baptised at Hales Owen Parish Church (on May 10th 1818 and May 16th 1830 respectively) when the family's address was recorded as Lapal. Christ Church The Quinton Register records the baptism of a third Sarah, daughter of James and Lucy Preedy on December 5th 1841, and Henry, registered as illegitimate son of (the second) Sarah Preedy on January 10th 1842. Henry lived only six weeks and was buried at Christ Church on February 20th 1842.

---

[346] Will of Joseph Darby, 23. 02.1837; proved Prerogative Court of Canterbury, 23.04.1838

By the next census, James junior and Lucy Preedy had both died (Lucy in September 1842 and James in March 1849); Sarah Preedy died aged 10 in October 1851. All three were buried at Christ Church. In 1851 grandson Joseph, now 11, was returned as Joseph Goode,[347] not Preedy. Also missing from Ridgacre township on census night 1851 was Benjamin Preedy. (By the census of 1861, grandson Joseph, now like his grandfather an agricultural labourer, was once again surnamed Preedy. Benjamin, like his late elder brother now a brick-layer was back at home with his nail-maker wife Jemima and sons Henry and Francis.) Two lodgers completed the 1851 household: Thomas Irons (50), a farmer's labourer from Hales Owen and Harriet Wheeler (27), employed as a nail-forger. in 1841 Harriet Wheeler had lived with her parents at plot 35 (12.03.12) and in July 1851 married Frederick Howard at Christ Church. (11.02.01)

Quinton Nail-makers age profile 1841-1861

6-year-old Amy Read (12.03.01) was the youngest of Quinton's nail-makers
and 86-year old John Read (12.03.04) the oldest

12.03.04   John Read

Not shown in 1844 but enumerated in the census of 1841 between the two households of James Preedy and Benjamin Hodgetts on plot 38 was the family of John Read. The identification and relationships of this family present some challenges. Listed first is Quinton's oldest nail-forger, 86-year-old John Read. He is followed by Elizabeth (36) and Mary (30) Read, both nail-forgers and presumably his daughters. They are followed by Amelia Read (8) and Richard Read (1), both entered in the female column. Amelia Read, daughter of nailer John and Elizabeth Read was baptised at Hales Owen Parish

---

[347] Two boys named Joseph Goode were baptised in Hales Owen in 1840. The first on January 12th was entered in the register as son of Sarah and the second, on May 31st as son of Lucy. No surnames were given for the mother in either case and only the first has a named father (James Goode). Both boys could be described as grandson of James and Sarah Preedy, as either the son of their daughter, Sarah, or daughter-in-law, Lucy.

Church on April 29th 1838, followed by Richard Read, son of nailer John and Elizabeth Read of Gosty Hill, on January 19th 1840. All of the Reads listed here in the 1841 census were identified as born within the county. None of them are present in Ridgacre township by 1851. It may safely be assumed that John Read had died. At the census of 1851, Elizabeth Read, widow, born in Rowley is head of the household at 11th house, 8th court, Smallbrook Street, Birmingham. Also present are her daughter, Amelia, born in Hales Owen, son, Richard, born in Rowley and 6-year-old daughter, Eliza, born in Birmingham. A 40-year old Mary Read (nailer) is shown in New England, in Hill township, living as a servant in the home of 40-year-old John Johnson (nailer). Three children, the eldest two of whom – Eliza (16) and Charles (13) – are also nailers, and, along with John (8), all listed as "born out of wedlock" made up that household. Ten years earlier, at Crook Street in Hill township, John Johnson (30), nailer, lived with Mary Johnson (30) and Eliza (6) and Charles (4). The identity of the two Marys and their link with Mary Read of Ridgacre township is a matter of conjecture. If Mary Read and Mary Johnson were the same person, then she was enumerated twice.[348]

12.03.05   John Sadler   Plot 38 (52°27'42"N 2°00'50"W)

John Sadler, listed as part-occupant of the house and garden at plot 38 in the tithe apportionments, was not resident there at the census of 1841. At that point, the enumeration route suggests that the residents were nail-forgers Benjamin (40), Fanny (20) and Thomas (15) Hodgetts along with three younger children, Sarah (5), Anne (3) and Jane (1 month) Hodgetts. Sarah Hodgetts, daughter of Benjamin and Sarah Hodgetts had been baptised at Hales Owen Parish Church on May 11th 1836 and was buried at Christ Church on August 28th 1842. Sarah senior's death was registered at Stourbridge in October Quarter 1837. The raw urgency of the mid-19th century nail-forging community is exposed by the seemingly immoderate haste with which the widower proceeded. On February 12th 1838 Benjamin Hodgetts married Fanny Coley at Birmingham's Parish Church of St Martin. Both bride and groom gave their address as Worcester Street, Birmingham and their occupation as nailer. Thus, Hodgetts becomes an apt paradigm for Francis Brett Young's brutalised nailer Tom Oakley who, on the day of his wife's funeral abandons his family commenting, "A woman's more use to me and I reckon it won't be long afore I get me another."[349] Benjamin and Fanny Hodgetts' children Ann and James were also baptised at Hales Owen: Ann on October 7th 1838 and James on May 23rd 1841. The final member of this household was nail-forger Thomas Sadler (20). All, apart from Benjamin Hodgetts, were returned as born within the county. Within five months of the census Thomas Sadler was dead and was buried at Christ Church on August 29th. No members of this Hodgetts family were present in Ridgacre township in 1851 nor, presumably, in 1844.

Occupant in 1844, Hales Owen-born John Sadler, at the 1851 census gave his age as 35, as did his wife Mary. Both were nail-forgers. Their 10-year-old daughter Mary, still a scholar, had been baptised at Christ Church The Quinton on May 2nd 1841. Three lodgers completed the household. The first two, also employed as nail-forgers were 18-year-old Ann Robinson, who presumably had moved from the Rose household a little farther along the lane sometime during the previous ten years (12.02.03); 14-year-old Elizabeth Robinson and 4-month-old John Robinson, returned in the census as "daughter-in-

---

[348] No appropriate death records for either Mary Read or Mary Johnson within the relevant time frame were identified.

[349] Young, F.B. (1937) *They Seek a Country*, pp 36-37

law's child". Prior to establishing themselves in their own home, John, Mary and Mary Sadler, along with Elizabeth Robinson, had lodged with their near neighbour, Mary Mason. (12.03.08.)

The Sadler-Robinson family relationship was obviously somewhat complicated. John Robinson died aged 18 months and was buried at Christ Church in May 1852. Within the same household in 1861 where the only adult male was still John Sadler, both Ann and Elizabeth Robinson were described as "daughter-in-law." There were two Robinson grandchildren: Sarah (6)[350] and another John (4 months). However, enumerator Thomas White was not necessarily over-concerned about the accuracy of his return as he listed the entire household, including the baby as nail-makers! In 1871 Ann and Elizabeth are both shown as: "step daughter-in-law" and there were two more Robinson grand-daughters: Eliza (7) and Mary Ann (2 months) in the Sadler household. It seems likely that Ann and Elizabeth Robinson were Mary Sadler's children from a previous relationship.

12.03.06   Thomas Andrews   Plot 37 (52°27'40"N 2°00'48"W)

Listed in the tithe apportionments as the occupier of one of the three cottages on this plot (measuring 1 rood 10 poles and belonging, like plot 38, to Joseph Darby) Thomas Andrews, from Carters Lane in Lapal township and then aged 31, gave his occupation as publican in the 1841 census. This would suggest that there may well have been an early beer house within the village centre to supplement the three inns located along the turnpike road. Though there are no claimants in 1851, at the census of 1861, William Yates (12.03.11), a close neighbour of Thomas Andrews, gave his occupation as publican and shop-keeper, with his step-daughter, resident at the same address, listed as bar maid. By 1871 Yates was the publican at the New Inns, Quinton, a hostelry which, as has already been established, was located in the south-west corner of the Glebe Land. (7.03)

At the 1841 census, the Andrews household also consisted of Thomas's wife, Ann (25) of no stated occupation and daughters Elizabeth (5) and Sarah (3 weeks). Elizabeth had been baptised at Hales Owen Parish Church on April 30th 1836, but by the time of Sarah's birth Christ Church The Quinton had been consecrated. There she was baptised on November 6th 1841, the register listing Thomas's occupation as nailer, which he declared himself to be in 1851. By this time, the family had grown to include two more daughters, Mary Ann (5) and Lucy (3), who, like their sister Sarah, had been taken to Christ Church for baptism: Mary-Ann on September 7th 1845 and Lucy on July 11th 1848. All but the two youngest girls were now working as nail-forgers. The Andrews household is one of the Ridgacre township units where the same nuclear family were the sole occupants of the cottage both in 1841 and 1851. However, a decade later they had moved on. Thomas, now a widower, with his daughters, Sarah, Mary Ann and Lucy were, at the 1861 census, living together in Bartley Green, where all four worked as nail-makers. On June 12th 1854 at Christ Church, nailer Elizabeth Andrews had married nailer George Hill of Carters Lane.

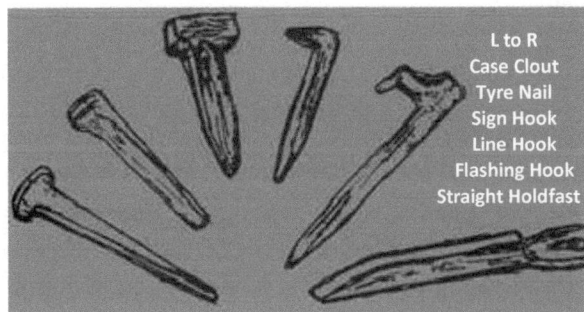

L to R
Case Clout
Tyre Nail
Sign Hook
Line Hook
Flashing Hook
Straight Holdfast

---

[350] Sarah Ann Robinson, daughter of Eliza was baptised at Christ Church The Quinton on November 19th 1858.

12.03.07   John Read   Plot 37 (52°27'40"N 2°00'48"W)

The fact that in the three censuses in which the Read family lived on plot 37 they were always enumerated second of the three households in this block, suggests that their home was the middle

Tenant and two stallers at work in a nail-shop – Harold Piffard

cottage. In 1841 their family unit consisted of just three members: nail-forgers John Read (65), his son, Enoch (20) and daughter-in-law, Elizabeth (20), all born in Hales Owen. Enoch, son of Ridgacre nailer John and Mary Read, had been baptised on September 6th 1818 at Hales Owen Parish Church, where on February 22nd 1841, he married Elizabeth White, daughter of labourer John White of Warley Salop. Enoch was literate, Elizabeth was not. John Read died in 1845 and was buried at Christ Church on February 16th. By the census of 1851 Enoch Read had become the head of the household. Five sons, each baptised at Christ Church had been born to Enoch and Elizabeth in the intervening years: John (baptised November 6th 1841), William (March 3rd 1844), Thomas (September 6th

1846), James (August 6th 1848) and George January 5th 1851). Sadly, William and Thomas had died within a week of one-another, in August 1847. Three daughters, all baptised at Christ Church – Sarah-Anne (April 3rd 1853), Mary (October 7th 1855) and Eliza (March 1859) were born during the next decade.

Though Enoch Read's children were baptised according to the rites of the Anglican Church he, presumably, worshipped with the Wesleyan Methodists and was the signatory to the ecclesiastical census return for Quinton's Wesleyan Chapel in 1851. (7.01) Despite the famed penury in which nail-forging families lived, the Reads opened their home to visiting Wesleyan preachers who came to lead services in Quinton. For this repeated generosity, they received financial remuneration on more than one occasion. "In consideration of the accommodation provided by Bro Read at Quinton for the Brethren appointed there, he be presented with ten shillings from our fund."[351]

---

[351] *Birmingham Local Preachers' Minute Book* (12.03.1852). A similar minute was recorded in March 1853. LB

By 1861, Enoch Read had exchanged nail-making for labouring at a phosphorous works,[352] with his son, John. James Read, however, now aged 12 had become a nail-maker. Enoch Read died in January 1863 and Elizabeth in March 1868. Both were buried at Christ Church. By 1871 only Sarah-Anne remained in Ridgacre township, now working as a nail-maker and lodging in the household of phosphorous maker, William Jones. John and James now had their own separate households in Oldbury (obviously to be closer to their place of work) with James having exchanged nail-making for an occupation as chemical labourer. With John and his wife, Emma, lived his sister, Eliza and with James and his wife, Mary Ann,[353] lived his brother, George, now a labourer. The remaining sibling, Mary, lodged as a general servant in Court Oak Road, Harborne in the household of laundress, Catherine Horton.

12.03.08   Mary Mason   Plot 37 (52°27'40"N 2°00'48"W)

Following the death of her nail-forger husband, Samuel, who died at the age of 75 less than three months after the 1841 census and was buried at Christ Church on June 27th, Mary Mason (70), who was not a native of Ridgacre, became head of the household, which occupied the third cottage on plot 37. John (20) and Mary (30) Sadler lodged with Mary Mason and worked at the nail hearth. They had two children, Ann (11)[354] and Mary (6 weeks). As we have already seen (12.03.05) by 1844 the Sadler family was established in its own household. However, another Mary Sadler (25) was also listed in Mary Mason's cottage as a nail-forger, with Ann Mary Chatwin (30) and four-year-old Betsy Robinson (who, by 1851, was living with John and Mary Sadler) completing the household.

By 1851, a new generation of Masons was listed. Home from the Royal Navy was Joseph Mason (50) an out-pensioner of Greenwich Hospital,[355] paid at Stourbridge. He was married to Ann (whose age, given as 37, was inconsistent with the previous and subsequent censuses); they had two children, Samuel (4) and Joseph (2) both of whom had been baptised at Bethesda Primitive Methodist Chapel: Samuel on January 31st 1847 and Joseph on July 1st 1849. The family unit was completed by nailer Martha Hyde (17), described as wife's daughter. Martha Hyde, illegitimate daughter of Ann Hyde, nailer of Carters Lane, had been baptised at Hales Owen Parish Church on June 14th 1834. In 1841 Ann (30) and Martha (7) Hyde were enumerated in Spies Lane in Hill township. Joseph Mason cannot be traced, as no provision was made in that census for recording sailors at sea. In April 1846, Joseph Mason married Ann Hyde at St Thomas' Church, Dudley. Joseph Mason died in 1853 and was buried at Christ Church on August 10th. In 1861, Ann Mason (50), and Samuel Mason, now aged 14, were both actively involved in the Ridgacre township nail-making community. Joseph Mason (11), described as

---

[352] This would almost certainly have been at the Oldbury works of Albright & Wilson. In 1842 Arthur Albright (7.03) had become a partner in the Birmingham chemical firm of John & Edmund Sturge, whose production of white phosphorous moved to Langley Green, Oldbury in 1850. In 1854 the partnership was dissolved and two years later Arthur Albright was joined by John Edward Wilson.

[353] Mary Ann Read (nee Jones) was the daughter of William and Myra Jones; Myra was the daughter of nail-forgers James and Elizabeth Hall, near neighbours of the Read family in Ridgacre township. (12.04.03).

[354] On June 12th 1848 at Christ Church, Ann Sadler was married to William Prosser of Warley Wigorn.

[355] Greenwich Hospital, the naval equivalent of Chelsea Hospital for soldiers was a home for retired Royal Navy personnel (in-pensioners) from 1694-1869. It was also responsible, under the terms of its charter, for paying out (via regional offices) meagre pensions to deserving applicants (out-pensioners) who had served in either the Navy or Marines and who "by reason of age, wounds or other disabilities shall be incapable of further service at sea and being unable to maintain themselves."

nephew and also working as a nail-maker, was living with William and Martha Sadler, illustrating the somewhat complicated family relationships within Ridgacre township in the mid-19th century. William Sadler, middle son of Joseph and Elizabeth Sadler (12.05.05) had married Martha Hyde (see above) who was, therefore, James Mason's step-sister, not aunt. Ann Mary Chatwin, who had been present in 1841, died in 1847 and was buried at Christ Church The Quinton on June 24th.

12.03.09   Joseph Goode   Plot 33 (52°27'40"N 2°00'45"W)

Nail-forgers Joseph (50) and Elizabeth (55) Goode shared their house on a plot of 36 poles, belonging to Sally Powers (12.01.05), with lodgers Benjamin (25) – also a nail-forger – and Sarah (25) Clay and their three children: William (5), Myra (3) and Anne (5 months) at the census of 1841. The two older children had been baptised at the Church of St John the Baptist, Hales Owen: William on November 4th 1835 and Myra on April 1st 1838. Anne was baptised at Christ Church The Quinton on February 7th 1841. By 1851 the situation was somewhat changed. Benjamin Clay, now working as a labourer on the turnpike road was established with his family in his own household. (12.01.07.) Nail-forger Hannah Coley (26) was now head of the household at plot 33 and was living here with her four-year-old daughter, Caroline, who had been baptised at Hales Owen on January 13th 1847. Still a nail-forger, Joseph Goode and his wife, Elizabeth, now of no stated occupation, were listed as lodgers. Elizabeth (Betty) Goode died in 1859 and was buried at Christ Church on 16th October. At the census of 1841, Hannah Coley who, like her daughter had also been baptised at Hales Owen's Parish Church of St John the Baptist (on May 14th 1826) had been living in her grandfather's household, with her parents and two siblings in neighbouring Warley Salop. In 1861, Hannah, who, on April 13th 1851 at Christ Church, had married Charles Haycock from Lapal township, was still resident in Lower Quinton, as was her daughter, Caroline. All three gave their occupation as nail-makers.

12.03.10   John Yates   Plot 33 (52°27'40"N 2°00'45"W)

John Yates was not a nail-maker but a farm labourer. However, he was obviously not the average farm labourer of the mid-1800s, as in addition to plot 33, jointly occupied with Joseph Goode's household (12.03.09), he also had the use of two other pieces of land. The first, plot 14 (52°27'44"N 2°01'21"W), a garden measuring 6 poles on the north-west corner of Thomas White's Further Mancroft, was actually Yates' own property. The second, Pleck, was a small field of pasture measuring 39 poles at plot 30 (52°27'39"N 2°00'44"W), rented from John White, on which John Yates presumably kept livestock, and for which he paid 1s in tithe rent to the Vicar of Hales Owen. At the census of 1841, Yates (aged 35 and, like all his family, a native of Hales Owen) lived with his wife, Elysa (25) and children, John (8), William (6) and Anne (2). The two younger children were both baptised at Hales Owen's Church of St John the Baptist: William on May 24th 1835 and Anne on December 9th 1838; on both occasions, John Yates' occupation was given as gardener. Two further children were baptised at Quinton Parish Church: Emma (June 4th 1847) and Henry (July 7th 1850), by which time the family had moved out of Plot 33 and into Long Lane in Hill township, where John Yates now gave his occupation as coal dealer.

In 1851 the Yates family was replaced at plot 33 by nail-forgers William (36), Elizabeth (33), Sarah (16), Joseph (13), Emma (10) and George (8) Rose. All were listed as born in Hales Owen. Ten years earlier this family had been living in Warley Wigorn, enumerated between the household of nail-maker David

Plots 37, 34, 33 photographed in mid-20th century

Payne (12.04.10) and Joseph Davenport's Four Dwellings Farm. (8.01.01) In 1841, only William Rose (who was then listed as not born within the county) had given his occupation as nail-maker. The three older Rose children had all been baptised at Hales Owen Parish Church of St John the Baptist: Sarah (April 12th 1835); Joseph (September 24th 1837); Emma (July 5th 1840).

By 1861, though still resident in Ridgacre township, the family had moved from Lower Quinton to Ridgacre. William and Joseph had become agricultural labourers. Elizabeth and Emma continued as nail-makers, as did Sarah Clay, nee Rose, since the last census married, widowed[356] and the mother of two children – Elizabeth (4) and Hannah (3). George had left home to work as a carter on John Hodgetts' farm in Warley Salop.

12.03.11   Benjamin Yates   Plot 31 (52°27'39"N 2°00'44"W)

This house and garden on a plot measuring 18 poles, the property of Ann White (4.04) was occupied in 1844 by four members of the Yates family: Benjamin (64), his wife Catherine (60), son William (35) and grandson John (8). A farm labourer in 1841, Benjamin was still following the plough ten years later. Though William was also a farm labourer throughout the ten-year period of the two censuses, John (who had been born in Hagley) did not take the occupation into the third generation but became, like so many other Quinton residents at this period, a nail-forger.

By one of two statutory declarations made by Benjamin Yates, who described himself as "yeoman," in 1857 and an indenture of the same date conveying "two messuages or dwelling houses, outhouses and buildings with gardens" which constituted plots 29, 30 and 31, more is known of this household.

---

[356] Sarah Rose married nailer Jesse Clay at Edgbaston Parish Church on May 12th 1856. Both gave their addresses as Edgbaston. The death of Jesse Clay was registered at Stourbridge in Oct/Nov Quarter 1860. Elizabeth Clay died aged 4yrs 6months and was buried at Christ Church on May 7th 1861.

Benjamin Yates had moved on his marriage in 1803 to this cottage, built and owned by Aaron White. (4.04) After Aaron's death, the property passed to his widow, Ann, otherwise known as Nanny, White. Yates' cottage is described as located in "an Occupation Road[357] leading from a certain lane called Court House Lane[358] at the Quinton."[359] For clarification, Yates adds that his home is opposite to Cutler's Farm.[360] In 1857, Pleck, the small field lying between plots 29 and 31, which in 1844 had been leased from Ann White by John Yates (12.03.10) was occupied by William Yates, Benjamin's son.

By 1861 William Yates, who gave his occupation as publican and shop-keeper, had become head of the household. He was now married to Sarah (46), widow of wood-turner David Smith. (11.03.03) Also in the household were Sarah's daughter, Fanny Smith (20), working as a bar maid and son Henry Smith (15), a spade tree maker. Benjamin, now a widower (Catherine Yates died in 1858 and was buried at Christ Church on December 1st) was still described as an agricultural labourer. John Yates, now a cabinet case maker, had left the family home and was head of his own household in Ledsum Street, Ladywood, Birmingham. Benjamin Yates died in 1867 and was buried at Christ Church on January 23rd. Plot 31 is one of the few township cottages occupied by the same family from 1841 to 1861, though only briefly in the period was the residence of a nail-maker.

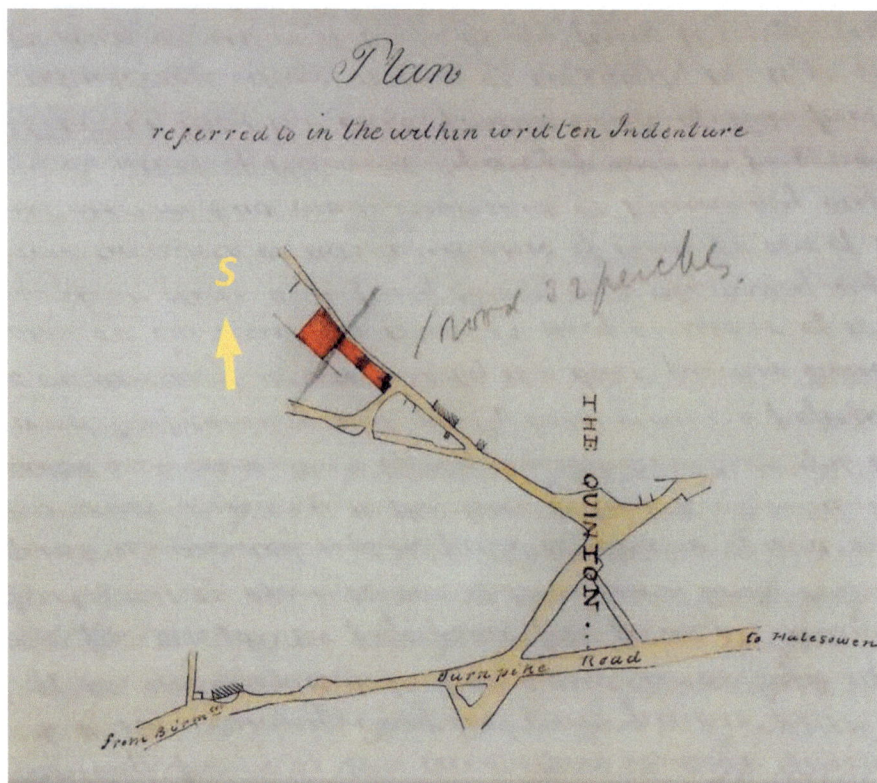

---

[357] An occupation road was a private road allowing right of access for the occupiers.
[358] No other reference to Court House Lane in Quinton has been identified.
[359] Conveyance of hereditaments and premises in the parish of Hales Owen in the County of Worcester: Messrs Burton, White and Others to Mr Richard Underhill (24.10.1857)
[360] Plots 19 (Lower Cutlers Leasow), 20 (Middle Cutlers Leasow), 21 (Little Cutlers Leasow), 40 (Cutlers Meadow) and 32 (Garden) which were directly opposite to plot 31 were part of the detached land of Hagg Farm.

I Benjamin Yates of the Quinton near Halesowen in the County of Worcester Yeoman do solemnly and sincerely declare as follows

That I am in the eightieth year of my age and since I was married in the year one thousand eight hundred and three I have lived in a cottage at the Quinton aforesaid opposite to the Cutlers Farm. The Cottage was built by Aaron White. The cottage adjoins to one now occupied by David Payne. William Newbold lived there when I first went to mine Nanny Bennett went there after he died My son William Yates occupies the little pleck adjoining my garden. I paid my rent to Aaron White during his life. The Cottage occupied by Payne and the little pleck also belonged to Aaron White in his life time. After his death I paid my rent to Nanny White his Widow

JM And I make this solemn declaration conscientiously believing the same to be true

Taken and solemnly declared at Birmingham in the County of Warwick this fourth day of September One thousand eight hundred and fifty seven

Before me

Thos. Martineau

A Commissioner to administer Oaths in Chancery in England

The mark ✗ of

Benjamin Yates

Statutory Declaration by Benjamin Yates, September 4th 1857 at Ryland & Martineau, Birmingham

12.03.12   Benjamin Wheeler   Plot 35 (52°27'41"N 2°00'43"W)

None of Benjamin Wheeler's family were born within the enumeration district where they resided in 1841 and where he was listed as occupier in 1844. Plot 35, with its house and garden, measured 30 poles and was the property of Lord Lyttelton. At the 1841 census, 60-year-old Benjamin Wheeler gave his occupation as nail forger. His wife Hannah (55) and their sons Edward (20), Thomas (20), William (15) and daughter Harriet (15), along with 5-year-old Rosanna Read completed the household. Apart from Benjamin, none had any stated occupation. By the census of 1851, with the exception of Harriet, who was now lodging with James and Sarah Preedy, (12.03.03) all had left the township. On July 20th 1851, Harriet Wheeler (whose occupation in both the marriage register and the census of that year was given as nail-maker) married Ridgacre tailor Frederick Howard (11.02.01) at Christ Church The Quinton.[361] In April Quarter 1845 the marriage of Edward Wheeler and Hannah Winwood was registered at Kings Norton. Giving their address as Moor Street, Edward and Hannah brought their children, Eliza and Michael David to Quinton's Bethesda Primitive Methodist Chapel for baptism on July 26th 1847.

By 1851, plot 35 had eight new residents who had moved in from Warley Wigorn. (12.04.10) Nail-forgers David Payne (36), his wife Phoebe (33) and their two older children, Elizabeth (14) and Sarah (12) had not yet been joined at the forge by the younger children, William (9), John (7), Myra (5) and Thomas (2). These four younger children had all been baptised at Quinton's Bethesda Primitive Methodist Chapel: William (December 19th 1841), John (January 1st 1844), Myra (August 23rd 1846) and Thomas (June 11th 1849). However, the older children had been baptised at Hales Owen Parish Church – Elizabeth on January 29th 1837 and Sarah on April 24th 1839. As Quinton's Wesleyan Methodist Chapel was available at the time of these earlier baptisms, it presumably did not appeal to David and Phoebe as much as the Established Church! In 1841, only David Payne had given his employment as nailer. By 1861 and (apart from Elizabeth) still in Quinton, all were working as nail-makers. Three further daughters, Mary Anne, Anne and Lucy, born since the previous census were baptised at Bethesda – Mary on September 21st 1851, Anne on April 17th 1854 and Lucy on October 13th 1856. Mary Anne Payne died aged seven months and was buried at Christ Church on February 2nd 1852.

12.03.13   James Cutler [E][362]   Plot 47 (52°27'42"N 2°00'43"W)

James Cutler was another Ridgacre township farm labourer who owned land. In Cutler's case, this was his own home and garden on the 26-pole plot 47. Aged 69 at the 1841 census, James lived with his wife, Hannah (also 69, but not from Ridgacre) and 9-year-old Joseph Yeomans, who like Cutler was born in Quinton. Could this Joseph Yeomans have been the son of neighbouring Thomas and Anne Yeomans (12.03.02) whose household of nine was no doubt crowded? James Cutler died in January 1848 and was buried at Christ Church where, in 1850 Joseph Yeomans married Harriet Read (12.03.01). Though in 1841 there were no nailers in this household, this changed ten years later with the arrival of a new generation of the Cutler family from Long Lane in Hill township.

---

[361] Benjamin Wheeler was evidently still living in July 1851 as his name appears as father of the bride in the marriage register. Frederick Howard's father, who had died, is not listed. However (apart from Harriet) it has not been possible to identify any members of the Wheeler family in the 1851 census.

[362] As owner/ occupier of freehold house in Ridgacre township. See 13.01

Nail forger John Cutler (44), born in Ridgacre township and his nail-forger wife, Hannah (42) from Warley, with their daughter Ann (13), son James (9), and daughter and son-in-law, Sarah (19) and George (27) Read, all born in Ridgacre and all nail-forgers now lived at plot 47. Sarah and Ann Cutler had both been baptised at Hales Owen Parish Church: Sarah on September 18th 1831 and Ann on November 26th 1837. The household was completed by granddaughter Hannah Read (14) born in Ridgacre, of no stated occupation, clearly not Sarah's daughter and unlikely to be George's, and 13-year-old nail-forger Sarah Read, born in Frankley, already working at the nail forge, and described as lodger. Ten years later, John, Hannah and James Cutler, George and Sarah Read were still resident in Ridgacre township and all were still working as nail-makers.

Plot 47 - Inglenook Cottage – N° 487 Ridgacre Road is one of only three extant buildings shown on the 1844 Ridgacre Tithe Map. An inspection in April 2017 by archaeologist Tim Cornah revealed that it contains some 18th century bricks and beams, with the side building being potentially older than the rest of the property

12.03.14   John Allen   Plot 47 (52°27'42"N 2°00'43"W)
[Hallen in Tithe Apportionments]

Cordwainer John Allen was the second householder on Plot 47. Unlike James Cutler (12.03.13) who is listed in the apportionments as both occupier and landowner, Allen is listed as occupier of a house, shop and garden owned by Francis Taylor. (4.17) In 1841, this household also consisted of Phoebe Allen who, at 41, was the same age as her husband; sons Henry (18) and Thomas (17), both of whom were working as nail-forgers, John (16) and William (9); and daughters Fanny (15) and Rebekah (8). Four of John and Phoebe's children were baptised at the Church of St John the Baptist, Hales Owen: Thomas on September 12th 1824, Fanny on April 15th 1827, William on September 1st 1830 and Rebekah on June 7th 1833. On November 6th 1842, at Christ Church The Quinton, Rev William Skilton baptised Francis, son of Phoebe and John Allen. The 1841 census records that John, Thomas, Fanny, Henry and John junior were born within the county, but that Phoebe, William and Rebekah were not. By 1851 the family were no longer living in Ridgacre township. On June 7th 1844 John Allen was buried in Hales Owen churchyard and in February 1847, Henry Allen (24), then resident in Warley Wigorn, was buried at Christ Church. In 1851 nail-forger Thomas Allen (26) born in Hales Owen, now married with a four-year-old son and two step-daughters was living in Cakemoor township but had returned to Ridgacre ten years later. It has not been possible to trace with any certainty the remainder of the Allen family.

As there are no unplaced residents of Lower Quinton in 1851, it would appear that at that census the Cutler family were the sole occupants of plot 47.

12.04 (Upper) Quinton

12.04.01   John Guest   Plot 43 (52°27'45"N 2°01'04"W)

The house, shop and garden occupied by the Guest family at the time of the tithe map stood on a plot measuring 22 poles, the property of Timothy Hill. Not present at the census of 1841, John Guest was dead by the census of 1851, by which time his widow, daughter and grandson had moved to plot 61 on New Road (12.01.05). The census enumerator's route suggests that in 1841 plot 43 was occupied by the household of Charles Clay.

Clearly having moved on by 1844, the Clay household was another of Ridgacre's migratory families. 25-year-old Charles Clay, who gave his occupation as labourer, shared his home with his wife, Elysa (25), sons Charles (5), William (4) and daughters Catherine (2) and Jane (6 months). All were born in Hales Owen, where William was baptised on May 13th 1838. When we next encounter the family in the 1851 census, they are in Hill township. Son Charles (who is now listed as Timothy) is working as a road labourer, as is his brother William. Catherine (now listed as Caroline) has become a nailer and there are two younger children, Joseph (7) and James (4). Head of the household is Eliza Clay, now widowed,[363] also employed as a nail-maker. By 1861, the family, minus James, are back in Quinton in Ridgacre township. Timothy is once again listed as Charles, though Catherine still appears as Caroline. All are now working as nail-makers.

In 1851, plot 43 is home to nail-forgers. James Jones (40) and his wife Phoebe (35) both work in the nail shop. Their daughter Myra (9) and elder son Adam (6) are at school and there is a younger son Elias (2). Myra Jones was baptised at Hales Owen's Church of St John the Baptist on July 31st 1842 and Elias Jones was baptised at Quinton's Christ Church on January 7th 1849. The Jones family are also birds of passage. In 1841, before the birth of their children, James, who then gave his occupation as labourer, and Phoebe lived in Carters Lane in Lapal township. By 1861, all of the family who had been at Ridgacre's plot 43 ten years earlier were now working as nailers in Combes Wood in Hill township. There were also now two younger children, Amelia (7) and James (4), born since the last census.

---

[363] The death of Charles Clay is registered at Stourbridge in January – March quarter, 1847.

12.04.02 James Hall **Plot 57** (52°27'48"N 2°00'51"W)

Listed in the tithe apportionments as a house, shop and garden on this 18 poles plot, property of Lord Lyttelton and occupied by James Hall, plot 57 was actually home to Bethesda Primitive Methodist Chapel. (7.04) However, that building was designed to provide living accommodation under its gallery: "kitchen and parlour; workshop adjoining, with other appurtenances."[364] This property attracted a weekly rental of 1s 8d. The census enumerator's route for 1841 would suggest that the tenant paying this sum at that time was Joseph Perry. Aged 20 at the time of the census, Perry lived with his 19-year-old wife, Sarah and one-year-old son, Thomas. Both Joseph and Sarah were nail-forgers, and they, along with their son, were listed as born within the county. Within three years they had left Ridgacre township. Thomas Perry had been baptised in Hales Owen in July 1840 and was buried there in August 1844. In 1851 and 1861 nail-makers Joseph (born in Hales Owen) and Sarah (born in Warley) Perry were living in Woodgate in Northfield parish. In 1851, the couple had three children: George (4); Mary Ann (2) and Henry (4 months). By 1861 all of these, still in Woodgate, were working as nail-makers. Three further sons – Jesse (7), Alfred (5) and Joseph (8 months) – now completed the household.

In 1851, adopting the same criteria, i.e. the household enumerated immediately before that of James Hall, the tenant of plot 57 would appear to be nail-forger Thomas Hall. Born in Quinton in 1800, Thomas lived with his wife Ann (52), also a nail-forger and identified in subsequent censuses as born in Pedmore. In 1851 their household included five children: William (26); Elizabeth (15); Thomas (13); John (11) and Sarah Partridge (28). All of these were born in Quinton and gave their occupations as nail-forgers. All had been taken to Hales Owen's Parish Church for baptism: Sarah on November 13th 1822; William on April 17th 1825; Elizabeth on January 24th 1836; Thomas on March 11th 1838 and John on April 12th 1840. Thomas and Ann had lost an infant son, Henry, who was baptised at Quinton's Christ Church on July 2nd 1843 and buried there on June 4th 1844. There were also two grandsons Henry (2) and William (4), both here surnamed Hall. Sarah's husband, Thomas Partridge, appears to have been living with his previous in-laws in Beech Lanes, where he is listed as a widower. (11.04.01) In 1841, Thomas, Ann, Sarah, William, Elizabeth, Thomas junior and John Hall had been living in Warley Wigorn, along with another son, Joseph (20) and two other daughters: Jane (9) and Etty (7). At this point only Thomas senior, Joseph and William were working at the nail forge.

Most of the family were still in Ridgacre township in 1861. Thomas, Elizabeth, Thomas junior and John all worked as nail-makers. Ann was a laundress. Two new grandsons John (10) and Harry (12 months) completed the household. Sarah Partridge had joined her husband in Beech Lanes, along with her son Henry and five other children, all baptised at Christ Church: Ann Elizabeth (March 7th 1852), Thomas February 5th 1854), John (September 2nd 1855), James (April 9th 1857) and Frederick (March 6th 1859). Thomas Partridge died, aged three, and was buried at Christ Church on April 12th 1857.

At the tithe apportionments, Thomas Hall also had the use of two garden plots. The first, his own property, measuring 11 poles was plot W93 (52°27'46"N 2°00'29"W) in Warley Wigorn township's large southern wedge of Quinton. Interestingly, this plot, which fronted the turnpike road, intruded into the Glebe Land (7.03) and was separated from Warley Wigorn land by a lane, was not acknowledged on

---

[364] Chambers, J. (1842) p 24

the Ridgacre tithe map. The second, and smaller plot 230 (52°27'51"N 1°59'19"W) in Ridgacre township, also near the turnpike road, measured 38 poles and was leased from George Birch. (8.01.03)

12.04.03   James Hall [E][365]   Plot 55 (52°27'49"N 2°01'55"W)

On a plot of land measuring 2 roods 11 poles, belonging to John Foley stood the cottage in Upper Quinton, where James Hall had lived for the whole of his life. Aged 59 at the time of the tithe map, James shared his home with his 58-year-old wife, Elizabeth (Betty), who came from Northfield, and their unmarried daughters, Harriet (23), Myra (17) and Mary (15). All members of the family worked as nail-forgers and apart from Elizabeth all were born within Ridgacre township.

By the census of 1851, Mary Hall was no longer at home and Myra was married to 24-year-old William Jones, a Hales Owen farm labourer. The household was completed by James and Elizabeth's 4-year-old grandson, John, listed here as Hall, but on the following census, presumably more correctly, as Jones. All still working as nail-makers in 1861, James Hall's household now consisted only of himself, Elizabeth and Harriet. In the adjacent household, William Jones now worked as a labourer in a phosphorous works,[366] Myra had been joined at the nail forge by John, now aged 14, and four more children Mary (9),[367] Kate (7), Sarah (3) and Harry (4 months) had been born since the previous census. Mary and Kate had both been baptised at Bethesda Primitive Methodist Chapel: Mary on August 22nd 1852 and Kate on an unspecified date in 1854. Elizabeth Hall died in 1864 and was buried at Christ Church on 3rd March and James Hall died in 1868 and was buried at Christ Church on 16th March.

The fragility of working-class family life in the mid-19th century is illustrated in that of Myra and William Jones. In October quarter 1849, the birth of their son Edmund is recorded in volume 18, page 431 of the Stourbridge register. On November 24th 1849, his death (at the age of three days, from convulsions which had lasted 48 hours) was also registered at Stourbridge. On the following day, his funeral service

Columns:-	1	2	3	4	5	6	7	8	9
No.	When and where died	Name and surname	Sex	Age	Occupation	Cause of death	Signature, description and residence of informant	When registered	Signature of registrar
215	Twenty fourth November 1849 Quinton Ridgacre	Edmund Jones	Male	3 days	Son of William Jones Labourer	Convulsions 48 hours Certified	The Mark of Harriet Hall Present at the Death Quinton Ridgacre	Twenty seventh November 1849	GG Fiddian Registrar

was conducted at Christ Church The Quinton by Rev William Skilton. The burial register gives his age as 48 hours, which is presumably a confusion with the length of his illness. Edmund's aunt, Harriet Hall, who had been present at the death, was the informant. His mother, presumably, was still recovering from childbirth and his father was at work. It is too easy to say that because such a death was

---

[365] As owner/occupier of freehold house in Ridgacre township. See 13.01
[366] See p 199, footnote 297
[367] Mary Jones subsequently married James Read, son of Enoch and Elizabeth Read (12.03.07).

commonplace, it was accepted. We cannot know what emotions it engendered or what were its consequences. Edmund Jones represents all those anonymous lives briefly spent on the Ridgacre and Warley Wigorn tithe maps, known only by entries in registers of births, deaths and burials. Nevertheless, each one of them is a part of the story which *Quinton in the mid-1800s* tells, and which itself is a microcosm of life in 19th century Britain.

County of
Salop

Be it Remembered, that on the *Twelfth* ~ ~ ~ .
day of *July* ~ ~ ~ ~ ~ in the year of our Lord 1832 .
. ~ ~ ~ ~ ~ at *Hales Owen* in the County of
. *Salop, Thomas Taylor* of the *Parish of Hales* .
. *Owen aforesaid Nailer* is convicted before *us Richard Brettle* .
. *and Michael Grazebrook Esquires two* of his Majesty's Justices
. of the Peace for the said County for that he the said *Thomas Taylor* .
. *did on the Eighteenth day of June last at the Parish* .
. *aforesaid in the County aforesaid unlawfully* .
. *and violently assault and ill use Betty Hall* .
. *wife of James Hall of the same parish Nailer* .
.   .
.   And *We* the said Justice *s* adjudge the said *Thomas* .
.   *Taylor* for his said offence to forfeit and pay the penalty of *Five* .
. *Pounds* ~ ~ ~ ~~and also the Sum of~~
.   ~ ~ ~ ~~being the value of~~
.   And also to
pay the Sum of *Seven Shillings and sixpence* .
.   ~ ~ ~ for costs. And in default of immediate payment of
the said Sums to be imprisoned in the House of Correction at *Shrewsbury* .
.   ~ ~ ~ in and for the said County and there kept to hard
labour for the space of *Two Calendar Months* - unless the said
Sums shall sooner be paid. And *We* direct that the said Penalty of *Five* .
. *Pounds* ~ ~ ~ shall be paid to someone of the
Overseers of the Poor of the Parish of *Hales Owen* ~
. ~ ~ to be paid by him applied according to the direction of the Statute
in that case made and provided. And ~~that the said sum of~~
.   ~~shall be paid to~~ .
. ~ ~ ~ And We order that the said Sum of ~ ~
Seven Shillings and sixpence for costs
shall be paid to the said *Betty Hall* .
     Given under ᵒᵘʳ my Hands and Seals the day and year first above-mentioned.

Richard Brettell ●

Michl Grazebrook ●

In 1832 46-year-old Betty Hall was violently assaulted by 27-year-old Hales Owen nailer Thomas Taylor,[368] lending credence to the violent lives 19th century nail-makers were reputed to lead in a township whose inhabitants "were noted for their wickedness."[369] Though later seen as a pillar of society "who never quarrelled with anyone," James Hall, at the time of the assault, was a new convert to Primitive Methodism. Prior to his conversion he had "the burden of guilt heavy upon him" and experienced "some struggling to step into liberty."[370] (In the terminology of contemporary religious literature, this may, or may not, have implied a dissolute life.) The circumstances of the assault are unknown, but Taylor was fined five pounds (a considerable sum for a nail-forger whose weekly wages were around eight shillings) with 7s 6d costs to be paid to his victim. Three months after his conviction the fine had not been paid and Taylor was committed to two month's hard labour in Shrewsbury Gaol.

James Hall was a Primitive Methodist Local Preacher and one of the founder members of the cause in Quinton. Between 1845 and 1850 his signature was regularly found in the Baptismal Register of Bethesda Chapel (7.04) He was also one of the applicants to the Bishop of Worcester for the recognition of a place of worship in the village in 1826. (7) Following his death, the *Primitive Methodist Magazine* published an effusive obituary.[371]

"Died happy in the Lord, at Quinton, March 12th 1868, aged 85 years, James Hall was for nearly half a century, a local preacher. In his every relationship in life, as a husband, parent, neighbour, nothing but good can be said; his example being most bright, illustrious and praiseworthy. It may be most emphatically said of him, that he walked with God and lived to do good. Loving all, he prayed for all, and was loved by all who knew him.

"His conversion to God appears to have taken place in 1831. At this time, there lived in Quinton, a very excellent Christian gentleman, Mr Samuel Chatwin.[372] Going to his home one morning, he said, 'James, I want you to do me a favour;' the reply given was, 'Well, Mr Chatwin, if I can I will; there is no person I would more gladly oblige than you.' Mr Chatwin then said, 'I want you to come with me to the preaching-house.' After some little hesitancy, our departed brother accompanied this good man to hear the Gospel; and the word preached proved to him the power of God unto salvation. But he had some struggling to step into liberty. He retired to rest with the burden of guilt still heavy upon him and in the visions of the night he wrestled with the great adversary. As the light of morning broke, the terror of the night was past – the darkness of sin was dispersed. Such had been his mental conflict that, when he fully awoke to his happy condition, he was as wet with perspiration as if he had been immersed in a pool of water.

"As a member of society, James Hall was in everything consistent; always punctual at the means of grace; he never quarrelled with

---

[368] There are three Hales Owen residents named Thomas Taylor identified in the 1841 census: - [i] a blacksmith of Long Lane, Hill township, living with daughter Sarah (18) and two sons (George (16) and Joseph (13); [ii] a blacksmith with no obvious family, lodging with Charles Deeley in Cornbow, Hales Owen township; [iii] a nailer living with his wife Ann in the wonderfully named Dogs Hole, Birmingham Street, Hales Owen township.

[369] Flesher, J. (1850), p 325

[370] Pugh, P. (1869), pp303-305

[371] ibid

[372] According to his tombstone (7) Samuel Chatwin died in October 1829

anyone; but was always agreeable, cultivating a spirit of love towards all his fellow-creatures. But it is as a preacher of the Gospel our late brother mostly claims our consideration. And here we may justly state that he shone amongst earth's noble worthies, a star of the first magnitude. Upon this dark benighted world, he scattered blessings in his path. It, perhaps, would not be too much to say that he was a great preacher – great in the strictest sense of the word – great in winning souls. It is true, he never scaled the heights of eloquence, or culled the flowers of learning to scatter them at the feet of his listeners. His was a nobler aim; that of winning souls to Christ. While holding forth the precious truths of the Gospel on one occasion the power of God was so manifested that sinners fell down before his feet and cried for mercy. As a preacher, his style was grave, sincere, homely and easy.

"Many long and wearisome journeys he had to make in his labours of love. He travelled on foot from Quinton to Darlaston, Bilston, Coventry, Bromsgrove and Redditch, places from 25 to upwards of 30 miles to and fro; returning with weary feet and enduring various privations.

"During the last two or three years of his life, his mental faculties weakened and his memory failed; but his love for the church and for his Saviour never abated. One of his sons became a very acceptable local preacher and died some time ago in the Lord. He has a grandson, a preacher, now with us; and many of his children and grandchildren are converted to God.

"In his short illness, it is a matter of question whether he suffered a real pain. When the doctor called the day before he died and asked him how he was, he said, 'O I am very well; I am going to heaven and hope I shall meet you there.'

"He was well provided for in his old age. A little property adjoining the chapel at Quinton, on which he lived all his days was purchased by the trustees of this chapel and so much per week, a comfortable living, was allotted him. After his funeral expenses were all paid, a considerable sum remained in hand, which, according to his will, is to be equally divided among his surviving children."

Baptismal records of James Hall's family suggest a religious conversion such as his obituary indicates. Harriet was baptised at Hales Owen Parish Church on March 15th 1820; Myra and a sister, Elizabeth[373] on June 6th 1830. That this may have been a purely nominal Anglican allegiance is indicated by James' grandchildren, Mary, Kate and Harry Jones, all baptised at Quinton's Primitive Methodist Chapel with which James was so closely associated: Mary on August 22nd 1852, Kate at an unspecified date in 1854 and Harry on September 17th 1861. The absence of baptismal records for John and Sarah Jones may confirm the obituary's comment that *many* of James' children "are converted to God."

12.04.04   John Foley [E,J][374]   Plot 55 (52°27'49"N 2°01'55"W)

Not occupied by nail-makers in 1841, the second house, plus yard and barn on plot 55 (measuring in total 2 roods 11 poles) was the residence of John Foley, first cousin once removed of John Foley of Monckton Farm. (See family tree – 6.03) The adjacent plot 54 (52°27'48"N 2°00'04"W), Top Meadow, at

---

[373] As no Elizabeth has been identified in the census and no record found for the baptism of Mary, they may perhaps be one and the same person, with a daughter Elizabeth called Mary to distinguish her from her mother.

[374] As owner/occupier of freehold land and buildings in Ridgacre township. See 13.01. Juror at Amy Read Inquest. See 13.02

1 acre 3 roods 3 poles, pasture on which tithe of 3s 6d was due to the Vicar of Hales Owen, was also in the occupation of John Foley, who was owner of both plots.

At the 1841 census, farmer John Foley, then aged 70, lived with Anne (55) and Thomas (10) Foley. John Foley had been one of the beneficiaries under the terms of his Uncle Ambrose Foley's will, who had left the residue of his estate to John's cousin, the second Ambrose…

> *…provided that he shall at the end of one year next after my decease pay to John Foley, son of John Foley, the sum of five pounds and so continue to pay the said sum each year of their respective lives. Also I give unto John Foley (my brother's son) my late brother's old wagon and all the old furniture now in my late brother John Foley's house.*[375]

John Foley died aged 74 and was buried at Christ Church on December 16th 1845. The sale of his property was advertised, in *Aris's Birmingham Gazette* of December 22nd 1845 for exactly one week after his funeral. It would seem that this John Foley, rather than his namesake at Monckton Farm (8.01.10) was the owner of plots 54 and 55 as Hales Owen Court Rolls for 1847 record the death of *John Foley the Nephew* (of Ambrose) and the admission of *William Foley the Nephew and next Devisee for Life* to his property and payment of the appropriate heriot and fine.[376] In 1851 Ann Foley was living as one of three lodgers at plot 63 in the household of her son-in-law, Henry Read. It would seem that Thomas Foley, now aged 20, was the second lodger, although the enumerator has entered Thomas Coley. No other possible candidates named Thomas Foley have been traced in the 1851 census (though there are several in subsequent censuses) and no death of a Foley were working as nail-forgers. Ann Foley died in 1869 and was buried at Christ Church on 31st July.

> **SALE AT THE QUINTON,**
> WITHOUT RESERVE
> TO be **SOLD** by **AUCTION**, by **JESSE WRIGHT**, tomorrow (Tuesday), December the 23rd, all the **HOUSEHOLD FURNITURE, FARMING IMPLEMENTS, LIVE** and **DEAD STOCK**, consisting two ricks of wheat, oats, rick of hay, and loose straw, all to go off the premises; four burrows of picked potatoes, two fat pigs, a large quantity of gearing, wheel ploughs, harrows, and variety other effects, belonging to the late John Foley, of the Quinton Farm near Hales Owen.
>   Sale to commence at ten o'clock in the morning. An early attendance is respectfully solicited on account of the number of lots.
>   Catalogues may be had upon the premises, and of the Auctioneer, Dudley.

By 1851, plot 55 appears to be the household of nail-forger George Smith. Aged 40 at this census, George lived with his nail-forger wife Eliza (39) and seven children, Jesse (12), Sarah (10), Daniel (7), David (5), Ellen (4), Esther (2) and Elysa (6 weeks). At this stage only Jesse had already joined his parents at the nail forge. Evidently the Smith family was amongst Hales Owen's itinerant population, but only within the confines of the manor. In 1841, they had been resident in Lapal township, which was Eliza's birthplace and also that of Jesse and Sarah. By 1861 they had moved, again a very short distance, to

---

[375] Foley, Ambrose (09.12.1826) LB
[376] Hales Owen Court Rolls, 1783-1915

Spies Lane in Hill township, the birthplace of George, who this time had become a tally-maker, which trade David had also embraced. Sarah, Ellen and Esther, however, had joined Jesse as nail-makers.

12.04.05   Benjamin Hadley   Plot 72 (52°27'50"N 2°00'47"W)

Situated just off the lane leading to Tinkers Farm (8.01.12), Benjamin Hadley's cottage and nailshop occupied a plot of Ambrose Foley's land south of Barn Close, put out to pasture as part of Monckton Farm. (8.01.10) At just 2 poles (giving it both a frontage and depth of approximately 7 metres) this was the smallest residential plot on the Quinton tithe maps.[377] Head of the household in 1841 was nail-forger, Benjamin Hadley (45). Also present were his wife Martha (43), daughter Hannah (18) and son William (10), none of whom had any stated occupation. On September 4th 1842, Sarah Jane, illegitimate daughter of Hannah Hadley of Ridgacre was baptised at Christ Church by Rev William Skilton. By 1851, Benjamin Hadley was working as a farm labourer, Hannah as a nailer, and William as a brick-maker's labourer. Martha still had no stated occupation. This census also clarifies that all four members of the family were born in Hales Owen. Still present in (Upper) Quinton in 1861, none of the Hadley family were now working at the nail forge. Benjamin was still a farm labourer, Martha still of no given employment and Hannah was now returned as a char woman. By this time William was married and, with his wife, step-daughter and two children of his own, living in Cocksheds Lane in Hill township.

Some entries for this family reveal that details given in census returns are often inconsistent from one decade to the next, either through the vagueness or ignorance of the person supplying the information or misunderstanding by the enumerator.

Name	Relationship	Age in 1841	Age in 1851	Age in 1861
Benjamin Hadley	Head	45	50	69
Martha Hadley	Wife	43	48	63

12.04.06   James Robinson   Plot 74 (52°27'49"N 2°00'47"W)

At plot 74, a house, shop and garden occupied by James Robinson, was part of Henry Foley Macdonald's Quintain Green estate (11.03.01) which, at 1 rood 28 poles was one of the largest non-agricultural plots in the village. However, like the household of Benjamin Clay (12.01.07) in New Road, this was an address which, even though enumerated consecutively, Macdonald chose to distinguish from his own establishment by listing it as Quinton rather than Quinton Green, which designation he reserved for his own household and that of John Foley.

In 1841 the Robinson family was eight in number. Nail-forger James (45), his wife, Sarah (40) and six children John (20), Caroline (15), James (10), Thomas (8), Eliza (5) and Abel (2). The family had moved to Quinton from Warley Wigorn in the two-year interval between the births of the third and fourth children. The four younger children were all baptised at Hales Owen's Church of St John the Baptist: James on October 21st 1827 (indicating the rounding down of his age in the census), Thomas on December 3rd 1833, Eliza on April 19th 1835 and Abel on May 19th 1839. In 1841, only James was returned as working. On May 18th 1846, at Christ Church, Caroline Robinson married Andrew Miner, also of Ridgacre township. By 1851, John Robinson was no longer at home and, with the exception of

---

[377] Plot W22, part of William Penn's Bearsland Wood, also measured just 2 poles.

12-year-old scholar Abel, all the family were working at the nail-forge. However, a number of significant changes had occurred ten years later, when only James senior, Thomas and Abel were returned as nail-makers. Sarah and Eliza now gave their occupation as washer-women; James junior was registered as a cripple and the family had been joined by a two-year-old granddaughter, Eliza's daughter, Sarah Ann, who had been baptised at Christ Church on November 19th 1858.

Eliza Robinson died in March 1870; James senior in March 1872; Sarah senior in May 1872 and Thomas in June 1882. All four were buried at Christ Church The Quinton.

12.04.07   Mary James

Not present in 1844, but enumerated in 1841 following the household of James Robinson, was the household of Mary James. This consisted of Mary James, Margarett Grovnor, Elizabeth Hutton and Joseph Hutton, whose ages were given respectively as 35, 40, 20 and 4. The three women, who each gave her occupation as nail forger, were all born in Ireland. Joseph is listed as born in the county of enumeration which, though technically Shropshire, sometimes actually meant Worcestershire, and which may or may not have implied Ridgacre township. No further reference to any of these residents has been found in subsequent UK censuses, which suggests that they may have returned to Ireland, where it has proved equally impossible to track them down. The Irish census returns for both 1861 and 1871 were destroyed shortly after recording; those of 1881 and 1891 were pulped during World War I to help address a paper shortage; apart from a few fragments the census returns of 1821-1851 were destroyed by fire in Dublin's Public Record Office on June 30th 1922 during the Irish Civil War. All this leaves a series of unanswered and perhaps unanswerable questions:

- Why was this quartet of residents living in Ridgacre township in 1841 and how long had they been there? (Clearly, they had departed by 1844.)
- Where had the women learned the nail-forgers trade and at whose Ridgacre forge did they practise it?
- Where, in Ireland, was their home?
- What, if anything, was the relationship between the three women?
- Could Mary James of Ridgacre be the Mary James (daughter of John James and Bridget Cavanagh) who was baptised at St Mary's Church Cork in January 1805?[378]
- Was, as seems likely, Joseph Hutton the son of Elizabeth Hutton? If so, had she come to England to escape disgrace at home, the forerunner of the many heroines of Anne Bennett's formular novels who, unmarried and pregnant, leave rural Ireland for the suburbs of Birmingham in the first half of the 20th century?[379]

It seems likely that these questions will remain unanswered and the enigma unsolved.

---

[378] This appears to be the only record in the Irish Catholic Parish Registers 1655-1915 (or indeed in any other available listing of Irish births and baptisms) that meets the known criteria.

[379] See, for example, Bridie McCarthy from Donegal in *Till the Sun Shines Through* (2003) and Agnes Sullivan also from Donegal in *A Daughter's Secret* (2007). N.B. A Joseph Hutton, son of Elizabeth and Thomas Hutton was baptised at Hales Owen Parish Church on Christmas Day 1836 and buried there on April 13th 1849.

12.04.08   James Cooper   Plot W119 (52°27'49"N 2°00'15"W)

In the tithe apportionments, this 39-poles plot with house, buildings and garden, the property of Stephen Grainger, was listed as occupied by James Cooper. (10.01.02) Farmer and victualler James Cooper was landlord of the Red Lion Inn in Ridgacre township just across the turnpike road from plot W119. Cooper was enumerated at the Red Lion in both 1841 and 1851, suggesting that he did not actually live at plot W119, but that it was sub-let. Given the Warley Wigorn enumerator's route from Hagg Farm to Upper Quinton, the mostly likely tenant would have been Thomas Hodgetts.

At the census of 1841, the household of 40-year-old nail-maker Thomas Hodgetts included Sarah (40), Thomas (15), William (15) David (11) and Joseph (7) Hodgetts, along with William Robinson (15). Thomas and Sarah Hodgetts and William Robinson were shown as born outside the county. Other records indicate that many of these census details are unreliable. Thomas and William Hodgetts were listed as nail-makers and William Robinson as carpenter. No other occupations were given. Baptism registers show Thomas Hodgetts born in January 1820, but not baptised until July 23rd 1837 at Rowley Regis.[380] William, David and Joseph were all baptised at Hales Owen Parish Church of St John the Baptist: William on November 17th 1822; David on February 3rd 1828 and Joseph on March 10th 1833.

By 1851, the household at plot W119 consisted of Thomas (54), Sarah (55), Thomas (30) and David (20) Hodgetts. All were working as nail-makers and all were listed as born in Hales Owen. William (29) and Joseph (17) Hodgetts were lodging in the home of coach-fitter Joseph Richards in Park Street Birmingham. Both brothers were working as nail-makers and both gave their birthplace as Quinton. Ten years on, none of the family remained in Warley Wigorn. Thomas (65) and Sarah (64) Hodgetts were shopkeepers in Shenstone Street, Hales Owen. Thomas's birthplace was then stated as Beech Lanes, Ridgacre and Sarah's as Quinton, Ridgacre. The younger Thomas, now married to Hannah, was still working as a nail-maker, but living in Moor Street. Also in Moor Street, at the Crown Inn, was David Hodgetts, now married to Alice and working as a victualler and poultry-dealer.

12.04.09   Thomas Haycock   Plot W87 (52°27'37"N 2°00'24"W)

Listed in the tithe apportionments as joint occupier of this plot measuring 1 rood 24 poles and containing two houses, shops and gardens, the property of George White, Thomas Haycock was tenant in both 1841 and 1851. At the earlier census, 60-year-old Thomas and sons John (30) and Thomas (25) all worked as nail-forgers. 65-year-old Sarah Haycock had no stated occupation. All were listed as born outside the county. John Haycock died in 1843 and was buried at Christ Church The Quinton on 15th June. In October 1847 also at Christ Church, Thomas junior was married by Rev William Skilton to nail-forger Elizabeth (Betsy) Dearn of Hill township. On June 9th 1850, their daughter Sarah was baptised at Bethesda Primitive Methodist Chapel, Quinton. Interestingly, the baptismal register records the Haycocks' address as Packs Hall, making this the earliest identified reference to Pax Hall, which is actually plot W91. Included in the list of founder-members of Quinton's Primitive Methodist cause 14 years earlier had been Sarah Haycock, possibly the child's grandmother? The elder Sarah Haycock died aged 84 and was buried at Christ Church on February 7th 1857.

---

[380] A chapel of ease was established in Rowley Regis during the reign of King John (1199-1216). An early building survived until 1840, when it was replaced. Rowley Regis became a parish in 1855.

Still present at plot W87 in 1851, Thomas (named as head of household) and Sarah Haycock were both then listed as "pauper, formerly nailer." Keeping the forge going were Thomas junior and Elizabeth Haycock. The household was completed by 10-month-old Sarah and farm labourer Charles Haycock (59), widowed younger brother of Thomas senior, who ten years earlier had been lodging in Ridgacre township at plot 235. (12.10.01) Thomas, Sarah and Thomas Haycock's birthplaces were clarified as Hales Owen, with Elizabeth, Sarah and Charles born in Warley Wigorn. By 1861 none of the Haycock family were left in Warley Wigorn. Now 81 years old and widowed, Thomas Haycock, "dealer in iron," had moved to the home of his son, Joseph, in the Quinton area of Ridgacre. Thomas, Elizabeth and Sarah were all working as nail-makers in Castle Lane, Warley Salop. Charles Haycock had become an inmate of West Bromwich Union Workhouse.

Status of Quinton Nail-makers 1841-1861

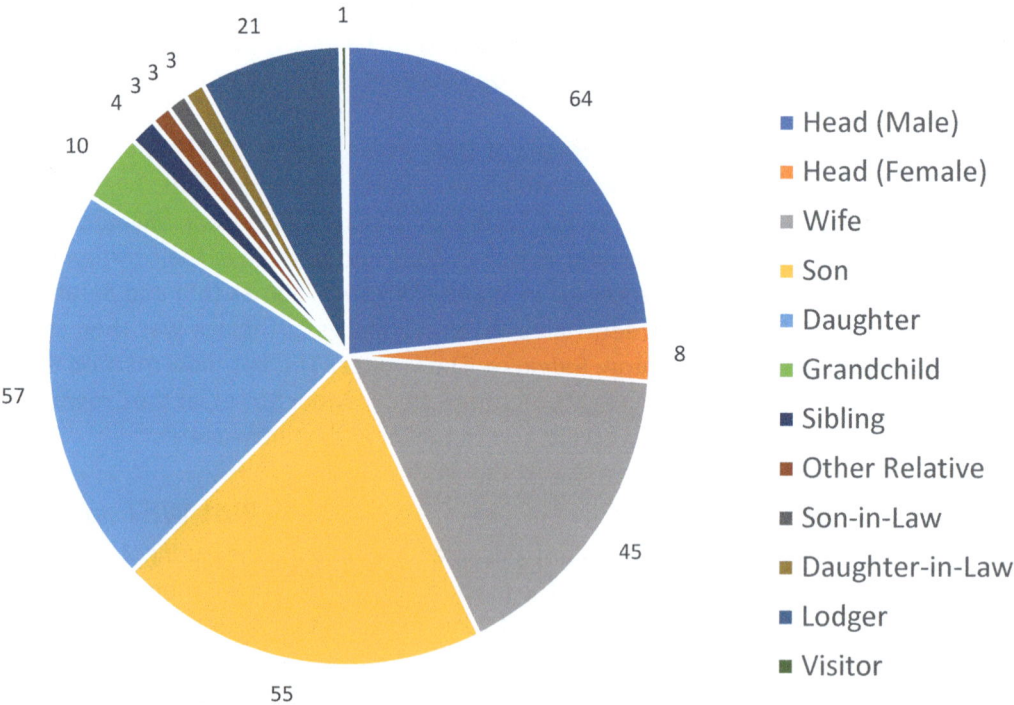

Legend:
- Head (Male)
- Head (Female)
- Wife
- Son
- Daughter
- Grandchild
- Sibling
- Other Relative
- Son-in-Law
- Daughter-in-Law
- Lodger
- Visitor

12.04.10   Charles Clay   Plot W87 (52°27'37"N 2°00'24"W)

The second of the houses, shops and gardens on George White's 1 rood 24 poles plot W87 was occupied in 1841 by 25-year old nail-maker David Payne, who was not born within the county. This household was completed by Phoebe (20), Elizabeth (4) and Sarah (2) Payne, all born in the county. Three years later there had been a change of residents, as the tithe apportionments list the occupant of plot W87 as Charles Clay, who also rented from George White a garden plot (W86 - 52°27'36"N 2°00'20"W) measuring 15 poles. The census of 1851 shows David Payne (Payne) and his family living at plot 35 in the Lower Quinton area of Ridgacre township. (12.03.12)

Clay family origins are unclear. The 1851 census lists 42-year-old farm labourer Charles Clay as born in Hales Owen. His household was completed by his nail-maker wife, Hannah (39), and daughter Caroline (11), and son William (8) scholar. Hannah, Caroline and William were all born in Warley Wigorn. On Christmas Day 1838, at St Martin's Church, Birmingham, Charles Clay had married Hannah Dearn. Both gave their occupation as nail-makers and gave Birmingham addresses: Charles in Worcester Street and Hannah in Bromsgrove Street. The fathers of both (Benjamin Clay and Robert Hadley) were also registered as nail-makers. On December 22nd 1839, Caroline Clay was baptised at Hales Owen. The family does not appear to be listed in the 1841 census, some two years before William was born. However, in 1861 all four Clays were still resident in Warley Wigorn, then given as the birthplace of them all. Charles was still employed as an agricultural labourer, William had joined his mother at the nail forge, which Caroline had abandoned to become a dressmaker, an occupation which would not seem to have much in common with the physical prowess demanded by nail-making.

12.04.11   Joseph Davenport

Plot W94 (52°27'46"N 2°00'27"W)

Ivy House in the early 20th century

Though the apportionments list Joseph Davenport (8.01.01) as occupier of buildings, offices and Ivy House on this 3 roods 5 poles plot belonging to William Spurrier, he is enumerated at Four Dwellings farmhouse which occupied the considerably larger (2 acres 2 roods 15 poles) plot W67. Clearly this was a much more likely place for him to live, leaving plot W94 available for sub-letting. That the property was sub-let is confirmed by advertisements placed in *Aris's Birmingham Gazette*.

Ivy Farm, Quinton, Halesowen, to be let and entered upon at Lady Day.
The Ivy Farm situate at the Quinton in the parish of Halesowen, in the counties of Worcester and Salop. This estate adjoins the turnpike road from Birmingham to Halesowen at the distance of four miles from Birmingham and consists of a very comfortable dwelling house with brewhouse, barn, two stables, a cow house, garden and thirty-two acres of excellent loamy land of the first quality and is well calculated for a person in trade, wishing to amuse himself with the culture of a small farm, and particularly for a person in the nail trade. For rent and other particulars please apply to Messrs Spurrier, Ingleby and Spurrier Paradise Street Birmingham.[381]

---

[381] *Aris's Birmingham Gazette*, January 12th 1824

The most likely candidate (extrapolated from the enumerator's route) in 1841 was indeed a nail-maker: 40-year-old Thomas Hall. His household consisted of his wife Ann (40) four sons: Joseph (20) William (15) – both also listed as nail-makers, Thomas (3), John (1) and four daughters Sarah (15), Jane (9), Etty (7) and Elizabeth (5). Apart from Ann, all were listed as born within the county. Their recorded birth years are somewhat approximate as the baptismal register of Hales Owen's Parish Church of St John the Baptist, where all of Thomas and Ann's children had been baptised, clarifies: Joseph (October 28th 1821); Sarah (November 13th 1822); William (April 17th 1825); Jane (June 7th 1833); Etty (May 5th 1834); Elizabeth (January 24th 1836); Thomas (March 11th 1838); John (April 12th 1840).

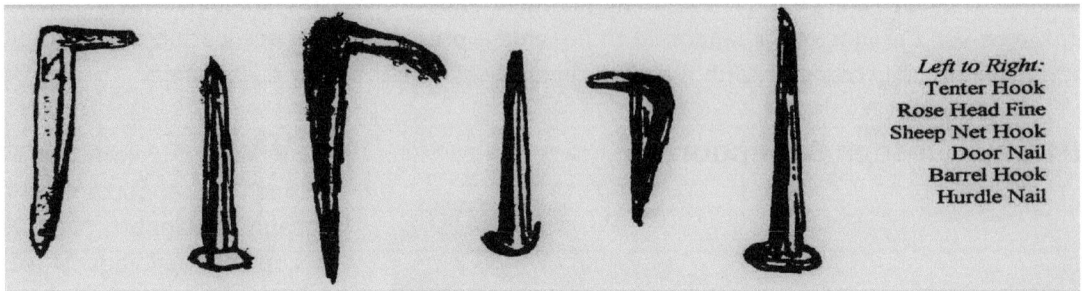

Left to Right:
Tenter Hook
Rose Head Fine
Sheep Net Hook
Door Nail
Barrel Hook
Hurdle Nail

On Christmas Day 1848, at Birmingham's Parish Church of St Martin, nail-forger Joseph Hall, with his siblings Sarah and William as witnesses, married Lucy Read, daughter of nail-forger Elijah Read. (12.06.03) Three years later Joseph and Lucy were living in Ridgacre township's Lower Quinton. (12.03.02) By 1851, the remainder of Thomas Hall's household had also removed from Warley Wigorn. Thomas and Ann Hall, with five of their children had re-located to Upper Quinton in Ridgacre township (12.04.03); Jane Hall was working as a servant at James Cooper's Red Lion Inn (10.01.02); Etty Hall in 1851 was living at Hawthorn Farm where she was employed as a house servant in the household of Henry and Rebecca Nicholls. (8.01.07) In a new advertisement, Ivy House farm had again been put on the market with interesting details of the current use of its ancillary premises.

> *Ivy House Quinton – Four miles and a quarter from Birmingham on the Hagley Road*
> To let at Midsummer next, the above desirable residence, comprising entrance hall, drawing, dining and breakfast rooms, and seven bedrooms, large coach house, and stabling for six horses, garden with lawn in front, piggeries and other outbuildings, now in the occupation of the Rev W.R. Skilton, rent £30 a year. A few acres of rich meadow land may be had adjoining if required. For particulars apply to Mr J. Davenport, New House, Quinton, or to Mr J. Robinson, Bruiton Mills Cut Nail and Rivet Works, Prospect Row, Birmingham.[382]

Adopting the same enumeration route criteria for 1851, suggests that plot W94 was no longer a nail-maker's home, but now the residence of accountant Thomas Southall and family. Apart from the perpetual curate and a succession of schoolmasters, Southall was the only Quinton resident with an occupation in the professions throughout the 1840s and 1850s. Perhaps the appeal of the *Aris's* advertisement suggested Ivy House to him as a house commensurate with his status. Whatever it was that brought the Southalls to Quinton, they became another of the township's transitory families.

---

[382] *Aris's Birmingham Gazette*, June 19th 1843

On April 16th 1846, Thomas Southall of Edgbaston and Julia Radenhurst of Aston Manor were married by licence[383] at the Church of St Peter and St Paul, Aston. Both the bridegroom and his father, Richard, gave their occupation as accountant; the bride's father was listed as gentleman, though he was subsequently returned as a clerk in the census of 1851. By this date Thomas (30) and Julia (27) were living in Quinton, Warley Wigorn with their two children, Julia (4) and Mary (11 months). On February 12th 1851, Julia and Mary had both been baptised at Christ Church The Quinton. (Joint baptisms were obviously a tradition in the Southall family, as on June 25th 1830 Thomas Southall, who had been born on November 11th 1820, was baptised along with two older and four younger siblings at St Philip's Church, Birmingham, when Richard Southall had declared his occupation as gun-maker.) Three other residents made up Thomas Southall's Warley Wigorn household in 1851: two-year-old Emily Jayes from Northampton, described as his niece, and two general servants: Ann Guest (60) from Kinlet, Shropshire and Emma Bolton (20) from Northfield, Worcestershire. No members of this household were still at plot W94 in 1861. Julia Southall, by then widowed, had become a boarding-house keeper In Sherlock Street, Birmingham, where she lived with her daughter, Julia. Amelia Augusta Jayes (aged 12, born in Northampton) – presumably the Emily of 1851 – was living with four siblings, a governess and servant at Holly Lodge, Moulton, Northamptonshire. Mary Southall, Ann Guest and Emily Bolton have not been traced.

12.04.12   Stephen Armes   Plot W121 (52°27'48"N 2°00'29"W)

Listed in the tithe apportionments as occupier of one of the two houses, shops and gardens on this 19 poles plot, the property of William Pritchett (4.18), was another of Quinton's migratory residents, Stephen Armes. Born in Hampstead, Middlesex in 1816/17, by 1841 Armes was working as a policeman and lodging in the household of butcher Joseph West in Romsley township. Two years later, on March 6th 1843, Stephen Armes and Ann Siddens, from Feckenham, Worcestershire, were married at Hales Owen Parish Church of St John the Baptist. The baptismal register of the same church records of April 17th 1844, "Sarah Ann, daughter of Stephen and Ann Armes, Quinton, Policeman of The Hill." In 1846 the birth of a second daughter, Susan, was registered in Aston, Birmingham and in 1851, by then with two more children, Stephen and Ann were living in Great Colmore Street, Birmingham, where Stephen gave his occupation as varnish maker.

At the census of 1841, Warley Wigorn's plot W121 appears to have been the home of single occupant, nail-maker Phoebe Hodgetts, then recorded as being 30 years old and born outside the county. Within three years she had obviously moved on and by 1851 could have been employed as a servant in Gigins Lane, Northfield in the farmhouse of Henry Ward. If this indeed was the same Phebe Hodgets (sic) then she was actually born in Hales Owen.

---

[383] Most 19th century couples were married after bans, called on three Sundays before the wedding in the church of the intended marriage and/or in the parish where the bride or groom lived. The alternative, under the 1753 Marriage Act, was by licence, generally issued by a bishop or archdeacon, following a statement under oath, usually by the bridegroom, that there were no impediments to the marriage. Licences cost more than bans and were often chosen by people with pretensions to gentility or who wanted a hasty marriage.

By 1851, 62-year-old nail-maker Thomas Coley, along with his wife Sarah (70) and niece Hannah (17) – also a nail-maker – had moved from Perry Hill where they had been living 10 years earlier, into plot W121. All three were native to Hales Owen. Hannah Coley, daughter of Joseph and Maria Coley (12.12.04) had been baptised at Hales Owen Parish Church on June 1st 1834. On June 4th 1853, aged 19, she married nailer David Deeley also at Christ Church. None of the representatives of the Coley family could write, those of the Deeley family could. The entry in the marriage register confirms that her father was Joseph Coley, presumably the brother of Thomas. Sarah Coley died, aged 71, in 1852 and was buried at Christ Church. By 1861, David (now Quinton's sub-postmaster and parish clerk) and Hannah Deeley were living in Warley Wigorn, with their three children all baptised at Christ Church: George, on May 28th 1856, Ann, on October 6th 1857, Elizabeth, on May 8th 1859.

12.04.13   Samuel Coles   Plot W121 (52°27'48"N 2°00'29"W)

The second occupier listed in the tithe apportionments of the two houses, shops and gardens on this 19 poles plot, the property of William Pritchett (4.18), was Samuel Coles, who has not been positively traced.[384] Once again the likelihood of the census enumerator's route suggests the occupants of plot W121 prior and subsequent to the enigmatic Samuel Coles.

The 1841 census offers no evidence of this plot being occupied by nail-makers. Its residents then appear to have consisted of 35-year-old wood-cutter Thomas Woodhouse born, as the next census reveals in Newcastle-under-Lyme, Staffordshire. His household included his wife, Phoebe (38) and children: Mary (12), Edward (10), Thomas (6), Phoebe (4) and John (2). None have any stated occupations. Mary, Edward, Thomas and Phoebe had all been baptised in Hales Owen – on April 26th 1829, April 24th 1831, October 19th 1834 and December 4th 1836 respectively. John was baptised at Christ Church The Quinton on October 4th 1840, when his father's occupation was stated as sawyer. By 1851 the Woodhouse family, now with three more children, had relocated to Fish Lane, Harborne, when the census supplies a few further details. Phoebe, whose occupation was then given as dress-maker and Edward were both born in Causeway Green; son Thomas and daughter Phoebe were born in Bristnall Fields, John and a further daughter, Amplias (9) were born in Quinton (all within Warley Wigorn township), with the two youngest children – Edgar (6) and Mira (4) both born in Harborne. It would seem, then, that the Woodhouse family is unlikely to have arrived at plot W121 before 1837. Plot W121 was occupied in 1851 by nail-makers John and Susannah Mason (12.01.04).

12.04.14   William Pritchett   Plot W125 (52°27'48"N 2°00'42"W)

The tithe apportionments list William Pritchett (4.18) as the occupier of Hales Owen Free School's 30 poles plot W125. However, as in both 1841 and 1851 he was enumerated in Lapal township at Boggs Farm, it is unlikely that he resided in Warley Wigorn. Again, the census enumerator's route offers the clues for his sub-tenants. The most likely occupants in 1841 are the family of nail-maker Samuel Coley. This consisted of 40-year-old Samuel (whom the 1851 census would reveal as born in Worlds End), his

---

[384] The most likely candidate would seem to be the Samuel Coles who in the 1851 census was a publican in Spring Hill, Birmingham, perhaps also identified as a chair-maker of Cross Street, Birmingham in the 1855 *White's Directory of Birmingham*, as a furniture-broker in the 1858 *General & Commercial Directory of Birmingham* and as a jet manufacturer of Tyndal Street, Birmingham in the 1861 census.

Quinton-born wife, Charlotte (35) and children Emma (18), William (10), Mary (8), Thomas (6), Samuel (4), Mira (14 months) and Lavinia (4 months). Mary, Thomas, Samuel and Mira had been baptised at Hales Owen Parish Church of St John the Baptist – Mary on June 6th 1833, Thomas on July 26th 1835, Samuel on March 21st 1837 and Mira on May 4th 1840. The registers of Christ Church The Quinton reveal the baptism of a further daughter, Agnes, on January 1st 1843, whilst the 1851 census lists the birth in Quinton of a further son, Joseph, in 1844. By 1851, the Coley family had left Warley Wigorn for Upper Lutley, where Samuel was then employed as a farm labourer and Charlotte and Mary (both now listed as born in Quinton) were working as nail-forgers. Mira (now listed as Maria), also born in Quinton, had no stated occupation. Brothers Thomas and Samuel were lodging in the household of Mary Whitehouse in Adams Lane Cakemore, where both worked as farm labourers. Emma, William, Agnes and Lavinia have not been traced.

In 1851 plot W125 appears to have been home to two households. The first was that of single occupant 28-year-old widower Edward Williams. Born in Bethnal Green, Middlesex, Williams was listed as a cabinet-maker. Ten years earlier, then described as a carpenter, he was living with his parents and sister in Newington Crescent, Finsbury. By 1861 he had left Warley Wigorn, making him another of the township's transitory residents.

The second household was that of Frederick Robins. Aged 27 at the time of the census, Robins, from Wickhamford, Worcestershire, was described as "labourer at chemical works." He lived with his nail-maker wife Jane (25) née Coley, whom he had married at Christ Church on August 5th 1849, and 2-month old daughter, Sarah. Frederick and Jane's first child, Frederick, had been baptised at Quinton's Bethesda Primitive Methodist Chapel on March 17th 1850 and buried at Christ Church The Quinton on May 31st 1850, aged eight weeks. By 1861, the family now with four more children had relocated to Ridgacre township. Two further children were born in the early 1860s. Baptismal records for all the children have been traced at Bethesda: Sarah (April 20th 1851), Joseph (May 8th 1853), a second Frederick (September 22nd 1855), Jane (November 22nd 1857), Ann (October 2nd 1859), Mary (August 25th 1861) and Elizabeth (December 20th 1863).

12.04.15   Joseph Salt   Plot W117 (52°27'51"N 2°00'13"W)

Listed in the tithe apportionments as occupier of this 1 rood 20 poles plot, with house and garden, property of Sarah Hudson (4.16) was Joseph Salt who does not appear as a Quinton resident in the censuses of 1841 or 1851. Though there are a number of possibilities, the most likely identification is of nail-maker Joseph Salt, born in Hales Owen in 1813, whose address changed at every listing. In 1841 he is found at Shut Mill Lane, Romsley along with his wife, Jane (25) and three children – William (5), Joseph (3), both born in Hales Owen, and Ann (1) born in Clent. The next census shows the family living in the delightfully named Sweet Turf, Dudley, with four more children: Helen born in 1842, Eli in 1843, Hannah in 1846 and Eliza in 1850. Helen, Eli and Hannah were born in Hales Owen, which would fit with a Quinton residence in 1844, whilst Eliza was born in Dudley. Continuing their itinerancy, the Salt family were at Netherton Hill, Dudley in 1861 and Wall Well, Hasbury, Hales Owen in 1871. The enumerator's route for 1841 suggests that the occupant of plot W117 in Upper Quinton was 65-year-old Richard Holloway, born within the county and of no stated occupation. No longer at plot W117 in 1844, Holloway died in 1847 and was buried at Hales Owen Parish Church on March 3rd.

The 1851 census, again following the enumerator's route, makes the residents of plot W117 James Gould and family. They are also entered as Gold and Goode in other records. With his age given as 32, his birthplace as Warley and his occupation as horse dealer, James Gould lived here with his wife, Sarah (32) and daughters Ann (8), Harriet (5) and Sarah (2) all born in Hales Owen, where Harriet was baptised at the Parish Church on May 6th 1846. In 1841, already working as a dealer, James lived in Spies Lane, Hill township, with Sarah and their infant son, Joseph, who had been baptised in Hales Owen on January 12th 1840, when his father's occupation was given as farmer and their address as Carters Lane. In 1851, 10-year-old Joseph Gould (Gold) was working as a labourer and lodging in the home of chain-maker Thomas Hickman in Woodside, Dudley.

Clearly, mid-19th century agricultural Quinton, with its 13 farms within the compass of the tithe maps had considerable need of horses. As we have already seen (9) at nearby Brandhall Farm, Richard Miller kept seven horses. As plot W171 offered no facilities for the stabling or grazing of horses and, unlike cattle-dealer James Pearman, James Gould apparently had no other land at his disposal, he perhaps plied his trade at horse fairs. Birmingham had hosted twice-yearly horse sales since the mid-13th century: one lasting for four days at Ascensiontide, and the other for three days at the Feast of John the Baptist; both were originally held in Ann Street (now Colmore Row). In the 18th century, the date of the first was moved to Whitsun week and the second to Michaelmas, with their location transferred to an area at the top of Smallbrook Street, subsequently named Horse Fair. Up to 3,000 horses were sold here annually in the mid-19th century when Gould was dealing, with the final fair held in 1911.[385] There would, then, have been ample scope for Gould's activities, though the buying and selling of horses would necessarily have involved, as would the buying and selling of cattle, the freedom and facility to travel away from home.

James Gould (Goode) died aged 41 and was buried at Christ Church on October 20th 1860. At the census of the following year, Sarah Gould (Goode) now head of household and with no stated occupation had relocated to Ridgacre township. Joseph, now employed as a carter, had returned home; Ann, Harriet and Sarah were all working as nail-makers.

12.05   Hawthorns

12.05.01   Daniel Read   Plot 90 (52°27'48"N 2°00'03"W)

The house and garden which lay behind the homes of Joseph Record and Samuel Hadley, near the Red Lion Inn, occupied a plot of 25 poles, the property of John White. In 1844 the tenant was listed as Daniel Read. At the census of 1841, the occupants were nail forger Enoch Read (49), his wife Diana (45) who came from Bewdley, and children Prudence (15), John (14), William (13), Anne (11)[386] and Joseph (8). Prudence, William and Joseph were all baptised at Hales Owen Parish Church – on June 11th 1826, May 11th 1828 and May 12th 1833 respectively. Amy Read died in October 1841, Enoch in December 1841 and Joseph in February 1842. All three were buried at Christ Church.[387] As no Daniel Read who

---

[385] Dudley also had held fairs for the sales of horses, sheep and cattle each April and September since the 17th century. An additional July fair was added in the 18th century.
[386] Ann is mis-named in the census. She was actually Amy, the girl who died in tragic circumstances – see 13.02
[387] See 13.02

meets the criteria has been traced, it seems likely that Diana has been wrongly transcribed as Daniel and that she was the tenant in 1844.

On November 14th 1847, Dinah (sic) Read, formerly Whitehouse, widow, married Charles Taylor, widower, at St Philip's Church (now the Anglican Cathedral) in Birmingham; neither were able to sign their names and both gave their address as Steelhouse Lane, Birmingham. This was clearly an accommodation address as the 1841 census shows Steelhouse Lane to be a long thoroughfare with numerous lodging houses and an eclectic mix of occupants, ranging from surgeon to spoon-maker, plumber to poulterer and encompassing brass-founders, gunsmiths, shopkeepers and labourers.

By 1851, the head of the household at plot 90 was Charles Taylor (37), a carpenter's labourer from Fillongley, Warwickshire. The household was completed by Charles's wife, Diana Taylor, her unmarried daughter Prudence, now the only resident nail forger, and a 5-year-old grandson, James Read. Diana's other children had by now left home, William (whose birthplace is now identified as Perry Hill) having become a servant – "all work" – at Warley Abbey, the home of John Edward Perry.[388] Ten years later, the remaining Taylor/Read family have relocated to Perry Hill, Warley Salop, with Diana now listed as Dinah and Charles Taylor and James Read both working as glasshouse labourers.

12.05.02   Joseph Record   Plot 91 (52°27'49"N 2°00'03"W)

In 1844, Joseph Record was the tenant of a house and garden at plot 91, which measured 21 poles, was the property of John White and occupied jointly by Samuel Hadley (12.05.03). Three years earlier, the head of the household had been 80-year-old William Record, who gave his occupation as nail forger. Also present were his 83-year-old wife, Hannah, along with Ann (50), Joseph (48) and William (20) Record. None of these had any stated occupation. William senior and Hannah both died within the space of three months shortly before the tithe map was drawn. Hannah was buried in the graveyard of Christ Church on January 7th and William on April 14th 1844, making Joseph the tenant in the apportionments.

Still the head of the household in 1851, Joseph, like his sister Ann was unmarried. William Record, who was Ann's son, was now described as a lodger. Two new members of the family were also present: Joseph Record (23), also listed as a lodger and Emma Cooper (5), listed as Joseph senior's granddaughter. In 1841 the younger Joseph Record had been working as a servant on Henry Nicholls' Hawthorn Farm, where he had been resident on census night. Emma Cooper was apparently his daughter.[389] All four adult members of the household now gave their occupation as nail forgers. On October 13th 1851, at Christ Church The Quinton, Joseph junior was married, not to Emma's mother, but to Mary Ann Cutler, also a nail maker, daughter of John Cutler of Warley Salop. Joseph senior died in 1856 and was buried at Christchurch on 24th February. By 1861 the head of the household at plot 91 was William Record, who shared his home with his mother, Ann and cousin, Emma Cooper. All three

---

[388] The Gothic Revival style Warley Abbey was built for the family of Hubert Galton, who moved there c1820 and remained there for around 20 years. After their departure, the Abbey was leased to a succession of families, until the estate was eventually sold off in the early 20th century.

[389] On April 13th 1868, Emma Cooper, nailer of Ridgacre was married at Christ Church The Quinton to William Painter, labourer of Beech Lanes. Her father is named as Joseph Record, labourer.

continued as nail-forgers. Joseph and Mary Record (now with four children) were still living in Ridgacre township, in Red Hill; Joseph, however, had reverted to his earlier occupation of farm work. Ann Record died in 1876, William in 1879 and Joseph in 1891. All three were buried at Christchurch.

12.05.03   Samuel Hadley   Plot 91 (52°27'49"N 2°00'03"W)

According to the tithe apportionments, the second household sharing plot 91 with Joseph Record (12.05.02) was that of Samuel Hadley. However, the 1841 census is confused as to whether Hadley had his own independent household or was part of that of Joseph Record. Given subsequent occupation, it seems more likely that the apportionments are correct.

Nail-forger Samuel Hadley was born within the county in 1781 and apparently shared his home with widowed Sarah Cooper, born in 1771, also within the county and, in 1841, of independent means. Sarah was still present at plot 91 at the census of 1851 when she was described as an annuitant. Samuel Hadley, however, had died a few days earlier and was buried at Christ Church The Quinton on Sunday March 30th 1851 (Ecclesiastical Census Day). Also present in 1851 was Sarah's granddaughter, Matilda Cooper who, ten years earlier was a pupil at a boarding school in Frederick Street, Birmingham. The household was completed by 54-year-old widow Mary Yeomans from Hales Owen who was employed as a servant. Mary Yeomans died in 1859 and was buried at Christ Church on August 23rd. At her death, Sarah Cooper, who by then had moved from Ridgacre township to Warley Salop, left effects valued under £600 – a not inconsiderable amount for the period. "Sarah Cooper late of Perry Hill near The Quinton in the Parish of Hales Owen in the County of Worcestershire, widow, proved at the Principal Registry by the oaths of Richard Cooper of Illy in the said parish, farmer, the Son and Charles Cooper of Northfield in the said county, farmer executors."[390] Sarah Cooper was buried at the Church of St John the Baptist, Hales Owen on February 26th 1858.

12.05.04   Joseph Harris   Plot 93 (52°27'48"N 2°00'02"W)

James Cooper was the landlord of the 21 poles plot with house, shop and garden next along the Turnpike Road towards Birmingham. Head of household in the tithe apportionments and in the censuses of 1841 and 1851 was nail forger Joseph Harris. Born, according to the 1851 census in Ridgacre, Joseph's age was given as 50 in 1841 and 64 in 1851. Joseph died in 1854 and was buried at Christ Church The Quinton on 2nd December.

Also present in 1841 were Sarah Harris (30), not a native of Hales Owen, Mary Anne Harris (15) and John Harris (10) both of whom were born within the county. Only Joseph Harris had any stated occupation. On March 24th 1845 at Christ Church The Quinton, Mary Anne Harris was married to Henry Pearson and in 1851 was living in Spring Hill, Hasbury. Sarah Harris died in 1846 and was buried at Christ Church on March 24th. By the census of 1851, the household consisted of only two members: Joseph Harris, still working as a nail-maker and a lodger, Henry Essex, also working at the nail forge. Essex is returned as born in Ridgacre and aged 28. Ten years earlier, with his age given as 15, Henry Essex is found employed as a servant to Thomas Nicholls at nearby Hawthorn Farm. (8.01.07)

---

[390] National Probate Calendar: England and Wales (08.05.1858) NB: In 1851 Richard Cooper farmed 25 acres at Illy Hall, employing one man and one boy; Charles Cooper farmed 248 acres at Weoley Castle, employing seven labourers.

Further light is shed by the 1861 census, by which time Henry Essex has become head of the household, now numbering three, all working as nail-makers. The other two members are his wife Mary Ann Essex (38) and nephew William Holloway (18). All are returned as born in Hales Owen. It seems extremely likely that this provides the link between Henry Essex and his landlord of ten years earlier, Joseph Harris. On July 21st 1844, at St Philip's Church Birmingham (now the cathedral), Henry Essex married Mary Ann Harris, who died 20 years later and was buried at Christ Church on 30th July 1864.

Mary Ann Harris, who was present at plot 93 in 1841, does not appear in any subsequent censuses, suggesting either that she had died or married. No matching death has been traced, further suggesting that she is the Mary Ann Harris who married Henry Essex (a rare name in the censuses of the mid-1800s) in 1844. Her non-appearance in the 1851 Ridgacre census (where Henry Essex is shown as married) means only that she was not at home on census night. The marriage register for Henry Essex and Mary Ann Harris names her father as George Harris, brick-maker, which sends out warning signals concerning the assumptions made about census information, particularly in 1841 where no relationships between members of households were stated. It is easy to assume, for example, that Joseph, Sarah, Mary Anne and John Harris are father, mother, daughter and son. However, Joseph and Sarah could equally be brother and sister, and Mary Anne and John their nephew and niece – or any other combination of relationships. Clearly, census details need to be treated with caution until confirmatory information becomes available.

12.05.05   Joseph Sadler   Plot 94 (52°27'48"N 1°59'59"W)

This is one of three households listed in the 1851 census as Hawthorn Cottage, the other two being those of Edward Thompson (11.03.04) and Richard Tomlinson (8.01.08). In 1841 nail-forger Joseph Sadler (45) shared his home at Hawthorn Cottage with his wife, Elizabeth (whose age is given as 46, but in the following two censuses as 60 and 70 respectively) and sons Joseph (17), William (12) and Charles (10). All three boys had been baptised at the Parish Church of St John the Baptist, Hales Owen. Joseph and Charles in infancy: January 11th 1824 and April 17th 1831 respectively. Though born on Christmas Eve 1829, William Sadler was not presented for baptism until October 30th 1837.

By 1851 the house, shop and garden on this plot measuring 24 poles, the property of Lord Lyttelton, had seen two changes. Elizabeth Sadler, now a widow (her husband had died in 1847 and had been buried at Christ Church on September 10th), was head of the household and with her three unmarried sons maintained the nail hearth. Also present in the household was her grand-daughter, 8-year-old Elizabeth Sadler. Nine months after the census of 1851, Joseph Sadler was married, at Christ Church The Quinton by Rev William Skilton, to Emma Guest, also of Ridgacre Township. (12.01.05 & 12.10.03) Their daughter, Ann, was baptised at Christ Church on October 1st 1854.

By 1861 this one household had become four – all within Ridgacre township. Remaining in Hawthorn and still head of household was Elizabeth Sadler, now sharing her home only with her grand-daughter, Elizabeth, but listed as Betsy, presumably to avoid confusion between the two residents. Both were working as nail-makers. Betsy Sadler was married to fellow nail-maker James Parkes at Christ Church on February 8th 1863; Elizabeth Sadler died aged 84 and was buried at Christ Church on March 13th 1874. Also in Hawthorn was Charles Sadler, now head of his own household, who had married Catherine Andrews on September 27th 1857 at Christ Church The Quinton, where their daughter

Catherine was baptised on February 2nd 1858. Charles' occupation was now given as agricultural labourer. Charles Sadler died aged 53 and was buried at Christ Church on April 12th 1884. The other two Sadler brothers are both found in Quinton. Joseph, now married to Rosannah (37),[391] his son Thomas (12) and daughter Mary (11) were all working at the nail forge. Joseph's daughter from his first marriage, Ann (6) was still at school. Rosannah Sadler died in 1871 and by 1881, Joseph Sadler was married to his third wife, Tabitha, born in Blackheath and also a nail-maker. They lived, along with Joseph's 16-year-old son, labourer John, at Hagley Road, Quinton, presumably the same address as New Road, where he was living in 1871.   The fourth household consisted of William Sadler and his wife Martha (27), both of whom were nail-makers, and daughter, Lucy (5) listed as scholar. William Sadler died aged 91 and was buried at Christ Church on January 10th 1918.

Nail-maker's workshop as shown at the Black Country Living Museum

12.05.06   Thomas Partridge   Plot W1 (52°27'46"N 1°59'52"W)

This 1 rood 39 poles plot with house, shop and garden, leased from William Grazebrook, agent of the trustees of Ferdinando Lea Smith, was occupied by Thomas Partridge, who was also tenant of the adjacent 25-poles garden plot W3. (52°27'46"N 1°59'49"W) In 1841, the household consisted of eight members, of whom two were listed as nail-makers: Thomas Partridge (50) and Samuel Allen (15). The other members were named as Linneus (45), Esther (15), Sarah (14) and Martha (12) Partridge and Jesse Allen (6). The stated ages of the younger generation were somewhat unreliable, as their baptisms at Hales Owen's Parish Church indicate. Esther Partridge was baptised there on July 27th 1823; Sarah Partridge on March 26th 1826; Samuel Allen on November 5th 1826; Martha Partridge on December 28th 1828; Jesse Allen on July 26th 1835. The parents of Esther, Sarah and Martha were named as Thomas and Mary Partridge; those of Samuel as Henry and Phelena Allen, and of Jesse as Henry and Paulina Allen. Clearly both clergy and enumerators had difficulty with this lady's unusual name.

---

[391] Joseph's first wife, Emma, died in 1855 and was buried at Christ Church on September 9th.

On December 29th 1839, at St Philip's Church Birmingham (Mary Partridge having died in 1838)[392] widower Thomas Partridge of Beech Lanes married widow Felina Allen (née Mucklow) of Quinton near Beech Lanes. Thus, Thomas Partridge's second wife was named as Phelena at her elder son's baptism, Paulina at her younger son's baptism, Felina at her second marriage and in the 1851 census, Linneus at the census of 1841 and Philenna in 1861. Phelena, Paulina, Felina and Philenna are easily mistakable homophones, but it is difficult to imagine how the enumerator arrived at Linneus!

By 1851 Thomas and Felina Partridge were both working as nail-makers at plot W1, as were Martha Partridge, Samuel and Jesse Allen. Their respective birth-places were also clarified: Thomas and Martha in Warley Wigorn; Felina in Rowley Regis; Samuel and Jesse in Quinton. Also born in Warley Wigorn was Thomas and Felina's daughter, Mary Ann, who had been baptised at Christ Church on June 5th 1842. Neither Esther nor Sarah Partridge was still living in Hawthorns by this census. On April 2nd 1848, Sarah's daughter, Mary Partridge, was baptised at Christ Church and on October 14th 1849, at St Martin's Church Birmingham, Sarah married sawyer William Powell. In 1851 William and Sarah were living in Beech Lanes, Warley Wigorn with daughters Mary (3) and Celena (9 months). On December 30th 1850, also at St Martin's Church, Esther Partridge had married labourer Joseph Hadley and in 1851 was living in Woodgate. Both couples had given their address as Broad Street Birmingham for the marriage register.

At the census of 1861, now widowed again,[393] Philenna Partridge was head of the household at plot W1. Also still present were her step-daughter, Martha Partridge (33); sons Samuel (34), Jesse (25) Allen and daughter Mary Ann Partridge (19). All five residents were now employed as nail-makers.

12.05.07 William Partridge   Plot W2 (52°27'46"N 1°59'49"W)

The second of the two Hawthorn residential plots lying within Warley Wigorn township was also leased from William Grazebrook, agent of Ferdinando Lea Smith's trustees. This house, shop and garden on a 37-poles plot, was occupied by the household of William Partridge, born in 1805 in Fermoy, County Cork, Ireland. On November 8th 1838, then living in Beech Lanes, nailer William Partridge had married Mary Gray, also of Beech Lanes, at St Philip's Church, Birmingham. By the census of 1841, along with their son Charles, who had been baptised in Hales Owen on December 8th 1839, William and Mary were resident at plot W2.

---

[392] Stourbridge register, April-June Quarter, 1838.

[393] There are two possible Stourbridge entries for the death of Thomas Partridge: April-June Quarter 1857 and April-June Quarter 1860.

Ten years later, the family had grown to include three more children, all baptised at Christ Church The Quinton: Ann (June 5th 1842), Joseph (May 5th 1844) and Elizabeth (February 7th 1847). In 1849, William and Mary had lost a fifth child. John Partridge had been baptised at Christ Church on May 6th and buried there, at the age of just 13 weeks, on July 1st. As the great cholera epidemic was sweeping the country, John Partridge, one of just ten burials at Quinton's Christ Church between July 1st and December 24th 1849, died of "inflammation of the chest," with no medical attendant present to certify the cause.

At the census of 1851, William, Mary and Charles Partridge were all working at the nail forge, with their three younger children listed as scholars.

The 1861 census reveals plot W2 as containing one of Quinton's most consistent and stable households, with all six members of the Partridge family still resident. William (56), Mary (50), Charles (21) and Ann (18) were all working as nail-makers. Joseph (17) was a brass founder and Elizabeth (14) was listed as house servant.

12.06 Upper Ridgacre

12.06.01   Thomas Coley   Plot 112 (52°27'27"N 2°00'11"W)

The tithe apportionments name Thomas Coley as the occupant of one of three cottages on plot 112, which measured 1 rood 14 poles and was the property of the trustees of Ferdinando Smith. However, the censuses of 1841 and 1851 identify only one Thomas Coley in Ridgacre during this period. He lived in the household of his brother, Josiah Coley, at plot 159 in 1841, 1851, and 1861. (12.12.01) The Warley Wigorn area of Quinton had two residents of the same name: six-year-old Thomas Coley who lived with his family at plot W125 in 1841 (12.04.14) and 62-year-old Thomas Coley who had previously been living in Perry Hill, but was head of the household at plot W121 in 1851. (12.04.12) As none of these appear plausible candidates for the tithe apportionment tenancy, the identity of this Thomas Coley remains a mystery.

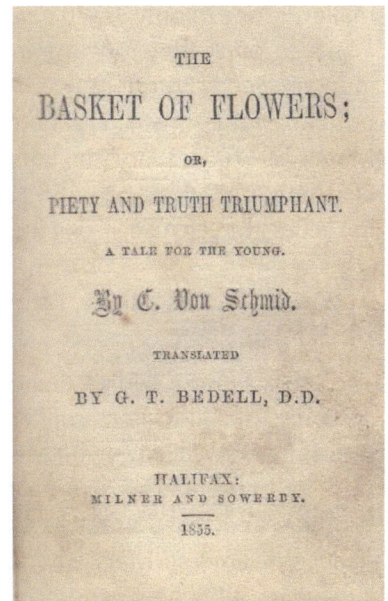

This tiny book (11 x 7cm) translated from French and published in England in 1855, was presented by Bethesda Primitive Methodist Sunday School Quinton in 1856 to Mary Coley. Though her great-granddaughter, Joyce Eccles, to whom the book belonged, believed that Mary lived in Worlds End, no-one of this name is listed in Quinton's PM baptismal register, nor in the censuses of 1851 or 1861 in the townships of either Ridgacre or Warley Wigorn – another Coley mystery.

At plot 112 in 1841 were farm labourer John Houghton, from Tardebigg in Worcestershire, his wife Charlotte, from Harborne, then in Staffordshire, their two-year-old son, John and a lodger, John Greaves (19), also a labourer. John and Charlotte are still in Ridgacre township (though moved to Upper Quinton) in 1851 and 1861, on both of which occasions Charlotte is listed as a nail-maker. In 1851, John Greaves is no longer present, but eight-year-old Alice Greaves (daughter of John and Hannah, baptised at Christ Church The Quinton on February 26th 1843) is now lodging with John and Charlotte Houghton and their son, now 12 and still at school. Ten years later, son John Greaves, now an agricultural labourer, married and with a son of his own, still lives in Ridgacre township, but by 1871, he has changed his occupation to phosphorous maker and his residence to Cakemore. Alice Greaves, in 1861, is working as a servant at the home of refinery foreman William Bromage in Icknield Square, Ladywood, Birmingham. John Greaves, now a coal-miner is head of his own household in Oldbury township. The link between Houghton and Greaves appears to be that Charlotte Houghton and John Greaves were both born in Harborne – perhaps brother and sister? – which, if John was Alice's father, is a plausible explanation for her lodging with her aunt and uncle in the absence of her parents. There is confusion over the ages of members of the Houghton family. John's age is given as 35 in 1841, 39 in 1851 and 48 in 1861; Charlotte's age reads 30 in 1841, 40 in 1851 and 58 in 1861. The younger John, who is 2 in 1841, 12 in 1851 has become 32 in 1861 and 33 in 1871!

The 1851 census identifies just three residents at this plot 112 cottage: 20-year-old farm labourer William Edmunds from Marsh Gibbon in Buckinghamshire, his wife, Sarah (19) and daughter, Fanny (3 months) both of whom were born in Hales Owen. Sarah Edmunds gives her occupation as spike maker,[394] one of only 3/270 nail makers (all women)[395] from the entire Ridgacre township and Quinton enclaves of Warley Wigorn from 1841-1861 involved in this heaviest section of the nail-forging industry. Fanny Edmunds was baptised at Christ Church on February 2nd 1851, as were her three sisters, born after the census. Elizabeth, who was baptised on April 2nd 1854 was buried at Christ Church on March 12th 1858, Mary Ann Edmonds was baptised on April 1st 1857 and a fourth daughter, also named Elizabeth, on October 2nd 1859. After leaving Quinton, William Edmunds, still a farm labourer is found in successive censuses living in Court Oak Road, Harborne.

12.06.02 William Goode   Plot 112 (52°27'27"N 2°00'11"W)
[Gould in the Tithe Apportionments]

The second house and garden on plot 112 was occupied by William Goode and his family. In 1841 this consisted of nail-forgers William (35) and John (40) the relationship between whom is not stated. Also present were William's wife Mary (35) and children, William (13), Sarah (10), John (7), Ann (5) and Elisa (2). The household was completed by Anne Goode (70). It seems likely that William and John were brothers and that Anne was their mother. On November 28th 1841, Mary Ann Goode, daughter of nailer William and Mary Goode of Ridgacre was baptised at Hales Owen Parish Church. She did not survive until the next census and was buried at Christ Church The Quinton on June 6th 1850.

By the census of 1851, still present in this household were William, Mary, William, Ann and Elisa Goode, all of whom were now working at the nail forge. William and Mary now had a 2-year-old son, Henry, who had been baptised at Christ Church on January 7th 1849. Still living in the household was Sarah (Goode), now married to nail-forger William Rudge (22), with their 1-year-old daughter, Jane, baptised at Christ Church on August 4th 1850. William and Sarah brought three more children to Christ Church for baptism during the decade: Ann on July 4th 1852; Emma on August 5th 1855; John on April 20th 1859. At the 1841 census, William Rudge had been resident in Lapal township with his parents and eight siblings. No longer at plot 112 in 1851 were Anne Goode, nor either the elder or younger John. The elder John, now working as a labourer, was established in his own household, with wife Mary (from Long Lane in Hill township) and an apparently pre-existent family in Camden Street, Ladywood.[396] The younger John, now following in his parents' footsteps as a nail-forger, was one of two lodgers in the Woodgate home of fellow-nail-forgers John and Elizabeth Stoker.

Ten years later, William and Mary were still nail-making in Ridgacre township. Eliza and Henry, both nail-makers, still lived in the family home, where their brother John had returned from Woodgate, but was now working as an agricultural labourer. William and Sarah Rudge were also still in Ridgacre, but now in their own household, still following the nail trade, as were their two eldest children, Jane (11) and Ann (9). This household was completed by Emma (5) who was at school and 12-month-old John. The younger William Goode, still a nail-maker, by 1861 was married to Mary (from Rowley Regis) and living with their three children in Ashes, Warley Wigorn. His father, also William Goode, who had been

_____

[394] Spikes were used for securing the iron chairs in which railway lines sat on the wooden sleepers. They were made from heavy rod iron, usually with the aid of an Oliver - a heavy hammer operated by a treadle.

[395] The other two were Sarah Hill (12.12.05) and Leah Deeley (12.12.06).

[396] Now in Hockley suburb, in the early 19th century, Camden Street was considered part of Ladywood. – See Chinn (2003) *The Streets of Brum* Part One, p 76

head of the household at plot 112 throughout the years of this survey, died, aged 64,[397] in 1867, and was buried at Christ Church The Quinton on 5th May.

12.06.03   Elijah Read   Plot 112 (52°27′27″N 2°00′11″W)

The large household of nail-forger Elijah Read (aged 43 in 1841), his wife Sarah (35), who, according to the 1851 census, came from Northfield,[398] and their nine children – Hannah (19), George (16), Lousey – presumably – Lucy (14), Harriet (13), David (9), Jesse (6), Reuben (5), Elijah (4) and Mary Ann (2) occupied the third cottage on Plot 112.[399] Only Elijah had any stated occupation, though it is extremely unlikely that the older children were not already at work and most likely at the forge. By the census of 1851, George Read, now identified as a nail-forger, was married to fellow nailer Sarah Cutler and living with his in-laws at Plot 47. (12.03.13) Elijah, Sarah and their large family had also moved to Lower Quinton, to Plot 41 (12.03.01) and their cottage on plot 112 was now occupied by the Mills family.

Farm labourer George Mills was one of Ridgacre township's incomers, having been born in Tamworth, Warwickshire in 1803. On April 21st 1839 at Hales Owen Parish Church, George Mills had married Sarah Hill, both with Ridgacre addresses. By 1851 they were living at plot 112 with 14-year-old Joseph Hill[400] ("son-in-law" – presumably Sarah's son from a previous relationship) also working as a farm labourer, along with children, Mary (11), David (8), Thomas (5) and Sarah (2) Mills. The three older Mills children were all at school. Mary Mills had been baptised at Hales Owen Parish Church on February 2nd 1840, but David had been baptised at St Michael's Church, Bartley Green on August 7th 1842, the family's address then recorded as Woodgate, Northfield. The two younger children had both been baptised at Christ Church The Quinton: Thomas on September 7th 1845 and Sarah on August 6th 1848. Still in the township ten years later, though without Joseph or Mary, David had now joined his father as a farm labourer, 12-year-old Sarah was described as a nurse, and Sarah senior had no occupation.

12.07   Muttons

12.07.01   Benjamin Hill   Plot 188 (52°27′37″N 1°59′36″W)

The house, shop and garden on this plot of 28 poles were the property of Timothy Hill, as were plots 189 (52°27′36″N 1°59′36″W) and 190 (52°27′34″N 1°59′36″W), *Little Meadow* and *Big Meadow*, held as pasture by Benjamin Hill. *Little Meadow* (2 roods 21 poles) attracted a tithe rent of 1s, whilst the much larger *Big Meadow* (1 acre 16 poles) was assessed at 2s, both sums payable to the Vicar of Hales Owen. Benjamin Hill returned his occupation in 1841 as "forger" (presumably nail-forger) and in 1851 as whitesmith. There were nine members of the household at each census. In 1841, Benjamin (48) shared his home with his wife Hannah (45), daughters Elizabeth (28), Sally (25), Mary (14), Louisa – also known

---

[397] Like so many ages listed in records during this period, this is inconsistent. In the census records William Goode's age is given as 35 in 1841, 48 in 1851, 54 in 1861, and 64 in the Christ Church burial register of 1867.
[398] The 1861 census lists Elijah Read as born in Northfield and Sarah Read as born in Ridgacre.
[399] Elijah and Sarah's four older children were all baptised at Hales Owen Parish Church: Hannah on June 2nd 1822; George on November 16th 1823; Lucy on Christmas Day 1825; Harriet on March 3rd 1828. Records for the next four boys – David, Jeffrey, Reuben and Elijah – have not been traced. Mary Ann and two further children – Enoch and Amy – were baptised at Hales Owen. (12.03.01)
[400] Joseph Hill died, aged 23, in1860 and was buried at Christ Church The Quinton on March 9th.

as Lucy − (7), Emma (4) and sons John (19) and Benjamin (11), none of whom had any stated occupation. All of Benjamin and Hannah's children had been baptised at Hales Owen's Parish Church of St John the Baptist: Elizabeth and Sally (Sarah) on January 11th 1818;[401] John on May 5th 1822; Mary on April 1st 1827;[402] Benjamin on October 4th 1829; Louisa on May 11th 1834 and Emma on August 6th 1837. Subsequent censuses would show that though nail-making remained integral to this family culture, Quinton's other staple occupation of farming also retained a hold, and that two of the daughters moved into the less physical occupations of dress-making and bonnet making.

By 1851 Sally had left the family home, having married William Downing of Beech Lanes at Christ Church on May 7th 1842. The younger Benjamin married Mary Lees (23), a nail-forger from Northfield, at Christ Church on February 9th 1851. Six months later the family extended to ten with the birth of Benjamin and Mary's son, William who was baptised at Christ Church on August 3rd. Their second son, Benjamin, was baptised at Christ Church on July 3rd 1853. By the 1851 census, John and Benjamin had joined their father as whitesmiths, whilst the three younger daughters (Mary, Lucy and Emma) who remained at home had each become nail-forgers. Hannah and Elizabeth still had no stated occupation. On May 11th 1851 came the third Hill wedding at Christ Church, when John Hill married Emily Monk, daughter of boat builder Joseph Monk and his wife Phillis, of Metchley Lane, Harborne. The 1851 census shows nail-maker Emily living at home with her parents, whilst the entry in Christ Church marriage register shows her as resident in Ridgacre and of no occupation.

Benjamin Hill senior died in 1860 and was buried at Christ Church on 16th December. At the census of the following year, Hannah Hill was now head of household, with her occupation described as "farming 9 acres." Still at home were Elizabeth (47) "employed at home;" Mary (34) "dress-maker;" Louisa (27) "nail-maker;"[403] and Emma (23) "bonnet-maker."[404] Though still in Ridgacre township, the two sons and daughters-in-law now occupied their own households. John and Emily Hill are listed in Red Hill, with John now working as a nail-maker and Emily of no given occupation. Still employed as a whitesmith, Benjamin Hill now lived with his wife, Mary (also of no stated occupation) and their children, William, Benjamin, Jane and Thomas in Beech Lanes. Hannah Hill died in 1862 and was buried at Christ Church on 19th May.

12.08 Lower Franks

12.08.01   Samuel Hadley   Plot 201 (52°27'43"N 1°59'38"W)

On a plot of land measuring 1 rood 18 poles, the property of Lord Lyttelton, just to the south of the wedge-shaped enclave of Warley Wigorn opposite Hawthorn Farm, at the apportionments of 1844

---

[401] The register notes that Elizabeth was born on August 27th 1813 and Sally on October 3rd 1815.

[402] At Mary's baptism the register lists her mother, Hannah, as Ann.

[403] Subsequently, Louisa Hill also changed her occupation. At her marriage to labourer Jesse Allen from Hawthorns at Christ Church on February 24th 1868, she is listed as "dress-maker." The register shows that like her brother and sister-in-law, John Hill and Emily Monk, Louisa was able to write her name; Jesse Allen was not.

[404] On September 21st 1863, Emma Hill ("milliner") married James Haglington ("boot and shoe repairer") of Beech Lanes at Christ Church The Quinton. Four and a half years later, Haglington was a witness at the marriage of Louisa Hill and Jesse Allen.

was the house and garden of nail forger Samuel Hadley. Though Hadley and his family had lived there in 1841, at that census, the household head was 70-year-old Mary Pitchford, listed as of independent means. Aged 35 in 1841, Samuel Hadley was married to Lucy (also 35), with daughters Anne (18), Mary (15), Sarah (3), Emma (3 months) and son Elias (9). The four older children, born before the building of Quinton's Christ Church, were all baptised at St John's Parish Church, Hales Owen: Anne on August 17th 1823; Mary on June 4th 1826; Elias on October 16th 1831 and Sarah on October 1st 1837. Labourer Charles Hadley (33) completed the household. Apart from Mary Pitchford, all the residents were born within the county and only Samuel had any stated occupation.

Ten years later, this same dwelling was registered as two households with a total of 14 residents. In the first were nail-forgers Samuel, Lucy, Sarah and Emma Hadley with two daughters born since the previous census – Ceyna (6) and Hannah (3). The three younger children, who had all been baptised at Christ Church (Emma on April 4th 1841, Ceyna on September 1st 1844 and Hannah on November 7th 1847), were listed as scholars. This household was completed by daughter Mary, now married to farm labourer John Haycock (31). Head of the second household was 35-year-old farm labourer William Haycock from Lye, his wife, Ann (27)[405] and sons John (8), a scholar at Quinton School and James (2). Also present was William Haycock's brother-in-law, 19-year-old Elias Hadley, now working as a nail-forger, and James Clark (29) from Standlake in Oxfordshire, listed as "visitor" and working as a labourer at Spon Lane Glassworks.[406] Charles Hadley was no longer listed in either household.[407]

Still in Ridgacre township in 1861, with their addresses now given as Redhall Lane, remained the households of Samuel Hadley and William Haycock. Samuel, Lucy, Ceyna and Hannah Hadley constituted one household, with Samuel, Lucy and Ceyna employed at the nail forge, and 13-year-old Hannah working as a nurse maid. Samuel Hadley died in December 1867 and Lucy Hadley died in January 1874. Both were buried at Christ Church. The next entry in the 1861 census is that of the household of William Haycock. No longer a farm labourer, William is now listed as a labourer at a forge. Ann Haycock still has no stated occupation; John Haycock is no longer at home;[408] 12-year-old James has become a photographic case maker and three children have been born since the previous census. William and Ann Haycock are the only couple of that name living in Ridgacre/Quinton between 1841 and 1861, so it is reasonable to assume that the following entries from Christ Church registers with Ridgacre addresses all relate to their offspring. Nine children were baptised during the two decades and four were buried, one according to the register transcriptions, three days before he was baptised! William and Ann were obviously desperate to have a son named William Samuel as, having lost two boys of that name in infancy, they used the name for a third time.

---

[405] Ann Hadley married William Haycock at St George's Church, Birmingham on July 10th 1842.

[406] Chance Glassworks was established in Spon Lane, Smethwick in May 1824.

[407] The only 43-year-old, Worcestershire-born Charles Hadley identified in the 1851 census was enumerated at Fore Street, East Stonehouse, Devon, listed as RM Pensioner, watch constable on duty in open air.

[408] The most likely 18-year-old John Haycock in the 1861 census was working as a servant (barman) in the household of publican Thomas Palmer, in Carver Street, All Saints Ward, Birmingham.

Name	Baptism	Burial or 1861 census entry
John	November 6th 1842	See footnote 352
William	December 13th 1844	December 10th 1844
James	June 11th 1848	Plot 201
Mary Ann	February 27th 1851	November 20th 1851
Ann Mary	March 12th 1852	Plot 201
William Samuel	August 6th 1854	April 2nd 1857
Sarah Ann	March 10th 1857	Plot 201
William Samuel	March 26th 1859	April 4th 1859
William Samuel	July 25th 1860	Plot 201

Also still in the township was nail-maker Elias Hadley, now living in Muttons with his nail-maker wife, Ann and sons George (2) and James (10 months), both of whom were baptised at Christ Church: George on November 7th 1858 and James on May 6th 1860.

12.09 Franks

12.09.01   James Partridge   Plot 205 (52°27'42"N 1°59'24"W)

Nail-forger James Partridge was 27 years old at the 1841 census; his wife, Lydia, was 25. The family was completed by 4-year-old Thomas, who was baptised at Hales Owen's Church of St John the Baptist on October 1st 1837. Also resident at this 23 poles site, comprising house and garden, the property of Timothy Hill, were nail-forgers John Cutler (18), David Guest (15) and 11-year-old Elysa Guest who was not listed as working.

In 1851 James Partridge gave his occupation as labourer/nail-forger, Thomas was returned as a scholar, as was his brother George (7). However, George's twin sister, Elysa, apparently was not at school. George had been baptised at Christ Church on May 5th 1844, but there is no similar entry in the register for Elysa. In 1851, all members of the Partridge family were listed as born in Beech Lanes. David Guest, still working as a nail-forger, was now living in the home of his brother-in-law, William Powell in the Warley Salop district of Beech Lanes. Elysa Guest has not been traced and John Cutler not positively identified.[409] George Partridge died, aged 11, in 1855 and was buried at Christ Church on 25th July.

In 1861, the Partridge family, now listed as resident in Red Hill (presumably an enumerator's quirk rather than a change of home) are all returned as born in Ridgacre. James's occupation is now given solely as nail-maker, at which trade he has been joined by his son Thomas, now married to nail-maker Mary from Northfield. Also working at the nail forge is 17-year-old Elysa Partridge, now listed as James' niece. This may suggest that she was actually the Eliza Partridge, daughter of Esther Partridge of Quinton, baptised at Hales Owen Parish Church on March 27th 1843. The 1861 household was completed by Thomas and Mary's children, 4-year-old George (baptised at Christ Church on April 5th 1857) and 12-month-old Betsy (baptised at Christ Church on January 1st 1860). James Partridge died in 1889 and was buried at Christ Church on 30th December.

---

[409] The most likely census entry is that for John Cutler (28), labourer, living with his nail-making wife Sarah, four children and two lodgers at Grove Lane, Northfield.

12.10 Red Hill

12.10.01   Ann Cutler   Plot 235 (52°27'49"N 1°59'28"W)

Ridgacre tithe apportionments list Ann Cutler as both owner and occupant of this house, shop and garden measuring 11 poles, immediately east of the wedge-shaped enclave of Warley Wigorn adjacent to the Turnpike Road. However, the 1841 census enumerates Ann Cutler in Quinton between entries for Benjamin Westwood (12.01.06) and James Robinson (12.04.06), some distance from Red Hill. In the same household were 20-year-old Edward Cutler and 50-year-old labourer Charles Haycock. Neither Ann nor Edward Cutler originated from Quinton nor had any stated occupation. Ann Cutler died, aged 76, in March 1850 and was buried at Christ Church. In 1851, farm labourer Charles Haycock was living in the Warley Wigorn sector of Quinton in the household of his brother, Thomas. (12.04.09) Edward Cutler has not been positively identified after 1841.[410]

Enumerated (sequentially with plots 233-234) as head of household at plot 235 in the censuses of 1841 and 1851 is farm labourer Richard Salter. In 1841 his age is given as 50, as is that of his wife, Ann. Completing the 1841 household are nail-forger John Cutler (25), Hannah (22), Joseph (20), Rebecca (14), Sarah (9) and George (4) Cutler. All, apart from Richard, are listed as born within the county. Subsequent censuses reveal confusion over Richard Salter's origins: in 1851 his birthplace is given as Welshpool, Montgomeryshire and in 1861 as Wollaston, Shropshire. George Cutler died, aged seven, in May 1844 and was buried at Christ Church.

Still present in 1851 are Richard (whose age remains at 50!), his wife, Ann, now working as a nail-forger, Hannah (here called Ann) Rebecca and Sarah Cutler[411] who were also employed at the nail forge. All three members of the Cutler family are described as "wife's daughter," which presumably means that Ann Salter was previously Ann Cutler. There are also three grandchildren present: George (3), Ann (18 months) and Eliza (8 months) Cutler. George Cutler, entered in the register as illegitimate son of Hannah Cutler, was baptised at Christ Church on November 15th 1847. Eliza Cutler died aged three years seven months and was buried at Christ Church5th 1854.

By 1861, the family is listed as two households. The first consists only of Richard and Ann Salter, both now 72 and still working. In this census entry (perhaps confused by his familiarity with Anglican liturgy) the enumerator, Thomas White, has altered the spelling of Salter to Psalter! In the second household Rebecca Cutler is now married to agricultural labourer John Jacques from Dordon in North Warwickshire. Two children Ann (11) and Elizabeth (11 months) Jacques complete the household.

The link between plot 235's long-term resident Cutler family and the tithe apportionment's owner-occupier Ann Cutler is unclear, but the fact that the name Ann Cutler is found here through three (possibly four) generations strongly suggests that one exists.

---

[410] The only possible Edward Cutler listed in the 1851 census is Edward Roger Cutler, living in Granville Square, Clerkenwell and working as an insurance office clerk. His age is given as 32 and his birthplace as St Brides.

[411] On August 9th 1852, at Christ Church The Quinton, a Sarah Cutler, daughter of Samuel Cutler, was married to Edwin Davis. Both gave their address as Warley Wigorn. Neither Cutlers nor Davis have been otherwise identified.

12.10.02   Thomas Haycock   Plot 233 (52°27'49"N 1°59'24"W)

Described in the 1844 tithe apportionments as a house and garden, the property of John Birch (4.07), plot 233, measuring 37 poles, was located just south of the turnpike road to the east of the wedge-shaped enclave of Warley Wigorn. The Ridgacre tithe map, however, marks no building on this plot. Listed as the occupant, Thomas Haycock would have been a comparatively new resident as, in 1841, he and his family were living in the household of Edward Smart at nearby plot 228. (12.10.06). Enumerated between the neighbouring plots 234 and 232 in 1841 were two households, the first headed by Mary Fox and the second by Thomas Fox, between whom no obvious relationship has been established.

Nail-forger Mary Fox, aged 47 and born outside the county, shared her home with 27-year-old Harriet Fox, also born outside the county and of no stated occupation. Blacksmith Thomas Fox, aged 38 and his nail-forger wife Harriet (40) shared their home with their eight children: William (18), Edward (16), Rebecca (15), Mary (13), Harriet (11), James (6), John (4) and George (3). In 1843, a ninth child, Owen, was born, shortly before the family left the township for Warley Wigorn. Thomas Fox died in 1850 and was buried at Christ Church The Quinton on 3rd November. In 1851 Harriet Fox, still working as a nail-maker, was head of a household in Londonderry, Warley Wigorn, of which Edward (puddler at iron works), Rebecca (nail-maker), Mary (nail-maker), James (labourer at glass works), George (labourer at iron works) and Owen were still part. George Fox died, aged 13, shortly after the census and was buried at Christ Church on July 31st 1851.

Plot 233 was occupied in 1851 by farm labourer Thomas Haycock (40) and his wife Ann (37), both from Lye, Worcestershire. Their two elder children Thomas and Mary (12.10.06) were no longer at home, their resident family now consisting of Harriet (10) and Elizabeth (7), both at school, and 8-month old John, all born at Red Hill. Harriet was baptised at St Peter's Church, Harborne on February 14th 1841; Elizabeth at Christ Church The Quinton on March 3rd 1844 and John at Christ Church on September 1st 1850. A further son, William was baptised at Quinton by Rev William Skilton on May 1st 1853. Though there were no longer any resident nail-forgers at plot 233, on census night 1851, 31-year-old nail-forger William Hadley was listed as a visitor.

Thomas Haycock died, aged 47 and was buried at Christ Church on May 10th 1857. This obviously led to the dispersal of the family and in 1861 scholars John (10) and William (8) Haycock were living in the household of their elder brother, agricultural labourer Thomas Haycock in Langley, Warley Wigorn.

12.10.03   Thomas Partridge   Plot 232 (52°27'50"N 1°59'23"W)

The next plot (measuring 38 poles) passed by the traveller who continued along the turnpike road towards Birmingham was also the property of John Birch. In 1841 this house and garden was the home of nail forger, 30-year-old Thomas Partridge, his wife Mary Anne (28) and son Joseph (4), who had been baptised at Hales Owen's Parish Church on November 6th 1836. Another son, William, born after the census but before the drawing of the tithe map, was baptised at Quinton's Christ Church on August 6th 1843, less than a year before his brother Joseph was buried there on May 26th 1844. Before William had reached his fifth birthday, his mother had also died. Mary Anne Partridge was buried at Christ Church on Boxing Day, 1847. 13-year old Emma Guest (12.01.05; 12.05.05) also lived with the Partridge family at the 1841 census. In 1851, Thomas (then listed as "labourer file cutting") and William Partridge were living at plot 216 (11.04.01) in the household of Benjamin Standley, Thomas's father-in-law, in Beech Lanes, where they were still to be found at the census of 1861. By this time William was working as a blacksmith, Thomas, by then head of the household and still a file-cutter had re-married and had five more children.

In 1851 the occupants of plot 232 were nailers John (55) and Sarah (60) Downing. Ten years earlier they had been living along with children Charles (20) and Mary (15) at End of Harborne Town in Harborne township. At this census, only John's occupation – nailer – was stated, and John and Sarah's ages were given as 50 and 55 respectively. Sarah Downing died in 1857 and was buried at Christ Church on 24th May. John Downing died in 1860 and was buried at Christ Church on 22nd April.

12.10.04   Thomas Page   Plot 232 (52°27'50"N 1°59'23"W)

Carpenter and joiner Thomas Page, born in Leominster in 1796, occupied a house and garden on a plot measuring 38 poles, the property of John Birch at Red Hill. Here he lived with his wife Hannah (42), son William (18), also a carpenter, and daughter Anne (10), all born in Beech Lanes, at the census of 1841. Ten years later, Anne, still at home, had become a nail-forger. William, who by 1851 was married, was living as the sole occupant at Back of N° 5 Sherbourne Street in the Ladywood district of Birmingham. His wife, Mary (24), whose occupation was given as joiner's wife, and three children, Joseph (6), Thomas (3) and Hannah (1) were all part of Thomas Page's household at plot 232 in Ridgacre township.

On February 3rd 1856, Ann Page, now working as a dress-maker, was also living in Sherbourne Street, from where she was married at St John's Church Ladywood to blacksmith, William Parkes. Thomas Page died in 1856 and was buried at Christ Church on 16th March. At the census of 1861, only Hannah Page, now returned as a nail-maker, remained at Red Hill, where she was living with Ann and William's daughter, Elizabeth (Betsy) Parkes, who had been baptised at Christ Church on October 5th 1856. Hannah's other grandchildren, Joseph, now 16 and working as a jeweller, Thomas (13) and Hannah (11), both still at school, were living with their re-united parents, William and Mary Page and a younger sister in the parish of Harborne. Hannah Page senior died, aged 78 in 1877 and was buried at Christ Church on 14th April.

12.10.05   William Fox   Plot 229 (52°27'51"N 1°59'17"W)

The tithe apportionments name William Fox as occupier of this house and garden on a plot, measuring 18 poles and belonging to George Birch, adjacent to the turnpike road on the edge of Redhall Farm. The only William Fox named in the censuses for Ridgacre township in 1841 and 1851 lived at nearby plot 223 but was only seven years old in 1844. Neither is there a William Fox in Warley Wigorn township during the same period.

The route taken by the census enumerator suggests that the occupier of plot 229 in 1841 was labourer, Joseph Workman, born within the county in 1801. Elizabeth Workman, presumably Joseph's wife, also 40 years old, was not born in the county. Enumerated as sole occupier of a single household between those of Joseph Workman and Edward Smart (12.10.06) was Nancy Fox, washerwoman, born in 1791, also outside the county. None of these three residents have been traced in subsequent censuses.

By 1851 the picture has become much clearer. Head of the household now is 36-year old nail-forger Frederick Hadley. Both he and his wife, Mary (25), also a nail-forger, give their birth place as Ridgacre. Completing the household are 7-year-old Mary Ann Downing and 4-year old William Hadley Downing, both of whom, the enumerator records, were born out of wedlock. Ten years earlier, Frederick Hadley, working as a nail-maker, had been lodging, along with nail-maker John Cutler, in the household of nail-maker Mary Richards in the Warley Salop area of Beech Lanes. At the same time Mary Downing had been living with her parents, John and Sarah (12.10.03) in Harborne, where both of her children were born. On September 13th 1847, Mary Downing married Frederick Hadley at St Martin's Church, Birmingham. Both bride and groom gave their address as Edgbaston Street, Birmingham. One of the witnesses was Ann Haycock, perhaps a Ridgacre neighbour? (12.10.02) Though Frederick Hadley was able to sign his name in the marriage register, neither Mary Downing nor Ann Haycock were literate.

The Hadley family was still present in Red Hill in 1861. Frederick had now become an agricultural labourer and Mary had no listed occupation. Their places at the nail hearth had been taken by 17-year-old Mary Ann and 14-year old William Downing. Three younger children Sarah (8), Betsy (6) and Emma (2) Hadley completed the household.

12.10.06   Edward Smart   Plot 228 (52°27'52"N 1°59'15"W)

The house and garden occupied by nail forger Edward Smart, at the angle of Upper Tolly Leasow (plot 224) and the turnpike road, measured 18 poles and belonged to Redhall farmer George Birch. Also resident at plot 228 at the 1841 census were labourer Thomas Haycock (30), his wife Anne (24) both subsequently identified as from Lye, Worcestershire, and their three children, Thomas (5), Mary (3) and Harriet (5 months), all born at Red Hill and baptised at St Peter's Church, Harborne: Thomas on January 24th 1836, Mary on July 22nd 1838 and Harriet on February 14th 1841. In the tithe apportionments, Thomas Haycock is listed as the occupant of plot 223 (12.10.02). Edward Smart died, aged 76, in 1845 and was buried at Christ Church on 21st March.

By 1851, plot 228 no longer housed any nail-forgers, now being the home of 42-year old farm labourer Henry Hunt from Inkberrow, his wife Ann (36) from Hanbury, and their children Jane (15), Mary (12), Henry (9) and Sarah (4) all born within the county. It is quite probable that Mary Hunt was counted twice in this census as 12-year-old Mary Hunt, born in Worcestershire is also listed as "house servant" at Hawthorn Farm just across the turnpike road. In 1841 the Hunt family had been living in Hagley Road, Edgbaston, with Henry's occupation given as "day labourer." By 1861, Henry, Ann and Henry junior were still living within Ridgacre township, but had moved from Red Hill to Quinton. Both Henrys were employed as agricultural labourers. The three elder daughters were no longer at home, but two younger daughters, Elizabeth (8) and Ann (4 months) had been born since the last census.

12.10.07   Joseph Butler

Not shown in 1844 but enumerated immediately after plot 217 and before Redhall Farm, were four households in 1841 and three in 1851. Only one of these, that of Joseph Butler, was a nail-forging household and had the same occupant at both censuses.

With his age given as 50 in 1841, nail-forger Joseph Butler who, like the rest of his family, originated from Hales Owen, is the only member of his household with a stated occupation at that census. His family consisted of wife, Maria (44), sons Edward (19), Joseph (11) and daughters 8-year-old Mariah (Mary Butler had been baptised at the Parish Church of St John the Baptist, Hales Owen on December 2nd 1832), and 2-year-old Sarah. Mary Butler died, aged 13, and was buried at Christ Church on March 29th 1846. By 1851, with his age now given as 66, Joseph Butler is listed as a pensioner of Greenwich Hospital[412], surprisingly the second resident of Ridgacre township to fall into this category. (12.03.08) Still present, Edward is now listed as a file-cutter, Joseph as a gun-finisher, with Sarah still at school. Maria again has no listed occupation. The 1851 household was completed by one of Quinton's migrant population, lodger, 36-year-old wheelwright William Evans.

Maria Butler died aged 60 and was buried at Christ Church The Quinton on March 17th 1857, when her address was given as St John's Ladywood, Birmingham, by which time the family had presumably left Quinton. In 1861, Joseph Butler junior, still a gun-finisher, but now married to 22-year-old Phoebe, was head of his own household at Highfield Terrace, Ladywood. Also present there were his two sons, Edward (2), who had been baptised at Quinton's Primitive Methodist Chapel on September 19th 1858, and Albert (8 months) along with his 76-year-old "Chelsea Pensioner" (which presumably, should have read "Greenwich Pensioner") father, Joseph Butler. Edward (38) still a file-cutter, and Sarah (22) now working as a warehouse woman, were both living in the household of their brother-in-law, carpenter William Spinks at Friston Street, Ladywood. As William's wife, Ann (39) is listed as born in Beech Lanes, it may be assumed that she was the elder sister of Edward and Sarah, who had left her childhood home prior to the 1841 census.

12.11 Beech Lanes

12.11.01   George Greenup

Not shown in 1844 but enumerated in the census of 1851 as the first entry for Beech Lanes, was the household of George Greenup. This consisted of 26-year-old blacksmith's labourer, George, whose birthplace was given as Penley, Flintshire; his nail-forger wife, Ellen (26) and 2-year old son, William, both born in Hales Owen. Completing the household was Erdington-born, 68-year old lodger and mother-in-law, Elizabeth Greenup.[413]   1851 is the only census appearance of the Greenup family in Ridgacre. However, George had presumably been present in the township for a few years prior to this, as on June 26th 1848, giving his address as Ridgacre, he was married by Rev William Skilton to Ellen Read, daughter of Enoch Read (12.05.01) at Christ Church. The witnesses were Prudence Read, the bride's sister and Henry Foley Macdonald (11.03.01).[414] Just over two months later, on September 3rd, George and Ellen's son, William was baptised at Christ Church. On August 29th 1850, Ellen Elizabeth

---

[412] See page 199, footnote 355

[413] In the mid-19th century "mother-in-law" was still used to mean "step-mother," as, for example by Dickens in *Pickwick Papers* chapter 27: "Samuel Weller makes a pilgrimage to Dorking and beholds his mother-in-law." The lady in question is "none other than the quondam relict and sole executrix of the dead-and-gone Mr Clarke," whom Sam's father, Tony Weller, had married.

[414] Henry Foley Macdonald was a frequent witness at weddings at Christ Church The Quinton, an obvious qualification for such a role being the ability to write.

Greenup appears in Christ Church's baptismal register and on September 11th 1850, at the age of just three weeks, in its burial register. Baptisms of two further Greenup children at Christ Church followed: George on October 3rd 1852 and Dinah on August 5th 1855. By the time of Dinah's baptism, the family's address was recorded as Birmingham.

George Greenup was a bird of passage, who sat lightly to such details as his own age and place of birth. The most likely census entry for him in 1841 is of a 19-year-old unmarried warehouseman, born in Lancashire, lodging in Gore Street, Manchester. At the census of 1841, Ellen Read had already left her childhood home to become a servant at Richard Tomlinson's Windmill Farm. (8.01.08) In 1861 George Greenup, giving his age as 32, his birth-place as Harley, Warwick and with a yet another occupation, was living in Cranford Street, Harborne, with Ellen, four children and a widowed sister. In 1871, now working as a striker, and with his age given as 48, George and his family were in Oldbury Road Smethwick. Interestingly, Ellen Greenup's given age remains consistent throughout the censuses.

12.11.02   John Fox   Plot 223 (52°27′52″N 1°59′12″W)

Timothy Hill was the landlord of the plot measuring 1 rood at Beech Lanes part-occupied by nailer John Fox, who also rented a garden – measuring 1 rood – jointly with Esther Cutler (12.11.03) and John Taylor (12.11.04) at plot 222 (52°27′51″N 1°59′12″W), the property of Lord Lyttelton. Aged 72 at the 1841 census, Fox shared his home with his wife, Elizabeth (77), and two younger generations of the Fox family: Henry (27) and 22-year-old Ann Maria (née Robinson); Ann (10), William Henry (4), who was baptised at Hales Owen Parish Church on August 20th 1837 and Anne Elizabeth (1), baptised at Christ Church The Quinton on June 7th 1840. All were born within the county.

By the census of 1851, John, Elizabeth and Henry Fox[415] had all died. Elizabeth Fox was buried in Hales Owen churchyard on February 10th 1842 and John Fox was buried in Quinton churchyard on July 18th 1849. John Fox was another of Quinton's residents to die during the great cholera epidemic. Aged 83 at the time of his death, the certified cause is given in the delightfully vague, but entirely appropriate term, "natural decay."

REGISTRATION DISTRICT					STOURBRIDGE UNION				
1849	DEATH in the Sub-district of Hales Owen					in the	County of Worcester		
Columns:–	1	2	3	4	5	6	7	8	9
No.	When and where died	Name and surname	Sex	Age	Occupation	Cause of death	Signature, description and residence of informant	When registered	Signature of registrar
167	Fifth July 1849 Beech Lane Ridgacre	John Fox	Male	83 Years	Nailor	Natural Decay Certified	+ The Mark of Ann Maria Fox Present at the Death Beech Lane Ridgacre	Twenty fourth July 1849	G G Tiddian Registrar

---

[415] There are two possible registrations for the death of Henry Fox in Birmingham: July 1847 and October 1850.

Ann Maria Fox, informant at the death of her father-in-law, was herself a widow at 31 and head of household at the 1851 census, when she was assisted at the nail forge by her 14-year-old son, William along with Anne Fox, now described as "relative/lodger" with her age given as 19. Elizabeth (11) was returned as a scholar, as were two further children, John (8) and Joseph (4) born since the previous census. Both of these younger children were baptised at Christ Church on June 6th 1847.

On November 26th 1854, Ann Maria Fox was married to 26-year-old bachelor John Birch at Bishop Ryder's Memorial Church, Birmingham.[416] Both gave their address as Princip Street. He was literate, she was not. At the census of 1861, carpenter John Birch (who came from Stoke Edith, Herefordshire) was head of the household in Beech Lanes. Also present were his wife Ann Maria, stepsons William, John and Joseph and stepdaughter Ann Elizabeth. Ann Maria, William and Ann Elizabeth were all working as nail-forgers. John and Joseph were screw wrench filers. By this date James and Ann Maria Birch had two children of their own: James (5) and Emily (12 months). Both children were baptised at Christ Church: James on April 4th 1858 and Emma on July 3rd 1859, which makes her more than 12 months old at the time of the census. Ann Fox has not been positively identified.[417]

Plot 223, photographed around 1930

---

[416] Commemorating Henry Ryder, Bishop of Lichfield, opened in 1838 and demolished in 1960, Bishop Ryder Memorial Church was located in Gosta Green's Gem Street, which disappeared in Birmingham's post-World War II redevelopment.
[417] On October 30th 1854, an Ann Fox, daughter of William Fox, was married to Joseph Yeomans at Christ Church The Quinton. Both gave their address as Warley Wigorn.

12.11.03   Esther Cutler   **Plot 223** (52°27′52″N 1°59′12″W)

The house and garden of Esther Cutler and her family was also located at Plot 223, the property of Timothy Hill. With her neighbours John Fox and John Taylor (12.11.02 and 12.11.04), Esther shared the 1 rood garden plot 222, property of Lord Lyttelton (52°27′51″N 1°59′12″W), immediately behind their cottages. In 1841, 54-year-old widow Esther Cutler whose occupation was given as nail-forger, lived here with her daughters Sarah (20)[418] and Emma (12).

Ten years later, Emma was no longer at her childhood home. On May 5th 1850, Emma Cutler in the registration district of Stourbridge, had married John Pratt at Hales Owen. At the census of 1851 this couple were living with their 7-week-old son in Lower Holt Lane in Cakemore township. Emma's occupation was listed as nail-forger. At plot 223, both Esther and Sarah were working as nail-forgers in 1851. Sarah's age was now given as 39.

A further ten years on, there are no members of this Cutler family enumerated in Ridgacre township. Esther Cutler died in 1860 and was buried at St Peter's Parish Church, Harborne on 30th September. Sarah Cutler has not been traced in the censuses of 1861-1881, but appears again in 1888, when in the register of Christ Church The Quinton is an entry for 30th April, recording the burial of Sarah Cutler, aged 75 of Beech Lanes.

12.11.04   John Taylor   **Plot 223** (52°27′52″N 1°59′12″W)

The third of Timothy Hill's properties on plot 223 was the house and garden occupied in 1844 by John Taylor, who shared with the other two households (12.11.02, 12.11.03) the garden plot 222 (52°27′51″N 1°59′12″W), belonging to Lord Lyttelton. At the census of 1841, nail-forger John Taylor was 66 years old. Also present in this cottage were Mary Taylor (66); Benjamin Hodgetts (37) and five members of the Hadley family: William (54), Sarah (53), William (21), Anne (26) and nail forger Andrew (22), the only other resident with a stated occupation. All of the members the household were listed as born within the county.

By the census of 1851, none of the above were still resident at plot 223. Mary Taylor had died in October 1841 and John Taylor in February 1848. Both were buried at Christ Church. Benjamin Hodgetts, whose occupation was now given as charcoal burner, was head of his own household in Birmingham Street, Hales Owen, where he lived with his nail-forger wife, stepson Henry Harley (8) and lodger, Betsy Hughes (48). Ridgacre nailer William Hadley was now an inmate (sick) of Stourbridge Union Workhouse at Kingswinford, where Sarah Hadley, whose occupation was given as domestic servant, was also an inmate. The younger William Hadley may well be the visitor listed on census night at the Red Hill home of Thomas Haycock. (12.10.02) Labourer and nailer Andrew Hadley, now married to 30-year-old Susannah, was head of a household at Carters Lane in Lapal township, which also included his step-daughter Emma Coley (10) and two lodgers, nail-forgers Joseph (50) and John (36) Coley. Anne Hadley has not been traced.

---

[418] This is presumably an enumerator's adjustment, as subsequent information indicates a birth year of 1812-13.

In 1851, this third cottage at plot 223 was occupied by the household of shoemaker James Male, his wife Mary and their seven children. Mary had no stated occupation; the eldest daughter, Rebecca (23) was the family's sole nail-forger. Sons Joshua (21), Alfred (18) and Joseph (15) were all employed as labourers in an Iron Rivet Manufactory.[419] Still at school were daughters Louisa (13), Mary (10) and Isabella (6), who had been born since the last census and baptised at Christ Church on November 3rd 1844. All nine members of the Male family were listed as originating from Beech Lanes. James Male had married Mary Parsons at the Church of St Peter & St Paul, Aston on June 6th 1825, when both gave their addresses as Aston Row. Rebecca, Joshua (though named as Josiah in the register), Alfred and Joseph Parsons Male had all been baptised at Hales Owen's Parish Church of St John the Baptist: Rebecca on December 9th 1827; Joshua on March 14th 1830; Alfred on December 2nd 1832 and Joseph on September 9th 1835.

At the census of 1841, James and Mary Male and their (then) six children were already living in Ridgacre township, occupying the house and garden on plot 34, measuring 15 poles, the property of John White. James, the only member of the household with a stated occupation, was then described by the much more picturesque title, "cordwainer" and Alfred was listed as Arthur. Mary, just three months old at the time of the census, had been baptised at Quinton on March 19th 1841. Born prior to the consecration of Christ Church, Louisa Male was baptised, like her four older siblings, at Hales Owen Parish Church on July 7th 1838 and was buried there on October 19th 1846.

By 1861 the Male household had changed again. In Beech Lanes, shoe-maker James Male still lived with his wife, Mary, son Joseph, now working as a sand-washer, and 8-year-old grand-daughter, Mary Pitt, who had been born in Dudley and was described as boatman's daughter. On August 16th 1852 at St Bartholomew's Church, Edgbaston, Rebecca Male had married Thomas Pitt. At the census of 1861, Thomas and Rebecca were living with two other children, Elizabeth (4) and Isabella (2) on board a boat moored at Burslem, Staffordshire. Both children, like their father, had been born at Mamble Hole, Staffordshire.[420] Thomas Pitt is described as master and his brother, 19-year-old Henry, also living on board, as mate. Now head of a separate household in Beech Lanes, was Joshua Male. On August 10th 1856, Joshua had married 17-year-old Jane Hall at Christ Church, with his brother, Joseph, as one of the witnesses. Joshua was described as employed in a glass works and Jane as a lacquerer. Their son, Thomas, was baptised at Christ Church on March 1st 1857. He died, aged six, and was buried at Christ Church on September 7th 1862. Of James' and Mary's remaining four children, Isabella died aged seven and was buried at Christ Church on October 26th 1851, but Arthur/Alfred, Louisa and Mary have not been positively identified after 1851.

---

[419] Two local rivet manufactories were listed in trade directories of the mid-1800s: *Thomas Parish, Nail Ironmonger and Factor and Tinman's Rivet Manufacturer* of Dudley Road Hales Owen and *Henry Holloway Manufacturer of Wrought Nails, Rivets, Tenter Hooks, Cable and Trace Chains* of Old Hill.

[420] The location is unclear. The village of Mamble, part of the Wyre Forest coalfield is in Worcestershire. In the 19th century a tramway linked Mamble colliery with Southnet Wharf on the canal at Marlbrook. The 1861 street index of Staffordshire lists three locations called Mamble in Dudley. The enumerator could, of course, have recorded *Mamble* Hole instead of *Bumble* Hole, the canal branch originally part of Dudley N° 2 Canal.

12.12 Worlds End

12.12.01   Josiah Coley   Plot 159 (52°27′18″N 1°59′24″W)

Josiah Coley also held plot 158, *Croft* (52°27′16″N 1°59′25″W), a field of pasture measuring 3 roods 4 poles on the corner of which his house and garden (measuring 36 poles) stood. Both were the property of John Whitehouse. Coley's cottage was located to the south of the lane running between George Birch's Redhall Farm and John Jakeman's Mockbeggar Farm. In 1841, Coley's household consisted of nail-forger brothers Josiah (45) and Thomas (35), along with John (30), who had no stated occupation. Also present was 70-year-old Hannah Coley, presumably their mother. She died five years later and was buried at Christ Church on June 8th 1846. By the census of 1851, only Josiah and Thomas, both still working as nail-forgers, were listed at plot 159. Also working as a nail-forger in 1851, John Coley appears in Carters Lane in Lapal township, as a lodger in the household of Andrew and Susannah (née Coley) Hadley. Ten years on, Josiah and Thomas Coley were still living in Worlds End, where Thomas continued as a nail-forger, but Josiah was by then working as an agricultural labourer.

12.12.02   David Lane   Plot 159 (52°27′18″N 1°59′24″W)

Not present in Ridgacre in 1841 or 1851 was David Lane, listed as the second occupier of John Whitehouse's 36-pole plot 159 in the 1844 tithe apportionments. In 1841, agricultural labourer David Lane, lived with his wife, Mary and three children in Harborne (Town). Ten years later they have moved to Webb's Building, Harborne Heath Road. How long they remained at plot 159 is unclear: the 1851 census lists 16-year-old William Lane as born in Kings Norton; 12-year-old Henry Lane as born in Worlds End; 7-year-old Mary Ann Lane as born in Harborne. If the enumerator's information is correct, then the Lane family must also have lived in Worlds End prior to their residence in Harborne (Town).

The census enumerator's route in 1841 suggests that the occupant of Ridgacre's plot 159 was 40-year-old nail forger John Hadley. The household was completed by John's children: Anne (20), George (15), Enoch (10) and Aaron (5),[421] none of whom have any stated occupation. By 1851, farm labourer Enoch Hadley, with his laundress wife, Jane and month-old daughter, Emma, would seem to have taken up residence in this cottage, with other members of the Hadley family having moved to plot 171. (12.12.03) The death of Enoch Hadley is recorded at Stourbridge in the January -March Quarter, 1852; Jane and Emma Hadley have not been traced beyond the 1851 census.

12.12.03   Void   Plot 171 (52°27′18″N 1°59′24″W)

Listed as void in the 1844 tithe apportionments, plot 171, near the south-east extremity of the map, on Joseph Wakeman's farmland was the property of Hales Owen Guardians of the Poor. This plot, containing a house and garden, measured 1 rood 3 poles. The number of households compared with the number of dwellings in Ridgacre township suggests that this was a temporary void and that the property was occupied at the censuses of both 1841 and 1851.

---

[421] Baptisms of George (December 11th 1825), Enoch (January 11th 1829) and Aaron (November 8th 1834) Hadley, children of John and Mary Hadley are recorded at Hales Owen's Church of St John the Baptist.

Consistency of occupation in neighbouring plots across consecutive censuses and the enumerator's route in 1841, indicate that the occupant of plot 171 at that point was Nathaniel Hadley. His all-male household consisted of nail-forger Nathaniel (40), along with sons Thomas (15), Joseph (13) and Edward (10), all of no stated occupation. No members of this family were still present in Ridgacre by 1851. At this census, Edward Hadley was living with his father, Nathaniel, in Kitwell, Northfield where both worked as nail-forgers. Thomas and Joseph, also still working at the nail-forge, were enumerated as heads of adjacent households in Woodgate, Northfield, where Thomas's household consisted of 25-year old Sarah Andrews, housekeeper, and her children, Eliza (6) and Thomas (2). Next door, Joseph was married to 26-year-old Hester and had two sons: Edward (4) and Joseph (2).

In 1851 the census enumerator's route again gives a clue to the occupant of plot 171, by which time it would seem that John Hadley had moved just across the lane from plot 159. (12.12.02) Still resident with their father were George and Aaron Hadley, both now, like him, working as nail-forgers. On February 8th 1842, at the Parish Church of St Martin, Birmingham, widower John Hadley had married spinster Harriet Andrews of Lapal. Her occupation in the marriage register was given as servant. By 1851 she also was working as a nail-forger, as was her 18-year-old son, John Andrews, born in Northfield, the fifth member of John Hadley's household. John, Harriet and George Hadley were still living in Worlds End in Ridgacre township and still working at the nail trade at the census of 1861. Aaron Hadley, now married to Emma had moved to Bartley Green, Northfield, where they lived with their three children: Emily (7); Lewis (4) and Eliza (2). Both Aaron and Emma worked as nail-makers. No longer employed at the nail trade and living in Little Moor Hill, Smethwick was John Andrews, his wife Mary Ann and their three children, the eldest of whom, Mary Ellen, was born in Worlds End in 1857. Jane (3) had been born in Warley and Kate (1) in Smethwick, suggesting that the Andrews family left Ridgacre township in 1857-58.

12.12.04   Joseph Wakeman   Plot 163 (52°27'12"N 1°59'17"W)

Though Joseph Wakeman is listed as the occupier of this house and garden, on a plot measuring just 37 poles, the property of William King, it seems extremely unlikely that Wakeman ever lived here. Situated adjacent to Old Road which led to William Johnson's Worlds End Farm (8.01.05), plot 163 is otherwise surrounded by fields also rented from William King by Joseph Wakeman. The bulk of Wakeman's farming interest, however, lay within Warley Salop, where he lived and was enumerated in the censuses of 1841 and 1851. (8.01.13) The likelihood, therefore, is that the cottage on plot 163 was sub-let to nail-forger Joseph Coley.

In 1841, the Coley household numbered seven: 45-year-old Joseph, Maria (39), Sarah (19), Jane (15), John (10), Ann (5) and Mary (3). Apart from Joseph, none had any stated occupation and all were born within the county. Still present in 1851, Joseph, Maria, Ann[422] and Mary Coley were all now working as nail-forgers. In 1845, Sarah Coley had married George Robins of Wickhamford, Worcestershire,[423] but was still living at Ridgacre's plot 163, with her children, 4-year-old George and 2-year old Anne Maria. George had been baptised at Christ Church on November 6th 1846, and Anne at Quinton's Bethesda Primitive Methodist Chapel on June 16th 1848. At the census of 1851, their father was working at

---

[422] On November 11th 1857, at Christ Church, Anne Coley of Ridgacre married Robert Lee of Beech Lanes.
[423] July-September Quarter, 1845; Stourbridge Marriage Register 18.528

Rosewarne Mansion, near Camborne in Cornwall.[424] No longer present at plot 163 were siblings Jane and John Coley.[425] On August 8th 1849, at Christ Church, Jane Coley had married Frederick Robins also from Wickhamford,[426] and in 1851 was living in Warley Wigorn. (12.04.14) John Coley, working as a miner and married with a 7-month-old son, was a visitor in the home of Thomas and Eliza Horton in Cross Street, Dudley at the 1851 census.

Ten years on, Joseph and Maria Coley were still working as nail-forgers and enumerated as one household. A second household at plot 163 consisted of nail-forgers Samuel and Mary Partridge and their two children, 2-year-old Anne and 4-month-old John. On June 20th 1858, at St Thomas's Church Dudley, Mary Coley had married Samuel Partridge of Hill township. Anne Partridge was baptised at Christ Church on December 4th 1858 and John on February 24th 1861.[427] George and Sarah Robins have not been traced in the 1861 census. However, four more of their children were baptised at Bethesda Primitive Methodist Chapel: Jane on June 20th 1851, Charles on April 13th 1856, Flora on August 5th 1866 and Ernest on August 29th 1869. In 1871, this branch of the Robins family was living in Spring Street, Oldbury, with George's occupation stated as manager.

12.12.05   Isaac Hill   Plot 174 (52°27'20"N 1°59'27"W)

Nail-forger Isaac Hill occupied this house, shop and garden measuring 1 rood 21 poles, property of Lord Lyttelton. At the census of 1841, the household consisted of just three members: 65-year-old Isaac; his wife Sarah (50) and David Deeley (15).[428] All three were born within the county. No explanation is offered in the census return for the presence of David Deeley at plot 174, However, Sarah Hill's maiden name was Deeley and the neighbouring household at plot 175 was that of George Deeley. It is likely that David Deeley (12.12.04) had moved in from next door to help at his relative's nail forge and relieve the congestion at home. Isaac Hill died aged 69 and was buried at Christ Church on June 8th 1844.

---

[424] Rosewarne Mansion, a building of some antiquity, had 18 occupants at the census of 1851. There were five female house servants, three of whom were native to Cornwall, one from Monmouthshire and one from Herefordshire; a footman and butler, both from Cornwall and housekeeper from Devonshire. The head of household was William Price Lewis, described as "chaplain at Rosewarne and committee to Mrs & WHH Hartley Esq." [NB "committee," now obsolete, is defined in OED as "a person to whom the charge of a lunatic or idiot is committed."] Lewis was born in Warwickshire, but his wife and youngest child were born in Camborne; two older children were born in Monmouthshire. Next listed are landed proprietors, 61-year-old widow Mary Hartley, also born in Camborne, and 27-year-old bachelor WHH Hartley, born in Bath: both are described as "lunatic, ward of Chancery." Also present were Henrietta Durban, born in the West Indies, companion to Mrs Hartley and Elizabeth Crawley from Cambridgeshire, attendant to Mrs Hartley. Last listed is George Robins, whose occupation is also given as attendant, which would seem to imply that he had some responsibility for the welfare, and perhaps safety, of WHH Hartley.

[425] On April 3rd 1853, at Christ Church, John Coley of Ridgacre married Ann Clark of Hill.

[426] The village of Wickhamford lies midway between Evesham and Broadway. Its population in 2011 was 735. George Robins was born in 1821 and Frederick in 1824; it may, therefore, be assumed that they were brothers.

[427] A further child, Joseph, was baptised at Christ Church on 30.10.1864, with three more children baptised at Bethesda Chapel: William (29.12.1869), Ann (16.04. 1871), Mary (28.11.1881), making this the second branch of the Coley family to transfer their allegiance from the Church of England to Primitive Methodism.

[428] David Deeley was baptised at Hales Owen's Parish Church of St John the Baptist on 05.09.1824.

By the census of 1851, only Sarah Hill remained at plot 174. Her birth-place was given as Hales Owen, and her occupation as spike maker, the physically demanding production of large and heavy nails. On December 8th 1852, at Christ Church The Quinton, widow Sarah Hill was married to widower John Jakeman. (8.01.09). By 1861, John and Sarah Jakeman were enumerated as heads of two separate Worlds End households (schedules 49 and 46 respectively): John still listed as a farmer, then living with his 13-year-old granddaughter, Emma Greaves; Sarah, living alone and of no stated occupation. John Jakeman died in November 1869 and Sarah the following month. Both were buried at Christ Church: John on November 12th and Sarah on December 30th.

12.12.06   George Deeley   Plot 175 (52°22'22"N 1°59'32"W)

North of the lane at the southern perimeter of George Birch's Redhall Farm, on a plot of land measuring 1 rood 34 poles belonging to Lord Lyttelton, was the house and garden of nail-forger George Deeley. Some ten years older than his wife, Elizabeth, Deeley was a native of Hales Owen, as were Elizabeth and their five children: Leah (15), Thomas (12), Sarah (10), Ann (7) and Phoebe (6). All of George and Elizabeth Deeley's children were baptised at Hales Owen's Parish Church of St John the Baptist: Leah on April 23rd 1826; Thomas on March 1st 1829; Sarah on June 5th 1831; Ann on January 19th 1834; Phoebe on April 26th 1835. Within ten years of the 1841 census, three members of the Deeley family were dead. Elizabeth died, aged 38, in December 1845, Thomas died, aged 19, in January 1849 and George died, aged 52, in June 1850. All three were buried at Christ Church The Quinton.

By 1851 the Deeley household at plot 175 had reduced to three. David Deeley had moved back from next door and was now working as a crank-iron-forger; Leah Deeley, listed as a spike-forger was still resident, with her 1-year-old daughter, Phebe Ellen Hicks Deeley. On October 13th 1852, Phoebe, daughter of Charles and Leah Hicks was baptised at Christ Church by officiating minister, Rev Charles Richard Hyde. On July 20th 1853, this entry in the register was amended by Rev William Skilton, to read "Parent's name: Leah Deeley; Trade: Nailer." Just over a year later, at Christ Church on October 16th 1853, Skilton officiated at the marriage of nailer Leah Deeley to labourer John Elliman from Yardley. The witnesses were Phoebe and David Deeley. All the members of the Deeley family were literate: Elliman was not. Leah Elliman died, aged 33 and was buried at Christ Church on June 19th 1859. At the census of 1861, John Elliman was living alone in Worlds End, Warley Wigorn.

Frontispiece to
The Mysteries of the Wrought Nail Trade Revealed
by Levett Nokes

On Christmas Day 1850, at St Philip's Church Birmingham, 19-year-old Sarah Deeley married 20-year-old William Edmunds. Both gave their address as Bishopgate Street, Birmingham. She was able to write her name; he was not. At the 1851 census, they were living in Ridgacre township at plot 112 (12.06.01), along with their daughter, Fanny, who had been baptised at Christ Church on February 2nd. During the following decade three more of William and Sarah's children were baptised at Christ Church: on April 2nd 1854, Elizabeth, who died aged four and was buried at Christ Church on March 12th 1858; Mary Ann, on January 4th 1857; and on October 2nd 1859, a fourth daughter, also named Elizabeth.

At the census of 1851, Ann Deeley was working as a servant in the home of jeweller, Ebenezer Timmins, in Coleshill Street, Birmingham, whilst Phoebe Deeley was similarly employed at the home of wine merchant Joseph Osborne at Camomile Cottage, Harborne. On November 21st 1858, at St Bartholomew's Church Edgbaston, Ann Deeley married agricultural labourer Richard Lewis of Northfield. She was literate, he was not. In 1861, they were living in Mass House Lane, Edgbaston. Also present in their household was Phoebe Deeley, along with her 2-year-old son, Thomas, who had been baptised at Christ Church on June 5th 1859. Phoebe was described in the register as "single woman."

12.12.07   John Westwood

Not shown in 1844 but enumerated in the census of 1851 immediately after David Deeley was the household of 37-year-old John Westwood, whose occupation was given as labourer in woodcutting. Also present were Westwood's nail-forger wife, Ann (30) and their three children: Aaron (8); Clara (7) and Campbell (5). The three children were all listed as scholars and, like their father, were all born in Harborne. Ann Westwood's place of birth is given as Warley. In 1841, John Westwood, then working as an agricultural labourer, had been lodging in Harborne Lane, possibly next door to the home of his parents and four siblings. All three of John and Ann's children were baptised at St Peter's Church, Harborne. Aaron (who, according to the register, had been previously baptised) on June 5th 1842; Clara on February 4th 1844 and Campbell on December 7th 1845. Presumably, the family moved to Worlds End sometime after this last date. In 1861, all five members of the Westwood family were still living in Ridgacre township, with their address shown as Redhall Lane. Campbell's occupation was then given as iron bedstead maker, whilst John, Ann, Aaron and Clara were all working as nail-makers.

12.13 Lower Dwellings

12.13.01   Thomas White   Plot W76 (52°27'19"N 2°00'27"W)

Though Thomas White is listed as the occupier of this 33-poles plot, with dwelling house and other buildings, the property of Aaron White, it is much more likely that Thomas resided at the farm house on plot W91, which abutted the foldyard of his Lower Quinton Farm at plot 27 in Ridgacre township. It would seem from the census enumerator's routes, that plot W76 was home to two sub-let households: first, that of Joseph Greaves in both 1841 and 1851 and second, of Isaac Partridge in 1841, replaced by Richard Fisher in 1851.

In 1841, the household of agricultural labourer Joseph Greaves consisted of himself, his wife Sarah (of no stated occupation) and 2-year-old son Owen. Sarah was listed as born within the county and Joseph and Owen from beyond its boundaries. The register of St Peter's Church, Harborne records the baptism of Owen Greaves on March 3rd 1839, following in the footsteps of his father, Joseph, whose parents Isaac and Sarah Greaves had presented him there for baptism on January 1st 1814. St Peter's had also been the venue for the marriage of Owen's parents, Joseph Greaves and Sarah Jakeman on November 15th 1836.

The census of 1851 expands earlier information. Joseph and Owen were both born in Harborne, Staffordshire and Sarah in Cofton, Worcestershire. Joseph was still working as agricultural labourer; Sarah and Owen were listed as nail-makers, as was 9-year-old James, who had been baptised at Christ Church The Quinton on March 6th 1842. Two further children now completed the household: 6-year-old Joseph and 3-year-old Emma. Both of the younger children were baptised at Christ Church: Joseph on December 1st 1844 and Emma on October 3rd 1847. Shortly after this census was taken, a further daughter, Jane, was born and baptised at Christ Church on September 7th 1851.

By 1861, the Greaves family, still largely intact, was enumerated at Muttons in Ridgacre township. Now only Sarah was employed at the nail forge. Owen and James had joined their father as agricultural labourers. Jane was still at school, as was 6-year-old Mary Greaves, who had been baptised at Christ Church on July 1st 1855. The younger Joseph had died in 1860 and was buried at Christ Church on November 13th. In 1861 Emma Greaves was living with her grandfather John Jakeman (8.01.09) in Worlds End in Ridgacre township, where she was listed as a servant. The unreliability of censuses in recording ages is illustrated by members of the Greaves family:

Name	Most likely birth year[429]	Census 1841	Census 1851	Census 1861
Joseph Greaves	1814	25	37	46
Sarah Greaves	1818	20	33	44
Owen Greaves	1839	2	13	22
James Greaves	1842	-	9	21

12.13.02   Thomas White   Plot W76 (52°27'19"N 2°00'27"W)

See introductory paragraph to 12.13.01.

The second household on this 33-poles plot, with dwelling house and other buildings, the property of Aaron White, appears in 1841 to be that of Isaac Partridge. Then listed as an agricultural labourer, 25-year-old Isaac lived with his wife, Ann (also 25), son John (5) and twin daughters Mary and Emma (3 months). The household was completed by 15-year-old Elizabeth Rose, listed as F.S.[430] Elizabeth, Isaac and John were all described as born within the county, whilst Ann was not. However, the next census identifies all the Partridge family as from Northfield, Worcestershire. This is corroborated by the record of John's baptism at Northfield Parish Church on July 19th 1835. Isaac Partridge seems regularly to have changed his occupation. In 1835, at his son's baptism, he is listed as labourer. At the 1841 census this is refined to agricultural labourer, most likely one and the same thing, as suggested in Christ Church The Quinton's register where, at the baptism of Mary (Marianne) and Emma Partridge on March 9th 1841, their father, Isaac, is again entered as labourer. On June 25th 1843, when Isaac and Ann's son, Charles, was baptised at Christ Church, Isaac was listed as nailer, but on July 2nd 1845, at the baptism of a further son, Isaac, his father was again described as labourer. At the census of 1851, by which time

---

[429] Taken from Civil Registration Birth Index 1837-1915 and Baptismal Registers of St Peter's Church, Harborne and Christ Church The Quinton.

[430] Some authorised abbreviations for occupations were used in early censuses, most commonly in 1841. F.S. indicated Female Servant. The practice gradually declined and by 1871 the only abbreviation mentioned was Ag. Lab. meaning Agricultural Labourer.

the Partridge family had returned to Northfield, Isaac once again was employed as a nail-maker, as were his wife, Ann and son, John. Charles Partridge died, aged 14 months and was buried at Christ Church on August 9th 1844 and Isaac junior also died in early childhood and was buried at Northfield Parish Church on May 5th 1847. From the above dates it is possible to narrow the period at which Isaac Partridge and his family lived at Lower Dwellings in Warley Wigorn. They arrived between July 1835, when John was baptised at Northfield, and March 1841 when Marianne and Emma were baptised at Quinton, just ahead of the census. They left between July 1845, when Isaac was baptised at Quinton, and May 1847, when he was buried at Northfield.

Northfield was also the place from which the later occupants of this second household on plot W76 had moved. In 1841, 25-year-old agricultural labourer Richard Fisher (born in Shipston-on-Stour, Warwickshire) had been living with his wife, Ann (also 25, but born in Northfield) and son Eli (1) at Merritts Brook, Northfield. Eli's baptism is recorded at Northfield Parish Church on May 3rd 1840. A second son, Stephen, was baptised at Quinton's Bethesda Primitive Methodist Chapel on November 25th 1849, by which time the family had evidently moved to Warley Wigorn, where the 1851 census shows Richard working as a nail-maker. His household was completed by Ann and a lodger – 30-year-old farm labourer James Harris from Gloucester. Stephen Fisher had died aged 18 months and was buried at Christ Church The Quinton on January 26th 1851. Eli had left the family home and was apprenticed to John Eden, shoe-maker of High Street, Hales Owen.

At the census of 1861, Richard, whose occupation had reverted to agricultural labourer, and Ann, now working as a nail-maker, were living in Spies Lane in Hill township. Two daughters had been born since the last census: Betsy, who had been baptised at Bethesda Primitive Methodist Chapel on June 1st 1851 and Harriet, who had been baptised at Christ Church on May 21st 1855. Both are listed as born in Ridgacre. It is interesting to note the family's association with Primitive Methodism around the time that Richard is known to have been working as a nail-maker, along with Harriet's Anglican baptism when her father had returned to the land. Evidently, religious affiliation could be as fluid as occupation.

Gender of Quinton Nail-makers 1841-1861

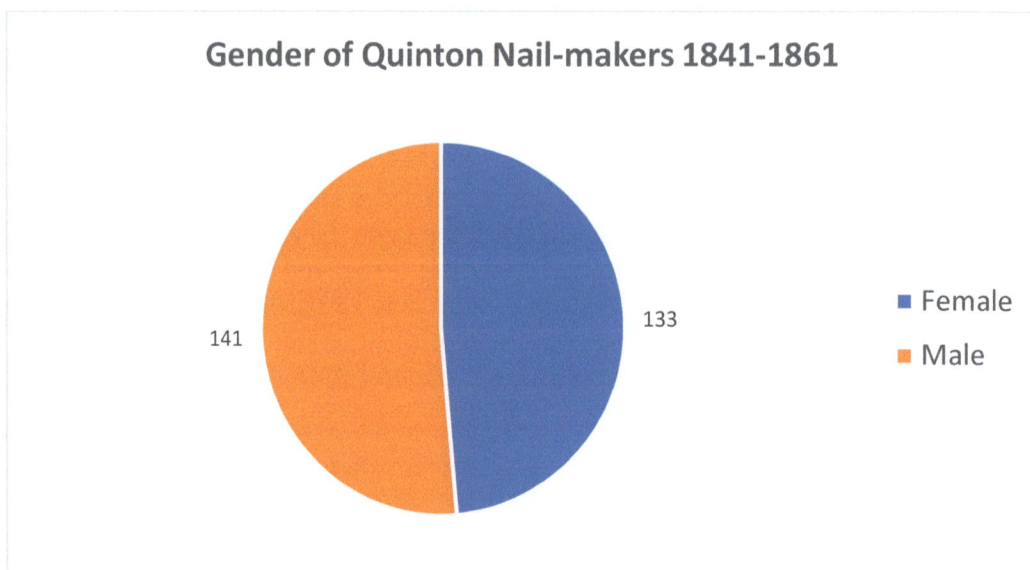

141   133

■ Female
■ Male

13   Appendices

13.01   Dudley Division Register of Electors 1836: Quinton

An Act to amend the representation of the people of England and Wales (2+3 William IV c45), better known as the Great Reform Bill 1832, brought the country to the brink of revolution. After its tumultuous passage through parliament, ministerial resignations and the intervention of the king, 56 boroughs, many with very few voters, were disenfranchised, 31 reduced to a single MP and 67 new constituencies, including Dudley with one MP, created. The electorate was increased from 400,000 to 650,000 men, of whom just 25 were Quinton voters. Multiple property owners were entitled to vote both in the constituency where they lived and in those where they owned property.[431] Thus only 60% of Quinton's voters lived within the village and John Monckton, resident in Northamptonshire, had two votes in Quinton – one in Ridgacre township and one in Warley Wigorn! For the first time, an efficient system of voter registration was introduced, administered by the overseers of the poor in every parish and township. The franchise was limited in boroughs to householders rated at £10 or more per annum and in the counties to £10 copyholders and £50 leaseholders.

The desire for reform had not initially found favour in Dudley. In December 1820 the mayor summoned a public meeting to the town hall to pass a resolution addressed to the king, concluding "We fervently pray that your majesty's reign may be long and prosperous – undisturbed by domestic factions; and that the blessings of our happy constitution – guarded from the machinations of the disaffected and the bad, by an indissoluble union of the loyal and the good – may descend, unimpaired, to our latest posterity."[432] Somewhat surprisingly therefore, when Dudley's newly enfranchised electorate went to the polls for the first time in 1832, the Liberal candidate, John Campbell, defeated his Conservative opponent by 318 votes to 229. When Campbell was appointed Attorney General in 1834, the resulting Dudley bye-election returned Conservative Thomas Hawkes, who held the seat for ten years. On his resignation in 1844, John Benbow was elected, continuing the Conservative representation until the by-election caused by his death in 1855 brought in Sir Stafford Northcote, Liberal Conservative. Northcote did not contest the seat at the general election of 1857, when an Independent MP, Henry Brinsley Sheridan, was returned. Sheridan, who stood as a Liberal after 1865, held the seat until 1886.

Voter	Place of Abode	Nature of Qualification	Property & Tenant
In Ridgacre township			
Birch, George	Reddall	Freehold land & buildings	Reddall, George Birch
Bissell, James	Webbs Green	Freehold Land	Quinton, James Cooper
Cooper, James	Perry Hill	Occupier of farm & buildings at £50 a year	Perry Hill, James Cooper
Cutler, James	Quinton	Freehold house	Quinton, James Cutler
Foley, Ambrose	Quinton	Freehold land	Quinton, Ambrose Foley
Foley, John	Quinton	Freehold land & buildings	Quinton, John Foley

---

[431] This plurality was not abolished until the Representation of the People Act, 1948.

[432] Cited by Chandler, G & Hannah, I (1949) *Dudley As it as and as it is Today*, p 109

Goode, Amos	Ridgacre	Rental of buildings & land upwards of £50 per annum	Ridgacre, Amos Goode
Grosvenor, John	The Firs	Freehold house	New Road, Crook-street, William Taylor
Hall, James	Quinton	Freehold house	Quinton
Jakeman, John	Worlds End Farm	Rental of land exceeding £50 a year	Worlds End, Ridgacre, John Jakeman
Macdonald, Henry Foley	Quinton	Freehold house & land	Quinton Henry Foley Macdonald
Millward, Robert	Beech-lane	Freehold house	Quinton, Joseph Sadler
Monckton, John	Fine Shade Abbey, Northamptonshire	Freehold land	Brant Hall, Henry Ward
Nicholls, Henry	The Hawthorn	Occupier of house & land above £50 a year	The Hawthorn, Henry Nicholls
Nicholls, Thomas	The Hawthorn	Occupier of house & land above £50 a year	The Hawthorn, Thomas Nicholls
Podmore, Thomas	Ridgacre	Occupier of house & farm exceeding £50 a year	Ridgacre, Thomas Podmore
Smith, Thomas	Quinton	Freehold house	Quinton, Thomas Smith
Tomlinson, Richard	Windmill Farm	Occupier of house & land at £50 a year	Ridgacre, Richard Tomlinson
White, George	Quinton	Occupier of house & farm above £50 a year	The Quinton, George White

In Warley Wigorn township

Davenport, John	Four Dwellings	Tenant & occupier of several messuages, farms & lands, freehold & copyhold, of the annual value & rent of £200 and upwards	At Warley Wigorn & Warley Salop, counties of Worcester & Salop, held by William Spurrier, John Davenport
Monckton, John	Fine Shade, Northamptonshire	Freehold land & buildings	Brant Hall, Warley Wigorn, Henry Ward
Spurrier, William	New-street, Birmingham	As owner of three messuages, farms & lands, with their appurtenances; part freehold & part copyhold	At Warley Wigorn & Warley Salop, parish of Hales Owen in the counties of Worcester & Salop, John Davenport
White, Edward	Romsley Hill	Freehold land	Four Dwellings, Warley Wigorn, George White
White, George	Frankley	Freehold property	Warley Wigorn, Sarah Gould
White, John	Aldridge	Freehold land	Hagg Farm, George White
Woodhouse, Benjamin	Hagg Farm	Rental of land	Warley Wigorn, Benjamin Woodhouse

13.02   Inquest: Amy Read

Amy, daughter of Enoch and Diana Reed (sic) was baptised at Hales Owen Parish Church of St John the Baptist on February 28th 1830. Her father's occupation was given as nailer and the family's residence as Quinton. Eleven years later, at the 1841 census Enoch and Diana Read, along with their five children, were enumerated at plot 90 in Ridgacre township. (12.05.01) However, their fourth child, an 11-year-old daughter, was wrongly listed as Anne. Tragedy struck the family on October 21st of the same year, when Amy was fatally injured when her clothes caught fire. Sadly, this was not uncommon in 19th century nail-making households, where children were exposed in confined spaces to the open forge. Though not the daughter of a nail-maker, five-year old Lavinia Macdonald would suffer a similar fate in November 1842. (11.03.01)

An inquest was held before the coroner, Hales Owen-born George Hinchliffe[433] (whose name would appear as informant on Amy's death certificate) with 12 local jurors. The court heard that Amy had survived for what must have been an agonising seven days and died on October 28th. A verdict of accidental death was returned. Three days later, on October 31st 1841, with Rev William Skilton officiating, Amy Read was buried at Christ Church The Quinton. Thus, entries in baptismal and burial registers, an incorrect census record, a death certificate and transcript of the coroner's inquest are the sole records of the life of this little girl, whose tragic death was of insufficient significance even to warrant a press report.

Sadly, Amy's death was not the end of tragedy for the Read family. Within six weeks – just two entries later in the Christ Church Register of Deaths, her father, Enoch, had also died at the age of 48. The cause of his death, suggesting that he was already ill at the time of Amy's accident, was given as dropsy. This is an archaic name for œdema, the abnormal accumulation of fluid beneath the skin, which causes severe pain and may lead to organ failure and cardiac arrest. Indeed, in the 19th century dropsy as a cause of death sometimes meant heart failure. Dropsy had a whole catalogue of possible causes, including insect bites, dermatitis and the chronic pulmonary disease to which nail-makers were vulnerable. It was also a term heard in the liturgy of the church, when, once during morning prayer in April and once during evening prayer in October, the gospel reading came from Luke 14, in which worshippers would have heard, "And behold, there was a certain man before him which had the dropsy... And he took him and healed him and let him go."[434] This was not to be the outcome of Enoch Read's illness, nor that of his 8-year-old son, Joseph, who also died of dropsy in February 1842. Like Amy, father and son were both buried at Christ Church, with Rev William Skilton officiating.

Diana Read, who had been the informant at of the deaths of both her husband and son remarried in 1847 and continued to live with her new husband, Charles Taylor, and her surviving daughter, Prudence, at Ridgacre's plot 90.

---

[433] George Hinchliffe (born c1794) lived in Paradise Street, West Bromwich. The census of 1841 describes him as solicitor and that of 1851 as solicitor and county coroner.
[434] Luke 14 vv 2,4 (King James Version)

Shropshire
To Wit

AN INQUISITION indented, taken for our SOVEREIGN LADY the QUEEN, at the Parish of *Hales Owen* in the County of Salop, on *Friday* the *twenty ninth* Day of *October* in the *fifth* Year of the Reign of our SOVEREIGN LADY VICTORIA, by the Grace of God, of the United Kingdom of Great Britain and Ireland, QUEEN Defender of the Faith, &c, before GEORGE HINCHCLIFFE, Esquire one of the Coroners of our said LADY the QUEEN, for her said County of Salop, upon View of the Body of *Amy Read*

then and there lying dead, upon the Oaths of *George Birch* *Henry Nicholls, Richard Tomlinson, James Wragg, John Birch Joseph Wakeman, Richard Branton, John Foley, Richard Underhill Henry Foley Macdonald, James Milner and Thomas Smith* good and lawful Men of the said County, duly summoned, and who being then and there sworn and charged to enquire for our said LADY the QUEEN, when and by what Means the said *Amy Read* came to her Death, do upon their Oaths say that the said *Amy Read an Infant of the age of eleven years on the twenty first day of October in the year aforesaid at the Parish aforesaid in the County aforesaid being near a certain Grate containing Fire it happened that the Clothes which the said Amy Read then and there had on her Body accidentally, casually and by misfortune caught, fire by means whereof and from the flame arising there Burnt of which said Burning the said Amy Read from the said twenty first day of October in the year aforesaid until the twenty eighth day of October in the same year did languish and languishing did live on which said twenty eighth day of October in the year aforesaid she the said Amy Read of the Burning aforesaid at the Parish and aforesaid in the County aforesaid did die.*

AND so the Jurors aforesaid, upon their Oaths aforesaid, do say that the said *Amy Read* in the Manner, and by the Means aforesaid, *accidentally casually and by misfortune* came to her death and not otherwise.

In Witness whereof, as well as the said CORONER, as the said JURORS, have hereunto subscribed and set their Hands and Seals, on the Day and Year, and at the Place first above mentioned.

George Birch	*John Birch*	*Richard Underhill*
Henry Nicholls	*Joseph Wakeman*	*Henry Foley Macdonald*
Richard Tomlinson	*Richard Branton*	*James Milner*
James Wragg	*John Foley*	*Thomas Smith*

Amy Read – died of burns October 28th 1841; buried October 31st 1841; Christ Church Reg 16

No.	When and where died	Name and surname	Sex	Age	Occupation	Cause of death	Signature, description and residence of informant	When registered	Signature of registrar
215	Twenty eighth of October 1841 Quinton Ridgacre	Amy Read	Female	11 Years	Infant	Burnt	Geo Hinchliffe Coroner	First of November 1841	J.D. Haslewood Registrar

REGISTRATION DISTRICT STOURBRIDGE UNION
1841 DEATH in the Sub-district of Halesowen in the Counties of Worcester and Salop

Enoch Read – died of dropsy December 5th 1841; buried December 9th 1841; Christ Church Reg 18

REGISTRATION DISTRICT STOURBRIDGE UNION
1841 DEATH in the Sub-district of Halesowen in the Counties of Worcester and Salop

No.	When and where died	Name and surname	Sex	Age	Occupation	Cause of death	Signature, description and residence of informant	When registered	Signature of registrar
283	Fifth of December 1841 Ridgacre	Enoch Read	Male	48 Years	Nailor	Dropsy	The mark X of Dianna Read Wife Ridgacre Present at the death Occupier Deceased	Twelfth of December 1841	J.D. Haslewood Registrar

13.03

Joseph Read – died of dropsy February 11th 1842; buried February 14th 1842; Christ Church Reg 22

REGISTRATION DISTRICT STOURBRIDGE UNION
1842 DEATH in the Sub-district of Halesowen in the Counties of Worcester and Salop

No.	When and where died	Name and surname	Sex	Age	Occupation	Cause of death	Signature, description and residence of informant	When registered	Signature of registrar
282	Eleventh of February 1842 Ridgacre	Joseph Read	Male	8 Years	Son of the late Enoch Read Nailor	Dropsy	The mark X of Dianna Read mother Ridgacre Occupier	Twenty fourth of March 1842	G.D. Haslewood Registrar

13.03   Other Residents

Compiled from Hales Owen and Quinton parish baptism, marriage and burial registers, Quinton Primitive Methodist baptism register[435] the following list is of Quinton residents not otherwise identified. Warley Wigorn residents having obvious links with other townships have not been included. No evidence has been found to suggest that those remaining did not live in Quinton.

Key:

bap = baptised   bur = buried   d of = daughter of   m = married   s of = son of
BPMCBapR = Bethesda Primitive Methodist Baptism Register
HOBapR = Hales Owen Parish Church Baptism Register   HOBurR = Hales Owen Parish Church Burial Register
HOMR = Hales Owen Parish Church Marriage Register   QCCBapR =Christ Church The Quinton Baptism Register
QCCBurR = Christ Church The Quinton Burial Register   QCCMR = Christ Church The Quinton Marriage Register

Name	Status	Date	Abode	Source
Alcock, Ann	m William Hill	29.12.1850	Warley Wigorn	QCCMR
Allen, Ann	m Richard Bennett	15.10.1843	Ridgacre	QCCMR
Allen, Elizabeth	bur 23yrs	16.10.1842	Warley Wigorn	QCCBurR
Allen, Emma	m William Foley	24.05.1847	Ridgacre	QCCMR
Allen, Henry James	bur 2yrs 6mths	29.01.1843	Warley Wigorn	QCCBurR
Allen, William	m Betsy Dicken	18.08.1850	Warley Wigorn	QCCMR
Andrews, Ann	bur 9mths	26.08.1856	Quinton	QCCBurR
Armstrong, Margaret	m Benjamin Cutler	08.11.1847	Warley Wigorn	QCCMR
Ashton, Annie	m George Alexander Rogers	03.11.1860	Beech Lanes	QCCMR
Baker, Richard	bap s of Richard & Mary	13.06.1855	Ridgacre	HOBapR
Barnes, Hannah	bur 40yrs	26.10.1851	Warley Wigorn	QCCBurR
Barnes, Henry	bur 9wks	18.09.1851	Warley Wigorn	QCCBurR
Barratt, Samuel	bur 86yrs	03.02.1857	Ridgacre	HOBurR
Bartlett, Henry	m Ann Haines	28.11.1843	Warley Wigorn	QCCMR
Bartlett, Sarah	m Edward Bowden	14.07.1845	Warley Wigorn	QCCMR
Bayley, Ursula	m William Lightwood	02.01.1853	Warley Wigorn	QCCMR
Bennett, Richard	m Ann Allen	15.10.1843	Ridgacre	QCCMR
Billingham, Sarah	m Joseph Thomas	16.11.1846	The Quinton	QCCMR
Bowden, Edward	m Sarah Bartlett	14.07.1845	Warley Wigorn	QCCMR
Bridgewater, Thomas	bur 74yrs	11.12.1859	Ridgacre	QCCBurR
Burton, Ann	m Joseph Burton	01.12.1845	Warley Wigorn	QCCMR
Burton, Edward	bur 85yrs	01.10.1843	Beech Lanes	HOBurR
Burton, John	m Sarah Whale	04.09.1848	Warley Wigorn	QCCMR
Burton, Joseph	m Ann Burton	01.12.1845	Warley Wigorn	QCCMR
Burton, Martha	bur 4mths	02.06.1844	Ridgacre	QCCBurR
Burton, Mary	bur 82yrs	02.10.1842	Beech Lanes	HOBurR
Cater, Martha	m John Dearn	07.07.1856	Ridgacre	QCCMR
Casterton, George	bap s of Henry & Mary	05.09.1841	Ridgacre	QCCBapR
Casterton, Joseph	bur 1yr 10mths	18.03.1842	Warley Wigorn	QCCBurR
Chambers, Ann	m Solomon Davis (Stourbridge)	20.04.1845	Warley Wigorn	QCCMR

---

[435] There are no extant registers for Quinton Wesleyan Methodist Chapel prior to 1872

Chatwin, James	bur 9mths	28.05.1848	Warley Wigorn	QCCBurR
Clark, Jane	bur 7mths	29.01.1854	Warley Wigorn	QCCBurR
Clay, Elizabeth	bur 4yrs 6mths	07.05.1861	Ridgacre	QCCBurR
Clay, William	bur infant	08.10.1856	Ridgacre	QCCBurR
Coley, Anne	bap d of John & Anne	??.??.1858	Ridgacre	BPMCBapR
Coley, Joseph	bap s of John & Ann	05.08.1855	Ridgacre	QCCBapR
Coley, Joseph	bur 3yrs	23.11.1858	Ridgacre	QCCBurR
Coley, Sarah Jane	bap d of John & Ann	06.08.1860	Quinton	BPMCBapR
Coley, Thomas	bap s of Elizabeth	13.07.1842	Quinton	HOBapR
Coley, Thomas	bur 14yrs	15.05.1853	Ridgacre	QCCBurR
Cooksey, William	bur 52yrs	10.07.1841	Ridgacre	QCCBurR
Cooper, Joseph Henry	bap s of Joseph & Anne	06.09.1857	Beech Lanes	QCCBapR
Cooper, Mary	m Benjamin Lowe (London)	18.03.1856	Ridgacre	QCCMR
Cooper, Sarah	m Henry Walker (Kingswinford)	18.03.1856	Ridgacre	QCCMR
Corbet, Mary	m Joseph Hulston (Hasbury)	18.05.1843	Warley Wigorn	QCCMR
Cove, Joseph	m Sarah Leighton	27.01.1853	Warley Wigorn	QCCMR
Cox, Isaac Lea	m Elizabeth Humphries	05.11.1848	Ridgacre	QCCMR
Cutler, Benjamin	m Margaret Armstrong	08.11.1847	WW	QCCMR
Cutler, Emily	bur 2yrs	14.02.1858	Red Hill	QCCBurR
Cutler, Joseph	bap s of Hannah	29.01.1843	Beech Lanes	HOBapR
Cutler, Joseph	bur 18mths	29.05.1844	Ridgacre	QCCBurR
Cutler, Mary	bap d of Samuel & Harriet	17.10.1841	Quinton	HOBapR
Davies, Andrew	m Mary Ann Northall	??.08.1846	Warley Wigorn	QCCMR
Dearn, John	m Martha Cater	07.07.1856	Ridgacre	QCCMR
Deeley, Alfred	bur 2dys	04.09.1860	Quinton	QCCBurR
Deeley, Emma	bur 11mths	10.04.1856	Ridgacre	HOBurR
Dicken, Betsy	m William Allen	18.08.1850	Warley Wigorn	QCCMR
Dingley, Mariah	m William Bates (London)	28.12.1859	The Quinton	QCCMR
Edmunds, William Joseph	bur 9mths	22.09.1856	Warley Wigorn	QCCBurR
Ellis, William	bap s of William & Caroline	04.08.1850	Ridgacre	QCCBapR
Evans, Anne	bap d of John & Sarah	16.11.1845	Crock Street	BPMCBapR
Evans, Jane	bap d of John & Sarah	04.04.1847	Crock Street	BPMCBapR
Evans, Phoebe	bap d of John & Sarah	10.06.1849	Crock Street	BPMCBapR
Evans, Sarah	bap d of John & Sarah	12.09.1841	Quinton	HOBapR
Evans, William	bap s of John & Sarah	24.05.1840	Quinton	HOBapR
Evans, William	m Martha Scott	14.10.1859	Ridgacre	QCCMR
Fellows, Kate	bap d of William & Prudence	04.07.1858	Quinton	QCCBapR
Fenton, Joseph	m Hannah Pickerill	07.12.1856	Warley Wigorn	QCCMR
Fingley, Benjamin	bur 7yrs	09.09.1847	Warley Wigorn	QCCBurR
Fleet, Thomas	m Ann Maria Hughes	10.10.1847	Ridgacre	QCCMR
Foley, Mary	m Joseph Harris (Causey Green)	20.03.1856	Warley Wigorn	QCCMR
Foley, William	m Emma Allen	24.05.1847	Ridgacre	QCCMR
Foley, William Henry	bur 39yrs	13.12.1850	Ridgacre	QCCBurR
Fox, Ann	bur 75yrs	16.09.1850	Ridgacre	QCCBurR
Fox, Charles	bur 2yrs 5mths	03.01.1841	Ridgacre	QCCBurR
Fox, Lavinia	bur 1yr 8mths	10.02.1848	Ridgacre	QCCBurR

Fox, William	bur 6mths	03.01.1841	Ridgacre	QCCBurR
Fulot, William	bur 4mths	04.04.1861	Quinton	QCCBurR
Garner, Charles	m Elizabeth Rutledge	24.05.1847	Ridgacre	QCCMR
Gill, Joseph	m Jetty Saunders (Germany)	25.12.1842	Warley Wigorn	QCCMR
Goode, Caroline	bur 13mths	17.05.1856	Quinton	QCCBurR
Goode, Jane	bur 1yr 5mths	10.03.1848	Ridgacre	QCCBurR
Goode, Joseph	bap s of Lucy	31.05.1840	Quinton	HOBapR
Goode, Sarah	bap d of Amos & Eliza	02.01.1859	Ridgacre	QCCBapR
Goode, Thomas	bur 5wks	10.06.1852	Ridgacre	QCCBurR
Gould, William	m Sarah Mason	21.08.1853	Ridgacre	QCCMR
Grainger, Harriet	m William Taylor	27.12.1852	Warley Wigorn	QCCMR
Gray, Rose Anna Jane	bur 8yrs 6mths	06.11.1847	Ridgacre	QCCBurR
Gray, William Edmund	bur 6yrs	06.11.1847	Ridgacre	QCCBurR
Grazier, James	m Betsy Williams	05.12.1849	Warley Wigorn	QCCMR
Greaves, Abel	bap s of John & Hannah	25.10.1846	Quinton	HOBapR
Greaves, Abel	bur 13wks	03.01.1847	Ridgacre	QCCBurR
Greaves, Hannah	bur 24yrs	27.12.1846	Ridgacre	QCCBurR
Greaves, Jesse	bap s of John & Hannah	06.11.1844	Quinton	HOBapR
Greaves, Jesse	bur 11yrs	09.12.1855	Warley Wigorn	QCCBurR
Green, Benjamin	m Mary Harvey	24.08.1846	Warley Wigorn	QCCMR
Griffin, Mary Ann	m Joseph Vaughan	18.01.1852	Warley Wigorn	QCCMR
Guest, Selina	bur 7mths	10.03.1852	Ridgacre	QCCBurR
Hackett, Mary	bur 3mths	26.12.1857	Quinton	QCCBurR
Hackett, William	bap s of Ann	07.11.1853	Quinton	HOBapR
Hackwood, Elizabeth	m William Henry Rudge	19.04.1845	Ridgacre	QCCMR
Haden, Joseph	bap s of George & Jane	07.03.1844	Beech Lanes	HOBapR
Hadley, Benjamin	m Sarah Rowley	??.08.1845	Warley Wigorn	QCCMR
Hadley, Joseph	m Sarah Hall	11.11.1844	Warley Wigorn	QCCMR
Hadley, Thomas	bur 7yrs	10.10.1850	Ridgacre	QCCBurR
Haines, Ann	m Henry Bartlett	28.11.1843	Warley Wigorn	QCCMR
Hall, Ann	bur 88yrs	19.02.1854	Ridgacre	QCCBurR
Hall, George	bap s of Ellen	12.07.1854	Warley Wigorn	QCCBapR
Hall, Sarah	m Joseph Hadley	11.11.1844	Warley Wigorn	QCCMR
Halton, Sarah	bap d of Thomas & Ann	31.03.1858	Red Lion	QCCBapR
Harper, Lucretia	bur 38yrs	05.02.1851	Warley Wigorn	QCCBurR
Harris, Sarah	bur 6wks	09.03.1843	Ridgacre	QCCBurR
Harry, Ambrose	m Elizabeth Knight	31.12.1855	Warley Wigorn	QCCMR
Harry, Thomas	m Mary Ann Newman	31.12.1855	Warley Wigorn	QCCMR
Harvey, Mary	m Benjamin Green	24.08.1846	Warley Wigorn	QCCMR
Hatton, David	m Phoebe Round	14.12.1846	Warley Wigorn	QCCMR
Haycock, Mary	bur 75yrs	28.02.1857	Ridgacre	QCCBurR
Haycock, Mary Ann	bur 1mth	12.03.1851	Ridgacre	QCCBurR
Haycock, Mary Ann	bur 11wks	20.11.1851	Ridgacre	QCCBurR
Haycock, William	bur infant	10.12.1844	Ridgacre	QCCBurR
Haycock, William S.	bur 2yrs 11mths	02.04.1857	Ridgacre	QCCBurR
Haycock, William S.	bur 2dys	04.04.1859	Ridgacre	QCCBurR

Hetridge, Henry	m Eleanora Spittle	14.08.1843	Warley Wigorn	QCCMR
Hill, Ann	m William Grazier (Cakemore)	25.11.1849	Ridgacre	QCCMR
Hill, Elizabeth	m William Ault Yates	04.06.1849	Warley Wigorn	QCCMR
Hill, Emma	bap d of Thomas & Elizabeth	03.09.1854	Ridgacre	QCCBapR
Hill, James	m Susannah Pritchard	22.01.1855	Beech Lanes	QCCMR
Hill, Thomas	bur 8mths	24.09.1857	Quinton	QCCBurR
Hill, Thomas	bap s of James & Mary	04.09.1859	Ridgacre	QCCBapR
Hill, William	m Ann Alcock	29.12.1850	Warley Wigorn	QCCMR
Hills, Mary	m Benjamin Timmins	07.10.1850	Warley Wigorn	QCCMR
Hodges, Maria	m Richard Yapp	29.11.1858	Warley Wigorn	QCCMR
Hodgkins, James	bur 38yrs	17.06.1854	Traveler	QCCBurR
Holland, Maria	m James Stevens	01.09.1845	Warley Wigorn	QCCMR
Hope, Henry	m Sarah Westwood	17.07.1853	Warley Wigorn	QCCMR
Houghton, Marilyn	bur 1yr 3mths	28.12.1858	Quinton	QCCBurR
Howton, Mary Ann	bap d of John & Ann	01.06.1856	Ridgacre	QCCBapR
Hughes, Ann Maria	m Thomas Fleet	10.10.1847	Ridgacre	QCCMR
Hughes, Hannah	m Joseph Ward	25.12.1852	Warley Wigorn	QCCMR
Humphries, Elizabeth	m Isaac Lea Cox	05.11.1848	Ridgacre	QCCMR
Hunt, Jane	m John James	22.12.1850	Warley Wigorn	QCCMR
Hunt, Robert	bur 8mths	05.03.1858	Quinton	QCCBurR
Hyde, Henry	bur 2yrs 6mths	11.06.1845	Ridgacre	QCCBurR
Hyde, John	bur 78yrs	31.08.1859	Quinton	QCCBurR
Insley, Rosina	bur 3wks	25.06.1845	Warley Wigorn	QCCBurR
Jakeman, Benjamin	m Jane Ward	25.12.1852	Warley Wigorn	QCCMR
James, John	m Jane Hunt	22.12.1850	Warley Wigorn	QCCMR
Jeves, Lucy	m William Jones	25.05.1846	Warley Wigorn	QCCMR
Jones, William	m Lucy Jeves	25.05.1846	Warley Wigorn	QCCMR
Jones, William	m Sarah Turton	25.12.1847	Warley Wigorn	QCCMR
Kinas, Eliza	bur 19yrs	22.11.1846	Ridgacre	QCCBurR
Knight, David	m Ann Stow	07.10.1855	Warley Wigorn	QCCMR
Knight, Elizabeth	m Ambrose Harry	31.12.1855	Warley Wigorn	QCCMR
Lawleys, Thomas	bur 1yr	05.03.1858	Quinton	QCCBurR
Lea, Walter	bap s of Ann	13.09.1851	Ridgacre	QCCBapR
Lee, Walter	bur 5wks	28.09.1851	Ridgacre	QCCBurR
Lee, William Joseph	bap s of Robert & Ann	29.03.1858	Ridgacre	QCCBapR
Lee, William	bur 1wk	02.04.1858	Ridgacre	QCCBurR
Lees, George	bur 8yrs	15.10.1858	Ridgacre	HOBurR
Leighton, Sarah	m Joseph Cove	27.01.1853	Warley Wigorn	QCCMR
Lewis, Elizabeth	bur 74yrs	16.05.1858	Beech Lanes	QCCBurR
Ligett, Elizabeth	m George Northall	01.06.1846	Warley Wigorn	QCCMR
Lightwood, William	m Ursula Bayley	02.01.1853	Warley Wigorn	QCCMR
Lowe, Amphillis	bap d of Joseph & Sarah	13.01.1854	Quinton	HOBapR
Lowe, Benjamin Richard	bap s of Benjamin & Mary	19.01.1859	Hawthorn	QCCBapR
Lowe, Charles Francis	bap s of Benjamin & Mary	19.01.1859	Hawthorn	QCCBapR
Lunn, John	m Eliza Smith	12.09.1860	Beech Lanes	QCCMR
Male, John	bur 3yrs	16.05.1858	Beech Lanes	HOBurR

Maltby, Hannah	m John Silk	01.07.1850	Warley Wigorn	QCCMR
Mander, Sarah	bur 78yrs	01.10.1846	Ridgacre	QCCBurR
Mason, Emma	bur 17dys	14.11.1859	Quinton	QCCBurR
Mason, Joseph	bur 3yrs	28.03.1858	Quinton	QCCBurR
Mason, Sarah	m William Gould	21.08.1853	Ridgacre	QCCMR
May, John	m Jane Portman	31.03.1851	Warley Wigorn	QCCMR
Millington, Joseph	m Phoebe Smith	06.10.1851	Warley Wigorn	QCCMR
Milton, William	bur 17dys	08.04.1854	Ridgacre	QCCBurR
Morrall, John	bap s of James & Sarah	30.03.1856	Crock Street	BPMCBapR
Morton, Hannah	bur 5mths	27.04.1842	Quinton	HOBurR
Neale, Isabella Lucy	bap d of Joshua & Jane	02.12.1858	Ridgacre	QCCBapR
Newman, Mary Ann	m Thomas Harry	31.12.1855	Warley Wigorn	QCCMR
Northall, George	m Elizabeth Ligett	01.06.1846	Warley Wigorn	QCCMR
Northall, Mary Ann	m Andrew Davies	??.08.1846	Warley Wigorn	QCCMR
Page, Ann	m Henry Slaughter	20.06.1842	Warley Wigorn	QCCMR
Partridge, Ann	bur 2yrs	28.03.1841	Ridgacre	QCCBurR
Partridge, Edward	bap s of Esther	04.04.1847	Ridgacre	QCCBapR
Partridge, Hannah	bap d of Martha	06.08.1854	Ridgacre	QCCBapR
Partridge, Hannah	bur 2yrs	08.07.1856	Warley Wigorn	QCCBurR
Partridge, John	bur 13wks	01.07.1849	Warley Wigorn	QCCBurR
Partridge, John	bur 2yrs	12.04.1857	Beech Lanes	QCCBurR
Partridge, Sarah	bur 3yrs	13.05.1841	Warley Wigorn	QCCBurR
Payne, Mary	bur 10wks	22.04.1860	Quinton	QCCBurR
Payne, Mary Jane	m Isaac Porter	27.01.1846	Warley Wigorn	QCCMR
Peplow, Eliza	m Isaac Westwood	21.03.1852	Warley Wigorn	QCCMR
Pickerill, Hannah	m Joseph Fenton	07.12.1856	Warley Wigorn	QCCMR
Porter, Isaac	m Mary Jane Payne	27.01.1846	Warley Wigorn	QCCMR
Portman, Jane	m John May	31.03.1851	Warley Wigorn	QCCMR
Powell, Ann Maria	bur 2yrs	16.05.1858	Beech Lanes	QCCBurR
Powell, Emily	bur 15mths	22.04.1855	Beech Lanes	QCCBurR
Powell, James Benjamin	bur 1yr	21.02.1858	Quinton	QCCBurR
Powell, Joseph	bap s of Elizabeth	31.08.1842	Beech Lanes	HOBapR
Powell, Joseph	bur 1mth	11.09.1842	Beech Lanes	HOBurR
Powell, Joseph	bur 6wks	14.07.1845	Warley Wigorn	QCCBurR
Prady, Henry	bur 6wks	20.02.1842	Ridgacre	QCCBurR
Pritchard, Susannah	m James Hill	22.01.1855	Beech Lanes	QCCMR
Pye, Edward	m Elizabeth Swan	22.09.1851	Warley Wigorn	QCCMR
Read, Elsie	bur 9yrs	07.05.1843	Ridgacre	QCCBurR
Read, Hannah	bur 7yrs	30.05.1857	Quinton	QCCBurR
Read, Mary	bur 62yrs	24.01.1841	Ridgacre	QCCBurR
Read, Mary Ann	bur 15yrs	19.09.1849	Ridgacre	QCCBurR
Reade, Hannah	bap d of George & Sarah	01.04.1850	Quinton	BPMCBapR
Record, Betsy	bur 13mths	13.01.1861	Ridgacre	QCCBurR
Ring, William	bur 7wks	21.02.1850	Warley Wigorn	QCCBurR
Ring, William	bur 8mths	25.12.1852	Warley Wigorn	QCCBurR
Robinson, Mary Ann	m William Sadler	13.02.1853	Warley Wigorn	QCCMR

Robinson, William	bur 1yr	08.04.1854	Ridgacre	QCCBurR
Robinson, William	bur 1yr 9mths	11.05.1859	Quinton	QCCBurR
Rogers, George Alexander	m Annie Ashton	03.11.1860	Beech Lanes	QCCMR
Rose, Amos	bur 5yrs	25.05.1858	Quinton	QCCBurR
Rose, Edward Joseph	bap s of John & Jane	02.12.1855	Quinton	BPMCBapR
Round, Phoebe	m David Hatton	14.12.1846	Warley Wigorn	QCCMR
Rowley, Sarah	m Benjamin Hadley	??.08.1845	Warley Wigorn	QCCMR
Rudge, William Henry	m Elizabeth Hackwood	19.04.1845	Ridgacre	QCCMR
Rutledge, Elizabeth	m Charles Garner	24.05.1847	Ridgacre	QCCMR
Sadler, Benjamin	bap s of George & Ann Rose	08.02.1858	New Road	QCCBapR
Sadler, William	m Mary Ann Robinson	13.02.1853	Warley Wigorn	QCCMR
Salt, Sarah	m Enoch Walters	04.05.1846	Warley Wigorn	QCCMR
Saul, Benjamin	bur 21yrs	06.03.1859	Quinton	QCCBurR
Scott, Martha	m William Evans	14.10.1859	Ridgacre	QCCMR
Shaw, Martha	m Christopher Waistell (Yorks)	20.12.1846	WW	QCCMR
Shipley, George	bur infant	09.03.1858	Quinton	QCCBurR
Short, Edward	bap s of John & Sarah	17.11.1858	Worlds End	QCCBapR
Silk, John	m Hannah Maltby	01.07.1850	Warley Wigorn	QCCMR
Slaughter, Henry	m Ann Page	20.06.1842	Warley Wigorn	QCCMR
Smallwood, Sarah	m John Benjamin Wright	14.12.1851	Warley Wigorn	QCCMR
Smith, Eliza	m John Lunn	12.09.1860	Beech Lanes	QCCMR
Smith, Henry	bap s of David & Mary	22.08.1852	Quinton	BPMCBapR
Smith, James	bur 18mths	02.01.1845	Ridgacre	QCCBurR
Smith, Phoebe	m Joseph Millington	06.10.1851	Warley Wigorn	QCCMR
Spittle, Eleanora	m Henry Hetridge	14.08.1843	Warley Wigorn	QCCMR
Stevens, James	m Maria Holland	01.09.1845	Warley Wigorn	QCCMR
Stow, Ann	m David Knight	07.10.1855	Warley Wigorn	QCCMR
Swan, Elizabeth	m Edward Pye	22.09.1851	Warley Wigorn	QCCMR
Taylor, Sarah	m George ? (Warley Wigorn)	??.09.1845	Ridgacre	QCCMR
Taylor, William	m Harriet Grainger	27.12.1852	Warley Wigorn	QCCMR
Thomas, Joseph	m Sarah Billingham	16.11.1846	The Quinton	QCCMR
Thompson, Sarah Jane	bap d of Henry & Sarah	08.02.1858	Beech Lanes	QCCBapR
Timmins, Benjamin	m Mary Hills	07.10.1850	Warley Wigorn	QCCMR
Tomlinson, Emily	m Edward White	17.10.1841	Beech Lanes	HOMR
Townley, Henry John	bap s of John & Eliza	06.03.1859	Holly Bush Hill	QCCBapR
Toy, Thomas	bap s of William & Eliza	07.07.1850	Ridgacre	QCCBapR
Toy, William	bap s of William & Eliza	07.07.1850	Ridgacre	QCCBapR
Turton, Sarah	m William Jones	25.12.1847	Warley Wigorn	QCCMR
Vaughan, Eliza	bap d of George & Susannah	06.08.1843	Ridgacre	QCCBapR
Vaughan, Joseph	m Mary Ann Griffin	18.01.1852	Warley Wigorn	QCCMR
Walters, Enoch	m Sarah Salt	04.05.1846	Warley Wigorn	QCCMR
Ward, Jane	m Benjamin Jakeman	25.12.1852	Warley Wigorn	QCCMR
Ward, Joseph	m Hannah Hughes	25.12.1852	Warley Wigorn	QCCMR
Watson, Emily	m James Pattison (St Helens)	17.06.1858	The Quinton	QCCMR
Wedge, Sarah	m William Williams	08.11.1857	Quinton	QCCMR
Westwood, Isaac	m Eliza Peplow	21.03.1852	Warley Wigorn	QCCMR

Westwood, Sarah	m Henry Hope	17.07.1853	Warley Wigorn	QCCMR
Whale, Sarah	m John Burton	04.09.1848	Warley Wigorn	QCCMR
White, Amplias Amy	bap d of George & Amplias	10.10.1852	Ridgacre	QCCBapR
White, Edward	m Emily Tomlinson	17.10.1841	Beech Lanes	HOMR
Wild, Henry	bur 5yrs	18.11.1846	Warley Wigorn	QCCBurR
Wild, William	bur 35yrs	23.04.1847	Warley Wigorn	QCCBurR
Wild, William	bur 3yrs	31.10.1847	Warley Wigorn	QCCBurR
Williams, Betsy	m James Grazier	05.12.1849	Warley Wigorn	QCCMR
Williams, William	m Sarah Wedge	08.11.1857	Warley Wigorn	QCCMR
Woodhouse, Charles	bur 2yrs 10mths	21.02.1847	Warley Wigorn	QCCBurR
Woodhouse, James	bur 33yrs	30.07.1847	Warley Wigorn	QCCBurR
Woodhouse, James C.	bur 10wks	17.10.1847	Warley Wigorn	QCCBurR
Woodhouse, Thomas	bur 15mths	22.05.1859	Warley Wigorn	QCCBurR
Woodward, George	bur 4mths	12.01.1842	Ridgacre	QCCBurR
Wright, John Benjamin	m Sarah Smallwood	14.12.1851	Warley Wigorn	QCCMR
Yapp, Richard	m Maria Hodges	29.11.1858	Warley Wigorn	QCCMR
Yates, George	bap s of John & Elizabeth	10.10.1841	Quinton	HOBapR
Yates, William Ault	m Elizabeth Hill	04.06.1849	Warley Wigorn	QCCMR
Young, Charlotte	bap d of Joseph & Jane	08.02.1846	Quinton	BPMCBapR

14.01   Bibliography

14.01   Books:

Allen, G.C. (1929) *The Industrial Development of Birmingham and the Black Country 1860-1927*, George Allen & Unwin

Amphlett, J. (1910) *Court Rolls of the Manor of Hales 1272-1307*, Part I, Worcs Historical Society

Amphlett, J. (1912) *Court Rolls of the Manor of Hales 1270-1307*, Part II, Worcs Historical Society

Askwith, B. (1975) *The Lytteltons: A Family Chronicle of the Nineteenth Century*, Chatto & Windus

Austen, J. (1813) *Pride and Prejudice*, T. Egerton

Baker, G. (1981) *Via Hales Owen Roads*, Dudley Teachers' Centre

Ballard, P. (ed) (2009) *Birmingham's Victorian and Edwardian Architects*, Birmingham Victorian Society

Baring-Gould, S. (1902) *Nebo the Nailer*, Cassell & Co

Bennett, A. (2003) *Till the Sun Shines Through*, Harper Collins

Bennett, A. (2007) *A Daughter's Secret*, Harper

Benson, J. (ed) (1809-13) *The Works of Rev John Wesley,* Wesleyan Conference Office

Billingham, J.M. (n.d.) *A History of Coal Mining in Hales Owen*, Hales Owen Teachers' Centre

Billings, M. (1855) *Directory and Gazetteer of the County of Worcester*, M. Billings

Bunting, T.W. (1990) *The Story of a Parish: The Quinton 1840-1990*

Bunting, T.W. & Taylor, B.J. (2005) *The Story of a Parish: The Quinton 1840-1990*, QLHS

Burritt, Elihu (1868) *Walks in the Black Country and its Green Borderland*, Sampson Low and Marston

Cameron, Kenneth (1977) *English Place-Names*, B.T. Batsford

Cassey's *Directory* (1850)

Cattell, J., Ely, S., Jones, B. (2002) *The Birmingham Jewellery Quarter*, English Heritage

Chandler, G. & Hannah, I. (1949) *Dudley As it was and as it is Today*, B.T. Batsford

Chaucer, G., (c1387) *The Canterbury Tales*, [Coghill, N. (1951) Penguin Books]

Chinn, C. (2003, 2004, 2006, 2007, 2009) *The Streets of Brum* Parts 1-5, Brewin Books

Creed, Kate (2008) *A Birth, a Death and a Barrelage*, Maxam Publishing

Crew, K. (1984) *Life at Hales Owen Abbey*, Hales Owen Local History Group

Curnock, N. (ed) (1938) *The Journal of the Rev John Wesley*, Epworth Press

Curry, K. (1965) *New Letters of Robert Southey*, Columbia University Press

Dickens, Charles (1837) *The Posthumous Papers of the Pickwick Club*, Chapman & Hall

Dickens, Charles (1853) *Bleak House*, Bradbury & Evans

Disraeli, B. (1845) *Sybil*, Henry Colburn

Dodd, J.P. (1979) *Worcestershire Agriculture in the Mid-Nineteenth Century: An Analysis of the 1854 Returns for Worcestershire*, Worcestershire Historical Society

Dryden, J., (1691) *King Arthur*, Dryden, J., (1691) premiere – Queen's Theatre, Dorset Garden, London

Eliot, George (1859) *Adam Bede*, John Blackwood

Fletcher, S. (1997) *Victorian Girls: Lord Lyttelton's Daughters*, Hambledon

Gaskell, Elizabeth (1851-53) *Cranford*, serialised in Household Words

Goldsmith, Oliver (1929 *The Vicar of Wakefield* and *The Deserted Village*, UTP

Grazebrook, H.S. (1873) *The Heraldry of Worcestershire*, John Russell Smith

Gray, Thomas (1751) *Elegy Written in a Country Churchyard*, Robert Dodsley

Gregory, K. (1996) *A Guide to St Mary's Abbey Hales Owen*, Hales Owen Abbey Trust

Gregory, K. (n.d.) *Halesowen Parish Registers: Baptisms, Marriages, Burials, 1559-1643*, HalesOwen History Society

Gregory, K. (n.d.) *Parish Registers of Halesowen, 1652-1661*, HalesOwen History Society

Gregory, K. (n.d.) *Halesowen Parish Registers: Baptisms, Marriages, Burials, 1665-1716*, HalesOwen History Society

Gregory, K. (n.d.) *Halesowen Parish Registers: Baptisms, Burials, 1761-1805*, HalesOwen History Society

Gregory, K. (n.d.) *Halesowen Parish Registers: Burials, 1813-1874*, HalesOwen History Society

Gregory, K. (n.d.) *Halesowen Parish Registers: Baptisms 1813-1861*, HalesOwen History Society

Gregory, K. (n.d.) *Halesowen Parish Registers: Marriages 1762-1861*, HalesOwen History Society

Hackwood, F.W. (1915) *Oldbury and Round About*, Whitehead Bros & Cornish Bros

Hale, M. & Williams, N. (1974) *By Rail to Halesowen*, Michael Hale

Hall, M. (1984) *Who Knows But It May Continue?*, Quinton Methodist Church Council

Hardy, T. (1895) *Jude the Obscure*, Osgood, McIlvine & Co

Hartley, L.P. (1953) *The Go-Between*, Hamish Hamilton

Hooke, Della (2006) *England's Landscape: The West Midlands*, Collins

Hunt, Joseph (1979) *History of Hales Owen Abbey*, Dudley Teachers' Centre

Hunt, Julian (2004) *A History of Halesowen*, Phillimore

Hutton, W. (1819) *The History of Birmingham*, J. Nichols and Son

Jeayes, I. H. (1893) *Descriptive Catalogue of the Charters & Muniments of the Lyttelton Family*, Charles J. Clark

Kain, R.J.P. & Prince, H.C. (1985) *The Tithe Surveys of England and Wales*, CUP

Kinvig, R.H., et al (eds) (1950) Birmingham and its Regional Setting, Cornish Brothers

Leatherbarrow, J.S. (1977) *Churchwarden's Presentments in the Diocese of Worcester c1660-1760: Hales Owen*, Worcester Historical Society

Mandemakers, K., et al (2013) *HSN Standardized, HISCO-coded and classified Occupational Titles*, IISG

Maxam, A., et al (2006) *Centenary of the People's Park*, Warley Woods Community Trust

McKechnie, C. (1892) *The Life of Hugh Bourne*, James B. Knapp

McKenna, J. (1986) *Windmills of Birmingham and the Black Country*, Brewin Books

Melville (1852) *Directory of Dudley and District*

Mills, A.D. (1991) *Dictionary of English Place-Names*, OUP

Murray, D.C. (1896) *A Capful O'Nails*

Nash, T.R. (1781) *Collections for the History of Worcestershire*, John Nichols

Nokes, L. ((1884) *The Mysteries of the Wrought Nail Trade Revealed*

Pitt, W. (1813) *General View of the Agriculture of the County of Worcester with Observations on the Means of its Improvement*, Board of Agriculture

Presterne, T. (1913) *Harborne Once Upon a Time*, Cornish Bros

Quinton Library (n.d.) *Around World End*, Birmingham Public Libraries

Razi, Z. (1980) *Life, Marriage & Death in a Medieval Parish*, CUP

Rosser, A.N. (1998) *The Quinton and Round About: Volume One*, Quinton History Society

Rosser, A.N. (1999) *The Quinton and Round About: Volume Two*, Quinton History Society

Rostow, W.W. (1948) *British Economy of the 19th Century*, Clarendon

Scott, Walter (1821) *Kenilworth*, A. Constable & J. Ballantyne

Scott, William (1832) *Stourbridge and Its Vicinity*, Stourbridge

Shakespeare, W. (1591?) *King John*, [ed Craig, W.J. (1905) OUP]

Sheldon, W.C. (1903) *Early Methodism in Birmingham*, Buckler & Webb

Sherard, R. (1897) *The White Slaves of England*, James Bowden

Somers, F. & K.M. (1932) *Halas Hales Hales Owen*, H. Parkes

Somers, F. (1952) *Halesowen Churchwardens' Accounts (1487-1582) Part I*, Worcs Historical Society

Somers, F. (1953) *Halesowen Churchwardens' Accounts (1487-1582) Part II*, Worcs Historical Society

Somers, F. (1955) *Halesowen Churchwardens' Accounts (1487-1582) Part III*, Worcs Historical Society

Spring, D. (1963) *The English Landed Estate in the 19th Century*, OUP

Stephens, W.B. (ed) (1964) *A History of the County of Warwick Vol VII: The City of Birmingham*, OUP

Storey, G., Tillotson, K, & Burgis, N. (1988) *The Letters of Charles Dickens Vol 6 1850-1852*, OUP

Thompson, A. (n.d.) *Registers of the Church of St John the Baptist, Hales Owen, 1736-1761*

Thorn, F & C (eds) (1982) *Domesday Book Vol 16, Worcestershire*, Phillimore

Tomkins, M.(ed) (2017) *Court Rolls of Romsley 1279-1643*, Worcs Historical Society

Tonna, CE (1843-1844) *The Wrongs of Woman – The Little Pinheaders*, WH Dalton

Upton, C. (1997) *A History of Birmingham*, Phillimore

Wilson, H.R. (1979) *David Parkes 1763-1833*, H.R. Wilson,

Wilson, R.A. (1933) *Court Rolls of the Manor of Hales 1276-1301*, Part III, Worcs Historical Society

Woodward, E.L. (1946) *The Age of Reform 1815-1870*, OUP

Yates DE & Halverson JD (1990) *The Gentry and the Clergy in Smethwick and Birmingham*

Young, Francis Brett, *Far Forest*, Heinemann, 1936

Young, Francis Brett, *They Seek a Country*, Heinemann, 1937

Young, Francis Brett, *Mr Lucton's Freedom*, Heinemann, 1940

Zaluckyj, Sarah (2001) *Mercia: The Anglo-Saxon Kingdom of Central England*, Logaston Press

- (1843) *Directory of Birmingham*, Wrightson & Webb

- (1845) *Post Office Directory of Birmingham, Warwickshire and part of Staffordshire*, W.Kelly & Co

- (1850 & 1868) *Post Office Directory of Birmingham, Staffordshire, Warwickshire and Worcestershire*, W. Kelly & Co

- (1855) White's *General and Commercial Directory and Topography of the Borough of Birmingham,* S. Harrison, "The Sheffield Times"

14.02   Articles

Aminzade, R. & Hodson, R. (August 1982) Social Mobility in a Mid-Nineteenth Century French City, *American Sociological Review*, vol 47, no 4, p441-457

Barr, D. (December 1890) Village Methodism: How Methodism came to Quinton, *Christian Miscellany*, pp 464-466

Chambers, J. (1842) An Epitome of the History of Primitive Methodism at The Quinton, in the Parish of Hales Owen, Shropshire *Primitive Methodist Magazine*, pp 23-25

Courtney, W.P. (1885-1900) George Wingrove Cooke *Dictionary of National Biography* Vol 12

Dingley, H. (1892) Recollections of Quinton and its Surroundings *Bourne College Chronicle Vol IV*, pp 132-133.

Heslop, T.P. (1866) The Medical Aspects of Birmingham Timmins, S. *The Resources, Products and Industrial History of Birmingham and the Midland District*, pp 689-703

Holt, H.M.E. (1984) Assistant Commissioners and Local Agents and Their Roles in the Tithe Commission 1836-1854, *The Agricultural History Review* Vol. 32, No. 2, pp. 189-200

Reynolds, S. (1964) Agriculture Stephens, W.B., *A History of the Country of Warwick*, pp 246-250

Underwood, E.A. (1947) The History of Cholera in Great Britain *Proceedings of the Royal Society of Medicine* Vol XLI, pp 165-173

Wright, J.S. (1866) The Jewellery and Gilt Toy Trades Timmins, S. *The Resources, Products and Industries of Birmingham and the Midland Hardware District*, pp 452-462

14.03   Newspapers, Journals & Magazines:

Aris's Birmingham Gazette (12.01.1824, 29.03.1830, 21.11.1842, 19.06.1843, 06.10.1845, 22.12.1845, 07.11.1868)

Birmingham Chronicle (02.03.1826)

Birmingham Daily Post (15.06.1872, 08.12.1944)

Birmingham Journal (13.04.1844, 19.06.1847)

Birmingham Mail (10.12.1918)

Blackcountryman, The: Vol 7, No 1 (1974)

Bourne College Chronicle: vol 1 (1888)

Hansard' Parliamentary Debates, vol 173 (08.03.1864), vol 182 (16.03.1866)

Lichfield Mercury (11.09.1886)

Primitive Methodist Magazine (1846, 1850, 1869)
Transactions of Midlands Record Society: vol iii, 13 (1889)
Wolverhampton Chronicle (18.07.1838, 03.06.1857)
Worcestershire Chronicle (15.12.1841, 26.07.46 04.07.1874)
Worcester Journal (25.10.1810, 29.07.1830, 12.06.1836, 14.07.1842, 23.12.1852, 14.05.1881)

14.04   Manuscripts:

Census

Office of Population, Censuses and Surveys, *Census Returns* (PRO)

Office of Population, Census and Surveys, *Ecclesiastical Census,* 1851 (PRO)

Church

Bethesda Primitive Methodist Church *Baptismal Register* 1841-1851 (LB)

Birmingham Local Preachers' Meeting *Minute Book* 1823-1949 (LB)

Birmingham West Wesleyan Methodist Circuit Quarterly Meeting *Minutes* 1830-1873 (LB)

Birmingham West Wesleyan Methodist Local Preachers' Meeting *Minutes* 1823-1949 (LB)

Hone, R.B., *Notebook* vol 1, vol 2 (DALHC)

Christ Church The Quinton, *Baptismal Register* 1840-1851 (LB)

Christ Church The Quinton, *Burial Register* 1841-1851 (LB)

Christ Church The Quinton, *Marriage Register* 1844 -1851 (LB)

Christ Church The Quinton, *Minutes of Vestry & Annual Parish Meetings 1842-1914* (LB)

Darlaston Primitive Methodist Circuit *Minutes* 1824-1832 (WLHC)

Quinton Primitive Methodist Quarterly Meeting *Minutes* 1901-1914 (LB)

Quinton Wesleyan Methodist Chapel *Minutes* 1877-1937 (LB)

Petition to Bishop of Worcester 1826 (LB)

Land Transactions

Glebe Land

Conveyance: *Revd Aaron Lewis Manby to Alexander Macomb Chance Esqre* 10.09.1889 (QLHS)

Letter: *Whitehall 376^D/$_3$ to Reverend A.L. Manby* 20.08.1890 (QLHS)

Indenture: *Arthur Albright, Alexander Macomb Chance and 10 others* 06.12.1890 (QLHS)

Correspondence: *Quinton Glebe sale from Holbeche & Son, Land Agents & Surveyors, Smythe, Etches & Co, Solicitors, Queen Anne's Bounty Office to Rev W.A. Rowlands 08.02.1923 – 01.09.1923* (QLHS)

Building Lease: *Rev Alfred Ernest Palmer to RH Bridge* 04.06.1931 (QLHS)

Building Lease: *Rev Alfred Ernest Palmer to Mr Douglas Harold Brindley* 17.10.1932 (QLHS)

Building Lease: *Rev Alfred Ernest Palmer to Mr Arthur Vernon Crowley* 31.03.1934 (QLHS)

Building Lease: *Rev Alfred Ernest Palmer to Mr William Thompson Yates* 24.04.1934 (QLHS)

Four Dwellings Farm

Abstract of Title: *Trustees of the Birmingham Freehold Land Society to Freehold Property known as the Quinton Estate situate at Quinton in the City of Birmingham* 1929 (QLHS)

Redhall Farm

Abstract of Title: *John White Esq to freehold property situate and known as Redhall Farm, Quinton in the City of Birmingham* 1933 (QLHS)

Abstract of Title: *Douglas Dyas James Esq to two pieces of land being part of the Redhall Estate Quinton in the City of Birmingham* 1934 (QLHS)

Abstract of Title: *John Douglas White and Mrs K.M. Orcutt to freehold property situate and known as Redhall Farm, Quinton in the City of Birmingham* 1935 (QLHS)

Hawthorn Farm

Sale Catalogue 1855 (LB)

Galton Papers 3101/A/B/7/13 (LB)

Windmill Farm

Abstract of Title: *Messrs H. Dare and Son Ltd to land and premises known as Windmill Farm Quinton in the City of Birmingham* 1937 (QLHS)

Mockbeggar Farm

Abstract of Title: *Freehold property known as Worlds End Farm, Quinton in the City of Birmingham* 1938 (QLHS)

Lower Ridgacre Farm

Abstract of Title: *Lower Ridgacre Farm, Quinton, in the City of Birmingham* 1938 (QLHS)

Abstract of Title: *Ridgacre Investments Limited to freehold hereditaments and premises situate at Quinton, in the City of Birmingham and known as Lower Ridgacre Farm* 1938 (QLHS)

Tinkers Farm

Abstract of Title: *Messrs L & G Rudge to property fronting Kingsway, Quinton in the County of Worcester* 1938 (QLHS)

Supplemental Abstract of Title: *J.H. Walters Esq and Mrs B. Walters to freehold property situate at Quinton in the County of Worcester* (1955)

Ordnance Survey

Staffordshire Sheet LXXII
Warwickshire Sheet XIII
Worcestershire Sheet V

Wills

Lee Crowder & Miscellaneous Papers (LB)
National Probate Calendar: *Index of Wills and Administrations* 1858-1966
Prerogative Court of Canterbury Will Registers, Class PROB11

Miscellaneous

Alehouse Recognisances (SA)
Calendar of Prisoners (SA)
Hales Owen Abbey Rent Rolls (WAAS)
Minute Book: *Birmingham - Hagley Turnpike Trustees* (WAAS)
Poor Law Commission (NA)
Parliamentary Papers Vol 33 19.01 – 22. 07 1847 (24th Report of the Commissioner for Improvement of road from London to Holyhead)
Record Commission: *Astle, Thomas; Ayscough, Samuel; Caley, John, eds. (1802). Taxatio Ecclesiastica Angliae et Walliae auctoritate P. Nicholai IV, circa A.D. 1291*
Warley Wigorn Court Rolls (WAAS)
Warley Wigorn Papers (WAAS)

Website

Natural Resources Conservation Service www.nrcs.usda.gov/Internet/FSE_DOCUMENTS accessed 17.08.2018

References:

DALHC = Dudley Archives and Local History Centre
LB = Library of Birmingham
NA = National Archives
PRO = Public Record Office

QLHS = Quinton Local History Society
SA = Shropshire Archives
WLHC = Walsall Local History Centre
WAAS = Worcester Archive and Archaeology Service

Plot Co-ordinates:

The accepted convention is that field co-ordinates relate to the north west corner of each plot. References are from Google Maps.

15 Index of Persons

269

271

276